Praise for *Raising Our Hands*

"Jenna has uplifted marginalized voices embodying a crucial sentiment of Malcolm X's: it is white people's responsibility to bring other well-intended white people to the social justice work of our time. *Raising Our Hands* is the urgent answer to our request."

—Angela Rye, CNN Political analyst, host of
On One with Angela Rye podcast, advocate, and attorney.

"The world doesn't have time to wait for you to decide that you're brave enough to do the work laid out in *Raising Our Hands*—you can't read this fast enough."

—Reshma Saujani,
bestselling author of *Brave, Not Perfect* and founder of Girls Who Code

"The wisdom in these pages will help you see the world, and your role in it, through a powerful new lens. If you want to raise your hand and step up to the frontline, this book will firmly point you in the direction of *how*."

—Sophia Bush, actress and activist

"This book is a valuable resource for people seeking greater understanding, and for white women who just need a little push. Jenna is a bold and brilliant writer who cleverly holds herself, her sisters, and the reader accountable to a higher standard by exposing paradigms that cannot and should not remain unseen. As a nonbinary person of color, I was surprised to see my own privilege reflected in these pages. *Raising Our Hands* is a helpful tool for confronting privilege and bias regardless of race or gender identity."

—Dr. Tiffany Jana, author of *Overcoming Bias, Erasing Institutional Bias*,
and *Subtle Acts of Exclusion* and founder of TMI Consulting

"Jenna tackles this topic with care and simplicity through an intersectional lens. I'm excited for people to engage with this much-needed conversation."

—Geena Roccero,
supermodel and first trans Asian Pacific Islander Playboy Playmate

"So many of the 'well intended' white women who have enthusiastically been marching over the past few years have been missing the urgent context of the foundational work that's needed today, which *Raising Our Hands* provides. This is the book that willing white women have needed for so long: directions for how to engage in the collective work of liberation for all."

—Tabitha St. Bernard-Jacobs,
director of community engagement for the Women's March

"At a time of division and uncertainty, we need true allies to hold their communities accountable and this book does just that."

—Jamira Burley, social justice activist and White House Champion of Change

"Arnold provides a useful and compassionate resource to guide readers seeking to transform themselves and their communities through self-examination, deep listening, and accountability."

—Jamia Wilson, author, activist, and publisher at The Feminist Press

"We have a great responsibility to the future. The time has come to address our past, our origin, and the ways it continues to dictate our choices. This book is an amazing starting point."

—Mesiah Burciaga-Hameed, Afro-indigenous youth advocate

"Jenna Arnold's *Raising Our Hands* is a daring call-out that bravely tells white women with supremacist sensibilities that the jig is up! Arnold beseeches white women to fess up to their role in keeping inequality, and as I've experienced as a black person, intentional and unintentional racial violence, alive today. This is the book I want all of my white friends to read—they will be forced to own their collective ability to challenge injustice in profound ways. Arnold has raised the bar for Quakers today; she's not just talking the talk of stewardship and peace, but walking the walk, and I welcome her Herculean effort in these charged times."

—Avis Wanda McClinton, Quaker anti-racist activist and preservationist

"To my allies we ask for the clarity and compassion that *Raising Our Hands* offers. It takes you into a history that gives you the space to reflect and unpack judgements, separation, and the below-the-surface hate that divides us. This book and books like this bring us to a space of collective healing so we can see how deeply dependent and connected we truly are. I applaud Jenna's delivery of a work whose time has come."

—Erica Ford, social justice activist and cofounder of the National Black and Brown Gun Violence Prevention Consortium

"It is time for action and young people are wondering where you are. *Raising Our Hands* is a user guide to how to be a great ally. Girls, especially black and brown girls, need your help and Jenna Arnold tells you how you can be your most effective selves!"

—Naomi Wadler, youth activist

"Funny, profound, and engaging, *Raising Our Hands* is a catalytic treatise for the future of ourselves and country. Through searing truisms, it challenges us all to think and behave deeply and to be . . . more. Every chapter takes us collectively one step closer to a reimagined us."

—Denise Hamilton, author of *When Sleeping Women Wake*, social justice facilitator, and CEO of WatchHerWork

"*Raising Our Hands* is bright as it is straightforward. This is exactly the type of content, matched with motivating instruction, that so many of us white women are eager to dive into—it answers so many questions we didn't even know we had."

—Reverend Amanda Hambrick Ashcraft, Baptist Minister

"This book is a call to action to raise our hands to say, 'That's me—I don't know what I don't know but I want to do better. I'm that white woman. I'm ready to do the work now.' It's for all of us who have marched and called our senators and raged on social media, but have not yet taken a deep, hard look at ourselves. Whether we like it or not, we white people are implicated at birth and it's gonna take all of us digging deep, decolonizing our minds, and dismantling the systems we are a part of to bring about the change we wish to see in the world. This book is a call to action to RAISE YOUR HAND and say 'that's me. I'm guilty but I'm also so willing. I'm that white woman. And I'm ready to do the work.'"

—Kerri Kelly, cofounder of Race & Resilience, author of
American Detox (May 2021), and host of CTZN Podcast

"Gripping. Urgent. Unflinching. A must-read."

—Marie Forleo,
#1 *New York Times* bestselling author of *Everything Is Figureoutable*

"Impressive in scope and effective in its simplicity, *Raising Our Hands* is the tool many willing Americans have needed for too long. There are so many willing women eager to do something besides march but they don't know where to start—I suggest right here."

—Rachel O'Leary Carmona,
COO of the Women's March and social-justice activist

"I've been telling Jenna for years, 'Go get your white ladies and do the work.' And *Raising Our Hands* is exactly that! Jenna takes white women on a journey through self-discovery by pushing them to see the world through a more equitable lens. She demands they listen, they learn, and they hold themselves accountable no matter how upside down it might turn their worlds."

—Paola Mendoza, artist, activist, and author of *Sanctuary*

"*Raising Our Hands* does not ask readers to do what the giants whose shoulders we stand on haven't done for generations, but it is a fresh and friendly reminder where exactly that 'work' might lie. After the 2016 election, we saw an influx of white women take to the streets and organize their communities, often without the grounding in history and our place in it that was needed to create real allyship. This book is a welcomed invitation to remind us all that we have learning to do and homage to pay to those who fought before us. *Raising Our Hand* does a great service in this education and provides an excellent road map on the work to do within ourselves and in the world around us."

—Sarah Sophie Flicker, activist, artist, and contributor to
the *New York Times* bestseller *Together We Rise*

"Racial justice is something that Black and Brown folks cannot achieve alone. We need white people to do the courageous work to confront problematic behaviors within their own communities and families. Jenna has raised her hand to do just that with *Raising Our Hands,* clearly outlining the mental and societal roadblocks for white women while emphasizing the potential tectonic shifts that could happen if they were removed. Hurry and read this book; we are waiting for you to join us."

—Carmen Perez, civil rights and racial justice activist, 2017 National Women's March co-chair, and CEO of The Gathering for Justice

"This is the book I give those interested in being part of the solution but don't know where to start on wrapping their arms around the complex social fabric of the United States. Presented through Jenna's engaging and simplistic lens, readers will draw complicated truths much closer."

—Tiphani Montgomery, founder of Millions Conference and faith-based motivational speaker

"*Raising Our Hands* is a firm, compassionate reminder to bind back to what is already so familiar to us humans if we consciously seek it out: compassion for each other and ourselves as we navigate what feels like the daunting complexity of life."

—Zoe Buckman, visual artist and activist

"Admittedly, I've become increasingly more suspicious about the societal rules that seem to have governed the cadence of my very white life (college, husband, house, kids (3!!!)) and *Raising Our Hands* has explained the reason behind so much of it. I live in one of the most conservative states in the country and this book has fundamentally shifted my understanding of the world around me and my role in it. I'm forever changed."

—Sara Williams, mother of three, Wyoming

"Think you're too busy to make a difference? Think again. In this insightful, inspiring book, author Jenna Arnold shows how to raise your hand and your voice to create a 'rising tide raising all people' conversation, community, and country. Read it and reap."

—Sam Horn, author of *Someday Is Not a Day in the Week: 10 Hacks to Make the Rest of Your Life the Best of Your Life*

"*Raising Our Hands* cuts beyond the kumbaya. It is a refreshing reminder that life is not *just* about trying to pick the perfect cause, organization, or candidate—it's about holding ourselves accountable for our words and actions every day. As a Jewish American woman from a proud interfaith family, this book provides a road map for me in navigating the many identities that I claim (or that others may assume about me) in today's complex world. This book challenges us to question and rethink how we show up in our day-to-day lives—so we can strive to do better for the world."

—Rachel Gerrol, cofounder of NEXUS and The Survivor Initiative

"This is what I have been looking for—clear insight layered with compassion about our past but straight shooting on what we need to do NOW."

—Alexis Jones, author, activist, and founder of I Am That Girl

RAISING
OUR
HANDS

RAISING

Our

HANDS

How White Women Can Stop Avoiding Hard Conversations, Start Accepting Responsibility, and Find Our Place on the New Frontlines

Jenna Arnold

BenBella Books, Inc.
Dallas, Texas

BenBella Books, Inc.
10440 N. Central Expressway, Suite 800
Dallas, TX 75231
www.benbellabooks.com
Send feedback to feedback@benbellabooks.com

BenBella is a federally registered trademark.

Printed in the United States of America
10 9 8 7 6 5 4 3 2 1

Library of Congress Control Number: 2019059828
ISBN 9781950665075 (print)
ISBN 9781950665242 (ebook)

Editing by Leah Wilson and Stephanie Gorton
Copyediting by James Fraleigh
Proofreading by Kim Broderick and Cape Cod Compositors, Inc.
Indexing by WordCo Indexing Services, Inc.
Sensitivity editing by Treasure Brooks, Holly Baird, and Mia Ives-Rubl
Text design and composition by PerfecType, Nashville, TN
Cover design by Oceana Garceau and Jenai Wadia
Raising Hand Woman emoji ©arizzonadesign/Adobe Stock
Author photo by Candy Kennedy
Printed by Lake Book Manufacturing

Distributed to the trade by Two Rivers Distribution, an Ingram brand
www.tworiversdistribution.com

Special discounts for bulk sales are available. Please contact bulkorders@benbellabooks.com.

to all those who have carried the torch of justice,
& to my children: this cycle stops w/ me.

CONTENTS

AUTHOR'S NOTE

This book is intended for women interested in exploring what it means to be white in the United States today. My target readers are primarily white women who are eager to learn more about their identity and its impact on the rest of the world, with context and suggestions for how to move forward civically in a way that considers the disenfranchised.

I am an upper-middle-class white woman raised in the suburbs of the United States. I have been exposed to and taught to live within a certain set of norms; in this book, I unpack and question those norms against the backdrop of our unequal society. Coming to the realities of this book through my life experience, I hope, might provide a helpful vantage point for some readers and increase the likelihood that they will start having challenging conversations they previously avoided or answered with silence. I cannot speak as anyone other than myself, but my goal is to support and inform other white American women who may receive the content more easily from someone like them.

My decision to direct my efforts and energy toward educating privileged white women, at a time when so many marginalized groups are suffering, is controversial. Yet I am doing so because I firmly believe the change we wish to see in the world is more attainable with white women engaged in conversations about injustice. If we fail to bring more white women into urgent conversations about their identity and the inequities in the world, we only continue to protect dangerous systems that have oppressed the marginalized for so long.

You cannot wake a person who is pretending to be asleep.
—Navajo proverb

INTRODUCTION

🐚. I've been waiting for you. So glad you're here.

Maybe someone gave you this book inside perfectly creased wrapping paper and a finessed bow. Maybe someone flung it on your desk or lobbed it at you, post–spin class, and said, "You have to read this." Maybe you're flipping through it at your OBGYN's office because your phone is dead and you have nothing else to do. Maybe you're side-eyeing the subtitle because you have too much on your plate already, or maybe you thought, *Why am I supposed to raise my hand and take responsibility for something I didn't do?* Maybe you're curious about where these "new" frontlines might be—and you're keeping your fingers crossed that I'm not about to ask you to board a seventeen-hour flight or empty your bank account. Maybe the part about "white women" gave you pause, because organizing people by race contradicts the rule you try to live by: everyone is the same.

This book might require you to question elements of your world that you prefer to ignore—those little white lies that keep life neat and contented enough—because if you knew the truth, you'd have to do something about it. Maybe it suddenly makes sense to see if the receptionist has a charger for that dead cell phone of yours after all.

But stick around—at least for a few more paragraphs.

I spend an exorbitant amount of time second-guessing my decisions, too, including the best use of my time. And I can tell you that what you will get out of reading this book is worth those minutes of your life. The payout will be more clarity about who you are and how you can change the course of history. No matter how you got to this sentence, or even if you don't know exactly why you're here, we (humanity, collectively—and yup, I'm speaking on behalf of every person in the whole wide world) need you, now.

There was never a clear "why we're marching" mission statement* for the original Women's March of 2017, the largest peaceful protest in history, which I helped organize. But there was, in my mind, some internal species alarm going off that screeched, "Something is very not right," that pushed us all out of our front doors to march, chant, and see and be seen by one another. In that moment, women all over the world gave ourselves permission to listen, to get angry, and to take to the streets in numbers that we hadn't in decades . . . or, arguably, ever. But since then, the next steps—the answer to the question, "Now what?"—haven't been particularly clear to the vast majority of those who marched that day: American white women.†

Yes, Americans are calling their representatives, donating money, mobilizing, and voting in numbers like never before. While all of those types of civic participation are crucial, my fear is that we think doing these things means we've done everything we can—and then, when we look hard at the state of the world, we freeze. Until there is a true understanding of how our country is, and becoming increasingly so divided, there is no way we can build long-lasting solutions that address the roots of the problem. Any smaller measure is like trying to fix a leaky roof with masking tape: it will buy you approximately .47 seconds of respite.

This book and its message aren't about the results of a past or future election. This is about the division and angst that pulsates through our streets and the purposeless lives that some of us feel like we are living, just comfortably jogging on the gerbil wheel of chores and never really seeming to make much progress in any one direction. And while we can't take our foot off the accelerator when it comes to calling, donating, and voting—because those things do make a difference—if those actions aren't accompanied by work we do on ourselves, we'll never fully address deep societal wounds and precipitate the collective leap we need to take in order to heal and move forward, together.

---

* There were the *Unity Principles*, but most marchers didn't know about them, nor were they a factor or source of direction in their marching.

† It's estimated that 85% of the 5.2 million (or more) who marched in the United States were women.[1] Of those, 86% (approximately 3.8 million) were white with a median age of 43.[2]

A reckoning is in order, but it requires that we take a peek at the parts of our history we've intentionally kept out of textbooks, so that we can better understand the structure of power today and the sources of the self-disappointment that might brew inside some of us. We need to understand how we got here in order to chart a new path for where we want to go and to craft the legacy we want to leave our children.

And while I joke about speaking on behalf of all humanity, really I can only speak with authority about one life experience: mine. What I understand to be true about the United States, and my place in it, has drastically shifted since my easy days as an average white girl growing up in the suburban American Dream. In fact, everything I understand about my own identity has changed so much in the past few years, that I felt I had to find out if other women like me were having the same experience—I wanted to take their temperature against the backdrop of a divided nation, as I was constantly checking mine.

listening circles

I decided to test my hypothesis that I wasn't the only one grappling with ideas that challenged my understanding of the white world in which I grew up. My life is comfortable enough; an ER, a roof, and enough food for myself and my children are within arm's reach, and I don't lose sleep over them. The catastrophic headlines I read seem completely unconnected to the lives of my larger family and social circles. In fact, my pleasant life is in complete contrast to the realities of so many others. I began struggling to reconcile this as a child and carried it on my shoulders for decades, and it wasn't until now, in this moment of societal turmoil, that I wanted to see if others who looked like me, who had the same privileged upbringing, who prayed to similar gods, were also haunted by the deep injustices they saw— and I wanted to know what they were doing about it.

So I began holding conversations with small groups of people identifying as white women in a variety of communities in living rooms across the country—Listening Circles, as I came to call them. I chose this demographic because I belong to it and I wanted to see how other white women were rationalizing their place in the world today, and also because, since 2016, journalists and pollsters have been quick to point a finger at the role of white women in electing US presidents and confirming Supreme Court nominees.

While I had spent a lot of time trying to understand our demographic as a voting bloc, I already knew intimately that white American women are no monolith. My mother is the eldest of her generation, one of nine. I'm the eldest of twenty-five cousins. My maternal family rolls deep—sixty-plus—so any family event requires restaurant reservations for parties of at least twenty. I know them all very well and I can say with certainty, they are all very, very different. Some of us are Catholic, others atheist; all fall on different sides of the political and socioeconomic spectrum; some co-sleep with their children, others never bothered breastfeeding. We are like many families: each member defines themselves, in part, by how they stand out from the others.

Yet the women in my family, at least, do share certain characteristics—habits, tendencies, deviled egg recipes—that make us all predictably uniform. Some of those cookie-cutter traits include avoiding the controversial, assuming roles like cooking and cleaning before the men have a chance to raise their hands, and performing some domestic ritual of attempted perfection—a casserole, a daughter's wedding, a window treatment. I saw a lot of my aunts' behaviors reflected in the many Listening Circles I hosted from the bluffs of Del Mar outside of San Diego to the suburbs of Raleigh, North Carolina, and the penthouses of Manhattan's East Village. My goal was to understand the state of the American white woman, to the best of my ability, and to see how this demographic was reconciling its power and privilege while so many others were suffering. I wanted to learn what keeps her awake at night and to see if that was the same as it was for me.

The women I spoke with all classified their socioeconomic status as lower middle class and above, but otherwise had a wide range of experiences and perspectives. They represented a vast array of religious and non-religious affiliations. Many were in committed relationships—some with men, some with women. Some of them were mothers, grandmothers, caregivers; some weren't. Democrats, Republicans, Independents, confused . . . all had strong opinions—some characteristically familiar, some original—about the state of the country and their role in it.

My commitment to these Listening Circles has meant many hours grazing cheese platters in Yankee Candle–scented, four-bedroom, center hall Colonials. Sitting cross-legged on high-gloss wood floors, benches at the feet of high-thread-count beds, and Carrera marble kitchen-island countertops, the women who generously invited me into their communities shared all they thought was wrong with the world—and often revealed the shame, regrets, or insecurities they secretly harbored about themselves, as well.

We discussed what stereotypes about "us"* are true and false, and attempted to define who the "other" or "them" really meant to us. Participants asked questions about race, gender, and class that they'd been wrestling with for years, sometimes decades, and didn't quite understand. Together, we studied our safe ambivalence and the toxicity of perfection seeking—the most insidious of all excuses, which keeps us tucked in our micro-suede couches watching Netflix series instead of getting up to do something about the injustices we know exist.

What I learned was this particular demographic—American white women—sometimes opts for silence because they're chasing some phantom ideal of perfection. They're unsure when it's their place to speak up, they struggle to wrap their heads around the very complex structures that produce and protect inequity, and though they want to do something to make the world better, they often don't know where to start.

Mostly, though, Listening Circle participants desperately wanted to keep talking. In some ways, the exercise of contemplation awakened a sudden drive to act substantively, to move to a frontline and make a mark—a longing that some hadn't realized was asleep within. This book outlines what I've heard in those closed-door conversations that might answer some of the questions you have about our world and your place in it. Who knows? You, too, might be ready to step up to intimidating tasks and into vulnerable places in ways you hadn't considered before.

when you know better, do better[3]

The very visible divisions that have always been integral to the American story are hard to sit with, let alone pick apart in detail. But if the past four years have taught me anything, it is that the comfortable silence that I have been able to sink into and out of at will for most of my life is no longer

---

* When I say "us," "we," "you," or "our," I am referring to the person who identifies as an American white woman. And when I say "American," I don't mean one's citizenship status—I'm referencing a life experience that people who reside in the United States might have. I intentionally use these terms broadly; they are meant to establish familiar identity markers, maybe ones that you might be able to relate to, but that aren't meant to qualify or disqualify anyone. I also make generalizations about myself, and sometimes who I am on Monday completely contradicts who I am on Tuesday—because, like you, I'm constantly trying to embrace my positive characteristics and (desperately) trying to adjust the negative ones.

comfortable. I can't pretend everything is rosy while I know there are people who love their children as much as I do—whose names and burdens and joys I'll never fully know—who are trapped inside a system of poverty and injustice, both in the same zip code and in time zones I don't even know exist. My turning around to avoid seeing, my keeping silent because it is easier than searching for what feels like an impossible solution, is the American white woman's crutch—and the country's Achilles' heel.

We are intimately familiar with competing priorities; the need to protect our own interests versus the desire to leave a meaningful legacy is just one example. We want to be everything to all people, but since our overrun to-do lists and lack of a clear path forward get in the way, we just stay in the easy lane, which encourages ignorance and apathy.

Some of us choose to sit out the seemingly unnavigable work of staying in tense conversations with people on the other side of the political spectrum, sifting through contradictory information about an issue we wish would just be solved already, or voicing a lone, unpopular opinion in a crowded room. We might become disinterested because challenging the status quo means questioning the comfy SUV in the driveway with the half-drunk bottle of water rolling around on its floor. We worry about what we could lose, or about admitting how we've been wrong, or that we (as individuals or as a country) might be causing harm to the defenseless. We're not sure we're willing to sacrifice cheap gas, Ziploc bags, or prep-school admission hook-ups. We might actively maintain distractions and choose to avoid headlines to dodge the fire hose of confusing news with no clear way forward. I get it (🫣).

When it comes time to assess our behavior or discuss an uncomfortable subject, either at the country club, in the gym locker room, or on the grocery store checkout line, we sometimes lean into our insecurity: *Who am I to say? I'm no expert. I care, but do I really know what I'm doing?*

But we can't afford to wait. We can't sit back and pretend to assume someone else has got "it" under control. They don't. If we delegate to a mythical "them," some government agency or smarty-pants academic, then we're being complacent, and complacency is the reason so many solvable problems aren't. There is no "them."

The American white woman is a powerful force—an essential participant—to mobilize on behalf of humanity and our planet, but based on what I heard and saw in the Listening Circles, I'm not sure we know it. It's like we're holding the key to one of the most expensive, sportiest high-performance cars on the planet, and we're too busy second-guessing whether we even know how to drive. We do.

Here's the proof, which was surprising to most of the women in the Listening Circles. Our purchasing power was estimated at $12.1 trillion in 2018[4]—which is $7 trillion larger than the economies of India and China combined.[5] That's a "t," not a "b." Men can't throw that "t" around like we can. We control 85%[6] of the share of purchasing power in the United States, and, consequently, we're the target audience for most ads.[7] Advertisers spend more time getting our attention than that of any other group of consumers, and we even get VIP treatment among demographic-data trolls, who purchase our online info in frightening volume, because they understand our influence even if we don't.

More than 53 million white women[8] reported voting in the 2016 election—a larger group than white men or any other voting bloc combined. In other words, *we* decide who becomes president of the United States. And, whether we like it or not, the American president has some of the most significant influence on political and environmental priorities around the world. Our environmental policies determine the air quality for billions,[9] we often drag dozens* or more countries into battle if we decide to go to war, and the atrocities our president decides to shine a light on can protect millions or leave them for dead. It's a shame the rest of the world doesn't get to vote for the American president given the dramatic implications the office has on their lives. Instead, it's America's white women who have historically decided elections, and I'm not sure we acknowledge that we carry that responsibility when we walk into the voting booth.

We American white women don't always recognize we have the influence we do. Instead we believe that because we work twenty-four hours a day (on the job, and as mothers, spouses, and life's general air traffic controllers), we are maxed out. And we are; I don't know a single woman who spends her time just focused on staying hydrated. Everybody has no time.

This is where I take aim at our assumption that if we had more time, we could do more good. Yes, more time potentially means more volunteer hours, but that's not exactly the work I'm asking of you—the new frontlines I'm pointing to are right there in the room with you. There is more foundational work to be done. Some of it can be done while folding laundry or

---

* 49 countries, known as the "coalition of the willing," joined the United States in the Iraq War.[10]

during your commute or sitting through a boring PowerPoint presentation. Some—the more existential questions that I pose in this book, or the ideas that will need deeper reflection or more research—require focused reflection. Many of them reveal contradictory truths, which can make our realities feel even more impossible to navigate.

Echoing so many religious texts, therapists, and self-help books, this work—or "the work," as I like to call it—requires that we remain committed to self-improvement while being gentle with ourselves, as we stumble through. It asks us to embrace the exploration of our own identity and our country's as a way to translate our privilege into active citizenship. This work is sort of like religion: there are times you show up to hear the words of inspiration, and other times you do the physical labor of taking communion. But religious lessons only truly blossom in the quiet moments, while you're brushing your teeth, before you lose your patience with the car in front of you, when you need a moral compass for a moment of confusion. The "work" I'll be asking you to do here will proceed the same way. Some of it is theoretical and will take some time to process (catching yourself when you're doing something un-useful because you're seeking perfection), and other points will inform immediate behavior change. When you know better you do better, and you will.

what's in this book

This book will walk you through what I learned when I stopped studying my pores and started admitting that my understanding of myself—my race, class, disability, and gender—might not be insignificant to how I operate in the world, or to how the rest of the world perceives me. In fact, my ignorance might be standing in the way of making meaningful change.

When I closely examined my privilege in the context of how the world got to the place it is today—have and have-nots, people suffering and people pretending nobody is suffering, more stuff than we need versus a planet that can't sustain our need to consume—I realized I was missing a huge piece of information about the role I, and women like me from the past, have played to get us to this exact moment. See, I'm a white, cisgender,* able-bodied (though I wear a wig—more on that later), nondenominational (unless you

---

* Identifying with the sex assigned to you at birth, as contrasted with transgender, or not identifying with the sex assigned to you at birth. The term is often abbreviated as "cis."

ask, and then it's an exhausting answer of how I've overcomplicated my relationship with lots of religions—so I just say "spiritual" since everyone just knows that to mean "gray"), resourced ("comfortable" but always a bit worried about money) woman wrestling with an identity crisis, along with what seems like many other demographics in America. I've personally become so overwhelmed by other people's stories about us that I chose to unpack our identity in the context of history and current affairs.

I spent my life making assumptions about the world, limiting my participation, and avoiding hard questions. Only in recent years have I begun to develop a practice of checking my privilege, catching my biases, putting fail-safes in place to prepare for blind spots, and developing language for difficult dialogues. I began raising my hand: I started buying books and taking courses; I spent time on the Navajo Nation and traveled to one of the first slave markets in Portugal, seeking insight from people who had perspectives on the complicity and potential of white women. I confronted the many truths we all occupy in this given moment and found a way to translate this very personal work into meaningful endeavors on frontlines I didn't know existed.

This book is meant to be a conduit for readers who might not know they're being called to the frontlines or where those lines might actually be located. The intention of these pages is to open the front gate of our collective white picket fence, guided by someone with a similar life experience, to gain greater insight into the role we've historically played and how that has translated to current realities of the world. I then invite you to have a seat right next to me as we learn from and follow the voices raising their hands to do the hard work of teaching us what we should have already known. Then, we'll look closely at how we should continue to move forward—because the American white woman is capable of a lot, and I'm wondering where we are.

This book poses challenging questions, many without easy answers, which may make the perfectionist in you (🫣) impatient. But all of the wrestling with ideas, the sitting inside the discomfort of what may be brand new ideas, the *not* putting the book down and plunging into the vapid social-media well—it's all part of what I'm asking us to admit and do. We may want to look away because being honest with ourselves about the work that lies ahead, and all that we didn't do in the past, is hard to own. This *ignorance dependency*, which clouds our vision and allows us to stay focused only on our jean size and follower count, makes the work in this book inconvenient.

Yet, instead of looking at the difficult questions I present as a chore, consider them a birthright—you live in a democracy, which means you've inherited the duty to participate. This, my friends, is a moral imperative.

The vast majority of white women benefit when we tell ourselves that because our relatives served in the world wars, our debts to society are paid; or that we're the "best country in the world," so there are no improvements remaining outside of a few poor blocks on the east side of Baltimore. Oh yeah, and saving the polar bears—I guess we'll have that on our shoulders for a while now, too, right? These are the dangerous old rationalizations and behaviors I hope these pages will provide the clarity to reverse. Together we'll find pathways and establish rules that will help us be in service to others and, in the process, come closer to our own humanity.

I'm not an expert on any one of the subjects that we'll discuss, but I am a curious student who knows how to nag academics and tap my Rolodex of friends on the frontlines of justice-based work in this country and abroad. My hope is that the foundational information in this book, presented through a lens you might find familiar, will help you gain a new understanding of topics you might be curious about and of the game you have the power to change. I've been there, and it took a variety of teachers—mostly, very generous people of color who shared perspectives I lacked or flagged my ignorant assumptions—to help me gain increased clarity and then support change accordingly.

The lessons in these pages are from my own (often mortifying) experiences, and the (sometimes contradictory) facts are from authors, PhDs, and entire university departments dedicated to studying these entangled past and present realities. There is a lot packed in here, and it's meant to be a starting place, your first-year, freshman class, *Intro to Being a White Woman in Today's World*.

Though we're exploring subjects like race and gender fairly broadly, we aren't going to handle any of them with kid gloves. You're going to feel all the feels, but you got this.

what's this "America" thing?

Many of us struggle with a deep sense of insecurity—a well-groomed American trait, born from a checklist created for white women many generations ago, that has morphed into something we think of today as acceptable, or even "proper" and "normal." When I was bored as a little girl, I would examine the tiny little weaves of my clothes, staring at them until my eyes pulled the threads into focus. There is so much complexity in a tiny square inch of fabric, when you examine it—so much technicality and art in the way threads dance over and under one another. In the same way, our society is woven together: the histories we want to tell ourselves; the consequences of our actions; our constantly changing identities depending on mood, people, and societal structure around us in that moment. Those complexities continue to reveal themselves as people intertwine in the course of daily life.

We talk about America* as if it is just a plot of land, with rules carved in stone. And while it is a physical place, one where you may have built your house or where your kids play soccer, in the end, that's just a patch of dirt. America is an *idea*, and that idea is still in development. We can debate its stage of construction: the foundation has been laid, but is the drywall really up? I know we're enjoying deliberating over the sectional versus the loveseat, but are we ready for that if we don't even know the size of the living room? Personally, I'm not sure the framing is as far along as we might want to believe. When was the last time you read the Constitution? (Let's be real, have you ever actually read it?) Because it needs work.

We might pretend that America is perfectly built so we don't have to face the parts of the house that need an upgrade, or even complete demolition. If we really looked, what we saw would force our hands into action. We'd have to do *something*, because the truth would lurk in too many of our quiet moments; we'd be too disturbed to do nothing. We'd have to change our assumptions and ways of life, and we'd have to work toward a different, collective goal. Maybe it's that we're all busy hanging out by ourselves, or moving to a different room of the house, so we don't have to face the truth 🫣.

I'm terrified about the state of the country—the dilapidated house—I am leaving to my children. My judgment day will come when my kids are old enough to interrogate me about the problems of the world I let fester on my watch, and rightfully so. We *have* to continue to renovate our home together—add more bathrooms, make room for new family members—if we're going to continue to chase the idea of America. And we can; the

---

* It's relevant to mention here that my use of the term "America/n" subordinates those who live in Central and South America. When I use the term "America" throughout the book it's in reference to the landmass known as the United States of America.

miraculous thing about humanity is our ability to self-correct and self-adjust when we decide to do so together, even if it takes longer than it should.

I've had a lot of different jobs. My first (and my most favorite, to date) was as a public school teacher, teaching first and fifth grades. But I've also worked in the halls of the United Nations and both Democratic and Republican White Houses. Sometimes it might feel that the problems being addressed in those buildings are too complicated to solve, or that there is too much gridlock to make any progress, but I can tell you from experience that's not true. During my time in those halls, I've worked with the bravest, most selfless civil servants, committed to positive change. Later in my career, as I've built both for-profits and nonprofits, I've learned that finding solutions requires patience, perseverance, and constant creativity.

And I've realized that the generation of top-down politics is over. The American house needs a serious gut renovation, and in some places, it needs to be rebuilt from the ground up. While construction is underway, we could really use another set of hands—so thanks for being here.

The only way to truly live up to the potential of America is for each of us to expand our sense of involvement and investment so that we can hold all the lovely and horrific truths that it contains. We must try not to compartmentalize any of these truths into absolutes—a well-refined habit of ours. We must be able to identify and acknowledge the social realities we live in so that we can re-weave our threads into the cultural tapestry we want . . . with patterns that bring us together rather than dividing us by race, gender, class, disability status, and religion.

your homework

Birthday party planning or organizing your closets—there is certainly something else this very second that you could be doing 🗑️. Still, there is something that led you here, something that's keeping your—and our—ears perked in a way that they haven't been for many generations. We know something needs to be done. The challenge is, we don't know what to do first, where to look first, who to trust, or how to embrace all the complex realities that require navigation, or how to address them without feeling overwhelmed or just plain defeated.

One of the things I enjoyed most as a first-grade teacher was finding ways to boil complicated concepts down to simple stories. You'll find a lot of that in these pages: complex ideas presented through the lens of one or two carefully selected, but unavoidably simplistic examples that can serve as a starting place for change. The only way we will move forward, together, is by understanding the role we, too, play in the American narrative: as a group and as individuals.

This work can bring up a lot of regrets, second-guessing, and self-doubt. That's okay—you're not alone. One eighty-four-year-old Listening Circle participant shared that, as she looks back on her life, she worries that she has not left a "real mark on the world." She has five children, loads of bubbly grandchildren, and family-filled holidays. She checked every box on the checklist society gave her. Still, instead of feeling pride, she looks back and wonders, "Where was I when decisions were being made for the country my children now have to live in?" Then she admitted with a sigh: "I was getting my hair blown out."

But we can start today by using an idea that activist and author James Baldwin offered in a 1984 essay, "On Being 'White' . . . and Other Lies." He wrote that humanity is "endlessly defined by those who do not dare define or even confront themselves." This, he said, "is the key to the crisis in white leadership."[11] When we avoid being honest about white supremacy in the world, we become a rudderless sailboat, floating in circles. By maintaining passivity and claiming not to know or understand even ourselves, we ensure the same patterns of injustice will endure.

America's lack of equality is perpetuated in part by white women's reluctance to truly know our past roles or potential power, in good and bad ways. If we truly understood our history and current influence, my hypothesis is that we'd have to act and do more. If you are like me, you were taught, growing up, to favor tidy behaviors and theories that made you feel satisfied for obeying the rules. Your textbooks told you a story of history that divided life into victor and conquered, into right and wrong, into "us" and "them." Such stories are what make it possible for power to remain in the hands of the powerful.

Some of the truths in this book were new to me, and some I've been wrestling with in my heart since second grade—maybe you have, too. These lessons may be overwhelming and infuriating, but I promise they will mostly be liberating.

My one request of you is that you stick with this book. It's going to be uncomfortable, and some of the information won't always feel applicable, but can we extend the possibility that we may be more flexible than we thought? Like that annoying burn during sit-ups, when the trainer claims the real strengthening and toning is happening—same concept here. The discomfort, pain, guilt, fury . . . all of it is where you make the progress. Just keep reading.

If you feel defensive, or possibly dismissive, remember the deal: finish the book first, and then tell me how I was wrong. I'm all ears.

the overview effect

As participating members of society, we are used to hearing messages that reaffirm the separations between us. We hold the assumption that there is a place where I (typically my body and possessions) begin and end and where you (and your things) begin and end. But my research—and, at times, hallucinogenic* experiences—prove we are undeniably connected.

I studied astrophysics in college and spent a lot of time obsessing over a metaphysical experience astronauts reported having in space, which scientists call the "overview effect." When in orbit and looking down on Planet Earth, hovering against the backdrop of infinity, astronauts reported a "perspective shift": a sense of overwhelming oneness with people and the planet they had never understood or experienced on land. When Edgar Mitchell, the pilot for Apollo 14,[12] tried to learn more about this phenomenon, academics he sought out found, in Sanskrit, the idea of *savikalpa samadhi*. This is when you see things with your eyes, but experience, physically, a sense of ecstasy and a total unity with the world around you.[13]

With an "overview" perspective, we are humbled by our insignificance as a tiny piece of an incomprehensibly large whole. But we also need to remember, when we zoom back in on ourselves, standing in our own shoes on the Earth, that each of us has the potential to change the course of history. We have to balance our desire to protect ourselves and our loved ones with an awareness of all the ways our behavior influences the world around us and of everything we cannot know.

These ideas aren't mutually exclusive or impossible to separate. Trying to ignore the connections between them is like saying you don't care about the toilet paper stuck to the bottom of your shoe just because you can't see it. Um, yes you do; take care of that, please.

---

* Yes, I did ayahuasca—one of three natural hallucinogens on the planet—and my parents will probably freak out a bit when they read this.

I believe that there is a reckoning in order for America and it must include the white woman. If you can buckle in for all the twists and turns we'll take in this book, you will gain a variety of perspectives that will help you better understand and embrace yourself. Moreover, you will take an active role—alongside all our brothers and sisters who have been expecting us for centuries—in defining the future.

This book is meant to be a first step in what, for all of us, is a lifetime of work. Come in, come see, come learn, and then go forth and do.

CHAPTER ONE

SILENCE(D)

Silence, I love you, and I hate you. Sometimes I work very hard to avoid you, and sometimes you're my most loyal companion.

Silence is a powerful and portentous concept. Many spiritual practices suggest the secret to happiness is embedded in its hollow caverns. Finding silence in tiny moments is grabbing the tail of time and yanking it back to the present, demanding that it stop moving forward. There are profound answers in silence—that is, if you can elbow your way through the ghosts of your to-do list and the demons of your insecurities first.

Sometimes we silence ourselves, covering our voice with a heavy, wet blanket so we don't run the risk of being embarrassed if we're wrong, or to pretend relationships and atmospheres are harmonious.

Sometimes silence is necessary, even essential. The only way you'll process the ideas in these pages is through silence—letting the ideas sink in, often while you're doing the mundane tasks of life. I have learned how crucial it can be for me, in my capacity as a white woman, to be actively silent—even though my mind is generating a red-carpet commentary on the daily nuances of life, particularly the confusing ones.

Occasionally, silence is painful. We've all gazed into the mirror in silent reflection, ambivalently disappointed about that C-section scar, or knowing that if we hadn't been so desperate to be tan in our youth, then we would have avoided the cluster of sunspots on our thighs. Perhaps we avoid the mirror at all costs, because who *is* that?! 🫠

I start here, with silence, because of its extraordinary power—both good and bad, and both personal and collective.

searching for the remote

If I'm on a business trip alone, surrounded by an empty hotel room, I quickly find myself in a torture chamber. This is when silence starts to harass me. I scramble for the TV remote, shushing the internal voice that reminds me of how germ infested it is, and fumble past the menu screen to any loud, busy channel. I hate the way a lack of sound leaves me to my thoughts, which can be dangerous, because sometimes my thoughts can get the best of me.

The irony is that I went to a school that raised me to seek out and embrace silence. In the Quaker school outside of Philadelphia that I attended as a kid, the entire student body sat in silence for forty-five minutes once a week. The point was to find yourself in that silence. Of course we kids resisted at first, giggling and making hand gestures to each other as if we knew what we were actually saying. The boys farted. Somehow, though, silence always won, settling over the room of two hundred elementary students. If anyone was moved to speak, by a sudden profound insight—if, as some Quakers say, they "were moved by the light"—they'd stand and share their brief thoughts.

As fourth graders, we stuck to processing the belly-up goldfish we'd found the night before. In middle school, we heard a lot about athletic-field failures; by high school, kids were coming out of the closet or wrestling with tensions at home.

My education taught me to value the power of silence, and yet, inside that collective silence, I sat in constant terror of sharing any insight. I had no way to overcome my self-doubt about sounding stupid by telling hundreds of judgey preteens I was losing sleep worrying about the decimation of Amazon rainforests. So I never spoke.

I pretended that I declined to speak because it was selfish to take up someone else's time by sharing what was on my mind. But in reality, I was scared I wouldn't express my thoughts in a way that would make me proud, after I sat back down. I thought I'd mess up somehow, the same way I do now. Instead, at that weekly meeting, I slouched into the safety net of silence, my insecurity suffocating the possibility of sharing ideas and building relationships with people in the community.

the privileged side of silence

Some of us have the freedom to choose when, and when not, to speak because our survival does not depend on it. This allows us to be selective about the truths we want to confront—the plight of the whales, for example, over that of children who might be going hungry a block away—and also about what we want to keep as zipped-up secrets, like admitting we don't actually know what to do about either. The ability to opt out of speech is the American white woman's perceived right, both a luxury and a trap.

More often than not, Listening Circle participants said they "don't see how politics affects their lives," and in some ways, they're right. When you are of a certain race and hover in a particular socioeconomic stratum, decisions that impact the public good don't always change your life significantly. That is privilege. Many of the Listening Circle participants I talked to could eke by on the swipe of a credit card if their teenage daughter needed an abortion, even if it meant flying to another country (on miles) to do it. If they had a beach house, their homeowner's insurance was a good enough backstop should rising sea waters flood their basements, but hey, they'd had some wonderful years at that place. One Listening Circle participant said she doesn't really see "how the presidential election impacts her life," though her increased tax rebate could finally get her the kitchen backsplash or repaved driveway she's been wanting.

Some argue the voluntary silence of white women is one of the country's greatest shortcomings, and I'm starting to agree. We seem only to speak, and are quick to shout, when there is an issue affecting our own routine, neighborhood, or kids; in fact, there is a whole collection of graphics and online posts about white women demanding to "see the manager." The internet likes to make fun of the entitled white woman who sees no problem berating workers for minor inconveniences or demanding an excessive level of attention, and with good reason. I remember loving the tweet of one online personality calling it like it is, suggesting that if white women used the "Can I see a manager?" tone with their husbands and with elected officials about the kids down the street that need their help, then maybe the world would be a bit better.

We can get nasty when inconvenienced in our own lives, but when someone else's kid doesn't have enough to eat for dinner, or is laying their head down in a violent home, we are suddenly very quiet. We become unhinged when something in our world is out of our control—like a school shooting in the suburbs that kills the same number of children who die from gun violence in Queens, New York, in a month. When something like this happens, we may believe it represents a break from what we have been promised. If my kid is running into the street or drowning, there's no choice but to scream. But when other people need help, it's optional?

Silence can be a recourse when we are "too tired" or when we're afraid of saying the wrong thing. When someone suddenly asks me "my opinion" and puts me on the spot, my hands get a little sweaty and I suddenly need some water. I choose my words carefully to prevent anyone from challenging me, and I kick myself—and even crumble—when I get a request I hate in response: "Prove it." *Abort,* I say to myself. It is definitely easier to dodge the conversation, retreat into the safety of silence, or change the subject to dinner plans, all while beating myself up for not being smarter and tougher and quicker.

The true gift of growing up Quaker-ish was that it forced me to see, and practice, facing the discomfort of silence, despite my preference for a constant soundtrack. But it wasn't until recently that I decided to dive into what really kept me on the bench in that meeting house for all those years. *As I explored my self-silencing, I realized my choice to remain silent wasn't solely internal; there are vast influences that were encouraging me to keep quiet.* I discovered that sometimes external rules and requirements were shushing me without my realizing it.

American white women tend to filter our words like we do clothing on a rack. We consider, exceptionally quickly, what something might look like on our body, which event it is appropriate for, how it will be received by certain audiences . . . a lot goes into the calculation. And we don't commit until we feel completely, 100% great about how an article of clothing will let us present ourselves to the world.

That's fine for dress shopping. It's not as fine when, you know, our voice could save a life? In our quest for perfectly structured arguments with impressively sourced statistics, we forget to wonder if all the time we spend picking and choosing the right words could be causing harm. Silence is also a procrastination tool—something that became clear to me in the Listening Circles. As I lugged impossible questions to dens and living rooms of beautifully appointed homes around the country, plopping them down on top of bowls of grapes and Werther's Original caramel candies, I began to understand both the causes and the impact of our self-silencing.

a perfectly warmed bench

The women who welcomed me into their communities suggested that we sometimes chill on the sidelines of the societal playing field. But is that because we want to stand there, or were told to, or is it a compromise we make because we're too anxiously occupied with creating a "good time" in unchallenging, comfortable ways, to consider the discomfort and risk of speaking up? The American playbook would have us believe that every debate has a winner and a loser, and that women are raised to be peace-makers: why would we create a circumstance where a sudden battlefield descends when and where it doesn't have to? Women are tasked with man-ufacturing and maintaining the peace in all of their domains. The result is soft smiles on our faces while low levels of anxiety are constantly coursing through our veins.

"I'm a peacekeeper. I don't like conflict in the family at holiday meals and things like that," said one woman who shared her views for a GAL-vanize USA[1] study that cited fear of conflict as a major reason why white women tend to align their political decision making with the men in their lives. Focused on our role as coordinators and cheerleaders, we avoid tense conversations, especially ones that could conclude in a tie; unre-solved, unsorted moments impede our ability to keep things sturdy. We are in charge of the cheese platters and spontaneous activities, so we leave complicated opinions alone for the sake of doing our job as coordi-nators and cheerleaders.

One Listening Circle participant said, "I'm at such a comfortable place I don't need or want to say anything to rock the boat—I don't want to lose the 'ease' of my cruise-controlled life." Other ladies shared fears like: *How am I really going to persuade anyone? What is the other person going to think of me?* We think twice before raising our voice—particularly if we don't have multiple PhDs in the subject. What comes out of this individual and collective unease is passivity—and the sacrifice of a moral compass to not use our voice to protect ourselves and others. This passivity creates a fertile breeding ground for voluntary complacency.

If, despite growing discomfort, you're still feeling hesitant, then that's because you are likely an excellent rule follower. We choose "nice" over "good" per the instructions handed down to us for generations—rules like what we are and aren't allowed to talk about at the table. No politics, sex, money, or religion, obviously. And we don't tend to tackle the upsetting subjects of race, gender, and class, either. Silence is the pathway to civility. White women sometimes find it hard to "express or defend" political views; 48% of us feel this way.[2] Since the ladies in Listening Circles did not believe they were properly informed about the list of overwhelming topics littering our headline news, they dodged difficult discussions at the school's band-camp fundraiser or in the staff break room. This habit of instinctive, fear-laced avoidance keeps our crucial voices out of most forums for discussion and inhibits us from stepping outside our safety bubbles to learn, engage, and challenge.

But are we as confused by things like world events and complicated systems as we claim? I am suspicious about our insistence that we don't "know enough." I do know we are statistically likely to be working all-around harder than our hubbies, live-in boyfriends, and male life partners,[*] which makes it more difficult to find the time to catch up on world events. We put in around four hours of unpaid work per day[4]—just think of how busy you stay, even after you get home from a day at work or schlepping the kids. None of us have much time to read longform journalism about the quality of our drinking water, the intricacies of assault weapons legislation, or the pros and cons of congestion pricing.[†] We can barely take in a sixty-second, five-step video about how to meditate as we scroll our Facebook feeds.

The United States is now ranked as the tenth most dangerous place in the world for a woman to live.[5] We are also tied for third (with Syria) in rankings of the most sexually violent nation, which I believe is due to the way we raise our boys (more on that later).[‡] With that in mind, are you really comfortable with maintaining your silence to keep the peace in your own home or family or workplace? How does your mindset change when you're fully aware of how the lives and experiences of women are devalued?

"You don't ever want to be that person who shows up at a cocktail party and talks politics," said one woman; the rest of the Listening Circle collectively nodded. "For anyone to bother listening, you really have to know what you're talking about." But who wants to deal with the risk of jeopardizing a

---

[*] Mothers spend nearly twice as long as fathers doing unpaid domestic work.[3]

[†] Congestion pricing is a strategy for reducing traffic and raising money for transit improvements by charging drivers to use busy roadways.

[‡] Quoting the website, "This includes rape as a weapon of war; domestic rape; rape by a stranger; the lack of access to justice in rape cases; sexual harassment and coercion into sex as a form of corruption."[6]

relationship when we're busy being pleasant? It's easier to avoid the drama and ask about the boss's daughter's college acceptance status or the weather during their last nine holes of golf.

If you are that person, you are the outlier (and a quick high-five for you). A full 74% of white women avoid conversations about politics because they typically lead to conflict.[7] That's seventy-four million* white women. Can we agree that's a really large number of us envisioning the gates to chaos cracking open if we so much as mention a subject that isn't universally neutral? No one wants a drama-filled impasse, right? And we as sure as hell can't be the ones to start the conversation, since our role is the glue that holds our family and group of friends "harmoniously" together.

to-do list, take me away

The first few moments of a Listening Circle can feel a tiny bit awkward; everyone is laser-focused on me, uneasy about where I'm going to take the conversation. They all know they signed up for an evening of asking tough questions of themselves and each other; this is no ordinary girls' night out. Feeling the discomfort in the silence, I ask: "How is everyone doing?" Lovely smiles form, but the participants' nods and quietly muttered "Good"s tell me they're performing, because really, who is "good"?

"No, really. How is everyone doing?" I repeat, and then there is the brave woman who answers, "Busy." This is an equally obvious response, and one that's intimately familiar.

A firestorm follows of "Ugh, I'm drowning," or "The kids have me running in circles," or "I'm on a really big case at work, so there's just no time." If I bump into a friend on the street or at school drop-off, their answer is the same: "Busy."

Every person I know has an endless to-do list, one that feasibly includes getting that year's holiday card photo taken even though it's only July. This list keeps us so occupied that we don't have time for anything else—especially our most insecure thoughts about ourselves and our relevance in the world. I know I can get pretty tied up when I'm trying to tune out the internal broken record grooving to "I'm not good enough" or "I can't figure this out so maybe I'm not worthy; I must not be needed." When that

---

* As of 2018, there were 100,127,799 white women in the United States.[8]

playlist starts, it's amazing how quickly I disappear into reorganizing the wrapping-paper drawer.

We're drawn to distractions like the television after a hard day because, as the renowned Buddhist leader and peace activist Thich Nhat Hanh says, "we know that when we turn it off we may have to go back to ourselves and get in touch with the suffering inside." What is that suffering? A Listening Circle participant said it's a question of "who am I, and it feels impossible to answer." We don't want to sit with ourselves, our thoughts, our outstanding questions about our lives—because that can quickly morph into the "not good enough" feeling that poisons our self-confidence. But when we use our to-do list or the latest Taylor Swift playlist to drown out those fears of inadequacy, we also block out our curiosity and the potential for self-improvement—our oldest habits allow us to self-silence.

New rule: Let's just accept that we've made ourselves, at times, unnecessarily busy. And let's no longer use that busy-ness as an excuse to not figure out, and then say, how we really feel.

it all feels like a lie-ish

Let's be honest: The maelstrom of conflicting cultural and political messages we receive—from news sources, partners, grown children, great uncles, and our own thoughts—is overwhelming. We all find a way to mute them at times; if not, we'd never get anything done. But muting them doesn't magically make them go away.

In addition to silencing ourselves to maintain the image that everything is just fine, we also fall victim to what political-behavior researchers describe as *cross-pressures*: instances where there are so many conflicting perspectives that it feels impossible to guide a group, or even just oneself, to a consensus. Studies, or just common sense, show that it's easier to just drop out of a conversation than it is to navigate all of its complexity.

No duh. I get it—one more thing for me to have to figure out, while I'm already juggling the birthday-party circuit over my anniversary weekend, when my best friends from college are in town. How am I supposed to choreograph any more in the world when I can barely keep the routines of my own life sorted? Plus, when there are entire aisles at bookstores dedicated to how today's labyrinths of crisis came to be? How are we supposed to be experts enough for our opinions to matter?

People who feel *cross-pressured* are less inclined to participate in politics or engage civically, even in the voting booth,[9] because they are overwhelmed and distrustful of the constant mixed messages.[10] It's like one of your kids demanding lemonade and the other apple juice, and since you don't feel like being a referee or coming up with an amicable compromise, everyone just gets water. We stick with the easy option when we don't feel like dealing 😊.

When we hear so much contradiction all the time, we get stuck. We tune out, and only tune back in when we hear WIIFM—the "What's In It For Me" station—playing. That is the only way we can rationalize the noise—by giving the complexity a relevant context (our own life) that makes information familiar and worthy of sludging through.

What's happened in political campaigns, unfortunately, is that they are all about catering to people in power, who often have wealth. In affluent homes, what's in it for them is the difference between that ski vacation in Aspen or just another cozy weekend in the basement screening room. The dichotomy structured by our politics and our winner-take-all, "look out for your own" culture has bred a national tendency toward self-centeredness that, I believe, is killing us.

In one Listening Circle in the suburbs of New Jersey, the participants were sharing their biggest concerns today. "Job security" and "access to healthcare" were at the top, followed by "education." But they'd never raised their voices about this issue. Why not? Because it didn't feel relevant enough to their daily lives.

The irony is that five of the fifteen participants' husbands worked at one of the two largest pharmaceutical companies in the country, located a few miles away. I reminded these five ladies—and the other ten, who are friendly with the first five's husbands—of their proximity to the people who set the cost for lifesaving and often prohibitively expensive drugs.*

---

* I can appreciate the millions of dollars that go into the research, development, and trials of drugs, and I understand how for-profit companies need to make their investments back. But it's impossible for me to rationalize the billions upon billions of dollars that Big Pharma makes every year while keeping the price for lifesaving pills so high that the people who need them can't afford them. Big pharmaceutical companies use something called "price discrimination" where drugs in developing countries cost less than they do in the United States. Even with these marked-down prices, many countries are still unable to afford innovative medicines being introduced to the market. According to the US Government Accountability Office, in 2015, pharmaceutical and biotechnology industries garnered $775 billion in revenue.[11]

As we talked, it became increasingly difficult for the women in this Listening Circle to reconcile their concern about affordable healthcare, knowing the role some of their partners had in pricing decisions. In these participants' defense, they were quick to make clear that none of their partners were on the "drug pricing teams." Still, it was a gentle reminder of their proximity to power. And when it comes to our silence, that proximity is a high stake. The closer we believe we are to power—often represented by the powerful men in our lives—the more silent we sometimes become.

who is the real Oz?

Proximity to power itself can make us powerful. We may not be the one with the job title, processing the paychecks, or with the important phone numbers in our phones. But just standing next to an influential person, or having access to some exclusive place, event, or thing, can increase the optics of our personal currency. Those who work in the White House often measure their power in feet, and sometimes inches, by how close they are to the Oval Office. Same rules apply outside 1600 Pennsylvania Avenue. Our access to the people who do hold that power gives us influence, and others may treat us accordingly. Though often temporary, and even false, this sense of influence can translate into assumed righteous behaviors and sometimes solicit responses from others that make us feel worthy.

It's like our fascination with "step-and-repeats"—the logo-covered canvases behind red carpets, where celebrities stand to be photographed. Every event I plan always has one of these—they're free PR in our selfie-obsessed world. And you'd be shocked by how eager everyone is to stand next to a step-and-repeat banner, regardless of the logos shown. It's photo evidence that your presence was requested—that you were wanted—by influential people, hip brands, the "cool kids" throwing the exclusive party.

Being seen there means that we are worthy. But, as gender studies scholar Ann Russo says, we need to "build critical consciousness about how the praxis of speech and silence are intricately connected with the power systems,"[12] because often the closer we, as women, are to those power structures, the more silent we become, in order to retain the validation of those affiliations.

Because proximity is power, we don't want to do anything to jeopardize our place on the "red carpet." Sometimes that just means making sure we have the Lilly Pulitzer–patterned dress for the BBQ, but other times it means laughing awkwardly at the misogynistic joke so we don't risk tarnishing the good mood of the man offering us prestige—whether it's the Oscar-winning actor headlining the event, our spouse, or their boss.

Whenever it's clear that a conversation has shifted into uncomfortable territory, and instead of acknowledging the tension, we whip out our magic wand* and change the subject, we are choosing an active kind of silence. We engage in a form of *intentional invisibility*—a term coined by a team of Stanford University researchers who study gender, health, and social inequality to describe how professional women employ "a set of risk-averse, conflict-avoidant strategies to feel authentic, manage competing expectations in the office, and balance work and familial responsibilities."[13] Sound familiar?

At work—and, I believe, everywhere we go—we might choose the safety of remaining behind the scenes over standing in the spotlight and asking the vulnerable questions or diving into debate. To us, being in control may not mean being onstage; instead, we're dripping with sweat as we yank levers behind a curtain, while all everyone else sees is a neat, easy performance of juggling it all. Everything is fine over here, so please hurry up and look away.

This projection feels crucial to us, and on some level, it is. It not only lets us maintain the currency of proximity; it also allows us to avoid backlash and side-eyes from frenemies and mothers-in-law. But really, what are we accomplishing? The same Stanford researchers found that while we're technically just trying to get through our days, these performances are actually helping maintain the status quo—and making it impossible for other women to share the benefits we enjoy from that proximity to power, as a result.[14]

we're all gold-medal gymnasts—watch this flip

Priya Fielding-Singh, a sociologist at Stanford University studying gender, health, and inequality, offered me a great term she developed for the way men and women alike work to rationalize inequality rather than change it: *cognitive acrobatics*. These mental somersaults and backflips are attempts to justify the unequal frameworks we operate in—though we wouldn't necessarily call it that. It's saying "It's just easier if I do it" to rationalize why you're the only one handling the buying of Christmas presents; "Women are more

---

* Hermione Granger's, to be exact.

in tune with kids' needs" to justify why you do most of the childcare; or the all-too-infamous "He doesn't know any better" to explain why we're the ones to ask the heartfelt questions of the grieving neighbor while he retreats into silence. It's when, instead of acknowledging and working to address inequalities in our own lives, or in the rest of the world, we rationalize them away.

"Women can feel safe and comfortable within their complicity, or even full participation in, gender inequality," Dr Fielding-Singh told me. "Whether this plays out in the workplace, at home, or in a marriage, the easiest response to the truth of inequality is to try to make sense of it. To make it seem like it's actually equal." So, we do somersaults to convince ourselves our "choices" are justified. Darcy Lockman, author of *All the Rage: Mothers, Fathers, and the Myth of Equal Partnership*, says there are "three broad explanatory categories for the tenacity [of cognitive acrobatics]: biology, cultural mandates around maternal devotion, and the ubiquitous prioritization of men's needs and desires relative to women's."[15]

. Many studies in the past decade* have tracked the extreme inequity of women's labor versus men's. Both a Pew[18] and an *Economist* study[19] have shown that men believe they carry equal weight in household chores, but women don't agree—particularly when children enter the picture. A study from Ohio State University found childless households with two heterosexual working partners each completed approximately fifteen hours of housework per week.[20] But once children arrived, women added another twenty-two hours of childcare, while men only added a small fraction of that number. And when we use these backflips and somersaults to justify the truth about our reality—and avoid rocking the boat by accepting the additional burdens and not asking for (and expecting) more from the men in our lives—we prevent change from happening, not just in our own households, but in society.

We can't make excuses for ourselves and expect the rest of the world to get better on its own. The best way to combat the deeply ingrained norms we use to justify our own positions is to see the patterns within our own self-talk and behaviors. In other words: Stop being silent and start flagging

---

* An Oxfam International report shows that women worldwide spend between two to ten times as much time performing uncompensated household chores and childcare as men.[16] The Organization for Economic Cooperation and Development (OECD) said in 2017 that the unequal distribution between men and women of unpaid work in the home is one of the most critical gender equality issues of our time.[17]

your own back handspring or aerial cartwheel. It's the only way we can design new processes that level the playing field for our daughters.

(written by . . . men)

The story that tells women we are expected to juggle so much without complaints is rooted in a message society teaches girls from a young age: you do not deserve the same power and freedom as your male counterparts. Think of all the micro-messages or blatant instructions in our religious texts (written by men), such as, God is assumed to be a man; the governing doctrines of many nations (written by men), such as "All men are created equal" in the Declaration of Independence; and how culture is perpetuated through our film, music, and art (mostly controlled . . . by men). Indeed, our world has been designed by men, for men. This system, which elevates male perspectives about everything from your period to your orgasm to who should be the breadwinner and the protector of the family, is known as the *patriarchy*.* It is the patriarchy that discourages us from speaking and allows the male voice to fill our void. In the words of Rebecca Solnit, an American writer on the topics of feminism, environment, and politics, "We know who has, mostly, been heard on the official subjects; who held office, commanded armies, served as judges and juries, wrote books, and ran empires over the past several centuries."[21] Men have made most of humanity's decisions from the beginning, so it should surprise no one that those decisions were made with men's best interests in mind.

The patriarchy was built on male-centered systems and women's forced compliance. Today, the patriarchy still thrives on our reluctance to speak, because when we don't, male voices replace our silence. While our silence is now theoretically a choice, it's a choice we've been strongly encouraged to make, all the while being told it was our idea. We think that we have the right to speak, to opt in or out of doing so, and we're not wrong; we have freedom of speech. But we often choose silence, performing little circus acts for ourselves for the comfort of men and our peace of mind. As a result, the male voice remains *more heard*, and the patriarchy continues to dictate all areas of our lives—from healthcare (even though 75% of all healthcare workers in the United States are women[22]), to education (despite women having

---

* A system of society or government in which men hold the power and women are largely excluded from it.

long comprised the majority of teachers), to the culinary arts (even though women are typically the ones who assume the role of feeding their families). And while one of our favorite acrobatic tricks is the line, "It's been this way for centuries," can we agree now, in this moment in time, that our settling for that excuse is partly to blame for the United States being at the top of the "Most Dangerous List for Women and Girls in the World," with no end in sight? Can we agree that what we've been doing for so long needs to change?

People of all genders who have challenged, and continue to challenge, the patriarchal system and demand that women's voices are heard are called *feminists*. From Abigail Adams, who reminded her husband, President John Adams, "Remember the ladies, and be more generous and favorable to them than your ancestors," to Maria Gallagher and Ana Maria Archila, who cornered Republican senator Jeff Flake in an elevator on his way to Brett Kavanaugh's Supreme Court Justice confirmation hearings, feminists recognize structural inequality and proactively work to fix it.

Defining feminism is like trying to define a religion. If you ask any one of the 2.2 billion Christians on the planet what Christianity is, you'll get approximately 2.2 billion answers. Despite the diversity of faiths, I feel I can confidently say: all of those 2.2 billion Christians believe, in some capacity, that Jesus lived a life we should all emulate.* Likewise, feminist scholars debate who should and shouldn't be able to consider themselves feminists based on the details of what they believe or the way they behave in various aspects of their lives. But I believe one universal tenet that all feminists share is that women's voices should be heard and considered in equal measure to those of men.

Even with the accomplishments of the many feminist movements† that have gotten us the right to work outside the home and run for office, and have protected us against many forms of discrimination, we can all agree: we don't have it as easy as men. Women contribute disproportionately more labor in the home, still get paid less than men for the same work, and are

---

* In fact, I'd argue many non-Christians would agree with that, as well.

† The feminist movement is divided into "waves." The first wave (nineteenth to early twentieth century) was focused on the woman's right to vote. The second wave (1960s through the end of the 1970s) revolved around equal legal and social rights, and the third wave (beginning in the 1990s) was a response to the second wave's focus on upper-middle-class white women. The third wave emphasized the need for an intersectional perspective on the oppression of women that demonstrated how race, class, disability, religion, sexual orientation, gender, and nationality are all crucial variables in discussing feminism.[23]

still underrepresented in nearly every government, military, and business in the world.

Maybe we're at the beginning of a new feminist chapter (some say the "fourth wave of feminism"), where marginalized voices are represented in decision making, centering the concept of intersectionality (more on that later). Or maybe we're still in the midst of the original, millennia-long battle of women wresting back their voice (fighting for the right to vote and the freedom to have their own credit cards, buy homes, and start businesses, among others) and dignity (the right to control their bodies and decide how they want to live their lives). Either way, our work—feminism's work—is not done. The need for us to raise our hands and position ourselves on the new frontline is as urgent as ever. And part of the work that remains is to dismantle a number of key systems, like the patriarchy, that—through our behavior and, often, our silence—we as white women operate within and prop up.

The *patriarchy* gets challenged whenever this silence is broken, and people who aren't male are controlling money, legislation, airtime on TV, pulpits, and attention on social media. Some women are already doing this work by speaking up louder, desperately trying to be heard in the face of incredible obstacles. Simultaneously, others—and I would put myself in this category—are still learning ways they are, and have always been, silenced, despite ostensibly being raised and encouraged to use our voices.

sweaty palms

In this particular social moment, we—okay, I'll qualify that as me, my friends, generations of my family, and close to every white woman I've spoken with in the past four years—are more vocally questioning the way our world works and our role in it. And I don't just mean in relation to the patriarchy, because for some, that is new terminology; I mean other systems that keep certain people constantly in positions of power at the expense of others. Another system that we might have been unknowingly protecting with our silence is widely referred to as *white supremacy*.*

---

* As summarized by Frances Lee Ansley, a critical-race scholar, and taken from a passage from David Gillborn, also a critical-race-theory scholar.[24] White supremacy is "a political, economic and cultural system in which whites overwhelmingly control power and material resources, conscious and unconscious ideas of white superiority and entitlement are widespread, and relations of white dominance and non-white subordination are daily reenacted across a broad array of institutions and social settings."[25]

I know these two words next to each other might make your palms sweat—it made a lot of participants in the Listening Circles uncomfortable. That's what used to happen to me. Now I'm grateful that I understand this framework; it's clarified so much. And maybe you'd argue that the term "white supremacy" is dangerous and should only be applied to the most outspoken extremists among us. So let me be clear: *white supremacists** are people who publicly voice their support for and actively protect a system of white supremacy. These are the people who want to keep America white and controlled by men (most white supremacists also believe that women are second-class citizens); these are the people who join white-nationalist hate groups. *White supremacy* is the societal structure they want to protect—one we are all swimming in now, whether we agree with it or not, because our laws and societal norms have given white people strong advantages over everyone else.

(This is often where white folk want to leave the conversation, but just hang on a few more paragraphs, so we're all working off the same set of vocabulary words. You are here, in the pages of this book, because you acknowledge that societal structures are not working and you are raising your hand to find out why.)

Being white and living within a system of white supremacy does not make you a white supremacist unless you are *actively*—and this is the key word—trying to protect it. However, there is a chance—like a really solid chance 🫣—that, despite not being a *white supremacist*, you are unknowingly behaving in a way that leaves the system of *white supremacy* intact, because you've been raised in a country that embedded these behaviors into the fabric of our culture.

This is one of the hardest concepts to recognize and absorb in anti-racism work—I'm still becoming aware of it in places I'd never expect, even though I've been doing this work for quite some time. And because white supremacy is so multilayered, and has seeped into so much of the foundation and processes of this country that there are no easy solutions to undo

---

* A racist belief that white people are "superior to people of other racial backgrounds and that Whites should politically, economically, and socially dominate non-Whites. While often associated with violence perpetrated by the KKK and other White supremacist groups, it also describes a political ideology and systemic oppression that perpetuates and maintains the social, political, historical and/or industrial White domination."[26]

its harm, it can be especially tempting to run away from . . . but it's one of the most crucial concepts to catch and examine.

A quick analogy: *White supremacy* is like the New York City subway system. I use it to get from point A to B, never really paying attention to the conductors or to the Metropolitan Transit Authority, which is constantly repairing tracks and building new ones. I am ignorant of what goes on behind the scenes to create and maintain the system; I just reap the benefits by riding the train, casually, when I need to. The *white supremacists* are the people driving the trains, or in the high-rise office buildings, actively lobbying for where tracks get laid—for instance, in neighborhoods where they will benefit one set of people and not others.

But here's the thing: even if I'm not actively participating in any decisions related to the subway system—I'm just a rider—I still benefit from that system. I *support* that system, by participating in it—by paying to ride. And when I don't pay attention to the behind-the-scenes decisions about how the subway system works—because, again, I only care if the train gets me from point A to B—I am letting the people who call the shots drastically impact the lives of other people even if those decisions weren't under my control or didn't happen on my watch.

While we aren't all actively undermining marginalized voices on our Facebook feeds, we did all inherit an infrastructure that put white people, and especially white men, ahead of everyone else, and we support it—both knowingly, like when we do cognitive acrobatics to laugh off dangerous jokes and behavior, and unknowingly. While we might not have carried torches in Charlottesville, Virginia, in 2017, we have been conditioned to make decisions that allow a system that supremely values whiteness and maleness to thrive.

What this kind of tacit support looks like, in the Listening Circles, is women complaining that their sons aren't getting into the universities they once easily did "because his all-boys Catholic school was a direct feeder to Notre Dame" and now there are new diversity requirements. It might be the smirks, raised eyebrows, and comments about paltry qualifications that tenured white professors exchange when a new faculty hire is announced—who turns out to be a person of color. We need to recognize that these benefits, dynamics, and stereotypes support white supremacist systems. For generations, we've passed wealth and opportunity down from one generation to another, whether through grandparents paying for their grandchildren's private school education, or through our calling in that favor to get our neighbor an internship.

We often think we're just playing the game that is laid out before us, and we are. We can't magically un-inherit wealth, race, ancestry, or being raised in the United States. But let's be clear: we protect these opportunities, this system, by oh-so-slightly bending the rules with our privilege to keep power in our own homes. And that is protecting white supremacy.

You might ask, "What's wrong with looking out for my own? Can you blame me?" And no, not really. As I write this book, my daughter, Ever, is in a private school with full Mandarin-language immersion. Having written part of my graduate school thesis on the benefits of multi-language learning in early-childhood education, I made a promise to myself that, no matter what it took, I would provide a dual-language education for my children. The best program I could find was in an exclusive private school that cost an egregious amount of money. Though my children won't spend their lives in the private school system, the fact that I'm investing even one dollar of my money in an education system that I know widens the opportunity gap contradicts my own values and causes me a lot of conflict.

I'm not a white supremacist, because I am not actively calling or working for a white-centered world. But am I protecting a white supremacist system? Yes. By sending my child to a private school, I am complicit in a system that causes harm. My actions, as we know, speak louder than my words. And I can scream all I want about the need for more resources in public school classrooms, but until I'm a public-school parent, my words are just that: words. I silence myself through my actions; I should be walking the walk of increased opportunity for all preschool students, which I could facilitate as an active parent of a public school classroom.

The New York City public school system, the largest in the country, is, in spite of the city's incredible diversity, also one of the most segregated. A 2010 UCLA study found that nineteen of the thirty-two New York City Community School Districts had fewer than 10% white students enrolled.[27] The range of experiences that children have within this system because of that segregation is an example of how the variables of race, class, and zip code connect—or, in the terminology that is often used today, how they intersect.

Intersectionality is the idea that the impact on a person or issue of any one aspect of identity (like race, gender, class, language, or religion) or experience (education in one zip code vs. another zip code) cannot be understood in a vacuum—*every* factor impacting someone or something affects the outcome, and thus they must all be considered together. I've talked earlier in the book about the impossibility of describing American white women as a homogeneous group. The same is true for Asian American women, or New York City public school children, or even the kids in a single Brooklyn neighborhood vying to get into the "best" public school in their zone—where one school might have a reading specialist (a service I desperately needed in elementary school as I battled dyslexia) while the other does not. Each of us has our own set of variables that play into the opportunities we receive and the decisions available to us in any given circumstance.

According to philosopher Amia Srinivasan, a global understanding of systems like the patriarchy and white supremacy gives us greater awareness of how our own experiences intersect with the diverse experiences of others. When we consider "the plight of women garment workers in Asia and women farm workers in North America, and the Indian rape epidemic," understanding intersectionality "allows people to ask whether some machine is at work that connects all the experiences they're having with all the experiences others are having."[28] The deeper I dive into this work, the more clearly I see our interconnectedness—my actions directly (both negatively and positively) impacting the lives of others around the corner and, sometimes, like voting for president, on the other side of the world. And, vice versa.

This awareness of shared experience can also help us gain a sense of relativity. We can better understand that some people, like those mentioned in the quote above, face greater obstacles than others at the nexus of white supremacy and patriarchy. We call groups of people who are facing some of society's largest barriers—people who are gender nonconforming,* disabled, stateless,† nonwhite, nonmale, and/or non-Christian—*marginalized* or *oppressed.*

Understanding how oppressive systems collide to keep certain groups of people suffering is key as we move through the pages of this book. Intersectional identities are endlessly diverse because every individual comes from a unique set of conditions. To take one example: the idea that all men

---

* "Gender nonconforming" refers to people who do not identify with the labels or characteristics associated with masculine and feminine gender norms.

† According the Convention of the Stateless, a stateless person is someone who is "not recognized as a national by any state under the operation of its law." Some stateless persons are also refugees.[29]

perfectly fit the cultural idea of a cis "man" disempowers every man who does not fit neatly into this category—which, based on the men I know, is all of them; not a single one of them is like the others. This feels like an obvious statement, yet we constantly bucket that gender together. "The notion that all men are a category in opposition to all women breaks down because not all men are men," said the feminist scholar Jacqueline Rose. "That is, not all men embody the kind of masculinity that men are supposed to inhabit."[30] In other words, the simple equating of physical characteristics with gender identity doesn't apply to anyone who is trans or nonbinary. Because of the binary-driven nature of white supremacy—that you're either one way or the other—the people who are often most marginalized, or who seem to suffer most in American society (as well as many other societies), are typically trans, indigenous people of color.

white lies beneath

My center-of-the-earth, molten-core point here is that any time society protects, makes room for, and encourages white, male voices and bodies over and at the expense of nonwhite, nonmale voices and bodies, it is the patriarchy or white supremacy—and often a combination of both—at work. And we, as white women, tend to protect this cross-section of power, because it often benefits us.

We are voluntarily engaged in a silent agreement with a system that sidelines us as women because ultimately it can benefit us. Because white men are one of the highest-employed demographics,* and most white men are married to white women,† more white women have a source of income. This means access to healthcare and, more superficially but not insignificantly, for some in the upper classes it can mean access to the country clubs, or "it" parties, that we use to validate ourselves. Counterintuitively, we also support it even when it doesn't benefit us.

Psychologist Terry Real, who has decades of experience as a couples therapist and whose work focuses on men's issues, crystalizes our protection of this system. I am drawn to his definition of *core collusion* to explain why we do this: "The *core collusion* is that whoever inhabits the 'feminine side of the equation'—whether it's a child to a parent, or a hostage to a

---

* In 2017, 71.8% of white American men were employed.[31]
† In 2016, 10.2% of marriages were interracial or interethnic.[32]

kidnapper—has a profound instinct to protect whoever is on the masculine side of the equation, even while being hurt by that person. That's true of children who are being traumatized, who are trying to regulate their parents. It's true of races who are trying to manage up to the ruling race or class that is oppressing them. It's true of women to men."[33]

I want to emphasize the power of his next point, so read closely: "This is one of the unspoken, most profound forces in human psychology and human history. The perpetrator is protected." When he comes home disappointed in his day so he's snappy with the kids, or when he monitors your spending but casually goes on boys' weekends without regard to the price tag, we may feel frustrated—but we already have well-worn coping mechanisms in place. Many women have a sense of "better the devil you know": the age-old rationale that shattering an entrenched inequity may just make room for an unfamiliar new oppressor.

It's important that we link our personal preference for keeping silent—in the sense of stifling ourselves—to its profound effect on the rest of society. Activists from across the spectrum have criticized what they call *white silence* as a form of complicity, and even as a form of violence. Author and antiracism teacher Layla Saad points out why: "But white silence is anything but neutral. Rather, it is a method of self-protection and therefore also the protection of the dynamics of white supremacy. It protects you, the person with white privilege, from having to deal with the harm of white supremacy. And it protects white supremacy from being challenged, thereby keeping it firmly in place." She goes on: "Here is a radical idea that I would like you to understand: white silence is violence. It actively protects the system. It says, I am okay with the way things are because they do not negatively affect me and because I enjoy the benefits I receive with white privilege."[34]

Albert Einstein, the world's most well-known theoretical physicist, who lived through Hitler's rise to power, builds on this in a quote that has always been especially resonant to me, as a Jewish person: "The world will not be destroyed by those doing evil but by those who watch them and do nothing." Here, I join the chorus of feminist voices who link the history of human rights with the history of being silenced, and share a determination to reshape the way we operate.

Society expects us to pretend that our silence is optional and well placed. This has been the case for so unfathomably many generations—but it's actually often enforced and unnecessary. The very reason the patriarchy needs this is because we, American white women, are one of the more powerful demographics on the planet, and if we truly stepped into that power, we could change the systems that keep so many in a constant state of suffering.

too powerful

Beyond the powerful currency that is our proximity to (white) men, I want to remind you about the power that we wield ourselves, whether we want to admit it or not: we control more money, votes, and education than our men.

Throughout this book, I'll further unpack what currency we have, but for now I'll just say this: white women, and the world, are marginalized by what we don't realize about ourselves. We give away our power to maintain civility, which is both caused by our cultural plague of self-doubt 🙆 and the continued source of it.

There is good reason for this. Our power as a demographic has been hidden from us, often intentionally, since our nation's founding; it's no wonder we now operate in ignorance of it. Just for a minute, go back to just after the Revolutionary War, and our country's vital first stabs at designing democracy. Enter the influential writing of French philosopher Jean-Jacques Rousseau. At the time, he had profound thoughts on how countries should be politically structured. Political theorist Judith Shklar summarizes Rousseau's thinking on the qualifications for democratic citizenship in this way: "Women must certainly be excluded, because they are psychologically too powerful and too domineering to be allowed to share political authority."[35] I just want to make sure you caught that: We are *too powerful*. And we are powerful in ways that can be hard to identify and quantify.*

I believe that we, women, would use this power to act on behalf of all,[38] which is a scary prospect for the few that are in power. Rousseau knew that and advised against it. "Our deepest fear is not that we are inadequate. Our deepest fear is that we are powerful beyond measure," begins a quote from author, activist Marianne Williamson, from her book *Return to Love*.

---

* A recent study suggests that female leaders are more persuasive, assertive, and willing to take more significant risks then male leaders. The same study also found women are more empathetic and flexible as well as stronger in personal skills.[36] Also, Catherine Hakim, a British sociologist, authored a book in 2019 about her theory of "erotic capital," also sometimes thought of as "sexual capital," which describes women's use of feminine allure to achieve their goals professionally, politically, and in other ways. She considers erotic capital to be an asset equally as compelling as financial, social, and cultural capital.[37]

It's been posted and shared so often for good reason; while it is spiritual in context, I also find it applicable to the ways women operate in political and civil spheres. The quote goes on to say: "It is our light, not our darkness that most frightens us. We ask ourselves, Who am I to be brilliant, gorgeous, talented, fabulous? Actually, who are you not to be? . . . Your playing small does not serve the world. There is nothing enlightened about shrinking so that other people won't feel insecure around you."[39]

Many of us—myself included—have been swayed by the idea that nature or evolution placed us in a passive, subservient role. After a Listening Circle in Virginia, in which we talked a lot about men's and women's roles in society, I spent some time with one of the participants' husbands. Standing next to his wife, he said, "It's always been the man's job to hunt and the women's job to gather—so let the men do the work." (You know, because gathering isn't work. Apparently.) Comments like these can give us permission to step down from the taller podium at home and in public when we're feeling self-doubt. It's a hall pass to be complacent when we're exhausted, confused, and feeling helpless 👀 in the shadow of problems that seem insurmountable. This isn't about who really "calls the shots" in your home—we are more likely to do that on all things related to logistics and kids—but about who forms opinions and makes decisions about how we act as individuals and as a family unit publicly, and about the state of our public systems, which is typically our fathers' and husbands' lane.

Our self-doubt is clear in the way we use social media—to compare our lives to other people's to see if we're measuring up. It is fueled by reality TV's hologram-ish portrayals of select people being "ordinary"—if that's not what our life looks like (you know they have hair and makeup teams there hours before the cameras go on, right?), then we've failed. Modern life keeps us strapped for time as we try to do it all (career, motherhood, caring for our elders), which means even though we're expected (and expect ourselves) to be perfect, we can't do everything (or anything) as well as we'd like.

I know self-doubt kept me quiet for a long time. But the comfortable silence I've been fortunate enough to know for most of my life as an upper-middle-class white woman is no longer comfortable. This echoed through Listening Circle conversations also: we want, desperately, to participate and engage, but we don't know where or how to jump in. We've been trained to be silent, the whole time believing it's our free will to disengage, when it's the patriarchal and white supremacist systems that have their hands on our jaws, forcing them shut.

It's time for us to stop having the conventional, passed-down-through-the-generations, society-approved, cognitive-acrobatic conversation with ourselves and each other. It's time to experiment and let our voices shake the Earth.

the power of shame

In the words of Rebecca Traister, author of many books on feminism and politics including the recent *Good and Mad*: "What is bad for women, when it comes to anger, are the messages that cause us to bottle it up, let it fester, keep it silent, feel shame and isolation for ever having felt it or rechannel it in inappropriate directions. What is good for us is opening our mouths and letting it out, permitting ourselves to feel it and say it and think it and act on it and integrate it into our lives, just as we integrate joy and sadness and worry and optimism."[40]

I think that large swaths of the American white female population are beginning to channel generations of uneasy compromise and silence into anger. And let me be clear: when I say we've been silent, I'm not saying we haven't raised voices to our husbands and sons for not cleaning up the garage or forgetting an anniversary. I'm talking about those moments when you debate the gun collection in the basement and whether he really needs it and he just wears you down so it stays there . . . sometimes unlocked . . . for decades. Or the times he and his friends are analyzing some cute twenty-one-year-old's body when you're at the bar, but you hide your annoyance because it's male bonding and he doesn't have a ton of friends. Or when he's standing next to his boss and they both agree there is enough diversity in the firm because a few of their executive administrators are women, and you stay quiet.

Those are the moments of silence that boil inside, individually and collectively, and over the past few years they have morphed into a new rage, a new chapter in the feminist movement, that is making the white supremacist and patriarchal hierarchies quiver.

Each of us has been raised with blind spots about how we should live well; presumably, without anger. Soraya Chemaly, writer and media critic, points out, "While parents talk to girls about emotions more than they do to boys, anger is excluded. Reflect with me for a moment: How did you first learn to think about emotions, and anger in particular? Can you remember having any conversations with authority figures or role models about how to think about your anger or what to do with it? If you are a woman, chances are the answer is no. As girls, we are not taught to acknowledge or manage our anger so much as to fear, ignore, hide, and transform it."[41]

But not knowing how to express anger has huge implications for our health. Our terror of open conflict, especially the kind fueled by our buried rage, is part of what preserves the patriarchy. When we've been vocal and loud and opinionated, we've also been punished and reminded we might not be good enough. We've been made to feel ashamed. "Shame is the most powerful, master emotion," says Brené Brown, a professor at the University of Houston researching courage, vulnerability, shame, and empathy. "It's the fear that we're not good enough." Shame traps us into getting stuck proving to others that we *are* good enough, nice enough, kind enough, generous enough, tidy enough—when we are capable of so much more than "enough."

Need something done? Give it to a busy, pissed-off woman. Something not working for you in your community or country? Plow past the embarrassment you might have in using your voice, the same way you would have no patience for a failed system at your kid's school, and assume your position in the new, often uncomfortable place on the frontlines.

your voice as a force for good

The tricky balance is that, once we come to terms with our marginalized voice, we have to be careful in how we deploy our latent capacities to use our voice. We need to resist the urge to now be suddenly loud when the new frontline might not be front and center in a public arena. Instead, it might be in quiet conversations with those in our lives with whom we've been reluctant to raise our hands to engage on a difficult subject; it might include being honest with ourselves about what we do and don't understand about our identity (self-selected or societally chosen); it might be taking a back seat to listen and learn from someone else about their views on the world.

And so: Just as I am telling you to go find your voice about parental leave or the division of labor at home and prop her up in the middle of the bar at Happy Hour for all to hear, I'm also requesting that you respect the role silence should take in making space for more marginalized voices. It's one way we can break oppressive systems and lift up perspectives that haven't had the chance to be heard. Advocate for other people and their challenges when they aren't there, but if they are, don't speak on their behalf.

Instead, sit your tush down and listen. Just think of how you'd feel if a man tried to tell the story of your labor. (Sometimes, when I am mid-story about one of my two labors, my husband gets excited and jumps in to share his side of the story, which is often how he had to "run in at the last minute and almost missed it!" or correcting when my contractions became intense or how many hours I was pushing—which feels like it undercuts the protagonist in the story: 😑.) There is a middle ground between saying nothing and being the one to say everything that needs to be heard.

You can tackle that knee-jerk response to speak by asking yourself: *WAIT* (Why Am I Talking)? When I find myself about to voice my opinion, particularly when my perspective might have been shared already by another, or when there is someone else whose experience is closer to the subject (i.e., me during labor vs. my husband), I stop and make sure: Am I genuinely adding something that hasn't already been said? Is it the right time for my perspective to be voiced? (My husband's experience during the births of his children is valid and relevant, but he should be telling his story—not mine.) Will my contribution be potentially counterproductive or harmful to the people in the room? I have a big "WAIT" on a yellow Post-It Note on the window above my desk, and it serves as an ever-present reminder to do less of what I've been taught is my role—voice my opinion, regardless of actual knowledge on the subject—and instead listen and pose clarifying questions.

That urge to be the one who has all the answers, right this instant, is a product of the "all-knowing" American system that we discussed: white supremacy. Taking it a step further: Any need to tidily divide concepts, ideas, perspectives—the belief that "either X or Y must be true" and never "both X and Y can be true"—is the result of a culture based on the idea that one thing or group is *always* right (whiteness) and other things or groups are *always* wrong. This is part of the work, to sit with a number of facts that are seemingly contradictory, and realize they are all true at once.

Part of the work is to start stripping from our minds the idea that there are clean-cut sides to any identity or issue, because then we can begin to sit with our confusion in a way that no longer feels so threatening. Just sitting in a place of contemplation is counter to the problem-solving methodology our education system fosters—not having the right answer right away can mean making room for others' ideas to flourish. If you're confused about something you hear, or just don't know, you can say: "I don't know what's actually going on with this." "I don't understand all sides of the issue." "I can't fathom the solution to this painful situation, but tell me more." We have to get comfortable with the imperfection of not-knowing.

Humanity is facing a lot of incredibly complex issues right now: the Arab–Israeli crisis; the melting icebergs; is the dress black and gold or blue and white? But leaving these confusing and intricate matters to the "experts" short-changes our own power and potential. We need to ask questions; we need to learn more. It's time for us to know our power and get in the game.

I spent the past six years trying to improve a medical bottleneck as the cofounder of the nonprofit ORGANIZE, which seeks to solve the organ donation crisis, and I don't have an MD (except when I'm diagnosing my kid's fever as fake as I push her out the front door to go to school). But my team and I saw a problem that needed solving, and so we just stuck with it, even though people told us we weren't allowed to play in their sandbox, that we had no place in the conversation, or—our favorite—that we hadn't "paid our dues." And guess what? We hung around long enough to see a system reformed that will save more lives.* It was hard and exhausting, and I wanted to walk away a lot because we were bullied and it felt dangerous. But even when things were at their most complex, we remembered that the goal of saving more lives was worth the constant difficulty of charging forward.

As I've worked in the end-of-life field, I've thought about my own death a lot. I'm not scared by the idea; I'm proud enough of the work I've done that I feel like I'll be leaving the world a tiny, *teeny* bit better than I found it. But I still fear irrelevance. And, if I'm being really honest with myself, I am even more haunted by the idea of my children or grandchildren cornering me at some point while I'm still alive to ask, "What the [fill in a curse word] were you doing when . . . ?" I want to be able to account for my time in this life in a meaningful way.

In one of my earliest Listening Circles, it wasn't just the woman who lamented wasting time getting her hair blown out that regretted her lack of involvement. All of the women over eighty years old, with expanding families they were proud of and well-manicured front lawns, all regretted not having done more "civically." They're wondering about their legacy while contemplating their own mortality; they're worried about the world they are leaving to their families. "Instead of perfecting my Bundt cake, I should have been

---

* The changes, we estimate, could save an additional 6,000 lives a year by increasing organ donation and transplantation from 36,000 to 42,000 by 2024. Communities of color will likely benefit the most, as they represent one-third of the waitlist for kidneys.[42]

in the cigar room debating the merits of our role in Vietnam or in the class-room helping the teacher," said one. "And not just planning the Halloween party but learning about a topic that I could teach the students—something that the teacher didn't have time to learn because she, too, was juggling a million things, including making sure my kid could read!" They all wish they had stepped in "back then." They wondered, "What was I waiting for?" Humans hate fear, but we should all be a bit terrified that we might be even more disappointed with ourselves at the end of our lives than we are now. (Gasp. Yup, I said it, and 😬.)

That's the tricky part about this silence thing: it's our task, for the rest of our lives, to take responsibility for how we use it. Be honest with your-self when you are opting for silence because you are scared of messing up. Choose silence when you aren't quite sure and need to listen. A good rule of thumb for me is, in the words of Quaker leader William Penn, "Don't speak unless you can improve the silence." And to that I'd add, if you can, do!

In other words, you have the power to use your voice as a force for good, even if it doesn't feel like it. And, if I can add my own two cents, know that we need you both to listen and to roar—now more than ever.

CHAPTER TWO

PERFORMANCE CHORES, PERFECTION & PRIVILEGE

've spent a lot of my life pretending. When I was eleven years old, the hair on my head profusely fell out. I have alopecia areata, which made me a bald preteen. Incurably so, despite the acupuncture and herbal concoctions my mom found in the deep corners of Chinatown. My parents spent money they didn't have on expensive wigs, made from real human hair, so I could at least present as though I was "normal."

If you've tried on a wig, you know how hot and itchy—and hot and itchy—they are. I got used to it—*ish*—but what surfaced in my mind every four to fourteen minutes was: *Is it secure? Could it slip off? Does Travis* [my seventh-grade crush] *know I'm wearing a wig?* I kept my head down and didn't talk about my shame with anyone—not even my mother. Instead, my strategy was to pretend that my twelve-year-old self actually had incredibly thick, never-needing-a-touch-up-on-my-highlights, always-perfectly-blown-out-and-ready-for-a-black-tie-affair hair. Always.

I would sit in Latin class, strategizing for the worst-case scenario—the wig coming off. My game plan: Wig in hands, I would make a beeline home via intricate pathways that crossed backyards and avoided major roads so that I never would be found, even if they sent out a search team. Then, one day, after a sweaty outdoor gym class, my best friend went to grab my shoulder, and her ring snagged my hair. Suddenly, the wig was lying at my feet, surrounded by fall's crunchy leaves. The only possible upside wouldn't be revealed for years: it was excellent fodder for my college-entrance essay 🦆. (And no, I didn't run home; I ran into the locker room instead.)

I was a master pretender, and the wig fostered a constant nervous energy that only dissipated when, at age fifteen, my hair mysteriously grew back. I had a full mane for twenty years—until I stopped breastfeeding my first child, and I had to buy another wig to cover what was clearly becoming the return of a bald head. Thanks to that wig, I could once again check that all-important box of "hair" on my list of what I "should have." There is certainly no box for an unexplained bald scalp.

To varying degrees, we are all spending an inordinate amount of time and money pretending to be some version of "perfect." Be it in beauty, career, or a casserole recipe, we are endlessly chasing a superficial set of what often feels like arbitrary standards. Our constant eye on that achievement, that performance of perfection, can serve as excellent fodder for procrastination so we don't have to spend time with ourselves long enough to realize we might not be creating the legacy we really want.

look this way and say "cheese"

Is there anything you are constantly trying to prove to the world, with new eyeliner or a handbag? Are you protecting a *perfection myth* about yourself that you are desperate to make true for the world to see? My research in the Listening Circles confirmed my intuition. Some white women's insecurities—*Am I a fair enough mom, wife, boss . . . ? Am I fit enough?* and in recent years, *Do I have enough "likes"?*—can take up a lot of space in our mind. It's noise that can often drown out more important questions we might otherwise consider asking about ourselves or our relationships, or the state of our communities, country, and world.

Sometimes the easiest thing to do is to pretend it's all okay. But what if it's not? And, a bigger question: What if our obsession with perfection is a part of the great American pretending—our insistence that, as long as we follow the set of rules embedded in the fabric of our culture about how we are supposed to navigate society and our place in it, the American Dream will be ours? For white women, there are a series of explicit instructions on how to reach that pre-designated life—the white picket fence, surrounding giggling children, with, ideally, not a care in the world. And for us, as for many other people, the only way to perform according to these guidelines is to apply some form of concealer.

It would have been revelatory for me to have taken off my wig and borne my shiny, bald scalp—to exist as I was.* And the truth is that this country is as wounded, confused, and as tempted to wear a wig as I am. We prefer to not look at the imperfections, to avoid talking about them, to cover them up with any accessory that suggests everything is "right on track." It's up to my fellow bald people whether they want to wear hairpieces or not; I'm not ready to let mine go. But, as an American who didn't know what I didn't know, I am now ready to take off our collective wig and be honest about our condition. As I aspire to have hair (via a wig or naturally), America has always aspired to live up to ideals of righteousness and equality. But if we truly care about this country, we must at some point learn to recognize how our reality diverges from this self-made myth.

So many women in the Listening Circles described constantly chasing a low level of buzzing "joy" that they nonetheless can never quite catch, or at least can never hold on to for long. But is life supposed to flow like a lazy river, with us floating, perfectly positioned, in our tubes? It seems so, from our vigorously manicured lawns, Norman Rockwell dinner-table scenes filled with children who always say *please* and *thank you*, and color-coordinated, strategically pieced together (please interpret as: totally spontaneous and effortless) family photos† from the summer beach home.

As one participant observed, "There's a woman in my neighborhood who is nice and pleasant.‡ She's always posting about her cruises and shopping

---

* There are plenty of strong women, men, and children who do this for a whole host of reasons.

† Some of the screaming matches I've witnessed during these khaki-and-white-button-down group photo shoots are my favorite: Moms and grandmothers threatening Christmas if kids didn't "look" happy at the camera. Truly, magical.

‡ Ah, the word "pleasant." The most mediocre dinner roll of compliments. Safe, acceptable, and totally bland.

sprees. It doesn't even seem to enter her consciousness that there are other problems in the world."*

If it's not your home or wardrobe where you're chasing perfection, then maybe it's being the best chef in your circle of friends. If it's not food, maybe it's the marathons you run or your son's new job. We're all performing perfection in some form: material goods, our body shape, our home and lifestyle, sometimes even our children. The Great American Pretending requires that we deliver excellence somewhere—in which lane, however, we're lucky enough to choose on our own.

check the boxes

American society has provided each of us with a list of suggested goals we should want to achieve in order to live "well." This blueprint—given to us as newborns with that first pink baby dress and reinforced through the stories we're told and the things we're praised for doing our whole lives—dictates the structures that we as individuals are encouraged to maneuver within. While there are incredible nuances to each of our lives, and varying requirements that our families and communities place on our shoulders, there are a number of expectations that many privileged American white women may find familiar: namely, that they complete some form of education, find a partner, and have children.

Of course, some of these rules may not apply to you, but since we're so good at pretending, let's see if the blueprint for my life does.

☐   In grade school, be sporty and cute. Get good grades and have lots of friends. Your arts and crafts and hoarding obsessions are welcome.

☐   As you move into middle school, have platonic (but secretly flirtatious) relationships with the opposite sex while maintaining those grades and athletics. By high school, you'll get asked about "boys" before your favorite subject in school. At a minimum, be "well liked" enough to choose where you want to sit in the cafeteria. If you want to be an overachiever, try and score the prom queen

---

* There are moments when I would kill for her life.

crown: it will protect your popularity and remind everyone else they're not as perfect.

☐ Go to undergrad* (maybe through a sports scholarship these days†) and, by sophomore year, you should be building your bench of potential life partners. And if this person is not in sight, you better have a strategy for how you're gonna find them.‡

☐ Meet "the One." If you find the right person—the one who will help make the rest of the checklist a reality—you are constantly asked when you will get engaged and if you are moving in together soon (or, depending on how traditional your family is, perhaps the other way around).

☐ Have a wedding that is just the right mix of traditional and unique. Everyone you know—and barely know—spends the entire engagement period grilling you on wedding details: DJ or band? How many people? The dress—strapless? Before you unwrap the last kitchen appliance, the question becomes (and when I run through this blueprint checklist at Listening Circles, they all uniformly

---

* Since the early 2000s, the wage gap between workers with only high school diplomas and college graduates has come to a halt; 25% of people with college degrees now earn no more than the average high school graduate.[1] As of 2019, Americans owed $1.56 trillion in student loans.[2] And according to Anthony Carnevale, director of the Center on Education and the Workforce at Georgetown University, "this [current] system is, in many respects, an aristocracy posing as a meritocracy."[3] Additionally, the phrase "bamboo ceiling" refers to the discrimination Asian Americans experience in the workforce; 31% of Asian Americans and Pacific Islanders reported experiencing discrimination in the workplace.[4] This discrimination arises because Asian Americans are perceived as unqualified for leadership positions, while being stereotyped into being good "subordinate employees," further decreasing the value of college and advanced degrees.[5] As Professor Chang noted, "Many Asian Americans have discovered that they, like other racial minorities, do not get the same return for their educational investment as do their white counterparts."[6]

† Investment in youth sports today is higher than ever. Parents are spending upwards of 10% of gross household income on elite youth sports to develop their children's athletic talent.[7] One study found 40% of parents believed that their child could get a scholarship; in reality, less than 2% of high school athletes receive even a partial athletic scholarship.[8]

‡ Go out to parties more, work harder to enlarge your friend circle, use more eyeliner . . . something. Just work harder, 'cause it's on you to deliver.

recite the next question without any prompting—they're well trained): When are you going to start thinking about kids?*

☐   Assuming you can conceive, about three months before your due date, you are asked the question you've been waiting to hear, the one you've long coveted, because it marks the crowning achievement for American white women—the question that means you've perfectly checked all other boxes of the blueprint checklist. You're finally getting that tiny gold star sticker, 'cause you've done it. You get to decide: Are you going to stay at home or continue to work? Then angels sing in the background. You have arrived.

You may, like me, have built—or be building—a life close enough to the checklist that you seem like a well-behaved, well-raised rule follower, that you're not going to be anyone's continued problem to solve. You've paralleled the checklist close enough that you're officially "launched." And, if you are a straight-A seeker, chances are you tried to get close to that perfect GPA on this report card, too—like landing a rich† and powerful man. If you are resourced enough (you made the money or inherited it, or your partner has a secure job with healthcare) to make the choice of whether to continue working or stay at home, you've summited the American woman's Mount Everest.

Bravo, mountaineer, enjoy the view—you've made it to a spot that most of the world's humans will never have the privilege to enjoy, and, if you've followed the blueprint according to the "right" timeline, you've done it all typically before you are, according to the blueprint, forty. In other words, you built the ideal life handed you through US laws and micro-messages from the Barbie Dreamhouse to TV shows like *The Wonder Years*. While the above checklist isn't the exact path of all of our lives—it surely wasn't mine (well, not entirely), nor the one I expect for my daughter—it is the one we measure ourselves against. It builds the lane many of us were broadly supposed to stay in, and did to some degree, or defines the boundaries we raise our hand to struggle against. It's part of the American Dream story we protect and export.

---

*   That's always the way it's phrased, isn't it? Truth is, I've been thinking about kids since I got my first baby doll when I was a toddler, so how exactly am I meant to answer that?

†   One Listening Circle participant reminded the room, "It's as easy to fall in love with a rich man as a poor man"; she said she reminds her daughters of that often.

Listening Circle participants admitted that after reaching this summit, they could then spend the next thirty, forty, fifty years—the remainder of their lives, basically—climbing the next mountain: guilt. The guilt sounds like this: *I'm working. Therefore, I'm an inadequate mom, wife, and friend.* Or: *I'm not working. Therefore, I'm inadequately informed and not smart enough to participate in conversations about current affairs.* Or worse yet: *I choose not to have children or get married, so I'm missing out on the central experiences of a woman's life, according to movies, commercials, and every last one of my grandmother's friends.*

Yes, the American white woman's blueprint has evolved over the generations to include more variety, more possibilities. When my great-grandmother had to work because her family needed two sources of income, it was a shameful family secret; my grandmother, her daughter, would pick her mother up at the bubblegum factory under the cover of darkness at midnight so nobody would see them. That stigma doesn't necessarily apply anymore (I'm not interested in the debate about staying at home versus working—let's leave that "mommy war" in the '90s where it belongs*); we have, as a society, matured into letting women work or stay at home or a combination of both. But even a broader blueprint acts as a set of guardrails—like bumpers in bowling—that constrain our choices. We're either checking boxes in some sequence, or we're wrestling with societal stigma or self-imposed shame of not checking those boxes. Many women 🙂 feel that if we're not working hard to check the boxes, or, for those of us overachievers, trying to secure a "perfect" score, then we're failing. We feel remorseful about our performance on this checklist, either quietly or out loud.

pineapple upside-down cake → kale smoothies

One Listening Circle participant, a real estate agent, said, "When I go to a listing appointment, almost every time, the women apologize for what the house looks like." The act of apologizing needlessly is what I like to call a

---

* I will say that the still-raging "mommy wars" are further proof of gender inequality: it's rare, though it is getting better, to find men grappling with the stay-at-home versus go-to-work decision. Yes, we are seeing more men as full-time dads: 7% as of 2016, up from 4% in 1989.[9] But if we were living in an "equal" society, many more men would be grappling with the same choice. I welcome all the dads who want to join the attempted "striking a balance" club, but since corporate parental-leave policies and our society's deeply entrenched ideas about gender aren't supporting the shift, we all suffer.

performance chore—when you have to say or do something that demon-strates your familiarity with the rules of the blueprint. The inability to take a compliment about a new haircut or outfit or looking more fit, the unso-licited apology for the state of one's house or a meal, the disclaimer for a present ("I've included a gift receipt, in case you don't like it!!") are some of any number of completely unnecessary chores we perform to hedge against failing in someone else's eyes, falling short of "perfection."

As the realtor continued, "The husbands never apologize or think to even call it out if it is a mess. Never! But I totally get it. The only time I feel Zen is when my house is clean and organized, but when I'm in other peo-ple's houses I could care less if things are out of sorts, even if I have to sell the damn thing." Even when we don't expect this from others, we assume the world expects us to keep organized and have clean homes all the time (which for me last year was exactly four times; I counted because, legit, it did feel so settling).

We are always identifying our shortcomings, real or imagined—the places where we've veered off course and are crawling to get back on track. Announcing our inadequacies is a kind of apology for imperfection that also highlights our efforts to stay inside the lines. Rarely do we willingly see or choose to acknowledge what is working in our lives, because often others' validation carries more weight; we're waiting for someone else to show up and cheer. When we apologize for the way our house looks, what we really want is for the real estate agent to exclaim, "It's in pristine condition!" so we won't beat ourselves up so much that evening. External validation can give us a sense of permission that our work is done—at least for a brief moment. As long as the real estate agent says what she's supposed to say—"it looks great" or "no worries"—we'll just keep the pile of unfolded laundry stashed in the back of the closet and turn on Bravo TV.

The prerequisites of perfection have evolved to include very modern requirements—a "clean" diet, core strength—but the myth itself, that perfection is achievable, hasn't changed. The women of earlier gener-ations may have yearned to be standing at the front door in an Empire skirt (my grandmother surely did) with their blonde children and their perfectly coiffed hair at their feet, waiting for their husband to step through the picketed gate as the sun scraped the horizon. Today, that Empire skirt is a pair of yoga pants from our "workout" earlier that day. And instead of waiting at the door, we're blending kale smoothies for our kids, who revolted against the meal we made earlier, while gabbing on our AirPods about our Etsy side hustle and gathering auction items for the school fundraiser.

Since perfection was always the deliverable, regardless of the task, as women's lives expanded beyond the domestic sphere, they kept exerting a set of impossible expectations on themselves with every new mold they broke. "What our grandmothers didn't do was lower the bar on quality," one Listening Circle participant said. "Even though she fought for us to operate in more lanes, it all still had to be perfect, all of the time."

Nothing has fundamentally changed about how we're supposed to behave: perfectly, in the kitchen and otherwise, with a pot filled with the guilty sense that we could do more constantly simmering on the back burner. We've just swapped the outfit and ingredients, tossed in a few more pieces of technology, and added some additional layers of guilt to our to-do lists.

Again, I say all of this acknowledging that each woman does put her own spin on perfection. If you're not looping about the state of your house or perfectly cooked, gluten-free meals, I'm willing to bet that there *is* something in your life that you feel driven to perfect in order to feel worthy, like a completed product of America. Whether it's your son's table manners or the size of the church fundraiser you're organizing or your Warrior II in yoga class, *something* has to be perfect, and you deny yourself any pride in your efforts until the rest of the world, especially that frenemy from undergrad, acknowledges it.

really, it's all so easy

It's easier than ever to pretend perfection to the world. Whether with our real-life friends or strangers on social media, we can pretend to the entire planet, from Bangkok to Dubai, that everything we do is light-touch and a joy to pull off. The crumb-free, white-sparkle granite counter we perch on for selfies; the tight abs under our carelessly loose tank; the brands we wear that scream *large bank account* even as we're chasing the kids around in the most relatable, down-to-earth of ways; thank-you notes branded with our trademark frog—promptly sent, of course . . . the list could go on forever. There is even a movement now in which social media influencers are making fun of their imperfect worlds 🐸—toddler disasters, delayed flights, delightful pups digging up garden beds—yet the well-filtered photos that tell those stories are still particularly, well . . . perfect.

The world can see, so we need to set the bar high and deliver. We do it all while meditating, maintaining an *amazing* sex life with our partner,* staying up-to-the-instant with the headlines on every global micro change, and all while tossing a salad from the garden in the backyard that we watered with the rain collected from our gutters.

I don't know about you, but this is definitely my life: just a snap of my fingers and it's all in place.[†]

Sady Doyle, feminist author and journalist, sums up the requirements for having it all with her description of the *Effortless White Woman*.[11] As Doyle describes her, she must:

- Have a unique job that's fun and fulfilling, answering urgent emails in the down moments of life, during penalties at soccer games, or while waiting for a taxi.
- Be married, typically to a white man.
- Be a mother—that's still a female responsibility—but not get too bogged down with baby-making challenges, pregnancy woes, kids' behavior challenges. Ideally the kids just sort of raise themselves.
- Make "a kajillion dollars at work," and have a wardrobe to match.
- "She must not ponder her children that much," because, of course, "her earning potential has not been compromised by them."[‡]
- "In between the time spent maintaining her children and her marriage and her job—this amounts, somehow, to endless free time," she can still take fun trips with her girlfriends and whip up dinner parties with intricate table settings.
- Mostly, though, she always "finds ways to enjoy and fulfill herself."[§]

---

* Sex has decreased in marriages: the number of young adults having sex at least once a week has fallen from 59% in 1972 to 49% in 2018.[10]

† I'm nauseated.

‡ Research by Sari Kerr at Wellesley College has shown that the gender pay gap widens by 35% between 25 and 45 years old—the period in which many women are likely to have children.[12]

§ And apply copious amounts of "self-care": face masks, and time focused on one's overall hydration strategy, which includes the best fruit-infused water for the moon cycle.

Today, women can have jobs as clergy* or in the military;† we can be presidents and CEOs of large corporations,‡ and as of the 1980 United States census[16] edit, we are even allowed to be the "head of the household." Yet, as the myth of the Effortless White Woman shows, we are still pursuing that impossible bar of perfection.

A Listening Circle participant described this in her own words: "Women are always saying, 'I got it,' they are always proving to themselves that they have it all under control. It's an optical illusion, 'cause they don't; everyone is a little bit drowning." Juggling all of it like it's no big deal is part of the facade. It's just another facet of the pressure to maintain public appearances that we discussed in the last chapter, part of the pressure put on us by the patriarchy to keep our image and behavior nonthreatening so as not to disrupt the grand American performance.

nobody's perfect (right?)

Even if we check our supposedly smudge-proof mascara thirty times a day or keep Windexing that countertop, or take our time selecting just the right filter for the family graduation photo before we post it, we know, intellectually, that perfection is an impossible proposition. Right?

That perfect "A" we're trying to get is impossible (thank God).§ This is even implied in the United States Constitution, in the wording "to form a *more* perfect union." Not a perfect union, because our Founding Fathers—giving them some gentle credit here—knew that was a fundamentally unattainable goal; they were realistic that the pursuit of perfection, particularly with regard to a union, would be ongoing.

---

* In 2016, women represented 20.7% of all clergy in the US, up from 2.3% in 1960.[13]

† When the draft ended in 1973, women represented just 2% of the enlisted forces and 8% of the officer corps. Today, those numbers are 16% and 18%, respectively, a significant increase.[14]

‡ As of May 2019, there were 33 female CEOs on the Fortune 500 list—or just under 5% of the total list.[15]

§ Logic systems *want* to prove all true statements and no false statements—that things are perfectly true. But the so called incompleteness theorems show perfection is unattainable because it doesn't exist, no matter how much we *want* it. As one blogger puts it, "incompleteness theorems show that pretty much *any* logical system either has contradictions, or statements that cannot be proven!" Phew.[17]

But even though we know there is no such thing as perfection, the ideal still holds the bar impossibly high for us, wreaking havoc on our psyches.*

The Effortless White Woman ideal, according to Doyle, "seemingly leaves women stuck in the familiar, dreary bind . . . hating ourselves, and hating other women† because they remind us of how much we hate ourselves."[18] Boiled down, our insistence that we can achieve perfection if we just tried harder, got up earlier, or were more friendly, dictates our sense of self-worth, self-esteem, and self-confidence, and makes receiving love feel conditional on an imagined set of impossible requirements.

While our perfect image is being constantly re-emphasized on social media, we are incurring the burden of living up to it. Scientific research is full of new statistics on how social media connectivity makes us feel lonely, envious, and addicted to constant feedback.[19] The unholy trinity of Social Media + Social Comparison + Self-Doubt = Our Misery. Our online lifestyle correlates with feelings of loneliness and envy—especially when we're passively engaging with the content,[20] and even though we're not actually interacting with people, just seeing how they've curated their lives in their own version of perfection. Through this endless, passive consumption and comparison, we are self-sabotaging by setting ourselves up to be disappointed with our own lives. The impact of all this pretending, and our disappointment with ourselves when we can't live up to an image of perfection that doesn't exist, is summed up by the political analyst Thomas Frank: "Our fantasies are driving us to an early grave."[21]

retail therapy

Having a set of rules we need to follow in order to be "a good white woman" is not a new one. In the '50s and '60s, a woman named Christine Frederick, who was helping her ad-agency husband (think the TV show *Mad Men*) figure out the best way to sell a blender,‡ had this insight: the best way to

---

* And in our digestive, nervous, and circulatory systems, according to research that links stress to disorders of all three.

† Just gonna toss Hillary Clinton's name in here. I promised myself her name would not be in the body of this book, but I made no such promises about the footnotes, so yeah . . . Hillary?

‡ This business exchange likely happened at a sea-green, Formica table top holding Pyrex dishes loaded with mashed potatoes, corn, and pork roast. Maybe an iceberg salad with Russian dressing, if her husband was in the mood.

sell home appliances is to target the woman of the house, not the traditional male consumer.[22] The attractive, docile, white actresses hired for the ads that followed sent a clear message to every female viewer who aspired to be perfect: "To maintain an orderly and happy home, you should buy every device [you] can afford,"* in the words[23] of author Julie Scelfo. Literally, that was the message Christine bestowed on American women, via appliance companies. To be a good woman (and patriot), buy everything. Hurry. The ads' over-the-moon success led sales dudes and advertisers nationwide to realize that the most powerful consumer when it comes to the home is the woman in it.

In speaking to a previously unspoken consumer—the woman—Christine "was instrumental in not only validating consumerism in the eyes of the American woman, but also building the idea in American minds that buying 'things' was a social, moral, and even maternal good,"[24] according to Scelfo. In Christine's case, she didn't live to see the effect rampant female consumerism would have on our climate, or the chaos that is our obsession with the size of our closets and the unnecessary items we shove in them. It reminds me of the story that one Listening Circle participant told us about how her mother brings her random produce from the grocery store. "Last week, she came over with more than a dozen limes," she said. "When I told her we don't need that many, she reminded me that they 'had been on sale.' I'm so desperate to move away from the knee-jerk reaction of always consuming more than we need because it's on 'sale.'" Thank you, Christine, for making us obsessed with consumption—even when we don't need any more damn limes—in an attempt to feel more whole about ourselves.

I've been trained very well, by my aunts in particular, to find joy in the art of shopping. I'd spend summers with them clicking hangers as we rummaged through sale racks at outlet malls or culling the long tables at garage sales on early Saturday mornings in Old Town, Virginia, searching for tiny trinkets that we (suddenly) "had to have" for the shelf in the perfectly presented living room. I started enjoying the high of consuming—which would last until we arrived home and showed off our new treasure to whoever was lingering in the house, and then it would evaporate once we placed the item on the shelf or in the closet.

---

* Insidious concept. I had to add it to show how one idea wormed its way into everything—especially how we feel about ourselves.

More recently, particularly when I felt a bit down, I always enjoyed the rush I got from shopping; at times I've used it to numb stress or quiet some voice in the back of my head. Consuming let me temporarily tap out of the realities of my world and avoid tasks and chores I didn't want to deal with. I have, at times, become addicted to this denial; opting for distraction, a.k.a. ignorance, is way easier than having to tackle reality head on. I've seen other white women in my orbit behave similarly, wrapping themselves in ignorance like a life jacket to avoid the labor of being human. This ignorance dependency, which we sometimes fuel through shopping or social media or TV series or . . . you pick a temporary source of distraction . . . helps us keep our head in the sand and avoid the realities of the rest of the world. Every hour we busy ourselves with frivolous pursuits is one hour less the world benefits from what we have the potential to contribute.

Christine wanted us to buy everything—and we *are*—but this wasn't, and isn't, just an advertising phenomenon.

how we bought in

You know who makes a lot of money from my insecurity about my body shape? SPANX.* Like, a lot. Companies profit from all of the ways society tells us we aren't good enough, especially when it comes to how we look. My mom has personally funded the electrical bills of many hair salons trying to achieve the exact right color of blonde.† When I was a teenager, I would sneak to the tanning salon after school; as a young woman, I would drop my babysitting money onto counters in exchange for fake eyelashes and the early-adulthood ritual of the oh-so-enjoyable bikini wax. We have been taught both to be disappointed in ourselves and that if we spend enough money, we can remediate the problem—ideas that comes part and parcel with perfectionism as a condition of a white supremacist, patriarchal culture.

I'll frame this loaded point with the way historian and author Nell Irvin Painter describes how the ideal image of a woman as fair-skinned, shapely, and quiet became idealized throughout the world in her book of *The History of White People*. Think of the nineteenth-century paintings of

---

* A company that sells body-shaping undergarments (think corsets but not as tight) for men and women

† Which is a constant conversation: *Is it the right hue? Is it too ashy? What about the dark roots? Too long?* Anyone, it seems, is always welcome to weigh in.

women that fill the halls of museums you have visited. There are a lot of voluptuous women—often naked or revealing large portions of "accidental" flesh—draped on all kinds of objects, tree stumps, each other, thin air. These are *odalisque* women*: plumpish because they weren't tilling the fields, typically looking like they can't really be bothered, but most importantly, white. Many paintings from this time period, of medieval serfs and tables with overflowing fruit platters, were meant to make onlookers a bit intimidated and envious of the rich and powerful. Same for the odalisques. These mostly naked women were designed to taunt the viewer, and their "pure," untouched beauty was meant to inspire the desire to conquer and possess.[26]

One of the definitions of the word *odalisque*, according to Painter, is "white slave woman."[27] The original women who posed for these paintings were slaves, primarily from the Caucasus mountain range,[†] who were concubines to near-omnipotent men in the polygamous households of the Ottoman Empire (centered in modern-day Turkey). And thanks to the nineteenth-century formulation of oil paint to make it last for centuries, rather than fade within years, these white female objects were cemented as the epitome of beauty, innocence, and purity.

These paintings became a precious trade commodity among the rich, comparable to the way the car you drive communicates financial status (as well as other forms of status: power, influence, and at least, performed respect). It was important to the elite to have these excessively pale and naked ladies hanging all over their homes, where the paintings sometimes remained for centuries. The lily-white lust objects became a powerful currency, and their suggested docile mannerisms and bright whiteness were the key ingredients that made these ladies shine down from dark castle walls.

The status symbol of Caucasian slaves and the portraiture tradition that followed was emblematic of a deeply entrenched, racist ideal of feminine sexuality. Those white odalisque women, representing the sexual fantasies of their buyers, became recognized as an aesthetic ideal to which

---

* O·da·lisque, \ō-dəˌlisk\, aka "concubine" or "part of a harem." According to Painter, "Each term refers to young white slave women, and each carries with it the aura of physical attractiveness, submission, and sexual availability—in a word, femininity. She cannot be free, for her captive status and harem location lie at the core of her identity."[25]

† Yes, this morphed into "Caucasian"; the description on some government forms to describe white people is derived from a 62-mile-long mountain range between the Black and Caspian seas.[28]

generations of women would aspire. All because of the staying power of oil paint and a group of gals from the Caucasus Mountains. Like billboards, TV shows, and Instagram ads do today, these paintings carried a compelling narrative about the standard we all should strive for: the white woman's fragility and sexual potential.

This is, of course, an impossible standard, because, well, not everyone is white and/or submissive. Unfortunately, the white requirement is extraordinarily dangerous, in particular, for nonwhite people. In the words of Staceyann Chin, author, artist, and activist, "For as long as I've known myself, the standards of beauty for women have been skewed towards [white women]—your hair, your skin, your body, your eyes—our mothers, our daughters, our sisters, our lovers have been rewarded for mimicking what you look like and punished for turning away and celebrating ourselves. Even the men who look like us have been taught to desire, and then be rewarded/punished for desiring/not desiring, you. Truth be told, some of the radical, black and brown queer and non-binary women who date women have looked to you for beauty."[29] We live in a culture that chooses "white-woman-ness," itself the ghost of a perfect ideal that really only existed in the minds of oil painters from centuries ago—and people are very literally dying because of it.

Let's take pale skin as an example. The status symbol of white skin was solidified during the eighteenth and nineteenth centuries when fair-skinned Europeans were colonizing much of the planet. Fair skin meant you were powerful and rich; in some countries, it meant you could afford to pay someone else to do the manual labor under the harsh sun that would tan skin over time. Today, the desire for white skin is particularly rampant in Asia* and India, and is now seeping into countries in Africa.† The global market for skin-whitening cream, one of the most popular beauty products in the world, is expected to reach $31.2 billion by 2024.[32] Worldwide, beauty counters and brands feature predominantly white models advertising the optics of purity—and with it, an easier life. On dating sites in India, women will describe the shade of their skin before they list their academic achievements; it's seen as the key to securing a wealthy, powerful man.[33]

This inherited, white supremacy–fueled obsession with light skin props up a lucrative industry of whitening pills, steroid injections, laser treatments,

---

* 44% of the female Chinese, Malaysian, Filipino, and South Korean population uses skin-whitening cream.[30]

† 77% percent of Nigerians who use face cream use one with whitening components.[31]

chemical peels, and skin bleaching that not only cause cancer[34] but also perpetuate the psychologically dangerous fallacy that lightness equates to increased worthiness. Inna Samson, a young woman in the Philippines, started taking skin-whitening pills when she was fifteen, thinking her parents "might show her off more" and wanting to silence family members who called her "little monkey."[35] Abhay Deol, a popular male Bollywood action star, has flagged the dangerous myths perpetuated in the elite and famous circles in India:* "Advertising preaches that we would get a better job, a happier marriage, and more beautiful children if we were fair. We are conditioned to believe that life would have been easier had we been born fairer."[37]

Here in the United States a number of black celebrities—including Michael Jackson, baseball player Sammy Sosa, and musician Nicki Minaj—have been accused of artificially lightening their skin.[38] A 2008 University of Georgia study[39] called the obsession around lighter hues of skin color in the black community "a well-kept secret . . . The hue of one's skin," the researchers wrote, "tends to have a psychological effect on the self-esteem of African-Americans." Ronald Hall, professor of social work at Michigan State University, also flags the physiological impact of encouraging skin lightening on communities of color: "It can also mean altering hair texture and eye color to mimic the dominant group. The rapper Lil' Kim, in addition to (allegedly) lightening her skin, has also changed her eye color and altered her facial features. The fact that so few in mainstream culture can even acknowledge the existence of the bleaching syndrome[40] is a testament to how taboo the topic is." While these figures have garnered scrutiny for their cosmetic alterations, it's important to bear in mind the way that skin lightening is a mere coping mechanism for the pressure placed upon people of color by white supremacy. Similar to women who get plastic surgery to keep up with patriarchal beauty standards, people who lighten their skin should not be antagonized but rather the social systems and conditions that made them feel they were flawed to begin with should be examined with more scrutiny. As long as light skin continues to be the ideal of the dominant group—white people—people around the world will go to extreme lengths, at great physical and economic expense, to try to achieve it.

---

* Ayurveda, traditional Indian medicine, tells pregnant women they can increase the chances their baby will be fair-skinned if they drink saffron-laced milk and eat oranges, fennel seeds, and coconut pieces.[36]

white privilege

So far we've seen how perfection was packaged and sold to us, and how the false, dangerous connection between perfection and whiteness has metastasized in our society and around the world. But we must also consider how our own lives are made easier precisely because of our proximity to a cultural definition of the "ideal": whiteness.

As mentioned, people with lighter skin in many countries are arbitrarily seen as more beautiful or more powerful—and this perception grants them more social currency. This is known as *white privilege*: simply being white gives you an advantage over nonwhite people. Feminist and antiracist activist Peggy McIntosh first wrote about the concept in 1988, citing her experience as a white woman: "I have come to see white privilege as an invisible package of unearned assets which I can count on cashing in each day, but about which I was 'meant' to remain oblivious. White privilege is like an invisible weightless backpack of special provisions, maps, passports, codebooks, visas, clothes, tools, and blank checks."[41]

In many parts of the world, including a lot of our own neighborhoods, people who are perceived as "white"* have unearned advantages because other groups have been systematically marginalized. This can be a really hard concept for white people to wrap their heads around, because until you learn to look out for it, you don't see it—when privilege is all you know, it can be difficult to recognize. It's not like there was a secret class in seventh grade where all the white people were told, "Okay, here are all of the rules of white privilege. Whatever you do, protect them at the expense of others and don't utter a word about this secret class." So, when we spend time unpacking these concepts in Listening Circles, there is often an air of defensiveness. The women feel like they are being accused of doing something wrong, when they didn't know there was an issue in the first place.

Listening Circle participants would become defensive partly because they were genuinely unclear about what these so-called privileges are. But once we get granular, all the blonde, brunette, and gray heads start to nod in unison. "I get it," they start to say.

So what are the privileges we experience simply because of the color of our skin? The answer is one that we'll spend the rest of our lives discovering.

---

* This includes people who are "white-passing"—individuals from ethnic groups or of mixed ethnicity who are considered to be nonwhite who can present themselves as white.

(I always say I am in first grade on this subject, and I might advance to second at some point in my life.) This is true in part because the privileges whiteness brings can vary, depending on where you are in the world or even what side of a city you live on. But it is safe to say that in mainstream American culture—and in most places around the world—whiteness has a very specific kind of beneficial currency. The more aware you become of it, the more you notice it everywhere, including in the most surprising and obvious places.

Just take the local pharmacy across the street from my house:

- The entire selection of "flesh-colored" Band Aids are roughly my skin color.
- The shampoo aisle has an overwhelming amount of options for white people's hair: many labels read "For regular hair," as if white people's hair were the standard. Meanwhile, the oils and treatments for "nonwhite" hair types (of which there are, I don't know, a ton) might be on a single shelf, or in its own, usually much smaller section.
- The makeup aisle has more concealer hues for lighter skin than for darker skin.
- This is the only one not about race, but is worth pointing out: The sea of English-language greeting cards has a very small section called "Mahogany," for black culture, and there are a handful of cards in Spanish. Eight hundred different languages are spoken in New York City alone,[42] yet Hallmark shoves 799 of them into one social envelope.
- While shopping, I can open a bottle of water or a snack to occupy my nagging kid* without store employees worrying about whether I'm going to pay for it. That's not necessarily the case for black shoppers. There are horror stories of managers harassing people of color for doing what I used to do all the time.†

---

* I've since stopped.

† This doesn't even scratch the surface of who is, or isn't, allowed to get their prescription drugs filled at the back of the store based on who qualifies and can afford health insurance coverage through government assistance programs. 59% percent of the 27.4 million nonelderly people who were uninsured in 2017 were people of color.[43]

The point is, I feel my privilege daily. And as icky as this is to admit, it does make my life easier, on so many levels. People hold the door for me; I can be short a buck or two at the coffee place and the barista will wave me through; my risk of being targeted by the police is lower than that of a nonwhite person. Still, that privilege may not feel relevant when you or a female colleague speaks up in a meeting, only to be dismissed as "shrill" or "bossy." Or when a doctor tells you a symptom is probably all in your head—something they have never told the men in your life. But in those contexts, and many more, people of color endure a level of bias that we white women never will.

Further, this privilege is not innocuous; it's toxic. As we benefit, others are systematically oppressed—and lives are lost. And the more comfortable we are with systems of oppression that benefit white women, the less aware we are of them, and the more deeply entrenched we become within them. When we refuse to question situations that assume white privilege is normal, we tacitly give our agreement. Our children—or anyone who considers us a role model—will absorb the complacency that we model for them. They will grow up without questioning the structures that shaped today's society, possibly even continuing to believe the myth that everyone has equal access to opportunity and safety. Over time, if the scientific evidence holds true, we will grow even more resistant to change—perpetuating a cycle of racism that reaches back to the founding myth behind the American Dream.

performing perfect privilege

Let's look at some of the beliefs and behaviors through which we, as white women, uphold patriarchal and white supremacist systems and how our behaviors might continue to contribute to the cycle of privilege:

1. we prioritize individual over collective accountability

Quoting john a. powell, leader of the UC Berkeley Haas Institute for a Fair and Inclusive Society (whose mission is "expanding the circle of human concern"), "We [Americans] still have the language of, 'You can be anything you want to be. You can control. You're in charge of your own destiny.'" This is the notion of *sovereignty*—supreme power, authority, or rulership— and it's a prime trait of white supremacy. In these views, it means that we consider individuals accountable for the conditions and outcomes of their lives, regardless of the bonds and circumstances they were born into. Conversely, if our own lives aren't perfect, then we've failed. powell continues:

"Whether it's a person, community, or a nation that holds it as an ideal, there's no such thing as sovereignty. We are in relationship with each other. It can be a bad relationship or a good relationship, but we are in relationship with each other."[44]

Another characteristic of white supremacy is a sense that we exist independently of one another and are therefore only responsible for our own actions.* The impact of our actions (or inaction) on others holds less weight in our society, and can be more easily justified within it, than the work we do in pursuit of a particular achievement. That ideology gives people in power—mostly white men—the freedom to worry only about themselves, their professional titles, and the digits in their bank accounts, without having to contemplate their impact on other people, let alone make room for them. As a result, white people, particularly those in power, aren't incentivized to actively confront the inequality of opportunity in our schools, workplaces, and financial and political systems.

2. the assumption that "only I can fix it" underlies everything we do
As a result of believing in our own white supremacy–supported sovereignty, we also believe that we're the only one who can solve certain problems. We get brownie points for being the hero, too, which is hugely validating, and drives us to "fix" things the same way we yearn for social media "views" and "likes."

Fixing things is also a way to center ourselves, making the problem and the solution revolve around us, as if we were spunky fictional heroines pulled straight off a fast-paced TV show or modern remix of a Jane Austen novel. As women, we do plenty of invisible domestic and emotional labor, for example, in full knowledge that it will not garner much recognition or appreciation from others. But when we feel that we don't receive the gratitude we're "owed" when we do a good deed beyond what's expected of us in our day-to-day, we are quick to play the "unappreciated" card. Perversely, that sense of being a martyr feeds our belief that we are "being the bigger person."

3. we avoid conflicts that we can't perfectly resolve
Remember in chapter one how we discussed letting our silence shield us from the consequences of not having the ideal solution to a social problem? For example, saying, "I'm not too familiar with the details"? Or not entering

---

* It's the opposite of the unifying "overview effect" that I talked about in the Introduction.

a conversation about, say, gun control, unless we can perfectly chime in (without rudely interrupting someone), perfectly explain gun safety legislation, perfectly persuade everyone of our position, perfectly correct anyone's challenge, and then perfectly exit? If we can't get an "A" on our performance, we'll sit silently, or stick to discussing recent finds at HomeGoods or the Saks Fifth Avenue sale rack—and that silence continues to make way for white supremacy to thrive.

4. we feel a strong sense of entitlement—and put the blame on others whenever it's obstructed

"Why me?!" we ask, when something doesn't go our way, or when we don't get something we believe we're entitled to. Which leads to "Why *not* me?!" and making lists of all the people whose lives—whose money or partner or job or house—we think we deserve. When this only deepens our sense of dis-ease and disappointment, we're led back to the start of the song: "Why me?!"

Then cue the blame-game. It's not our fault we didn't know we had to sign up for a class by a certain date so missed the chance to enroll, or that our license had expired so we have to pay that fine in addition to the speeding ticket, or that our focus on sorority/fraternity mixers over our GPA meant we didn't qualify for that summer internship. But this sense of entitlement, which has its roots in white supremacy, is unfounded. We don't deserve the bus driver waiting just a few more minutes for our kids or to get the aisle seat we wanted on the airplane. Though our governmental systems can be outdated and slow, we are no more victims of their inefficiency than anyone else, and our wasted time is no more precious than anyone else's.

the perfect candidate

This set of behaviors has given us permission to opt in or out of being active citizens, depending on how convenient it is for us to raise our hands, and on how likely it is that doing so will boost or detract from our ego—and that can lead us to inaction. "I didn't vote in 2016!" blurted one Listening Circle participant at the end of a session, as we were gathering our coats. She didn't vote, she said, because there wasn't a "perfect candidate." I get it.* This behavior is common among white Americans. We're five times as

---

* I've never seen a perfect candidate, in any election. I can tell you what she *would* look like, but I genuinely don't think she will ever exist.

likely as black Americans to say we didn't vote because we "did not like candidates or campaign issues."[45]

The reason? Perfectionism helps us navigate moral ambiguity—or more precisely, avoid having to grapple with it. *Moral ambiguity* is what we experience whenever there is no clear right-or-wrong answer to a complicated subject. White supremacy tells us a mutually exclusive binary always exists—but it rarely if ever does. When we face moral ambiguity, rather than act counter to our ethics and conscience—in other words, rather than risk acting imperfectly—we freeze. Without a perfect choice, we feel it's impossible to say what is right, and use that ambiguity as an excuse for inaction, rather than risk our self-image or admit our confusion. But sometimes we have to choose the lesser of two evils.

Let's get real for a second about the position in which society traps politicians. Though we know our own lives are often fraught with moral ambiguity, we don't extend this compassion to our elected officials. So much of their work and performance depends on having to strike balances in what feel like no-win situations. They cannot admit to not knowing the answers, to any imperfection or frailty. They cannot change or grow as human beings, alter course, or in any way divert from the party script or the role they've established. And, most of all, once they make a judgment call, they can never later say—or at least, not without being chastised—"I was wrong and I'm sorry." We know, deep down, that these standards we hold our politicians to are impossible to meet . . . but rather than radically alter them and recognize our own responsibility in our communities, we point out how the person or the whole political system is inadequate, turn our backs, and go play tennis instead. I'm not letting politicians off the hook here—they are raising their hands for leadership roles that require tremendous reserves of self-sacrifice, accountability, and grit. But let's stop pretending they are supposed to be perfect so you can stay checked out.

life, post-perfection

Life is not perfect. We know it, even as we strive for perfection anyway, having been sold the idea that it's the key to happiness. As Rebecca Solnit points out, "We hear constantly about happiness: 'Are you happy?' Its emotions are mutable, and this notion that happiness should be a steady state seems destined to make people miserable."[46] I think this is why white women by and large hate to be asked if we're "happy." Of course we *say* we're happy, thanks to the performance-chore side of us, but in our pursuit of what we think happiness is, are we actually making ourselves miserable? We know deep down that happiness is not about stuff or followers or awards or any number of other distractions that we use to avoid confronting the complicated truth. As I've mentioned, I heard over and over from Listening Circle participants who have lived for seven and eight decades how much they regret having focused on performance chores earlier in their lives instead of studying the world around them, contributing op-eds, running for office, or, at bare minimum, asking harder questions.

We need to see "pretending" perfection and happiness for the millstone it is: a heavy, inescapable responsibility we wear around our necks, the blueprint that we sometimes fixate on to hide our unhappiness and disappointment that, in fact, things just aren't perfect. Can we grant ourselves the freedom and grace of imperfection? Because the more we are able to embrace our imperfections, mistakes, and even failings, the more we leave the burden of perfectionism in the dust of our newfound authentic joys— and the better we can begin to understand how we as a country got to the place of division we are in today.

CHAPTER THREE

WHITE LIES

M s. Arnold here, former first-grade teacher. It's been my favorite job so far because I loved teaching history, but guess what: I taught it all wrong.

Before I give it another try here, with you, I'll pose a question, a theory I'm wrestling with: Are we humans at a moment in our evolution as a species where we can look at our past—our incredible accomplishments as well as our grave missteps—hold the disappointment, and finally be strong enough not to look away? What do you think? Is our collective psyche still too fragile, or are we ready to take off the oversized shame-filtered sunglasses and peer at our pedigree?

Though the roads each one of us has walked have not been pristine, either in their circumstances or in our choices, we've largely tried to be decent people along the way. All of us, I can say with confidence, have decisions and accomplishments we're proud of, and we also have those moments that we replay over and over and wish we could re-do. Like any personal history, American history is littered with contradictions. We've been visionary and forward thinking in our ideals of freedom and equality; we've also been negligent at best, if not a deliberate part of the problem, in the face of human suffering, both around the world and in our own backyards.

In the Listening Circles, it was nearly inevitable that someone would moan about "our divided country." A typical excuse from another participant was, "Humanity has always been like that." *Really*, I'd silently respond. That seems like an easy way out of this mess: blame it on how "it's always been." In all seriousness, when did inequality begin? There had to be a moment when someone first took more than they needed and let someone else suffer as a consequence? To understand who we are individually and collectively, I believe we have to keep searching for that moment, just like a therapist might ask you to find the incidents, relationships, and forks in the road that changed it all.

It's impossible to see how we got here until we take a closer look at where we've been.

Let's start with the biggest picture. There are the things that make us human, regardless of the land or language in which we were raised—common characteristics that root us in ourselves and amongst one another. Music universally binds us, sex draws us closer, the sound of a baby's laugh makes us all smile* . . . and the pressure of our ego on our psyches historically has built gauntlets of extreme oppression.

Yet, I still wonder, if we can look back at the good and bad about us as a species, at its past and potential, if now might still be a different moment than we've had before? We know enough about how we operate psychologically, and what we need nutritionally and medically to survive. We know we long for one another's attention and love. We can communicate across vast distances, faster than ever before. Can we take all of those hard lessons from the past and the data we hold in the palm of our hand, and turn the corner into the next phase of our story? Can we create a way forward that doesn't require relearning the same lessons over and over, at the expense of one another and the planet? I feel like this is an easy "yes," and yet some of us are behaving with the same level of complicity as the "well-intentioned" bystanders did in the years prior to World War II.

To truly move forward, we can't just peek under the corners of some rugs we've been walking delicately around. This won't change the cycle of white supremacy that has us, as James Baldwin has written, "trapped in a history [we] don't understand."[2] And so long as that is the case, we won't use the lessons of the past for the sake of future generations.

---

* The sound releases endorphins that act as natural painkillers and brings instant joy.[1]

People have very different stories about how and why they arrived in this land known as the United States. There's no easily skimmed common story that tells everyone's truths. While each person's attempts to survive are worthy and no more important than another person's, at times, these truths compete with one another. While each person's attempts to survive are no more important than those of others, we cannot avoid the often-damaging ways in which these truths, when lived out, vie for primacy in America's story.

The indigenous peoples were here first. The Europeans came seeking better lives for their families. Both are true. Neither contradicts the other. But it is also true that, in seeking better lives for their families, those Europeans stole and killed in unquantifiable ways.

We understand that important moments, people, and decisions have been edited out of history and textbooks, and that those decisions were made based on who was holding the pen.* But many of us don't revisit the facts of our nation's founding as adults, even when we're more fired up than ever to change the world around us.

If you've picked up this book, you've likely rotated the prism through which you see the world and your role in it, and now want to know and do more. We must also look back with newfound urgency; to solve today's problems, we must be clear from where and why they initially blossomed. There are miraculous accomplishments we must continue to cherish and atrocious decisions we should consider giving our lives to avoid repeating. So here we go.

America, #nofilter

We've been fed a highly curated, relentlessly sanitized series of stories about America. We maintain our notion of America the same way we curate our Instagram accounts—only the flattering angles, no muffin tops or wrinkle-enhancing shadows. We all know those social media accounts that *clearly* use a portfolio of apps to erase imperfections. But when you see that woman over and over again, maintaining the act that

---

* Historically it's been curated by a panel of twelve people—mostly white, mostly male—on the State Board of Education in Texas, a state that consumes more textbooks than any other, so they get to decide what information lands on the page.[3]

she has it all together, you might actually start to believe it. Or, worse yet, you stop questioning the way she is editing the photos she wants you to see—you just take her at face value because you can't be bothered to question it anymore.

That's sort of what we've let happen to our nation's history. People micromanaged the social media account over the generations, and we only get a few well-filtered photos that make our story look too perfectly neat to question. We need to rummage for the truth if we're ever going to move forward, but if you are like me and most of the well-intentioned, well-educated women I know, you likely did not get this context from your K–12 education. And how would you? You didn't spend all of your formative years in history class—you also had to learn the quadratic formula and papier-mâché and the periodic table. Unless you raised your hand to dig deeper, there was likely no point in your life when the information would have just landed in your lap.

We have to hold up a mirror not only to ourselves and our performance chores—deciding what tchotchke to bring to a friend's house for dinner 🪆, or most of all being appropriately, or, even desperately, *nice*—but also to the history we're taught. If we really spent some time pushing beyond our ignorance dependency and thinking about our history, it might be tougher to justify all of that scrolling and equivocating. I believe that if we really did take some time to sit with all the truths layered in our history, then we, white women, would not stand for so many of the brutal injustices happening just out of our view.

To help you relate to our history in a tangible way, I'm bringing some of the past to the present—identifying the exact cross streets where key moments, especially brutal moments, in American history unfolded, so that they can't stay in the "long time ago" category. I'm telling these stories a bit differently so you understand in just a few pages (remember: don't put the book down, even if you might want to). There is blood in the soil of this land, including where your house 🏠 likely sits.

Before we start, it's imperative that I flag that this is where we enter a dangerous part of this conversation: I, as a privileged, white, cis woman—one with a book deal, and this podium—am about to cherry-pick a handful of historical truths from the endlessly complex sweep of the country's past. It's by no means meant as a summary of our whole history. I don't spend nearly as much time as I'd like talking about the breakthroughs or the unjust plight of Asian Americans and Pacific Islanders'* struggles (and their triumphs), as well as the urgent crises facing the Latinx† community, particularly the refugees at our southern border. In fact, I have focused on early instances of theft and oppression by white people and their effects on those who lived or were brought here. I chose the stories in the following pages not because they were concepts you might not know—likely you're familiar with all of them—but because I wanted to recontextualize that somewhat familiar history in light of today's problems.

No, these events are not our fault. But they did happen on some of our ancestors' 👁 watch. We can't be held directly accountable, and yet pretending like these things don't still carry weight—an art we're masters of—and ignoring their implications today *does* make us guilty, even if not legally. We have to be really honest about whose land this really was, how it was taken, and who benefited and thus preserved privilege and power, just so we can live this somewhat superficial American dream filled with "likes" and Instagram filters that still have us feeling unfulfilled.

We know that most human beings want the same things—job security, healthcare, education, and brief moments of joy. Are we willing to come face to face with our history, remind ourselves of its lessons—those rooted in kindness and those in cruelty—and use them as a way to approach the

---

* Starting in the mid-1800s, immigrants from any one of the forty-eight countries in Asia were characterized as the "model minority" for their "docile" nature. (The term AAPI—Asian American and Pacific Islander—once a political tool to fight oppression, has been de-weaponized for use by the government and others to show how well some people of color are doing while ignoring that the group has the widest income gap of any group.) White Americans reduced Asian Americans to second-class citizenship through a number of policies as they were constantly seen as competitors in the workforce. This competition for jobs has exploded into anti-Asian violence, as recently as 1982: Victor Chen, a Chinese American, was beaten to death that year by two men who blamed him for the Japanese taking jobs from the auto sector. Political commentary today leans on scapegoating Asians for stealing jobs from working- and middle-class Americans when it's actually wealthy, often white business owners making these decisions on their companies' behalf to take their firms abroad. A tried-and-true technique of white supremacy is using racial minority groups against one another to try to keep them apart. This endures today—for instance, stoking anti–affirmative-action feeling among Asian Americans by giving out incorrect, biased information about how it works. Many Asian American social justice groups use the term "not your wedge" to address this and show camaraderie with black and brown individuals.[4]

† A gender-neutral term used as an alternative to the gendered terms "Latino" and "Latina." The term has garnered popularity in recent years due to the growing visibility and advocacy of the transgender and gender-nonconforming community.

new frontlines with the wisdom from our past? My assumption is if you are at this sentence, you're game (woohoo, let's do this).

One of the most often-cited Bible verses, John 8:32, ends this way: "the truth shall set you free." In the interest of coming closer to the truth, as scary and complicated as it may be, we will need a very good GPS. First stop, obviously 🌎, is NYC.

New York, New York

Important caveat: I'm writing this book from the best city in the world.* I don't need to brag about the food or the fashion houses or the lyrics booming from Broadway or the politics of the world at the United Nations or cancer breakthroughs at our hospitals. I'm one of the millions of New Yorkers who feel what happens here matters disproportionately more than what happens anywhere else in the world.†

Here's another striking fact about New York: we have the largest population of homeless people in the country—larger than the whole population of Philadelphia.⁵ One hundred thousand of our children float in and out of temporary housing each night, and one in three of our babies is born into poverty.⁶

It's a devastating contrast of the best and the worst in one place. For example, some wealthy New Yorkers can opt to be ignorant 364 days a year, and then absolve themselves by showing up at a fancy fundraiser and cutting a huge check.‡ There is so much self-assigned urgency in our steps, and yet, in between our hurried subway rides and crowd dodging, we often ignore the desperation on our sidewalks.

Additionally, only a fraction of us actually know or spend any real time considering the history of the island. When we look at the time of those

---

* Tiny bit biased. I don't even welcome complaints about Times Square (you're right) or the fast walkers (you're right) or the stinky trash piles (you're right). It's perfect. Period.

† #biased

‡ Every year, thousands of privileged New Yorkers attend a gala held by the Robin Hood Foundation—a who's who of the city's philanthropists—in support of the organization's exceptional work addressing the needs of the city's most disadvantaged. In one evening Robin Hood raises anywhere from $100 million to $200 million more than any other charity in the country—all fueled by the ultra-high-net-wealth, ego-based competition of who can write a bigger check. The irony is that, en route to the annual event at the Javits Center on the West Side of Manhattan, guests pass extraordinary examples of poverty.

early settlers—our "Founding Fathers," as they are so often referred to—we see only the noble beginnings. We prefer to keep our story neat and brave, spearheaded by pure men on behalf of some divine vision.

"Our" story of America typically starts when the Europeans first sailed the bows of their ships onto these shores. How convenient to skip over the first thirteen thousand years these lands were already inhabited,* and the six-hundred-plus indigenous tribes[8] thriving here prior to Columbus's "discovery."†

Since I'm a self-centered New Yorker, I'll zero in on what went down in Manhattan, also called Turtle Island by its inhabitants. When the Dutch first arrived in Lower Manhattan, they were met by the Lenape, a popu-lation numbering around 7,500 (possibly more) who lived in areas today known as New York City, New Jersey, parts of Pennsylvania, and Delaware.[10]

In 1626, Peter Minuit of the Dutch West Indies Company "purchased" Manhattan from the Lenape for some number of goods—tools, bowls, knives, beads—worth about sixty Dutch guilders[11] (about $24 then, approx-imately $1,000 today[12]). The average square foot in this city right now goes for $1,773.[13] Twenty-four bucks for the island . . . You're probably thinking, *That's a steal.* 'Cause guess what—it was.

The Lenape may not have had the same definition of "ownership" that the Dutch did. Or they may have thought the goods the Dutch offered were just to thank them for the hospitality they'd provided.[14] Either way, it's clear the two parties involved in this exchange weren't on the same page about the "terms." It's as if someone knocked on your door and offered a bag of sticks—or something else you didn't need‡—to "own" the air in your living room.

Imagine that same person hovering around until you agreed to the deal, or just started behaving as if you'd accepted it, even if you wanted nothing to do with them. And then, over time, they tell you how you are allowed to walk through the living room to sit on your couch or how you're allowed to

---

* Starting with the Clovis people, whose bones were found in what's now Clovis, New Mexico—though there's evidence there might have been people here as long as 24,000 years ago.[7]

† You cannot "discover" land occupied by other people. Oh, and footnote to this footnote, Columbus was actually lost at sea—he was asked to find a western sea route to Asia. Besides, concrete proof exists that the Vikings traveled to North America five hundred years earlier, and some scholars suggest the Irish and Celts came here even before that.[9]

‡ What were the Lenape going to do with sixty guilders?

breathe the air—if you are allowed to at all. And then, finally, they push you and your family into one square foot of the room and say, "Live here, but you get no running water."

We typically hear a much more romantic story of indigenous people and early colonists. It's the "Thanksgiving" story: settlers off the Mayflower, with those wool Empire skirts and freshly starched bonnets that didn't get dirty at all on their months-long voyage across the sea, seeking new adventures and helped by the friendly locals. A seamless transition into friendship at a table with bountiful gourds and zero tension about whose spinach casserole recipe was used. It all sounds so lovely.

This history of the feast is rooted in some truth: There likely was a meal in 1621 in New England, possibly in the Cape Cod area.[15] It was a celebration of a productive harvest, and there were some Wampanoag* in attendance. And then, a year later, as Tommy Orange, a member of the Cheyenne and Arapaho, puts it: "The Indian Wars began. Native people were systematically erased."[17] The holiday as we know it today (eating until we're out of commission, then waking up for bargain shopping) didn't become a holiday until during the Civil War,[18] when Abraham Lincoln needed a way to unify America. So, at the suggestion of a media campaign,[19] he reached back into the history books, picked a random meal that mostly English settlers enjoyed, and branded it as a "big family, we are one, everything was very mutual, sorry about that disease and what I'm about to do to you (that's coming on the next page) meal, so we can pretend to feel good about ourselves" holiday. Bravo, Abe.

Let's just be crystal clear about the source of this event the next time the holiday comes around, and we dive into the artichoke dip 🥣 with the soundtrack of America—the clicks of football helmets (and skulls) crashing into each other—on in the background.

Even worse, this type of behavior was not anything out of the ordinary. Europeans' belief that they were entitled to colonize territories of people who weren't Christian dates back to a declaration† made by Pope Nicholas

---

* A tribe of approximately fifty thousand that lived in what is now Rhode Island and Massachusetts.[16]

† A papal bull to be exact, which is a type of decree or grant of authority by the pope. Today it's comparable to a presidential executive order; it's not law, but it gives agencies and elected officials permission to behave, and allocate money, accordingly.

V* in 1452.[20] This belief was based on the pope's likely "interpretation" of passages like Deuteronomy 20:16-17† that advocate and cement the relationship between God and his chosen people as contingent upon them taking land and "completely destroy[ing life] . . . [as] God has commanded you." The Christian Europeans who comprised most of the colonizer population were under the belief that their relationship with God, and vice versa, hinged on their conquering and settlement of the *Promised Lands* (which eventually also included the United States). Their service to God required them to subjugate, conquer, and enslave the original inhabitants of those lands at their leisure.[21] This moral air cover‡ from the Church§ blew wind into the sails of European colonizers throughout Africa and India—as well as the Americas.[24]

Many of the early European colonizers believed they were chosen and responsible for manifesting the expansionist destiny that God (well, Nicholas V) had preordained. The same sort of logic shaped the concept of "manifest destiny," what a nineteenth-century US newspaper editorial proclaimed was the right of settlers in America "to overspread and possess the whole of the continent" (#CognitiveAcrobatics, anyone?) to advance its

---

* Originally written to justify war against Muslims and pagans, the bull, *Dum Diversas*, issued June 18, 1452, authorized King Afonso of Portugal to "invade, search out, capture, vanquish . . . reduce their persons to perpetual slavery . . . and to apply appropriate to himself and his successors the kingdoms, dukedoms, counties . . . and goods, and to convert them to his and their use and profit."

† "However, in the cities of the nations the Lord your God is giving you as an inheritance, do not leave alive anything that breathes. Completely destroy them—the Hittites, Amorites, Canaanites, Perizzites, Hivites and Jebusites—as the Lord your God has commanded you" (Deuteronomy 20:16–17).

‡ Also known as the Doctrine of Discovery: a collection of papal bulls from the Church to the people of Europe saying that wherever you go, whatever land you find not occupied by white, Christian rulers, those people are subhuman and their land is up for grabs. This collection of documents empowered Europeans to colonize and enslave people across the entire continent of Africa, India, and the Americas. These documents, my friends, are some of the earliest artifacts of written white supremacy.[22]

§ As described by Steve Newcomb, a Shawnee Lenape scholar and author of *Pagans in the Promised Land: Decoding Doctrine of Christian Discovery,* "the Doctrine of Discovery is premised on the claim by Christian nations that they had located ('discovered') the lands of 'heathens' and 'infidels,' for the benefit and profit of the Christian world. That way of thinking is premised on the idea that Christian nations supposedly had the right to establish a system of domination over any non-Christian lands on the planet and over the non-Christians living there."[23]

"great experiment of liberty."[25] Much later, this perspective mutated into the dysfunctional concept of American *exceptionalism*, rooted in the belief of early colonists (and, dare I say, some Americans in 2020) that white conquerors bring enlightenment to other peoples and places.

There you have it: the "hall pass" white male Christians needed to do whatever they want. Their chosen-ness and entitlement to new Promised Lands, wherever they might be, was driven by their interpretation of divine will. This in turn supported the notion that they were particularly exceptional, while excusing their brute-force white supremacist policies as the advent of "civilization."

the "whitewash" setting

This is where I'd like to provide context for most of us who don't know all these intricate details.

I learned in fourth grade that the early colonists were heroes: God-like, strapping figures who were hardy and good at building cabins.* While studying indigenous people, we made construction paper headbands in the shape of feathers. Mine was perfectly frayed. Surely, a cornucopia billowing with fake food in a mock Thanksgiving Day feast—a Common Core–required fourth-grade activity—doesn't exactly frame what happened.

Similarly, in my school, we covered the enslavement of black people in fifth grade. We used the word *slavery* then, but I use *enslavement* now to emphasize the fact that this was something done *to* people, who were brought here involuntarily—it's not a title they'd give themselves. We didn't have to really talk about the horror in detail—that would be "too hard" to navigate. Instead, we read the book *Follow the Drinking Gourd,* about a group of enslaved people following the North Star to freedom. The unit culminated with my blonde hair and blue eyes and I playing the role of Mollie, the eldest daughter, fleeing north during a play for the third-grade class. It seemed like a fun adventure: building forts in the woods and log rafts to cross rivers, running from some "bad guy." It was a perfect example of how "we celebrate the heroes who escaped slavery long before we explain to children what slavery was," says Maureen Costello, director of the Teaching

---

* Pennsylvania State Standard, along with forty-two other states, teaches fourth-graders the subject in elementary school.[26]

Tolerance Project at the Southern Poverty Law Center.[27] That decision is just one more example of our habit of whitewashing the truth.

People typically use the term *whitewashing* to describe the process of covering something up, toning it down, making it seem less vivid and, overall, just more pleasant (where, culturally, "more pleasant" is usually more white, able bodied, heterosexual, and Christian, and more apt to put an optimistic gloss on complex topics). It's a key strategy in maintaining that ignorance we're so dependent on. I'm using the term to mean the way we present history, or the present day, in ways that makes us (usually "white people") feel most comfortable.

One way we whitewash the issue of inequality is by sticking with the illusion that we're all treated "equally"—that everyone has the same access to opportunity.* But taking a blinkered approach erases the ongoing effects of enslavement. For example, we put on pedestals the handful of individuals who have broken barriers—the women of color leading Fortune 500 companies,† a gay Presidential candidate,‡ or a theoretical physicist with motor neuron disease.§ Or, Will Smith. They all did it, so everyone must be able to. We're good. Problem fixed (or nonexistent). But their individual successes don't erase the existence of the barriers they had to surmount.

In our heads, we think, well, if this exception made it, then surely other Muslims, disabled people, and transgender people, for instance, will be able to climb their way up the proverbial mountain, just like every other hard-working American can. If they don't, it must be their own fault. And that assumption makes it harder for us white people to consider the possibility that, for example, black people are still having to deal with unjust consequences of racist policies from generations ago—because, you know, that all ended in 1865.¶

---

* 65% of all elected seats in the United States are occupied by white men[28]—71 of 100 Senate seats to be exact,[29] 72% of Fortune 500 companies are likely run by white men,[30] yet they only make up 30% of the American population.[31]

† Which is exactly two at the time of this writing, Joey Wat of Yum China and Lisa Su of Advanced Micro Devices.[32]

‡ Pete Buttigieg, mayor of South Bend, Indiana.

§ Stephen Hawking, who lived with amyotrophic lateral sclerosis (a.k.a. Lou Gehrig's disease) for more than fifty years, eventually only able to communicate via a speech-generating device linked to a single cheek muscle.

¶ It never came to a complete end, as we'll see in chapter five; there are laws that still provide loopholes that keep people enslaved in a system generation after generation.

The most obvious *whitewashing* is what we do to our American icons. We have done an excellent job of making some of the most radical figures of our history "safe" by whitewashing them. Many Americans today count Dr. Martin Luther King Jr. among our most important American heroes,[33] but during his life he was deeply despised and seen as a serious threat by many white people around the country. We have a national holiday in his honor, for which people are quick to post memes about equality and justice— neither of which are being received by the demographics he sought to protect. White people generally stick to sharing Dr. King's most platitude-heavy messages; they are often surprised to learn of his disappointment for white moderates, whom he condemned as being "more devoted to 'order' than to justice."[34] Sharing his image, or his words, has become another decoration, right next to the photos of ourselves, protesting, which allows us to pretend inequity is in the past—that it's "over." We've whitewashed ourselves into a place of comfort.

We have done an excellent job of making some of the most radical figures of our history "safe" by whitewashing them—like Jesus of Nazareth, who has been completely Anglo-fied despite being from the Middle East, making it very likely he had brown skin (at least). My favorite example is Santa Claus—a character based on St. Nicholas, a Turkish, dark-skinned saint who is now the color of snow. White supremacy has conditioned us to believe that heroes have fair skin and that evading historical accountability is a routine part of making white people comfortable. Being white and fitting in with a certain image is seen, at least in our mainstream cultural narrative, as more important than being faithful to all the facts. To take one example, United States president John F. Kennedy, had a 58% approval rating when he was killed in 1963, yet today the entire political establishment fawns over his legacy even though we now know he was a serial adulterer.

Clearly I, and most products of American education standards, have internalized many of these whitewashed stories. I had a diluted education about the Genocide of Native Nations,* which I have come to learn is the more accurate way to think about the orchestrated killing of millions of people.[35] (I will say more about that very controversial word, "genocide," and the reason why I use it so intentionally, later in this chapter.) Our education system shielded me from learning the true atrocities of our past that

---

* There are a number of different terms used for the slaughter of the indigenous population: War of Manifest Destiny, Genocide of Turtle Island, and Native American Genocide.

kept us centered. And that gave me little context when it was my turn to stand in front of the blackboard as a teacher, decades later. I recently came across a sign I made to teach my first-grade students about the "Indians" in 2003, which read: "Indians, Indians dressed in brown come to visit Plymouth Town." It was laminated, so I could use it year after year.

There are so many problems with the way our curricula came to be. First, many natives have no use for the word "Indian" or "America/n."[36] "Indigenous" is one of the more accepted terms to describe a continent filled with thousands of cultures, religions, and languages—many more different from one another than French is from Chinese. (And, yes, the Smithsonian museums and other institutions across the country use a combination of "America/n" and "Indian"—and if you ask any number of indigenous peoples from across the country what their preferred terminology is, you're likely to get a variety of responses. It's important, however, to remember that any name or term given to the original inhabitants of this land we refer to as America comes with the baggage of colonialism.)

There are reasons why we teach the way we do. As the storybooks of our country, textbooks are simpler when they focus on history's victors as heroes.* And elementary educators can't conveniently dive *that* deeply into the necessary and horrific details of the Genocide of Native Nations or what enslavement really looked like for students so young.† So the school boards that create the K–12 curriculum schedule‡ make sure we don't have to get into too much complexity, allowing us to continue to whitewash our way through the not-so-simple chapters of our history.

For example, it's easy for our textbooks to say, "Yes, there were enslaved people in America. But, don't worry, everyone is free now [they're not; more on that later]—thank you, Lincoln." It's harder to hear, "Lincoln didn't think of black people as equal to white people; he made the decision to free the slaves for political advantages."

---

* One book that takes a different approach, Howard Zinn's A People's History of the United States, has been routinely banned from libraries and was even the subject of proposed legislation outlawing its presence in Arkansas public schools because it was too honest. "Honest"? Please—it's part of the perfection performance.[37]

† I'll whip out my two academic degrees in early education to confirm that the gruesome details are not appropriate for eight- and nine-year-olds, if avoidable, though the oppression should be taught ASAP.

‡ The subjects *are* casually woven through middle and high school curricula, but not in meaningful ways.

How does an average American woman 🙄 who became an elementary school teacher emerge from her cloud of ignorance? For me, it took a series of life experiences and brave and patient friends of color who grabbed my hand and said, "Please go look at what you clearly don't see," and my being so infuriated at the thought of living in a system where some people are actively discarded that I had no choice but to act. Sometimes the experience of being called to a new frontline, hearing their shouts of "Wake up!," was (and is, and always will be) jarring. Yet this is what they've always been asking us to do.

This is hard and urgent work. Again, I'm so glad you're here.

let's get on the same page

I want things to be rosy for my kids, too, the way my parents made sure they were for me. Part of me wants them to believe only the shiny parts of the American idea, the characteristics I was taught:

- America is a land of freedom and equality for all.
- American heroes have always stepped up to save those who need saving.
- Everything in our nation's past was a necessary step in our advancement.
- There may have been injustices in our past, but we have always corrected them.
- If you work hard enough, you'll achieve your dreams.

It pains me that I have to sit down with my kids and walk them through the complicated truth.* But while I do that, I can also tell them—and we can remind ourselves—that we are still writing American history today. Only by knowing our past as it was—and not how we want it to be—can we understand our present in order to solve for the future.

"Where common memory is lacking, where people do not share in the same past, there can be no real community," wrote theologian H. Richard Niebuhr.[38] It's a powerful idea that was later reiterated by Mark Charles,

---

* As another example of white privilege, this is a conversation that parents of color, especially black and brown parents, are forced to have just to keep their kids safe.

Navajo* activist, pastor, and coauthor of *Unsettling Truths: The Ongoing Dehumanizing Legacy of the Doctrine of Discovery*, who argues that all America's problems with race, gender, disability status, and class come down to the fact that we as a country lack this common memory.

Instead, he says, we have "single stories," like the Thanksgiving story or that of the Underground Railroad. They're passed down just like, in my family, Van Morrison's "Brown Eyed Girl" is: my great-grandmother knows it cold, so do the two generations in between her and me, and I just taught it to my daughter (in an attempt to get her excited about having brown eyes instead of my blue ones). She's listened to it a few times, and she's almost got it down. Handing cultural artifacts down from one generation to another is just that easy.

These individual stories in and of themselves aren't the problem. It's not that they're incorrect. It's that they're *incomplete*. When these stories become the *only* stories, we think in limited ways. If we want to build a unified community,† we have to move past the stories and song lyrics we have memorized and accepted as truth. We have to uncover and take to heart the real range of intentionally hidden histories—the ones that can give us a blunt understanding of the world today.

oh, Abe

Many of us can parrot enough of what we learned in grade-school history to demonstrate some semblance of having paid attention. A favorite exercise of mine, inspired by a question Mark Charles posed initially, is to ask participants of a Listening Circle, "Who is the most revered American president?" They look at me with the typical, "Oh no, I hope I get this right . . . actually, let me sit here silently and let someone else answer, 'cause I'll probably get this wrong" kind of look. I tell them there is no wrong answer,

---

* While the origin of the name "Navajo," bestowed by Spanish missionaries, is well known, some believe it is a word for clasp knife, promoting a stereotype of the Navajos as war-obsessed aggressors. The name members of this group use for themselves is "Diné" (pronounced din-EH), which is a word from the Athapascan language, spoken by indigenous people from Alaska and Canada to the Southwest United States. This word is defined as "man," and is translated as "the people."[39] Diné is an affirmative way of referring to the Navajo people.[40] However, it is much more complicated than that; "Navajo Nation" is what is recognized by the Tribal Nations, and some still refer to themselves as such.[41]

† I'd argue that this is key to reweaving our societal fabric.

that I just like to play this game to see how the participants will respond, so just "blurt out whatever name is now in your mouth." Eighty to 90% of participants answer with one gent: Abraham Lincoln.

"Why?" I ask . . . and then I get some iteration of how he ended slavery and the Civil War, blah, blah, blah. Few of us are called to learn more about Lincoln after we've put required classes behind us, so nobody can really deliver anything beyond those arguments.

And, yes, Lincoln ended the Civil War* and moved us one step closer to salvation by making slavery illegal in a handful of states.† But as I'll detail, it was also under his orders that indigenous populations were tortured and annihilated as America continued to expand west. Some consider this part of history a genocide on American soil.‡ I do.

I'm using that term *genocide*§ very intentionally and carefully. I spent a good part of my graduate education studying this subject. I've written curriculum about it, I've published articles about crimes against humanity, and I know the kind of fire I'm playing with in making this claim (alongside many other people much smarter than me). *Genocide* is always

---

* The war ended in 1865. But Lincoln's goal in ending slavery, as he describes it, and which is now displayed on a bronze plaque at his monument in Washington, DC, was to "save the Union, and it is not to save or destroy slavery. If I could save the Union without freeing any slave, I would do it; and if I could save it by freeing all the slaves I would do it; and if I could save it by freeing some and leave others alone, I would also do that." The fate of the slaves always comes second to the need to save the Union.

† Lincoln needed to keep some of the states—Kentucky, Missouri, Delaware, and Maryland—happy because they hadn't technically joined the Union—the northern part of the country that was posturing as anti-enslavement. Because, let me be clear here: white Americans were killing each other not over whether or not to free the slaves; they were fighting over how to keep white supremacy intact. Lincoln didn't think the country needed to enslave people to keep the country united and stabilized, though his Democratic opponent, Stephen Douglas, did. This was not a war about equality; this was a war about keeping all of the states in the country under one flag. Slavery was the wedge issue (more on that in chapter seven).[42]

‡ In 2013, the National Congress of American Indians passed a resolution calling upon the Smithsonian to establish the National American Indian Holocaust Museum. In the resolution, they describe what happened to indigenous people in America as genocide, and the slaughter of indigenous people as a holocaust. As of the publication of this book, the Smithsonian has not accommodated the request.

Experts have a series of arguments for why the term genoicide is accurate—see the endnotes for their perspectives.[43]

§ Which the United Nations Office on Genocide Prevention defines as "acts committed with intent to destroy, in whole or in part, a national, ethnical, racial, or religious group."[44]

a contested description because it means a tremendous number of lives were systematically ended over their ethnic, racial, or religious background, or disability status.

In my research to understand what happened on this land before the Europeans arrived, I kept coming across conflicting estimates for the size of the pre-colonized indigenous population of what is now the United States. I spent the first few months wrestling with two figures: one scholar suggested the number was one million, whereas others suggested it as high as twenty million.* Right before I submitted the manuscript for this book, I received an email from another scholar suggesting the number could have been closer to 120 million.

The exact number is not for me to weigh in on—I'll leave it to the experts. The bottom line: A significant population lived on this land before they were methodically erased. The number, which is almost definitely in the many millions, qualifies what took place in our country as a genocide. And it happened on a number of our presidents' watches, including that of everyone's favorite: Abraham Lincoln.

Under Lincoln's direction, our railroads pushed further west† onto Indigenous land, displacing some communities. "Well," you might say, in the midst of some cognitive acrobatics, maybe a high-beam twist, "it was a necessary step to build train tracks from the Atlantic to the Pacific." It was indeed, and that is still how many of our made-in-China sneakers get to New York City. We can justify the need for expansion and industrialization to create jobs and thriving economies all we want. But we can't hide behind railroad building for what happened next. The approach of Lincoln and his generals—particularly James Carleton, who said, "All Indian men . . . are to be killed whenever and wherever you can find them"[46] involved more than just laying tracks for commerce.

Lincoln's men forced the migration of Indigenous populations, pushing them from their homes and communities and requiring them to walk inhumane distances each day. You might be familiar with the Trail of Tears,‡

---

* Scholars have different algorithms for arriving at estimates of the loss of life; see the endnotes for one calculation.[45]

† The Pacific Railway Act of 1862.

‡ In which, under President Andrew Jackson's rule, 17,000 Cherokee were forced to walk over a thousand miles from their territory in Georgia to new lands in Oklahoma. An estimated 4,000 people died.[47]

which does appear in our history books. That forced migration, thirty years before the ones ordered by Lincoln, was only one of many. And while its inclusion in the curriculum is a good first step to greater clarity about our past and the footsteps we also walk, our version blames the vast loss of life on disease rather than brutality. During these death marches, pregnant women, children, and elders who couldn't keep up were left behind as everyone else did their best to maintain the pace of the Yankee generals flanking them on horseback.

One walk, the Long Walk of the Navajo in 1864[48]—the year Lincoln was reelected—resulted in two thousand Navajo and Mescalero Apache people dying from the physical and environmental conditions.[49] There are terrible stories from this event, so brace yourself: In one, soldiers refused to stop the march for a pregnant woman in labor. She told her parents to go on without her; perhaps it would work out somehow. They did—and the parents had gone only a short way before they heard a gunshot. The soldiers had killed her.* The spot where she and her unborn child died is estimated to have been somewhere in Santa Fe, possibly across the street from the Starbucks on West San Francisco Street, adjacent to the ATM and next to Thunderbird Bar & Grill . . . at the corner of Lincoln Avenue.[51]

This was genocide. They and so many others on these marches died because they were not white or of European ancestry. And this genocide was possible because of a culture that believed that white people of European ancestry were preordained to identify *Promised Lands* and know the best means to take and control them, as was their commitment to God (and he to them). The assumption that "real" Americans are of direct lineage from this chosen European demographic is a belief you still see in our white supremacist culture today.

Our ancestors were told of their exceptional privilege by their ancestors, who heard it first from Pope Nicholas V on behalf of the Church, which gave them permission to commit these heinous crimes. In the words of Pastor Mark Charles: "*Exceptionalism* is the coping mechanism of a nation in deep denial about its genocidal past as well as its current racist reality." He goes on: "The reason we cling to the narrative of exceptionalism is if we don't have a special relationship with God that justifies our past then we're just another colonial, genocidal, murderous nation, and that notion

---

* According to historical researcher Jennifer Major, who approximates that between fifteen to twenty-five women would have died this way on this particular walk.[50]

is unfathomable to people." We avoid that truth because, for many of us, it defies everything we believe to be safe about our identity as Americans. And faced with reality, we just don't know what to do with it.

The indigenous people weren't passive in this torture. They retaliated, and colonists' and settlers' lives were lost,* as well. The difference was that the European settlers—and, later, the Americans—had one thing that the natives didn't have: guns. Bullets and gunpowder intentionally extinguished indigenous lives, leaving room for one narrative to take center stage: the white man's.

victors get to tell their story

Western civilization has used religion as a means to justify its territorial expansion,† as have many others, throughout human history. The story we tell ourselves—not just about our actions on the continental United States, but globally to this day—is that when human populations are invaded, they sometimes fight back, get hurt, or are displaced, but that is an unfortunate by-product of expansion. (What we also know, but don't often discuss, is that when a people are invaded, women and children always suffer the most.) We knew people were suffering then, and we know it even better now. We can't change what happened then—but can't we do better now? Can we stop making excuses for our behavior then, or use it as an excuse for how we do things today? Our history is not a permission slip that makes continuing to do those things okay.

We must also acknowledge how different the story would be told if there had been a different outcome. Mark Charles posed a question to a group of people at the Trinity Evangelical Divinity School Conference in 2019, asking, "What if Hitler had won World War II? What would be

---

* For example, 490 settlers died in the Santee Sioux uprising in 1861. But even here, the truth is complicated. It's critical to remember that at the time, the Dakota were starving to death. What's more, the US government retaliated. 303 Dakota people were arrested for their role in the uprising. Those who were arrested didn't speak English, and were not given legal representation or processed in a proper court of law; instead, they were prosecuted in military tribunals and sentenced to die. Lincoln, in a last-minute show of sympathy, pardoned 265 of those sentenced, but 38 were executed, in what remains the largest mass execution in American history. And then Lincoln's Congress went on to remove all the tribes that had settled in the area, even the ones who'd had nothing at all to do with the uprising.[52]

† The Doctrine of Discovery and Manifest Destiny, as mentioned on page 77.

our understanding of his motive?" Hitler's story would look a lot different, wouldn't it? As a Jew, I can't quite fathom what that would be: Would non-Christian, nonwhite people, people who identify as LGBTQ, and disabled people have been globally exterminated at this point? As a victor, how would he have promoted a narrative to convince the world that his success was justified by nature and destiny? It's a question worthy of consideration—I surely don't have the answer.

The victors in the case of the settlers versus the indigenous certainly told the story the way they wanted to. Check any fourth-grade textbook and you'll see "that the Indian problem was dealt with nicely," says Lisa Wade, who examined academic standards on the subject in fifty states.[53] The "Indians" would tell the story differently. Still today, there are neighborhoods within reservations that have severely limited access to running water[54] and the indigenous have the highest rates of suicide in the nation.[55] The deprivation of resources contributes[56] to particularly frequent drug use, sexual violence, and murder on the reservations we marched their ancestors to because then, as now, we provided only nominal means of support (more on this later). But our state-sanctioned ignorance allows us to sleep better at night.

We have to be careful not to perpetuate the myth that native communities are either "extinct" or universally "destitute"—neither is true.* I share this heartbreaking information to make the clear point that in mistreating the native population, our ancestors knew better, and so do we. But neither can we pretend these problems, which we as a country have caused, do not exist. Just about every sitting president and soccer mom alike has cruised right through these truths—the tragic past as well as the current scars on our country's face—with little pause, despite little drive to address the blood on all our hands. The first step to remedy the inherited plight of the indigenous today is admitting that our ancestors took lives and land under a banner of entitlement ("we know better than they do") via interpretations of the Doctrine of Discovery (that many denominations and individual congregations

---

* To mention two signs of progress, past due but nevertheless important: Representatives Deb Haaland of New Mexico and Sharice Davids of Kansas made history in 2018 as the first indigenous women elected to Congress. Also, there's evidence that the gap between indigenous people's life expectancies and the average American life expectancy, which was about twenty years in Lyndon B. Johnson's day, is now only five years.

have rightfully renounced verbally—though they haven't always translated this into concrete action[57]).

Mark Charles offers a metaphor: "It feels like our indigenous peoples are an old grandmother who lives in a very large house. It is a beautiful place with plenty of rooms and comfortable furniture. But years ago, some people came into her house and locked her upstairs in the bedroom. Today her home is full of people. They are sitting on her furniture. They are eating her food. They are having a party in her house. They have since come upstairs and unlocked the door to her bedroom, but now it is much later, and she is tired, old, weak, and sick; so she can't or doesn't want to come out."

past is present

Sometimes, in the Listening Circles, women will ask why black folk can't just "get over slavery." It's something from the past, they say. Why do we still have to wrestle with it in our day-to-day discourse? And it is technically accurate that it is illegal to own other humans or keep them against their will. But that is in no way the end of the story.

A friendly reminder: To curate a story about our collective past that I don't think we know enough about, I've selected a few historical truths from under the umbrella of "colonialism," to demonstrate my point that the land in which we focus on our core in Pilates class, lick drippy ice cream cones, fill up our cars with gas, and have sex has been home to countless people before us, many of whom were subjected to extraordinary peril so we could live in our McMansions pretending everything is "new."*

This is what I do when I lay with my babies on the grass in front of my parent's home in Pennsylvania. We'll study a small patch of earth, maybe

---

* Some additional key points of our history we are quick to forget, as Frederick Douglass outlined in his *Douglass Monthly* back in 1862: "We had bought Florida, waged war with friendly Seminoles, purchased Louisiana, annexed Texas, fought Mexico, trampled on the right of petition, abridged the Freedom of Debate, paid $10 million to Texas upon a fraudulent claim, mobbed the Abolitionists, repealed the Missouri Compromise, winked at the accursed slave trade, helped to extend slavery, given slaveholders a large share of all the offices and honors that we claimed for ourselves, paid their postage, supported the government, persecuted free Negroes, refused to recognize Hayti and Liberia, stained our souls by repeated compromises, born with Southern Bluster, allowed our ships to be robbed of their hardy sailors, defeated essential road to the Pacific, and have descended to the meanest and degradation of negro dogs, and hunted down the panting slave escaping from his tyrant master—all to make the South love us; and yet how stands our relations?"[58]

a foot by a foot, in search of the creatures milling about the bases of grass stems—and I think, who else's bare feet stepped right here? Was their blood drawn here, that the rains pushed further into the soil invisible to my eye? What did the Lenape do—is this where they built their homes or birthed their babies? Did the enslaved hide behind that boulder on their way in between the Quaker meeting houses sprinkled all over the area? That's my way of bringing history into my living, breathing present; it is the only way I can carry the behemoth of our past and make sure it lives in the now so I never forget.

I am not asking you to wallow in the past for its own sake, without turning that knowledge into a constructive resolution for the future. But as part of the work I asked you to do earlier in the book, the next time you're outside, take a moment to hold these paragraphs in mind—and don't forget whose footprints you are walking in while enjoying your freedom.

And, while I have no idea how we reconcile these past truths with the ones we create while moving through our lives, I do believe that we need to hold history closer as we think about our own behavior. We're not working off a clean slate here. This moment in time is just the latest building block on top of the stack, and if we don't balance ourselves correctly, the whole thing could still collapse. We can't ignore the lessons from our nation's scars or we'll end up hurting people all over again. Let's continue this here—in one of the harder chapters of the book. We're more than halfway done.

A final caveat: I'm walking on particularly thin ice in this chapter because the previous and the following stories aren't mine to tell. These are not stories of my ancestors. Their pain and perseverance are not mine to lean on; their trauma isn't still in my bones. In fact, I'm still benefiting from their torture, regardless of how much I wish that weren't true. I can look at their stories with empathy, and with the intention to use that knowledge to raise my hand to dismantle my own misconceptions—but I will never really know these experiences.

I don't know their pain, and I never will, but I can hold a part of their humanity next to mine.

As I tell the Listening Circles, the reason why the period of enslavement cannot be left in the past is that we share a country with a huge population whose ancestors were brought here against their will and whose descendants can't "just go back to Africa"—just like the members of countless indigenous nations whose lands were stolen, and who can't "go back" because they are now full of strip malls and cul-de-sacs. The more than 330 million of us living in this country are immigrants 🔍, yet we act like we own the place. We have inherited consequences of decisions that caused extraordinary pain then and continue to cause extraordinary pain now. We may try to avoid inflicting the same harm as people who lived and died before we were born, but the descendants of those victims can rightly hold us accountable for what we *aren't* doing to clean up the legacy of that harm, a legacy that still benefits us. That, my friends, is on us.

At the Women's March on Washington, before a crowd of millions, Tamika Mallory, one of the organizers, said, "To those of you who experience a feeling of being powerless, disparaged, victimized, antagonized, threatened, and abused, to those of you who for the first time felt the pain that my people have felt since they were brought here with chains shackled on our legs, today I say to you: Welcome to my world. Welcome to our world." Her words rattled my chest bone.

our path here

Throughout history, people have conquered other people using divine right as justification. We've established that. We've also established that that's wrong and we shouldn't do that anymore. Sometimes "conquering" has meant killing or enslaving others. Sometimes skin color had nothing to do with it. In other words: Slaves weren't, and aren't today, always what the American culture has defined them as. The word *slave* is often said to come from *Slav*, the term used for Slavonic people—some of whom were taken as slaves during the eighth and ninth centuries. All these people were light in skin color, what we call "white" today.[59]

In this land that is now the United States, there were enslaved people of various colors from the beginning. The Dutch brought enslaved Africans when they arrived in the 1600s,[60] but they also brought enslaved people from India[61] and Asia.[62] There were also many *indentured servants* of many different nationalities and skin colors. Unlike people who were enslaved and held as property, indentured servants worked under contract with their owners for a period of years, often in exchange for something like passage to the states or land ownership. It was a temporary condition, a debt of sorts that could be repaid and the contract ended.

As British settlers arrived and formed colonies, producing raw materials to send back to England, there was high demand for labor to harvest the crops grown in the colonies—tobacco, cotton, and rice. And a variety of people from several countries—including England, Scotland, Ireland, and Germany—came as indentured servants to fill that demand.[63] In the mix were white homeless children from London, impoverished white women, and white convicts. In the early 1600s, Virginia, like all the colonies, didn't distinguish between indentured servants of different skin colors. All toiled together in the fields, all were looked after, and all became free when their contracts ended.

A high-profile escape attempt in 1640 changed the system. Three indentured servants fled their plantation. Two of them, both white, were punished with an additional four years on their contracts. The third, a black man named John Punch, was forced to remain in service to the plantation owner for the rest of his life. It was the first record of a shift to enslavement in the colonies' actual law—and it fell upon a black man.[64] This was a significant moment: the first recorded case of a man of color being treated differently from a white man in a court of law.[65] This ruling gave permission to elite and slave-owning households to treat their indentured servants, particularly people of color, as brutally as they wished, knowing the law would be heavily weighted on the white man's side.

In 1676, there was another fork in the road: Bacon's Rebellion. Nathaniel Bacon, a wealthy landowner frustrated that indigenous people were occupying lands he wanted to exploit and leading raids on Virginia's settlers, issued a challenge to the governor of Virginia, William Berkeley, to remove them. (Berkeley preferred to deal with the indigenous people without violence[66]—imagine that.) When Berkeley failed to resolve the situation to Bacon's satisfaction, Bacon gathered a volunteer militia of indentured white and black servants and enslaved black people,[67] all of whom were also looking for a means to more freedom and prosperity, to fight Berkeley and the colonial elite. Ultimately, Bacon's militia burned down the colony's capital, Jamestown. The uprising terrified other property owners. It further fueled elites' determination to divide the power of the laborers, lest they team up again, and the easiest way to do that was based on race.

The elites thought that if they could firmly designate all black and mixed-race people as "slaves," and if poor whites could be made to police them and keep them "in line," they could keep the lower classes from organizing against them en masse again.[68] They were right. By pitting the enslaved and indentured against each other, it broke their collective power. (Sound familiar?)

White servants often became responsible for overseeing the enslaved, thus cementing another layer of white supremacy and creating further division. White people were also given greater access to lands taken from indigenous people, further distinguishing them from their former peers. And though the lives of poor white folk didn't improve by *all* that much, the benefits they did receive made it worth their while not to make trouble again. (This was another of the many key moments in the process of white people *dehumanizing* and "othering" people who are nonwhite.[69]) One major benefit white servants did receive was getting to avoid the most brutal agricultural labor, which was instead performed by *enslaved* Africans. Poor whites increasingly embraced racism because it gave them a sense of superiority in society where they were otherwise the lowest rank. Rather than addressing the true perpetrators of their misfortune—their fellow white man—they accepted the lie that people of color were somehow the problem.

The consequence of manufactured race-based division, as we all know, was horror after horror.

The reading of these next few sentences is pivotal to our moving forward—commit to this work of looking at the truth of our past, so we can start to undo the oppression we see in the world today. It's important that we internalize this history, not put it on shelf like a dusty trinket that we glance at when we're not busy with life; we need to let these truths—many of which most of us haven't visited with since grade school—soak into the collagen of our flesh, make them part of the prism through which we see the world so we can't see the world without this history. It's one of the tiny ways we restore what has been done. Apathy has no place in our bodies or the world anymore; let's continue.

Some mothers from the west coast of Africa, desperate to spare their babies from being shackled in the bowels of a dank ship surrounded by corpses and whatever survivors clung to life, and to protect them from a life of torture, reportedly killed them.* Some of the enslaved died soon after they arrived, having been suffocated in close spaces with no ventilation; slave traders justified this treatment by claiming black people were naturally better at withstanding heat (a bias that still exist today).[71]

---

* In 1660, Charles II of England issues a charter to launch the Royal African Company, which was dedicated exclusively to increasing the British share of the slave trade. Over the next fifty years, the annual number of captured Africans from all different backgrounds and tribes brought to the British colonies had risen to 45,000.[70]

In one center for trading enslaved people, Shockoe Bottom in Richmond, Virginia, as many as three hundred thousand human souls, and likely more, were sold into slavery. Both adults and their children were sold on the auction block; people stood by while babies were ripped off their mother's nipples, never to be reunited. (The market site is now buried under a six-story parking garage for Virginia state employees. You can learn this spot's history by visiting the sculpture and plaque in the Reconciliation Triangle at the corner of the garage property, or the historical marker facing it across the street. The millions who zoom above it on eight lanes of Interstate 95 likely never will.)

For generation after generation, slavery meant inhumane work and living conditions, sexual exploitation and rape, and extreme physical and mental abuse. Enslaved people lived in cramped quarters providing the bare minimum to keep them alive enough to work.[72] Women who fought back against sexual assault were punished. Records show an enslaved woman named Celia killed her white owner after he raped her for years; the state of Missouri executed her.[73] One Kentucky woman, known only as Sylva, killed all thirteen of her children "rather than have them suffer in slavery."[74]

To keep enslaved Africans under control, in the mid-1600s the colony of Virginia passed laws to codify the practice of slavery and established that, once purchased, enslaved people were considered property, and the owners could do with them what they chose in perpetuity.* Once that was written into statutes, one of the great foundational injustices of America was firmly in place.

Enslaved Africans built the original railroad routes[76] Amtrak still uses, as well as the United States US Capitol building, on the steps of which we still inaugurate each new president.[77] They produced all of the cotton, sugar, and tobacco that the south sold to the north and abroad, which produced the money that built cities like Birmingham, New Orleans, and Atlanta.

White women are plenty aware of racial and class divides today. They're evident when we drive from our suburbs to dinner downtown or when we're watching almost every scripted network show on television. But we sometimes forget the painful causes of those divides. We forget those whose lives were tormented and cut short on the land that is now some of our front lawns. So when white women in a few of the Listening Circles commented that slavery is over, I remind them: it's not.

---

* See endnotes for the sequence of laws quickly passed to protect the powerful.[75]

our inheritance

We will look at today's societal consequences from our past systems of enslavement in chapter five. For now, though, just know that, as the writer Rachel Elizabeth Cargle says, "There is a very real connection between today's continued deep racial tensions and our passive acknowledgement of our very ugly history."[78]

Most of us know that the United States Constitution starts with a sequence of words, words that we occasionally boast about as if they'd been dropped from heaven onto parchment paper: "We the people." But the Constitution that we celebrate and revere was written to protect the interests of white, land-owning men—and it is doing just that. "He," "him," and "his" are used fifty-one times to describe who has the freedom to own land, run for office,* and be protected by the law.

The Declaration of Independence says, "All men are created equal," but the document signed on August 2, 1776, also calls Indians "savages" and bears no mention of women (👋, hey there). Only white men could vote, and in measuring the population for taxation and representation purposes, each slave was counted only as three-fifths of a person in the Constitution.†
In other words, the founding documents only protect white men, and the system we know as white supremacy.

To date, none of its articles or amendments reflect any other aspiration. Even amendments aimed at extending rights to others have had unsatisfying results in terms of making social justice a reality. The marginalized demographics, mostly people of color, have moved from being enslaved in the fields to being incarcerated in jails. There are exactly zero female pronouns throughout the entire document, so it should be no surprise that women, particularly women of color, were completely disenfranchised until a century ago‡ and still make as little as $0.53 for every dollar a white man makes for the same job.

---

* Article 2, Section 1 reads, "He shall hold his Office during the Term of four Years" . . . which raises the question, is the electoral college in violation of the Constitution if a women gets elected president?

† Article 1, Section 2

‡ It is worth noting here that black and indigenous women in the United States furthermore didn't get full voting rights until the 1965 Voting Rights Act, despite the passage of the Nineteenth Amendment in 1920 that grants all American women the right to vote—and there are still many millions of women disenfranchised today.

The Constitution, as Mark Charles reminds us, "is doing exactly what it is meant to do—it is protecting the interest of landowning men. The Constitution is working." And there are so many ways in which it must be improved.

Just as it was the task of past generations to abolish slavery, it is now our generation's task to abolish the systems that continue to protect the white supremacist ideals of our country's founders. We must pull ourselves up to that frontline and question our deeply ingrained motives—not from a survival perspective, but in terms of wealth creation and maintaining power. We have spent too many generations telling ourselves that our history was rosy and fair. And now that is over.

People of color, women and gender-nonconforming people, disabled people, and new immigrants have constantly been subjugated so that white men could maintain the lion's share of resources. Did you know that for most of the 1850s, Chinese Americans were forbidden to testify against whites* and were forbidden to go to public schools? And that Native Nations don't own their land, it's in a Federal Trust—and they *still* aren't permitted to sue the government?

We need to do more than just embrace the shame of our past. We need to take responsibility for its legacy and stop it from continuing any further into our future. Let's connect the dots between what happened then, on this land we call home, and what is happening now to marginalized people here and around the world; we can't keep tucking these truths into the creases of our history books from a time long gone, because humans are still suffering. Let's think about how our relationships with countries in the Middle East depend more on the price of a barrel of oil and not on whether they let women drive, or, I don't know, prevent the flow of food to starving children.† Let's learn about the lives and needs of mothers in war-torn countries (beset by conflicts often started or exacerbated by the policies of powerful Western nations), who have bombs dropping on their children's nursery schools; of displaced women who carry their babies hundreds of miles toward the safest border; of moms living in under-resourced communities watching their sons pick one of two options—a gang or a prison cell.

---

* *People v. Hall* in 1854.

† As in Yemen, where Saudi Arabia–led blockades and bombing campaigns have deliberately targeted the distribution of food and water, resulting in what the United Nations has called "the worst famine in the world in 100 years." All, I might add, very preventable.

The poet Marilyn Nelson offers one powerful example of how we can learn to own our past, in order to better understand the state of our world today. In a September 2018 episode of the podcast *On Being*, Nelson talked about working with a church community in Lyme, Connecticut, to explore slaveholding in their past, as they celebrated the church's 350th anniversary. They learned Church members had enslaved people. Their first pastor had owned people; they'd lived in the attic of the parsonage. Many parishioners hadn't known any of this history. Nelson also said the group discovered that many of their homes in the surrounding neighborhood are located on land once set aside for the indigenous.

Some families had lived in the area for three hundred years, in the houses their ancestors had built. They struggled with how those ancestors had participated in an inhumane institution, and how their families still benefited from those decisions today. And the work they did to come to terms with that was exactly the work I'm talking about here: difficult, confusing, embarrassing, painful, necessary . . . and repeat. The most impressive people I know are the ones who can detach themselves from shame so they can continue to learn. In her nonfiction book, *The Meeting House*, Nelson chronicles how the church community actually did the work on themselves while in community, coming face to face with their privilege, and one of the reasons they were able to do that work is because they weren't willing to look away. This is part of the new frontline, not looking away—which is one of the early first steps in restorative justice.

When we look at our history, particularly when we summarize unimaginable suffering in a few sentences as I have done here, it's hard not to feel ashamed—not just that this happened in a land on which you might feel entitled to call home, but also that you, as a human, are in any way connected to such a brutal, bloody, and unfair history.

We try to protect ourselves from feeling too much self-hate by leaning, again, into ignorance, and not really looking. And in the process, we end up whitewashing our past, individually or through policy and curriculum. Reading and experiencing the words on these pages—together—are crucial to us breaking our silence 🔇 and stopping the unintentional perpetuation of old norms. And even if you are alone while reading this, know that you are doing this work in community with millions of others consciously rising from the ashes of our very settled past. Your participation is seen and needed. Thank you for getting through chapter three. Onward.

CHAPTER FOUR

GO WHITE-SAVIOR YOURSELF

Pretty girls are bad in bed." That is *exactly* what one Listening Circle participant said.

"Whhhhaaaat?" I asked the Listening Circle participant, intrigued.

"Yeah, whenever I watch the Victoria Secret Fashion Show, I always think, 'Those girls don't have to work particularly hard to get men, so they don't have to work in the bedroom, either.'"

"Gotcha," I said, totally baffled that this was her answer to my question about what biases the group had, yet tracking her point. "Anyone else want to share any biases they might have?" I asked, hoping some would offer a more constructive insight. "Feel free to be brutally honest."

"Men who wear tassels on their loafers have small penises," belted someone else. "I have no idea where I got that, but it is what I think." She followed with, "And all Italians are good in bed!"

"They also cheat on their wives," volunteered someone else, with a mouth full of brie, from the loveseat on the other side of the room.

Long pause. I had officially lost control. I sat there with a soft grin on my face, pretending I wasn't screaming confused curses in my head. They were right that these were all examples of bias. I was just hoping for racial, gender, or religious biases—not opinions about the size (and ability) of people's penises.

We spend our days moving through the world, juggling tasks, driving, adjusting the Sirius XM station, foraging for dinner, and constantly processing a tremendous amount of information, including up to 12 hours[1] of media a day. The messages we receive about race, gender, and other identifiers are sometimes very obvious (pink is for girls, blue is for boys) and sometimes more subtle or hidden (like the way you're more likely to think of your female college instructors as "teachers," and your male college instructors as "professors.")*

Some biases, like the ones offered by the Listening Circle participants about pretty girls and penises, are called *explicit biases* because they are accessible. By asking ourselves, "How do I feel about a specific demographic?" and giving ourselves a few minutes, we can typically unearth at least a handful of sweeping *stereotypes*†—about sex, but also about race, gender, religion, disability, and class.

We're generally aware of explicit biases, especially those we've collectively been groomed to think are "okay" to have: women aren't as good at sports, black people are better dancers, the French make the best love (throwing a bone to those who would rather read about sex than bias). Other explicit biases we're very careful not to share because we know they are negative: Jews are cheap, Asians are bad drivers, Muslims are terrorists.

But there's another category of bias that is possibly even more alarming: *implicit biases*. Implicit biases are ones we don't know we have, and that we sometimes work really hard to convince ourselves don't exist. Implicit biases can be the same in content as explicit ones ("black people are dangerous") but differ because they influence our behavior without us catching them (white people call the police on black people more quickly than on those of other races). Taken together, both biases contribute to the high numbers of innocent people of color dying by the police. We treat these biases not as beliefs we hold, but as facts about the world, like the presence of oxygen in the air we breathe—except, for some people, they can be deadly.

The first time I realized I had an implicit bias about race was (and still is, let's be real) one of the more embarrassing moments of my life. Six years

---

* "The misattributions are linked to the imputed statuses 'teacher' for women, and 'professor' for men, regardless of the actual positions held or the credentials earned by faculty members and graduate student instructors."[2]

† A generalized, overly simple picture we have of a particular person or group of people, or of a thing.

ago I was at an annual gathering, surrounded by activists, mostly of color—friends whom I've spent years with, whom I love, and who I know care for me. Many were venting about the white population's general disregard for anything related to race or racism. I, along with the fifteen other white people in the room of about a hundred, sat quietly. I assumed the speakers were frustrated with people outside of the room—people I probably didn't even know. The "other" white people. Not me, obviously.

Then, figuring it was worth voicing my own enlightened opinion (because, back to that list item at the end of chapter two—"I can fix it"!), I chimed in, "I'm not racist. My parents worked very hard to make sure I was raised with an understanding of 'we are all created equal.' I don't see color." I sat back, satisfied I'd helped them see I, at least, was in the right, and on their team. That I was a "good" white person, and damn those other racist white people. I gave myself a mental high-five.

One of the participants, with tears pooling in her eyes, stood up and left, clearly disapproving of my response.

I didn't say anything more, embarrassed that there might be something I wasn't seeing, though still convinced I was right. I silently ran through argument over argument for why she shouldn't have been upset.

It took about a year for me to finally conjure enough bravery to ask for a clarification.*

"I thought we weren't supposed to see color," I told one of my black girlfriends who had been in the room a year earlier. "I thought we were supposed to see everyone as equal, regardless of race?"

"Jenna," she generously explained, "race is not the problem. *Racism*† is. We can and *should* acknowledge the ways that we're all different and still be able to access the same, equal, opportunities. I'm proud of the fact that I'm black and *want* others to acknowledge that part of me, too. Blackness doesn't just define my skin color. It's my culture, my heritage—it affects how others see me and how I see myself. By saying you 'don't see color' you're trivializing the way race shapes my life in positive and negative ways.

---

* I should have gone to Google that night. The machine had the answer; instead, I just stewed.

† Racism can refer to the racial prejudice and institutional system of oppression that denies rights and privileges to some groups because of their race. It can also refer to direct violence (verbal, physical, or otherwise) directed at someone due their race. Racism is a white supremacist construct.

You're telling me my bloodline—surviving abduction, enslavement, and centuries of second-class citizenship—is the same as white people's, when your ancestors came here by choice? It's simply not the same, and pretending not to see it ignores all of the joy and complexity that comes with being a black woman trying to build a career and life. My race is a part of me, so if you don't see it, you don't truly see me."

Long pause.

"Ohhhhhhhhh."

She continued, "But, I'm really proud of who I am, and I want you to see my pride reflected in the color of my skin."

Seeing past my friend's skin color, a crucial part of her identity, denies her of her dignity and the path that she's had to walk. Pretending her race doesn't impact the way she moves in the world protected me from having to reconcile how the world responds to my race—white—a designation I only confront on medical forms and school applications. Admitting I see the blackness of her skin would require that I then see the whiteness in mine. Acknowledging that the world responds differently to her because of her race meant admitting that the world responds in a certain way to me because of mine.

One of the more powerful places I can start is by raising my hand to admit that pretending "not to see color" gave me the freedom to ignore my race—and the benefits that I receive because of it.

As you know, it takes years for a true friendship to develop—and it had taken years for this friend to trust that I would listen to and believe her. The timing worked out for us: when she was ready to speak, I was ready to listen.

Conversations like the one we had do not surface casually. Even when they do, it's hard for words to always land exactly as they are meant to, in ways that are always useful. I was blessed to have a friend in my life willing to share her painful truth, one that she (rightfully) felt should have been obvious to me. But we can't just wait until *enough* white people are in close enough proximity to people of color to build these types of relationships, where it's easier for us all to be honest with one another about our confusion—and pain. It is also not our friends' jobs to educate the ignorant, particularly on any subject that is an emotional and mental burden for them. Carri Twigg, a former special advisor to President Clinton and director of public engagement for Vice President Joe Biden, has said, "Even if you have black friends it doesn't mean you don't have racial biases and say things that cause harm. I have loads of white friends and colleagues, but they still make comments, tell jokes, make assumptions that they assume I'm cool with. I'm not. My silence is not my approval, it's me being exhausted from constantly having to explain the pain."

Why should our friends of color carry any additional weight outside of just trying to survive in a white supremacist world that wants to keep them compartmentalized—especially when all of the education you need is in the palm of your hand, with many very willing educators of color producing content constantly? I used the term "generous" before in describing my friend's willingness to catch me—she didn't have to, I 🫠 should have preemptively done the work on myself to learn what I was ignorant about. Learn this lesson from me, so we can all get to work: as my friend so wisely put it, equality shouldn't be dependent on sameness. And we all have racial biases that will take time and effort to shake. That doesn't make us racists, just as benefiting from a system of white supremacy doesn't make us white supremacists. But it's time to get real about the ways our beliefs and behaviors may be perpetuating harmful cultural norms and propping up the companies and laws that keep certain demographics down.

no color, really?

Once I began exploring my biases, the perfectionist in me was relieved to learn that, by "not seeing color," I had been following the rules as they used to be (though this isn't an excuse for having been wrong). In the '80s, according to john powell, the position was "to notice race is bad, so let's not notice it anymore."[3]

The challenge, as powell points out, is that, unless you have some sort of visual impairment, it is impossible to not see characteristics like race, gender (unless it's intentionally ambiguous), or disability. These things "are deeply embedded in our biology, structures, and arrangements."

It is not that the message of equality I internalized as a kid was wrong—every human *should* be treated equally. It's that people *aren't*, and failing to recognize that prevents us from being able to make things as equal as we can. Race, gender conformity, disability, and class, among other factors, dictate how we are received by the world and how we are allowed to operate in it, whether we like it or not. Race is way more complicated than just the color of one's skin.

Author Tom Vanderbilt notes that it's natural for our brains to categorize—and we tend to spend more time thinking about subjects that are easy to sort: "The human brain is a pattern-matching machine. Categories help us manage the torrent of information we receive and sort the world into easier-to-read patterns."[4] Whatever is hard for us to wrap our brains around, we avoid spending our time on. Constructs like race, ethnicity, disability, gender conformity, sexual orientation, and religious affiliation can be so complex, our natural inclination is to quickly oversimplify instead of anticipating and embracing intersectionality. I love john powell's analogy that race is like gravity—"we all have weight so we think we understand it, but in reality, it's so complex that only a handful [of scientists] actually do."[5]

Noticing differences is natural. Experts in the field of antiracism are now arguing that noticing differences is also needed, so we can understand how our broken systems impact the full range of American lives. Saying you don't see racial difference is the same as saying you don't see *any* difference. And I'm pretty confident that, on the bus, you *see* and offer pregnant and elderly people your seat. Just a hunch. You see it all, we all do, and precisely because we've been pretending to ignore "differences" for so long, we're now overwhelmed with the idea of reteaching our brains to notice and reckon with them. Its daunting enough to abort the entire project and go back to the "not seeing color, I treat everyone the same" shtick. Sorry, brain—deal.

We need to pose questions so we can continue to learn, peel back the layers of our biases, and be better. It is key that we hold ourselves in a constant state of inquisition—specifically, by asking, "Why?" Take my three-year-old, Ever, who has a PhD in inquiry. Right now, she's bombarding me with questions about the behaviors of sharks in bathtubs and whether unicorns like pink or purple better. While these are in the realm of imagination, her dedication to understanding the nuanced angles and perspectives of this subject is both impressive and . . . exhausting. While this isn't directly comparable to the work of understanding intersectionality, the constant digging for truths is what we have to raise our hand to do. Just as we might never get to the bottom of the color preference of unicorns, we will never fully understand the source and capacity of biases in our processing and behavior. But we *can* keep asking questions and learning.

As Patricia Devine, a professor of psychology who researches bias at the University of Wisconsin–Madison's Prejudice and Intergroup Relations Lab, puts it: "You *will* see color because you're a human being who has vision.* You *will* hold certain associations with the things you see, because you live in a culture. It's what you *do* about the things you see and the associations that arise for you that matter. That is habit, and you can break a habit."[6]

implicit and explicit bias

Implicit biases are pervasive, and they form early. Researchers have seen infants as young as six months show preferences between different races and genders, as demonstrated by the length of time the babies spent looking at individual photos of a group of diverse, unfamiliar faces.[7] Race-based biases appear to be directly influenced by the amount of contact children have with people from different racial groups;[8] to quote one study, "children growing up in multiracial environments generally learn racial labels and distinctions sooner than those in monoracial settings."[9]

Three decades of research focused on infancy to early childhood suggest that white children show more of a preference for their racial in-group† than their black classmates do.[10] Similar research has shown how "pro-white bias in our society also influences African American children's intraracial attitudes."[11] Black children demonstrated a preference for photos of lighter skin tones instead of those with darker skin tones when hypothetically selecting teachers, neighbors, and playmates.[12]

Each of us grows up watching commercials, noticing the colors of the faces in our classrooms, and listening to our uncle's jokes at holidays, all of which contribute, one message at a time, to the way we think about different people, including ourselves.

I was recently going through the jury duty interview process, when one of the attorneys read off a clause—something like "you must give unequivocal assurance that you can set aside any bias and give a verdict based on the evidence and evidence alone." The case at hand was dripping in stereotypes: it was a third-degree rape case (defined as an assault in which the victim didn't consent verbally, but the intercourse wasn't forced), in which a black man was accused of raping a white woman in a nightclub bathroom stall, after they had both voluntarily done cocaine in the stall.

---

* With the caveat that not all people do.
† Meaning, the group you identify with and consider yourself part of.

I laughed out loud when the judge* later asked the panel of jurors to "surrender all bias." Each one of us who sat on that bench had come in with our racial biases about black men and those who party at clubs. We held gender biases and victim biases (because we often blame women for putting themselves at risk in these sorts of situations). Add in the fact that both the man and woman were voluntarily doing cocaine (we have biases about drug users), and it's biases on parade: to set them aside, where would one actually start?

I told the judge, prosecution, and defense lawyers it was impossible for me (or anyone) not to bring every one of those biases into the courtroom, though I'd try to avoid letting them influence my judgment. To my heart's dismay, they disqualified me as a juror—despite the fact that the awareness of my biases, I'd argue, makes me more able to form fair opinions.†

In our courts of law, when we're selecting jurors to determine the life-long fates of the people involved, we ask jurors to "surrender all bias"? Please. This is why biases can be so dangerous: we don't always know when they slip in to trigger a decision, and in a jury's case, a verdict. Part of our new frontline is catching them, almost like a goalie would a soccer ball, snagging each one before it impacts our actions. As we get more refined at identifying implicit biases, we convert them into explicit biases, because we identify and source them, which is part of stripping them of their power and protecting others in the process.

if Beyoncé said it . . .

> "It's been said that racism is so American that when we protest
> racism, some assume we are protesting America."
> —Beyoncé[14]

As easy as it would be to wrap up our conversation about implicit biases here and just go back to talking about sex, we can't. We have to talk about race.

We tend to avoid having the racism conversation with ourselves and others because it is difficult to contemplate that we might hold racist

---

* According to the Kirwan Institute for the Study of Race and Ethnicity, "Implicit biases are pervasive . . . Everyone possesses them, even people with avowed commitments to impartiality such as judges."[13]

† I don't know what happened to either party but I think of them both, often.

beliefs. But you're here, in this book, to push through to new frontlines, particularly to question those prisms through which we see our world and that hold harmful myth-based perspectives. And we need to run at those with laser attention.

By now, we've had several difficult conversations, and there are more ahead. In the first chapter, we talked about our dependence on silence, and the ways in which it causes harm. In chapter two we talked about our tendency, specifically as privileged women, to seek out opportunities to perform perfection, and how we sometimes use that as a way of opting out of paying attention to the rest of the world. In chapter three we called into question our founding documents and gained new insight on the genocide and other horror woven into America's history, so we never forget and bring those lessons forward into the future. In chapter five, we'll take a closer look at class. But in this chapter, I want to explore bias through the lens of race—the place where I started unpacking my own biases.

The subject of race used to make me nervous: I see the same thing happen in every Listening Circle. I used to be the uncomfortable white person preferring to dodge the topic, because, you know, we elected a black man as president . . . and where did I put my phone again? I wanted out of the conversation, too.

In *White Fragility: Why It's So Hard for White People to Talk About Racism*, Robin DiAngelo, a writer and educator on social and racial justice, says that white people think of racism as a question of "nice" and "mean" people.[15] We assume "racism" looks like isolated individuals performing specific actions: a lone white man burning down a black church or decorating his car with swastika bumper stickers. But it's not. Racism operates on every level of culture, politics, and policy.

I believe white people don't feel comfortable talking about this subject for two reasons: an inherited sense of culpability for what we've done (more on that later), and because diving into this space means running the risk of pointing out an imperfection in our performance—revealing that we know life is more difficult for other people, and we may not have done much to make it any easier. I know this from first-hand experience. When I'm gently reminded that a term I've used is offensive or biased, I can get snappy and defensive, ready with several well-scripted rebuttals.

In the Listening Circles, there was a fear that anyone who was white could be accused of "being racist" if they admitted to racial bias. The topic sent the micromanagers in all of us into a tailspin. One said she knew she wasn't "good enough" to have the conversation and feared she didn't know what to do when it came to the subject of race, so she never engaged with the three black moms in her daughter's dance troupe. She is right that she isn't going to be able to resolve the centuries-old injustices around race—but that is not an excuse to sit solo in the corner. And, as we've discussed in chapter two, she was so afraid at failing that she opted out, sitting complacently the same way people had before her, pretending nothing was wrong.

As Listening Circle participants talked about times in their lives when they believed they had experienced *reverse racism*—discrimination against white people—*white fragility* reared its head. White fragility "is triggered by discomfort and anxiety, it is born of superiority and entitlement" writes DiAngelo. She goes on to explain, "There [is] both knee-jerk defensiveness about any suggestion that being white had meaning and refusal to acknowledge any advantage of being white. Many people claimed white people were now the oppressed group."[16]

One participant used the example that her son, whom she said was in the minority at his school, wasn't allowed, as a white student, to participate in the affinity groups* that facilitated conversations for students of color about discrimination they were facing. She made the argument that he was being excluded (which, let's be clear, he was) because he was white (also true).

However, *reverse racism* is not a thing. Racism is about a system—about a history of laws, ideas, and institutions, about the flow of money and power—that excludes certain groups of people from having equal access and opportunities based on their race. If you are not part of those groups of people intentionally excluded, you can't be the victim of racism—and "reversing" it won't do the trick, either.

I had a hard time wrapping my head around re-reversing myself out of this concept, too. I thought the words *racism* and *discrimination* just described actions that kept a person out of a space because of their race—the specific race was irrelevant. But when I once suggested a mutual friend was being racist by excluding me from a conversation because I was white, my dear friend Angela Rye, an activist and on-air commentator, offered this

---

* *Affinity groups* bring together people with something important in common—race, age, disability, gender, sexual orientation, religion, and the like. Members of this group may share a common identity, but it does not mean they have all had the same universal experience. These groups recognize that their common identity impacts the way they move through the world and is worthy of collective reflection, discussion, and support.

explanation: "By definition she can't be racist because minorities generally lack the institutional capacity to cause economic and systemic harm to the majority [white people]." Remember, *racism* is designed to privilege white people over nonwhite people. Period. *Discrimination* describes patterns of oppression of nonwhite people within that system. So it's inaccurate to apply these terms to white people (no matter what the dictionary technically claims), because *racism* and *discrimination* exist for the sole purpose of protecting the supremacy of white people—as designed by the papal bull in 1452 and every other system since that has elevated white, male, land-owning, Christians.

So when white people aren't included in affinity groups, that is just us not being invited. Same as when men aren't allowed on our girls' nights—we need a place to discuss subjects that only women can relate to without having to explain our perspective or defend our position.

"all of my decisions are driven by guilt"*

As DiAngelo notes, and as the Listening Circles have proven, many white people find even the smallest amount of racial tension intolerable. The mere suggestion that being "white" has meaning often triggers a range of defensive responses.[17] This is likely because we're only now being confronted with words and ideas for concepts we didn't know existed—like the privilege that comes with being white, which is not connected to the fact that we as individuals are uniquely exceptional or deserving, but is instead an attitude that we inherited from our ancestors, and that was written into the Constitution. When our defenses are up, it can trigger emotions such as anger, fear, and guilt, and behaviors such as arguing, silence, and avoidance—and, I might add, a rush toward distraction.

White women can feel particularly fragile when we first see that others' suffering, particularly that of children,† could be directly connected to our silence—which it is, as we discussed in chapter one. The consequences of these complicit behaviors—behaviors from which we might be benefiting—quickly become too much to handle, and we fall back on old habits by looking away; or, if we can't look away, by deflecting.

---

* Said one real-life Listening Circle participant . . . to which I can totally relate.

† It's why I'm only using examples of women & children when I give quick anecdotal case studies; I know what pierces your heart the fastest. 🖐

Listening Circle participants often talked about how hard their parents, grandparents, and they themselves have worked—"My grandfather was a police officer and worked so hard!" or "My mother was a nurse and raised all five of my siblings after my father died when I, the oldest, was just thirteen." Nobody is denying that you have worked your ass off. Life is *hard*. But life is hard*er* when you're also having to survive under discrimination. Both things can be true.

Here is why we deflect, according to Tema Okun, an antiracist and anti-oppression activist, in her article, "From White Racist to White Anti-Racist: The Lifelong Journey": "When we begin to hear about systemic, racist barriers to achievement and success, we begin to wonder if that means we don't deserve and didn't earn what we have, making it even more difficult for us to identify as part of the white group, since doing so erases our precious individuality."[18]

Okun describes the American "pull yourself up by your bootstraps" mentality in which we may notice differences in life outcomes among different racial groups, but wrongly believe those differences are acceptable because everyone started from the same place and had equal access to the same range of opportunities. This reaction is strengthened by the way in which Western culture prizes individuality and meritocracy.* It encourages us to believe our race has nothing to do with our success and that we got to where we are thanks to our individual merits. The question isn't whether you worked hard for what you have; it's whether "working hard" in Beachwood, Ohio, or the Mainline outside Philadelphia, looks the same as it does in Chicago's Englewood neighborhood or Brownsville, New York. It's whether every classroom or doctor, home or job, treats every person with dignity.

In many cities the poverty rate is disproportionately higher for black residents. In Cleveland, for instance, the poverty rate for black residents is 34.2%, compared to 9.3% for white residents. In Milwaukee, 30% of black people in the metro area live in poverty, compared to just 1.2% of white residents.[20] These cities are highly segregated; that segregation didn't happen because of tendency or universal preference, but was the result of racist policies that were enforced. But the fact that we continue to live in clustered communities (like in Chicago, and Detroit,[21] and, and, and . . .) has

---

* A system that fosters and rewards personal effort, ability, and talent through competition to determine social standing.[19]

another consequence: it makes it incredibly difficult for large swaths of the population to have a real understanding of the boundaries and challenges others face, simply because we don't see them. Our assumption as white people is that "the access enjoyed by the controlling group is universal," writes DiAngelo[22]—when it's not.

The truth is, not all obstacles can be overcome with "hard work." For some people, the cards are stacked against them to a degree that no matter how hard they work, they cannot get ahead. Add a disability or a stigmatized gender identity, and forget it. While every one of us has navigated challenges in her life, not all disadvantages look the same. Not being able to get the job you want because there was a lot of competition isn't the same as not being able to get a job because of a prejudiced system. Hearing that someone helped us cheat, unbeknownst to us, to get that "A" we thought we earned on merit can be, um, infuriating.

The realization that we have succeeded where others didn't not because we are special, but because we faced more surmountable obstacles, makes us feel suddenly inferior. It can also make us feel really guilty. Essayist Eula Biss defines *white guilt* as the discomfort a white person feels knowing that regardless of how hard they've worked, their current comfortable life is the result of having had a leg up at the expense of marginalized demographics.[23] It's the guilt and embarrassment 😳 that arises when we learn a system we've been told all our lives is "fair" benefits us, as white people, more than it benefits people of other races or classes.

I recently facilitated a Listening Circle where one of the participants spoke about the diversity of her neighborhood, but was taken aback when her daughter reprimanded her, "Mom, just because there is one Muslim family in the neighborhood does not mean you have diverse friends. You don't even know the dad's name!" The daughter is right. This is a standard deflection attempt—"these behaviors of white people don't apply to me because of my neighbor." Whose name she apparently didn't know.

We try to "fix" *white guilt* by desperately trying to contribute something in a "positive way." As Biss says, "Guilty white people try to save other people who don't want or need to be saved, they make grandiose, empty gestures, they sling blame, they police the speech of other white people, and they dedicate themselves to the fruitless project of their own exoneration. But I'm not sure any of that is worse than what white people do in denial. Especially when that denial depends on a constant erasure of both the past and the present."[24]

I understand why people want to avoid the truth about our society's injustices, why they work very hard to pretend to be asleep. Frankly, there are days I wish I didn't "know" and could just focus on the latest items on sale at whatever clothing company was spamming my inbox that hour. In graduate school I wrestled with the realities of these contradicting desires— wanting to be asleep to the realities of the world but wanting to be awake to do something about them. How was I supposed to sit in class, studying the impact of war on the faces of children with missing bottom lips, limbs, ears, and parents, and then just go pick up my dry cleaning afterward? And I wrestle with a similar dissonance now. How can I want to make the world better while still knowingly inhabiting one that benefits me at the expense of other human beings? I want to keep the privileges of being white—the ease of walking through airport security, being able to talk my way out of a speeding ticket—but not at the expense of others' suffering. Like you, I can't live with that.

That feeling, that sense of *white guilt*, can be useful when the tension we feel inspires us to change our behavior and be more aware. But we have to be careful, because it can also cause its own share of problems. Stay with me.

shove your good intentions

As we've discussed, the idea of bias and the complex ways we have ben- efited from it can make us very defensive. We scramble to put up all the well-intended points on the "why I'm still a good person!" scoreboard. I believe most people are well-intentioned, and this includes the white family who raised me—who taught me to help an old lady cross the street, to not laugh if someone awkwardly falls (though you might giggle a bit inside), and to occasionally "share the damn remote control with your little brother pla-hese." They represented their churches and synagogues at food banks, they bought Girl Scout cookies when they were on diets, and they reposted my pleas for donations to Syria relief efforts on Facebook, even though they couldn't find Syria on a map.

But good intentions can fail. In fact, they fail frequently, often because they don't always result in the type of help needed. My great uncle, for exam- ple, is an incredibly generous man who likes to buy my kids gifts. We once had a conversation where he offered to buy them new pajamas. I thanked him but declined; we already had a good pajama rotation working and, because I'm a minimalist, everyone gets exactly what they need and no more.

You can probably guess where this is going. One day, a large box of kids' pajamas showed up—many more sets than my kids would ever need. Those pajamas were a "nice to have," not a "need to have," and thus became a burden. We live in a small New York City apartment; each of my kids gets one drawer for clothes, and we didn't have anywhere to put them.

Of course I was grateful for my great uncle's generosity. But I kept thinking, *This is what people in need experience all the time, when well-intentioned people show up with their solution to a problem you don't have.* My great uncle's well-intentioned desire to help with our tight budget and be generous only meant extra work for me: having to find a spot in which to store the superfluous pajamas or make sure they landed in the hands of someone who genuinely needed them.

We charitable white people often behave this way. We show up with what we've decided is a source of support that, while well-meaning in nature, actually becomes a burden. This plays out in a wide range of examples, from extreme weather events to the individual on the street corner asking for support. It seems that every natural disaster site is flooded with nonessentials such as stuffed animals or bathing suits, sent by people who think they're helping but are really using the emergency to clean out the bottom of their closets and "just send everything, someone will need it!" In my case, my kids needed new socks and bike helmets, not pajamas.

Too many of us assume "good intentions" should be praised even if the actions associated with them are more about doing what's convenient and optically pleasing for us rather than taking the time to listen to what's truly needed—which, yes, is usually things that can't be ordered on Amazon and delivered in a box: a job, a student loan . . . a house. Carefully listening and parsing someone's real needs is the authentic frontline; that is where we should all work.

The most overt expression of good intentions can even lead us into acting as *white saviors*, a topic on which I'm an expert 🙋.

go white-savior yourself

My incredibly supportive parents were always the first to raise their hands to coach one of my sports teams. My dad would make elaborate "happy b'day" and "welcome home" signs and would constantly tell me how "special" I was. It helped to have parents always telling me "I could do anything," particularly when I was navigating early adolescence bald. Believing

I was special and capable gave me the confidence to walk into a room pretending everything was fine, even though I was a preteen trying to keep a wig attached to my head. But it also meant that I felt entitled to a position of control even in situations where I should have taken a back seat.

We, in our country, often believe our way of life, our notions of democracy and personal freedom, are entirely American and entirely brilliant 🤦. This pretense has long been the basis of our foreign policy.* We know what's best for the world, and we're gonna do it whether or not it's welcome. It also lets us celebrate our do-goodery when we're the ones who established those boundaries in the first place.†

Most of us were raised with this ideology of *American exceptionalism,* which Dartmouth professor Donald Pease says "has been taken to mean that America is either 'distinctive' (meaning merely different), or 'unique' (meaning anomalous), or 'exemplary' (meaning a model for other nations to follow), or 'exempt' from the laws of historical progress (meaning that it is an 'exception' to the laws and rules governing the development of other nations[25])."

In other words, we've been told there is always a correct solution to a problem, and we are the ones that know the best way to fix it. That America is exceptional, and therefore we have a responsibility to intervene in conflicts and export our ideals for the benefit of all. This is a complicated subject that defies "right" and "wrong" because any circumstance is ultimately extraordinarily gray and always subjective. For generations of "well-intended American do-gooders," that has meant traveling to the other side of the world to do charity work, often to the exclusion of addressing problems in own cities and states.

In the late '80s and early '90s, when I was an elementary school kid seeing photos of starving children in Ethiopia and, later, Somalia, I felt a pull on my heartstrings and a strong desire to act. According to my parents, I could do anything. And I believed that I had to do everything I could to fix the problems I saw. Charity brochures arrived in our mailbox with images of white people in fluorescent vests handing out food to black children with distended stomachs. The commercials in between segments of *Full House*

---

* Another legacy of Pope Nicholas V's 1452 bull.

† It's like when Ever creates a game, changes the rules in the middle, and then self-declares herself the winner when she wants to start the next activity. Winners all around—thank goodness she can't write or maybe she'd be documenting her noble accomplishments and how she's graciously bestowed them upon us all. Sound familiar?

panned across a stretch of refugee tents as far as the eye could see—and the white people who had come to help. I drew two significant conclusions from all this: that the "most" critical problems needing attention were those in far off places, like "Africa,"* and that white people could help solve those problems. The message sent—"white people" save desperate nonwhite people—perpetuates a dangerous myth known as *white saviorism,* which I unknowingly embraced.

It wasn't until my senior year in college, while I was studying education, that I was assigned a student-teaching position at a school near my home outside of Miami with kids who faced severe socioeconomic challenges. The opportunity to help students who were experiencing food and housing insecurity and sexual abuse quickly relocated my "savior" goals to the streets of an American city.† But the complexity of working with kids living under the hardships of an unequal society requires a PhD in social work, not thirty credits in elementary education. To quote educational researcher Ken Zeichner, "Although race and race-related issues permeate and influence every social institution, any White teachers currently teaching in schools have had little exposure to a type of education in which the impact of race on classroom practice and student development was systematically examined."[26, 27] I realized that my ability to help lagged far behind my ambition. There was so much structural work to be done in America—in my zip code to be exact—that my bubbled life had shielded me from ever encountering.

Yet I carried my "savior" mentality to a job as an education and media specialist at the United Nations, where the problems became intimidatingly more complex. I stuck with it, still not realizing that the reason I wanted to help had more to do with my childhood desire to "save" others—to be that savior in the brochures—than with realizing how I caused harm just by being. I didn't know I had work to do on myself beyond learning more facts and figures. And why would I have? I'd gotten the grades and enough of the friends and boyfriends to keep me from being a red flag for any teacher or family member. I was checking every box and pretending perfection whenever my blueprint was on display—until that moment when I beheld a sea

---

* And while we're at it, let's stop grouping fifty-four sovereign countries under the umbrella of one name: "Africa." Instead, let's start referencing countries on the continent by their unique names, given how drastically different so many of them are.

† I was living out my superhero daydream as Michelle Pfeiffer, star of *Dangerous Minds*, a movie about a blonde, blue-eyed inner-city teacher.

of pink pussy hats from the stage at the first Women's March and realized that most of those white ladies were showing up at this moment to fix some "political problem" when we hadn't ever been forced to question whether or not we *were* the problem 💁.

I am the one who needs saving—saving from the distorted prism through which I was seeing myself and the world. Within the past few years, as friends, wise teachers, and books have helped to educate me, I have begun to understand Gandhi was right (sigh): "You must be the change you wish to see in the world." If I want to truly make a difference, then the most urgent work I had to do began with the woman looking at me in the mirror.

progressive white women 💁 can be dangerous

While organizing the Listening Circles, I strove to include a wide cross-section of white women. Women from the suburbs of Raleigh, conservative moms from Dallas, Jewish hipsters from Brooklyn—I sliced and diced the demographic carefully. The only constant variable was that people involved identified as both white and women. But I admit, I was generally the most surprised by the responses of the women who considered themselves politically progressive—the women who were a lot like me.

These women were quickest to put into words their heartbreak over the angst and confusion swirling around our country, but they also seemed confident they had done everything they could to make it better. They had protested and donated money; they'd called their elected officials and voted. They were also the most surprised (and a bit offended) at the idea that they might be part of the problem, and the least open to seeing and confronting their own biases. While the more conservative-leaning women would get right into asking clarifying questions about their biases, the women who considered themselves liberals just looked at me blankly, avoiding voicing any confusion they might genuinely have. They were the first to say "Not me!" and the most determined *not* to continue this part of the discussion.

Activists are constantly speaking about this danger: "White progressives cause the most daily damage to people of color," says DiAngelo.[28] Why? Because we are more likely to believe that, because our social media feeds are filled with reposted left-leaning news articles, we don't still have work to do. We go to extreme lengths to prove to the world that we care about social justice. The energy we put toward justice work is sometimes more about showing the world who we are and who we're not than about the work itself; we have to be perfect in our outward performance so we can better accept ourselves when we're alone.

I'm all for marching, obviously, but when a recent anniversary of the Women's March came around, I saw so many people who seemed most energized about posting perfectly filtered selfies with their creative signs on their social accounts. The day after the forty-fifth president's inauguration, those of us on the 2017 Women's March team aimed to get people marching. But in the long run, we failed to convert that energy into a more mature kind of action. We didn't convert white marchers to the next frontline of work: looking within, to challenge oppressive systems—to do the work I describe in this book.

Our complacency about those systems—our belief that we're already doing enough—is the reason these vicious systems continue to exist. That's why it's so critical that you are here, reading these words. You know you have work to do, and you are ready to do it. You know that even more important than marching, voting, calling, and signing petitions is also holding a mirror up to ourselves and asking how both our showing up and not showing up might be causing harm. As Rachel Cargle says, "You have to go and break something down. You can't nice racism." Thank you in advance.

Remember, white supremacy and the biases it is designed on and protects are incredibly complex, and they're unfortunately something within which we've all been raised. There is no going back. Think of it this way: Not so long ago, people didn't know that it was important to put your kid in a car seat, or even to wear a seatbelt. And yet now this safety precaution is the cultural norm, and you're judged harshly—and rightfully so—if you don't do it.

We became aware of the problem. We made changes. Now we are all safer because of it. In the same way, you may not have known that you do, in fact, see color, or think that women are poor leaders, that Democrats are bleeding hearts and Republicans only care about their wallets, or, of course, that the size of a penis can be discerned based on the presence of leather tassels. You may not have recognized the source of discomfort when it comes to race, whether you're experiencing white fragility or white guilt or a toxic mixture of the two. But now you know. So let's take the knowledge of our past we gained in chapter three, and our new awareness of our biases from this chapter, and apply both to the world in which we're all living today.

CHAPTER FIVE

KKK & KALE SMOOTHIES

ach of us is shaped by the structures of our childhood homes, schools, and religious institutions. Our perspectives on ourselves and our roles in the world are influenced by the messages we receive from the people who make up these intimate-to-expansive networks.

In your house growing up, were there strict curfews? Could you take sips of alcohol with family members before turning twenty-one? Were there predetermined chores, or did someone always pick up after you? The norms we inherit and the behaviors we observe dictate how we operate as adults, how we design our lives, and the ways in which others see us and we see them. For example, the fact that one of my exes didn't know how to load a dishwasher because his mother coddled him and his siblings so much was one of the first red flags for me.

A country is no different. America is still navigating the structural decisions made by our ancestors, even those from hundreds of years ago. And those choices impact our lives as white women differently than they do the lives of other white people, or the lives of people of color across the gender spectrum.

Probably in fourth grade, and more recently in the last few chapters, you learned that slavery ended in 1863 with the stroke of a Presidential signature on the Emancipation Proclamation. While the Civil War feels distant, and, at least for me, has always been couched in "another time, in another place," it's not. The Thirteenth Amendment, which made it technically illegal to own humans, is law in the United States today.* But we are still evolving beyond the racist, sexist, and classist biases (among many others) that underpinned our societal and economic infrastructure when these documents were first signed more than 150 years ago. That is part of the work of this book: to see some of the glue used then, and see how it's still holding parts of our systems together today, so we can start to peel it off.

In the South, for example, the dynamics of social inequality are complex—but a few major factors can be traced back to the Civil War era. In losing the war, the South was not only humiliated; it was economically devastated. Plantation owners were forced to give up the key resource that made them rich and powerful: free human labor. From the late 1860s, white supremacists came together in terrorist mobs that specifically targeted African Americans, like the Ku Klux Klan (KKK†). White nationalist perspectives still speak to a shocking number of people today, and their ideology and influence are on the rise.

What might have gotten glossed over in fourth grade is how, in the late 1800s, as continued retaliation for the end of slavery, Southern legislatures passed discriminatory laws, known as Jim Crow Laws.‡ Payback for the Thirteenth Amendment included laws that barred white people and people of color from playing billiards together, drinking from the same water fountain, or sitting on the same park bench.[4] Voter registration fees prevented blacks (and poor whites) from democratically changing these laws, which helped white landowners regain the power they lost when slavery ended.

---

* Though it's worth noting that, in 2016, 46 million people worldwide were still enslaved in the form of "human trafficking, forced labor, bondage from indebtedness, forced or servile marriage or commercial sexual exploitation," with an estimated 18 million of those in India.[1]

† The Ku Klux Klan is an American white supremacist group founded in 1865. They have committed numerous hate crimes against racial and religious minorities, particularly African Americans, through the present day.[2]

‡ Hundreds of Jim Crow laws of varying types were enacted throughout the South after the Civil War. Most were repealed by Supreme Court decisions and legislation such as the Civil Rights Act of 1964 and the Voting Rights Act of 1965.[3]

Four million slaves were freed, but laws and discrimination kept them from dignified opportunities well beyond where they were allowed to sit—they were denied access to quality education, home loans, and healthcare. Our history books frame Jim Crow laws as being in the past; while some have been overturned, their legacy of cruelty still lives on today. Understanding how the scramble to establish discriminatory laws that kept power and currency in future generations of white, landowning families gives context for how we can examine the structure of the world today.

the thirteenth in 2020

You might be surprised to know that the Thirteenth Amendment includes a loophole—one that has preserved a trap of poverty and inequality for millions of Americans to the present day. While declaring "slavery" and "involuntary servitude" unconstitutional, the Thirteenth Amendment also allows these penalties "as a punishment for crime whereof the party shall have been duly convicted." Using this exception, white people have clung to *some* of their lost sense of dominance by imprisoning the formerly enslaved—based on often made-up charges—who were then forced to go back to the fields and work. And guess what? That clause still exists today.

Today, prisoners are legally required to perform cheap labor.* Inmates do menial tasks for pennies like shrink-wrapping computer mice, packaging meat, and constructing handcuffs,[6] none of which are likely to increase postincarceration job prospects.† The incarcerated are paid anywhere from $0.23 to $1.15 per hour for this work[8] (as of this writing, federal minimum wage is $7.25 per hour). Companies like Walmart, Starbucks, Victoria's Secret, and Microsoft purchase inmate-made products from the prison operators—whether the state, the federal government, or a private corporation—at a deeply discounted rate. The prison owners make a hefty margin; the prisoners, on the other hand, can't afford a chocolate bar[9] at the commissary on an hour's worth of work. My good friend Chris Wilson, a one-time prisoner serving a life sentence, writes in his book *The Masterplan*

---

* Federal Prison Industries, a US-owned government corporation, earned $500 million in sales in 2016 by brokering deals between the federal government, the prisons, and the corporations.[5]

† Inmates have been used as firefighters, most recently in dangerous California fires, but aren't allowed to join fire units upon release.[7]

about how he had to ration his salary to borrow books from the library[10] so he could complete his GED and still afford to make phone calls[11] home.* Technically, the inmates doing this work are being paid for their labor. But the whole situation looks an awful lot like slave labor to me: the prisoners do the work, whether they want to or not, while the prisons reap the financial rewards, leaving the prisoners with no skills or money upon release.

If I haven't been clear already, let me drive this point home here: The Thirteenth Amendment permits the use of prisoners as modern-day slave labor.†

Whenever a system is profitable, there's an incentive to keep that system going—in this case, to arrest people for minor "crimes" like jaywalking[12] or being unable to pay a parking ticket—thus increasing the supply of free labor. The people profiting from prisoner labor today, like those former slave owners looking to regain power during Jim Crow, look for reasons to imprison people long term (rather than, say, rehabilitating them or the system, or addressing crime through community programs). And who are the people they target? People of color, often those who have been stuck in this cycle for generations.

Jim Crow hasn't gone anywhere.‡ We may decry vocal advocates of white supremacy, but we ignore people, institutions, and companies that more obliquely preserve racial and class disparity. We avoid affiliating ourselves with people who wear their racism on their sleeve but leave the rich

---

* Inmates are charged money to send emails, anywhere from $0.35 to a couple of dollars per email. Checking a book out of the library could also cost them money. All of this is deducted from a monthly allowance that comprises their scant wages and whatever funds people outside the prison contribute to it.

† This takes a number of different forms, but it includes any involuntary, labor-intensive, physically violating work that may or may not be compensated. This includes forced labor (work or services that people are forced to do under threat of some form of punishment if they don't cooperate), debt bondage (when people are forced to work after not being able to repay borrowed money, often because the terms of the loan are unrealistic; sometimes these debts travel from one generation to another); human trafficking (transporting, recruiting, and harboring people for the purpose of exploitation, sometimes in the form of sex, and using coercion as the main means for control), and child slavery (when children are forced to be soldiers, sex partners, or marital partners).

‡ Suggested reading: *The New Jim Crow: Mass Incarceration in the Age of Colorblindness* by Michelle Alexander.

folk who profit from racist institutions, like the for-profit prison system,* to themselves, maybe on their yachts in the Mediterranean. We spend more money on our prisons than our schools.† Yup, I'm pissed 😠. The United States incarcerates more people‡ than any other country in the world.[15] We spend about $80 billion a year on maintaining our prison systems, between $14,000 and $70,000 per inmate, depending on whether it's a state or private prison and what health and education services are provided.§ A lot of people are continuing to make a bunch of money[17] on the shoulders of primarily black and brown people whose ancestors were never given an equal chance to prosper, even post Emancipation Proclamation.

As I noted, keeping these prisons full means policing low-income communities for low-level crimes because they typically don't have the resources to hire mouthy private lawyers, post bail,¶ or pay fines. Their parents are also less likely to golf with the attorney general, who needs their contribution to get reelected. Very different from the kids I knew in high school and undergrad, who were enjoying and dealing the same substances young people of color end up in jail for all the time.

Black people are incarcerated most often—at five times the rate of white people.[19] Are any of your explicit biases starting to roll through? Here is one of mine: "Well, black men commit more crimes than white men, so of course they're jailed more often." Black men do commit more crimes than white men—though only 2% of black men commit violent crimes at all.[20]

---

* Prison operators Core Civic and its closest competitor, GEO Group, collectively manage over half of the private-corrections contracts in the United States, with combined revenues of $3.5 billion in 2015. Core Civic maintains more than 80,000 beds in over 70 facilities, including prisons, immigrant detention, and reentry centers. GEO Group operates a similar number of facilities.[13]

† The United States Department of Education found that correctional spending rose 324% from 1976 to 2012, going from $17 billion to $71 billion. Educational spending, on the other hand, grew by only 107%.[14]

‡ In 2019, the number of people in prison is 2.3 million (along with 840,000 others on parole, and 3.6 million people on probation).

§ The exact annual spend depends on whether the prison is state operated or private and what health and education services are provided. According to the Vera Institute of Justice, "the total cost per inmate averaged $33,274 and ranged from a low of $14,780 in Alabama to a high of $69,355 in New York."[16]

¶ One in four women jailed cannot afford bail.[18]

We're primed to accept this disparity as natural by the messages we receive from the world around us. Crimes with black perpetrators, for example, often get more airtime on the news.[21] And these messages have other consequences. Black men are killed by law enforcement at *twenty-one times* the rate of white men because of implicit biases baked into both the laws and the psyches of police officers—even black ones,[22] because even people of color can have biases against their own affinity groups.

Even African American police officers might adopt prejudices held within the institutions of law enforcement that contribute to the over-representation of inmates of color in our jails. Dennis Parker, director of the American Civil Liberties Union's Racial Justice Program, says, "When you're talking about police interactions, in many ways the color blue becomes more important than black and white." He continued, "People identify more with their role as a police officer and all of the cultural things that entails more than their race."[23] Taken together, these factors begin to explain why black people represent roughly 40% of the prison population.*

I wrestle with large numbers—light-years, tons (literally, I can't grasp the weight of a ton without measuring it in the approximate weight of cars in my head)—and the idea that a black man is twenty-one times more likely to be killed by law enforcement than a white man . . . that's millions of human beings who don't get to build businesses or make art or console their babies in the middle of a nightmare.

Even though we've made some progress in addressing police violence, taking measures like installing body cameras[26]—though that step by itself has limited effectiveness—officers' implicit biases remain. This is also true of judges and juries in the sentencing process. Black men, for instance, receive sentences that are nearly 20% longer than those white men receive for the *same* crime.[27] In other words, two identical crimes are not always considered in identical ways, depending on how the intersection of race, class, and other variables impact the defendant's life.

I'm the oldest of twenty-five grandchildren. One evening, at my grand-mother's beach house, a big group of my cousins and I were laughing and

---

* According to the Federal Bureau of Prisons, 37.8% of those 2.3 million incarcerated people are black,[24] though black people make up just 13% of the United States population. The incarceration of Hispanic people isn't as well studied, but an estimated 32.3% of incarcerated people are Hispanic, though Hispanic people make up just 18% of the United States population.[25]

sharing their stories of getting in trouble when the conversation morphed into secrets about their run-ins with the law (ones their parents preferred they keep secret from the larger family because even though we're very close, we're still performing for each other). One of my cousins admitted to being arrested for having a fake ID at a beach bar, then trying to run from the police in the rain (she is painfully unathletic, so she didn't get very far before she was arrested); another had brought alcohol to a sweet-sixteen party, and one of the girls who attended ended up having to have her stomach pumped. In both cases, their parents—my aunts and uncles—were instantly by their children's sides, paying fees to pull them from their cages; ultimately, the charges were thrown out. As I was poking fun at them for their immature choices, I couldn't help but think of all of those who do the same but suffer much harsher consequences.

I also remembered my own missteps, during my freshman year at the University of Miami. There was one time I (stupidly) agreed to pick up someone else's drugs from a dealer; I wanted the extra cash to buy a Prada handbag to be more like the older sorority girls I was hanging out with, and was desperate to fit in with. Had I been caught and prosecuted to the fullest extent of the law, I wouldn't have been able to get that teaching job at a public elementary school—a position I was very good at and loved. I wouldn't have gone to grad school, I wouldn't have worked at the United Nations . . . and I probably wouldn't be writing this book. But even if I had been caught and arrested, I likely would have received a lighter sentence, if I were even convicted at all—unlike a black or brown person caught doing the same thing.

Though I'm not condoning it, people do occasionally break the law—sometimes on purpose, sometimes by mistake, sometimes out of desperation or for survival, and sometimes just to feel like they're part of the crowd (we're all longing to be part of something bigger than ourselves). The difference is that the police aren't circling white kids' neighborhoods as often, or with the same biases and protocols. It's the same reason I'm not likely to get pulled over no matter where I'm driving, as long as I'm following the speed limit, whereas black drivers cannot say the same.

In Listening Circles, when the #BlackLivesMatter movement came up, some participants asked, "Don't all lives matter? Why just black lives?" The #BlackLivesMatter movement isn't saying that nonblack lives don't matter. It's saying that black lives are the ones most in danger from the current policing system. Yes, police officers* and firefighters†—and now, elementary school teachers‡—have lost their lives in the line of duty. But those numbers don't come close to the number of the black men who lose their lives—*senselessly*—at the hands of police officers every year. There's also a big difference between being the victim of a tragic accident or losing your life protecting the community, and being the target of strategic, systemic, historically state-sponsored attacks on an entire race.§ And situations like the latter happen much too frequently, specifically to black people, for us to think in good conscience they are part of the same conversation as keeping police officers safe.

The way I connect these statistics to the urgent need for the #BlackLivesMatter movement and the conversation around it is to tell the women in the Listening Circles a story I once heard about ten men sharing the burden of carrying a very large log. On one end of the log were nine of the men, and on the other end was one man.

"Who needs the most help carrying the log?" I ask the Listening Circle. "The nine carrying one end or the one on the other end?" The answer seems quite obvious: the single man who is burdened with 50% of the weight of the log. If we support the people carrying the heaviest burden, everybody can move forward fairer and faster. This is why we have to prioritize the population of humans that are most at risk—in this case, people of color. Our society's treatment of black men—their subjugation, imprisonment, and murder—is a remnant of those same Jim Crow laws from after the Civil War designed to help white landowners maintain their power and wealth.

The resulting rate of incarceration touches all in the community, especially children. One in 10 black children has a parent who is incarcerated, in comparison to 1 in 60 white children.[31] One in 13 black folks lose their

---

* 132 police officers died in the line of duty in 2019; 47 specifically by gunfire.[28]

† In 2018, 82 firefighters died from activities related to an emergency or from activities at a fire scene.[29]

‡ No source has compiled a clear total of teachers and school administrators killed in school shootings, but the number is significantly more than zero; there were 25 school shootings in 2019 alone, killing or injuring 51 people.[30]

§ In just one instance: Trayvon Martin was an unarmed seventeen-year-old black boy who was shot and killed walking home from a convenience store in 2012. The shooter, George Zimmerman, was a member of the neighborhood watch team and pursued Martin against the orders of the 911 dispatcher. Zimmerman was acquitted of murder, a verdict that sparked outrage across America.

right to vote because of a past conviction.[32] Formerly incarcerated people face high rates of unemployment;* as a result, women of color and immigrant women are most often the main or even only breadwinners in these homes,† in addition to being the main caregivers. And precisely because they also earn less than white men and women, they have the highest chance of living in poverty, too, not to mention having to work harder for the same dollar.[35]

Many who walk the poverty line are an unexpected $500‡ expense away from a financial crisis, such as choosing between diapers and food. That's a phone being dropped in the toilet by a toddler, an old washing machine that floods because a stray penny jammed the drain, or an unexpected eye infection that keeps a child home from school and you out of work until it clears—not to mention the cost of the antibiotic. For the wealthy, $500 is a massage and the gift shop upsell of the face-oil made from unicorn tears. For many in the middle class, this can be a few months' setback—but not the difference between having a place to live or not.

they get you where you live

Of course, I am oversimplifying here in order to prove my point. No single factor can determine all of the cascading effects that I just listed, and there are many exceptions to the trend. Sometimes we can look at specific data to compare specific experiences—the rate of incarceration for white men versus men of color, for example—and then there is the reality of life experiences, in which many moments and decisions and facts intertwine or intersect to make people and communities into who and what they are.

Intersectionality is the key concept here: the idea that a combination of societal factors—including gender, race, class, sexual preference, religious

---

* 35% for the men, 44% for the women (compared to 23% for white women and just 18% for white men in the same situation).[33]

† 87% of family members who cover costs of prison phone calls, visiting costs, ancillary expenses related to sending new socks or help with those library books, are women, 91% of whom are black, African American, Latinx, or Hispanic.[34]

‡ As explained to me by Michelle Rhone-Collins, CEO of LIFT, an organization that provides, among many other services, "direct-cash-transfers to women who need money for first/last month rent, an academic certificate to qualify for a job or childcare during the summer months can make or break ends meeting for so many families throughout the country" (private interview with Michelle Rhone-Collins).

orientation, disability status—work together to dictate the steepness and height of each individual's mountain to stability.

That's why people of color who are also part of the transgender community,* for example, are even more at risk of experiencing systemic bias. In just the stories I know about, one woman had her welfare benefits terminated when she showed up at a mandatory "workfare" but was marked as absent; the supervisor had listed her as not "work ready" because she was wearing women's clothing. Another trans woman was denied access to a domestic abuse shelter, and still another was forced into a men's homeless shelter where she knew she'd be targeted with violence.

Transgender people are also significantly more likely to live in poverty than non-transgender people. Roughly 30% of all transgender people have experienced homelessness and poverty at some point in their lives, largely because there aren't enough social and legal protections put in place for them. Employers have been known to terminate transgender employees on the basis of their gender, causing the unemployment rate for trans people to be three times the rate of the general population. Unable to hold traditional jobs due to discrimination, many trans women turn to sex work to earn an income—a line of work that not only puts them in harm's way, but that also makes them significantly more likely to be arrested. Due to the conjoined oppressions of racism, sexism, and transphobia, trans women of color are particularly susceptible to being murdered as well as incarcerated.[36]

You may be thinking, *How does the oppression of transgender people have anything to do with race?* Despite what our patriarchal society would like you to believe, it has *everything* to do with race. Gender, just like race, is systematically constructed. The way that we understand the concept is neither universal nor natural; it, too, was a European concept. In fact, prior to European colonization, many indigenous societies did not organize themselves in terms of "men" and "women." On the contrary, many cultures had multiple descriptors for people's gender identities. Nor did those communities adhere to binary labor roles: the person who was best with a bow and arrow (👀 . . . if I do say so myself)† hunted, the person best at wrangling children did so, and the person best at designing and constructing shelter did that work. This started changing when Western cultures arbitrarily

---

* "Transgender" describes those who are assigned a gender at birth that doesn't fit their true gender identity.

† Women are better shots then men—the idea they didn't hunt is a patriarchal myth.[37]

confined women to the home. It was not until indigenous people were over-taken and influenced by the West that two binary genders and traditional gender roles—with women at home and men in power—were cemented. This colonial gender enforcement was carried out across Africa, indigenous America, and most parts of the world.[38]

Based on the conversations in the Listening Circles, it seems most people have arrived at the conclusion that homosexuality is not a choice; it has been normalized through the characters we see on TV and in film, and same-sex marriage is no longer a hot button political topic. But many older women in the Listening Circles really struggled with the subject of transgender rights. One participant said, "I'm all for people loving whoever they want, but it's a choice for [transgender] people to go through the con-version. Why can't they just love who they want but skip the surgeries?"

There's an exercise I often use with women who do still talk about sex-uality as being a "choice": the next time you're having sex, try to fantasize about the gender you're not attracted to—see how far you get. My hunch is that there are probably a few people and scenarios that really are not of interest to you in the "really don't turn you on" department. Imagine if society insisted you conform and like something sexually that you really just aren't attracted to.

It's a harder thought exercise, but now try imagining being assigned a version of a gender that currently feels very opposite to you in this moment. Insisting someone who is transgender just be okay with remaining the gen-der they were assigned at birth can exert an extreme mental and physi-cal toll. People who are transgender describe feelings of "intense longing," "shame," and "distress," and have more instances of suicide, anxiety, and depression.[39] Trans people are often denied life-saving services because of the way gender markers on identification documents are used to divide people up in sex-segregated facilities.

In one Listening Circle we discussed a fear that taxpayers are suddenly going to have to pay for an astounding number of human beings to transition. Recent research, however, suggests that it's cost effective for transition to be covered because there would be an associated decrease in mental health challenges. So while the United States spends $2.6 billion on printing (for-get about the number of trees they kill) a year,[40] the country nonetheless balks at being asked to consider spending around $198 million for transition surgeries and additional programming for 9,000 gender reassignments—ignoring how much in mental health expenses this would save.[41]

Each of us is dealt a proverbial set of cards—based on where we are born in the world, the norms that prop up that societal structure, the ways we present (race, gender, disability), what we've been able to accrue (resources, power, influence), and certain lifestyles we choose (religious community, wellness habits). Taken together, these determine the societal obstacles we face as we move through our lives. The cost-benefit analysis of validating and supporting the transgender community, particularly when it comes to better mental health outcomes, clearly indicates that we Americans should see this movement as an urgent civil rights frontier.

who gets a roof?

A lot of the Listening Circles I attend are in comfortable homes in the suburbs, with lovely lawns and seasonally appropriate wreaths on the door. Homeownership has been a primary source of affluence in this country for generations, but the most frequent owners have been white people. Not indigenous people, from whom the land was stolen. And not the formerly enslaved, who were not given the forty acres and a mule after the Civil War in 1865, as General Sherman had promised.[42] If they had, it would have changed a lot of things for a lot of people.

Our cul-de-sacs are segregated because of systems that were designed—wait for it—hundreds of years ago. They are a direct by-product of segregating populations based on race and class—rules that were imported via ships like *Niña*, *Pinta*, and *Santa Maria*. And this is still the case in the suburbs, as well as in our urban centers, in which we largely continue to live separately along racial lines.[43]

To get specific, 48.4% of black Chicagoans are confined to the city's South Side, known as the "Black Belt."[44] This is the result of longstanding discrimination that was formalized after the National Housing Act of 1934, a practice known as *redlining*—the systematic denial of services like loans and other forms of credit to nonwhite residents or aspiring residents of particular neighborhoods. "Lines like these, drawn in cities across the country to separate 'hazardous' and 'declining' from 'desirable' and 'best,' codified patterns of racial segregation and disparities in access to credit"[45] and prosperity, and are responsible for so much of the economic disparity in the country today, according to financial analysts.

The most significant period of redlining was conducted by the Federal Housing Administration in the 1930s, established by the National Housing act in an effort to fix the housing shortage created by the Great Depression. Researchers estimate the maps drawn by planners, developers, and landlords back then account for 15 to 30% of the segregation we see in major cities today.[46]

As we learned in the previous chapters, I and people like me—white people—have opportunities that increase our prosperity and protect our power. The legal and business decisions my ancestors made—the ones that marginalized and continue to marginalize people of color and other minority groups—also put me, and others like me, in a better position to have access to, receive, and capitalize on opportunities when those opportunities are presented. Sometimes we even take credit for that privilege, believing it was earned. As Jim Hightower once said about President George W. Bush, and one could say just as easily about me, "[He] was born on third base [but] he thought he had hit a triple."[47]

There have been a number of key forks in the road throughout history that have determined who is able to hoard power and wealth, who is permitted by the powerful to enter their spaces, and who is not. There are many ways to deny rights: not allowing everyone to vote, have bank accounts, or, as we'll see, gain fair access to housing and education support, which the federal government provided to white veterans returning from war while doing nothing for those blocked from owning a home by redlining or unable to go to college because their families needed another income.

One of the more significant government subsidies for returning military after World War II was the GI Bill, a program that helped veterans gain access to low-interest mortgages to buy a home, low-interest loans to start a business, and tuition for college or vocational programs. This led to the rise of the middle class—the foundation this country is built on—but this middle class was carefully selected to be white. The Veterans Association openly encouraged African American veterans to apply for vocational training instead of college and had no resources for challenging housing segregation. Take the story of Eugene Burnett, a returning serviceman who tried to buy a house in Levittown, New York, in 1949: he was denied because the brand-new community, which was specifically planned and built for returning servicemen and their families, was closed to black applicants.[48]

My grandparents were able to secure a home equity loan when my grandfather came home from World War II—not directly sponsored by the GI Bill, but unhindered by racial bias. They bought a lovely three-bedroom, one-and-a-half bath in the Philadelphia suburbs with a front porch that had lots of potted geraniums. That neighborhood was zoned to a school with small classroom sizes,* often a prerequisite for attracting teachers committed to locking in decades-long careers in education. My father was processed through this school system; he received good-enough grades and played soccer well enough to secure admission to a state school.

The home ownership subsidies in the GI Bill led to similar stories for millions of working class, mostly white families in the '60s, '70s, and early '80s.† With their degrees in hand, those veterans' kids were able to secure steady enough jobs (my dad was an architect, my mom a labor and delivery nurse) to access their own housing loans, which put their children (👶) right back into those small classrooms . . . and the cycle continued for the next generation. My parents leveraged their major asset, our home, to qualify for the student loan that I used to get an undergraduate degree at the University of Miami, which helped me get financial aid for my graduate school at Columbia University's Teachers College, which led me to where I am today, writing this sentence . . . and so on.

However, the opportunities afforded by the GI Bill were not equally accessible to every veteran. The funds for these programs were federal, but local officials controlled how they were distributed, and soldiers of color rarely benefitted. Those who served alongside my grandfather returned home to discrimination; they struggled to secure home loans after World War II. GI Bill benefits were declined for approximately 1.2 million black veterans,[52] and they also had to contend with redlining, among other obstacles stemming from structural bias. In the 1950s, when the American middle class was forming, people of color were systematically left out, often forced to take on low-paying, unskilled jobs like janitors or dishwashers.[53]

---

* I can speak from experience, when your classroom size breaches twenty, you spend more of your time wrestling behavior management than creative lesson planning, and after years of the battle, some tap out.

† By the time the original GI Bill ended in July 1956, 7.8 million of 16 million World War II veterans had participated in its subsidized education and training programs.[49] Also, 4.3 million took advantage of the GI Bill's $3.3 billion in home loans. Ira Katznelson explains in his book, *When Affirmative Action Was White: An Untold History of Racial Inequality in Twentieth-Century America*,[50] there was "no greater instrument for widening an already huge racial gap in postwar America than the GI Bill" (p. 122). As a consequence, the extreme wealth gap between black and white Americans continues to thrive. According to the Census Bureau, the median income for white households in 2017 was $68,145; for black households, it was $40,258.[51]

Fast-forward to the present day, and black home ownership is now at an all-time low (41%, compared to 73.2% for white people[54]), while communities of color continue to be discriminated against in lending. They are given more expensive loans[55]—ones that require less money down, but end up costing more in interest—or they're denied loans altogether.* The outcome, decades later, of these discriminatory policies, is that people of color nationwide are disadvantaged when it comes to homeownership—traditionally, one of the major means of ensuring financial stability and upward mobility for American families.† The knock-on effect is staggering. Today, in America, white families hold 90% of the national assets;[60] black families hold just 2.6%. For Hispanic families, the share of national prosperity is even lower: 2.3%.‡

wellness smoothie

Which brings us to another basic human right, wellness—who we allow to pursue it, and why. Living in New York City, one encounters a wide spectrum of skin colors and life experiences. I live in Chelsea, a neighborhood in the borough of Manhattan that is slightly central and a bit west on the narrow island. It's a particularly busy part of town: below the Lincoln Tunnel; incorporating Twenty-third Street, one of the city's few four-lane crosstown roads; and ten blocks south of Penn Station and Madison Square Garden. Because of the connectedness of this neighborhood, I am constantly surrounded by the diversity of my fellow New Yorkers.

My office overlooks one of the few helicopter pads transporting ultra-high-net-wealth individuals to and from their homes in Connecticut or the Hamptons, and when I walk Ever to school, I pass neighbors who are

---

* White families are offered loans at 2.7 times the rate black families are.[56] And, the more black and Latinx people there are in a given neighborhood, the more loan requests will be denied—even after controlling for things like income. Black and Hispanic people are 21 and 15% more likely, respectively, to be denied a loan than white people.[57] Race isn't the only factor affecting loans, of course. Gay couples are 73% more likely to be denied a home loan compared to a heterosexual couple, with women (regardless of relationship status) 33% more likely to be denied a loan than men.[58]

† Over half of black homeowning households were "cost-burdened"—meaning they spend over 30% of their income on monthly costs, compared to just 36% of white households, which puts them at risk of losing their homes to foreclosure.[59]

‡ And as of 2018, there are 84,681,000 white households, 16,997,000 black households, and 17,318,000 Hispanic households.[61]

homeless, including a double-leg amputee in his wheelchair often asking for money outside our local grocery store. And while I don't have to wrestle with the justification of having my own helicopter when so many people are in poverty, I still struggle with the extreme disparity I see as I walk to my favorite vegan café or Bikram yoga class. White supremacy has always afforded me resources and freedom, even granting me the option to consult exotic spiritual healers in remote towns around the world or make an occasional on-a-whim visit to the tarot card reader on my block.

Well-being is a very broad concept. Today, the "wellness" buzzword gets a lot of play, suggesting that "health" is not just the absence of disease but, according to the National Wellness Institute, "an active process through which people become aware of, and make choices toward, a more successful existence."[62] Today's wellness industry (juice bars, day spas, silent retreats) is booming; it's a $52.5 billion market in the US, a $4.2 trillion. market globally, and one of the biggest growth sectors in the economy, increasing by 12.8% between 2017 and 2019.[63] That's a lot.

In the end, though, "wellness" often reflects the concerns of, and is isolated to, a small, specific niche: white, wealthy, female. It provides us another benchmark for measuring whether we are good enough, and another set of products and services to buy—crystals, meditation classes, grow-our-own-mushroom kits for the kitchen counter—in order to fix ourselves. It's another example of how we'll do anything, literally, to make the high-expectations, anxiety-inducing array of choices easier. The wellness craze tells you to drink that $9.00 kale smoothie with a few drops of CBD oil, or to hurry and take that $35 spin class set to girl-empowerment beats 🍵. And yes, I usually do feel better after all of that: healthier, calmer, more energetic. But it's never a sweeping solution for maintaining my mental and spiritual health, and even if it were, it's something that requires the luxury of time and extra cash that not everyone has.

Consider yogi, organizer, and activist Kerri Kelly's interpretation of the current wellness movement, which is that well-being is very much shaped by systems of access and privilege: "There is a deep paradox in this world that sells the concept of wholeness by making consumers feel incomplete. Any version of wellness that only benefits some and excludes others is not just limiting, it's harmful. A wellbeing gap that leaves some people behind hurts all of us—it destabilizes our economy, it causes stress which makes us sick, it fuels higher rates of crime and violence, it holds back our children, and it separates us from each other. The most unhealthy systems (the ones that are really making us sick) are white supremacy, patriarchy, and capital-ism. Let's start there."[64]

It was impossible for me to un-see the suffering in our news feeds and, in my case, twenty-five yards from my front door. Given that suffer-ing, the constant barrage of messaging to my demographic to eat organic, hold people and your thoughts in the "light"—and don't forget about that juice cleanse—all started to feel like a myth, not to mention another source of pressure. Kerri explains further: "Our culture tells us 'we're not good enough.' They say 'buy this and you will be happy,' 'do this and you will feel beautiful,' 'eat this and you will be healthy,' 'read this and you will be enlight-ened.'" It is a storyline sponsored by a system that profits from our sickness. Yes, I endorse supporting local farmers and avoid high-fructose corn syrup. But those decisions don't exempt me from cultivating an authentic moral compass and acting on it—it wouldn't mean much if being part of the trend, or checking another box, is the driving motivation.

I can't lean on wellness as a "spiritual bypass," as John Wellwood, a Buddhist teacher and psychotherapist, calls it, to forgive myself for my complacency. Faith and spirituality can present possibilities for growth, but we can't get there passively by praying our way out: no amount of hours on a pew, on our knees in conversation with any god, or repenting in a journal will break these systems.

Those self-reflective exercises are crucial, and I mean core, to the work I'm asking us to do in this book—to challenge the inner voices of self-doubt, to make greater peace with our individual imperfections. But we also can't forget the way that some practices designed as philosophies to help us have become a commercial industry that capitalizes on our self-doubt, all while setting the prices for "whole living" out of reach of many people.

healthcare: you get what you pay for

No juice regimen is a cure-all, but the fact remains that when people have money and resources, they live longer. Did you know the wealthiest 1% of American women live 10.1 years longer than the poorest?[65] Ten years—that is a lot of family holidays and watching your daughter's kids when she has to work. That's a lot of opportunities to offer wisdom to younger generations and to be the glue that so many women are in their families and commu-nities. This inequity exists in large part because the healthcare systems we've inherited—which, while well intentioned, have been fraught with inequality since their founding—also determine who gets to be well, and who doesn't.

Before the Civil Rights Act of 1964, black people could only be treated by black physicians—a law put in place during Jim Crow[66]—which were hard to come by, due to a range of factors including education and segregation.[67] Many black patients suffered indignities like having to be treated in cold hospital basements and stuffy attics. Others died because of unequal, basic healthcare: for example, lack of access to standard vaccines, surgeries, and antibiotics.

Unequal healthcare access persists today: 59% of Americans are a $1,000 medical bill away from financial crisis[68] with or without health insurance; medical bills are the number one cause of personal bankruptcies.[69] That's a slip on an icy sidewalk, an unresolved ear infection, or the flu. Because the poor don't have the same quality of education, their job prospects tend to be limited, leaving them with lower-paying careers. Even those lucky minimum-wage workers with decent health insurance can't afford chronic illnesses that lead to increasing health complications, leaving individuals and families in debt, often in perpetuity.

We also see major inequities in health outcomes. Diseases like type II diabetes, in particular, disproportionately strike underresourced and low-income Americans of color, partly owing to a lack of access to healthy food (which I'll return to). Which brings me to organ donation.

Being involved in the organ donation world for many years made me intimately familiar with the number of people waiting for a lifesaving organ transplant.* And in the deepest, most judgmental recesses of my mind, regardless of how much I wrestle with my biases, I do get judgey when I see someone—anyone, regardless of what they look like—walk out of a Starbucks with a venti mocha frappe blah-blah with caramel oozing all over the whipped cream. *I'm gonna have to find you a damn kidney now, too,* I can't help but think. And it's not like kidneys are easy to come by. To keep someone who needs one alive without a transplant can require a grueling regimen of dialysis—three to five hours of in-clinic treatment, two to five times a week.[71] That's a time commitment equivalent to a part-time job, and unsurprisingly only 19% of people who start dialysis ever return to the workforce.[72]

---

* As of this writing, 113,310 people.[70]

The costs involved are staggering. American taxpayers spend $110 billion each year on kidney disease—more than what we spend on NASA,* the National Institutes of Health,† and the Department of Homeland Security‡ *combined*. But that amount of money, which could on its own lift whole communities in this country out of poverty, is only a temporary Band-Aid for people simply waiting for a life-saving kidney transplant.

Now, I've wrestled with my waistline, and consequently, my self-confidence, just like some of you may. I have no willpower when it comes to Krispy Kreme donuts. Another guilty pleasure, being a Philly girl, is a properly loaded steak sandwich with nuclear-colored Cheese Whiz (so. damn. good). But the kind of poor health decisions I'm talking about, and their long-term health consequences, often have less to do with giving in to cravings and more to do with access—not just to healthcare, but to healthy food.

In 2018, 5.6 million[76] Americans are "food insecure"—meaning that members of the family may have gone without food entirely because of how hard it is to find and afford. And even among those who can afford to eat, more than 23 million[77] of our fellow Americans live in places called *food deserts*: areas, occupied predominantly by low-income people, that have half as many supermarkets as those occupied by high-income people.[78] Race is a factor here, too: just 8% of black people living in low-income communities have a supermarket within a mile of their homes, compared to 31% of white people. A recent study found that Native American families are 400% more likely than other US households to report not having enough to eat, "largely as a result of living in remote,§ isolated locations where food supplies and jobs are scarce."[80] There we go again, another incomprehensible figure.

In many cases, the grocery stores in the middle of these food deserts that low-income people *can* access tend to stock more long-lasting, cheap

---

* NASA's 2020 budget is $22.6 billion[73]—and they *explore and send people to space* (my dream job).

† The National Institutes of Health had a 2019 budget of $39.2 billion,[74] and are responsible for all federally administrated medical research, including curing cancer, AIDS, and research related to infant mortality rates.

‡ The Department of Homeland Security has requested a budget of about $51.7 billion for 2020—and they're meant to keep us safe from terrorism![75]

§ Many in the indigenous community live on designated plots of land known as reservations in isolated parts of the country, making it difficult for the private sector to invest in local businesses, including supermarkets and other societally dependent conveniences.[79]

ingredients on the shelves[81] and fewer fresh fruits and vegetables. When the only place where you can get affordable food is a convenience store, and you're stuck with either mac 'n' cheese, Doritos, or Twizzlers, quality of health decreases, medical bills go up, debt gets larger, and it is impossible to get off the hamster wheel of financial, emotional, and healthcare despair. The younger generations of hungry mouths also suffer from the same lack of availability of healthy food and are supremely targeted by Big Food Companies, which lure their curious eyes with flashy packaging and gregarious characters, convincing them a cereal or a candy bar leads to adventure and fun.

How well you do, and how well you *are*, depends in large part on access afforded to you based on your position on the socioeconomic ladder. And as we've seen, thanks to systemic historical inequities like limited access to home ownership, this position can have a lot to do with race, gender, and ethnicity. We are in an opportunity crisis where people can't get food, jobs, and healthcare not because they don't want them and wouldn't work for them, but because their opportunities have been restricted.

in search of numb

These examples show just how dependent we are on health, financial, and food distribution systems to provide stability and support—and how having them in place can free us up to focus on other pursuits to further enrich our lives and the world around us. For those of us used to having those systems working for us, when things in our lives are not so easy, we tend to get angry and point fingers at others. The assumption that it's someone else's job to make our lives easier is often on display when people try to outmaneuver one another for a parking spot outside of Home Depot or when drivers exhibit a lot of road rage. Sitting passenger-side, I can't help but question: *Why do they think they deserve a closer parking spot than someone else?* Or *Why should they have the right of first refusal to every road in the country?* This "it's all mine first" mentality—this sense of entitlement to material goods, knowledge, and power—is insidious and pervasive.

This attitude of entitlement spews a "you owe me" belief that the "system" should be automatically at your service, and it is a white supremacist construct. I don't think we're wrong to ask people to participate in the systems if they benefit from it—the problem is the white, wealthier people have far greater ability to influence the evolution of those systems to ensure they benefit the most from them. Granted, all of those systems, from public education to Social Security, are designed by humans, so all are naturally imperfect; others are also outdated or redundant. It's still on us to solve them—it always has been.

This dynamic extends to how we raise our children. We hope they grow up to be accountable and independent, but one thing is for certain: they learn their attitudes about entitlement from us. Teachers aren't supposed to raise your children; they're trained to make students understand primary colors and the speed of light and hopefully help them fall in love with learning. Your doctors can't and shouldn't be fully responsible for your health—study your own disease and make better health choices, when possible. Nor is your partner or spouse fully responsible for your happiness—go find that yourself. This idea that we are owed something from other people or some government agency is a false promise from your ancestors. The high levels of angst and resentment that can result when that promise goes unfulfilled, bringing a wave of disappointment and resentment, can morph into corrosive and sometimes deadly stress.

Robert Sapolsky, a neuroscientist at Stanford University, explains how stress is supposed to exist in a few-minute window of "fight or flight." It's not supposed to be days, months, or years of worrying about surviving, or whether you're good enough. "Stress is not the enemy here," he says. "It's the constant, never-ending 'toxic stress'—that's the stress that'll kill you."[82] That type of chronic, toxic stress is exactly what the blueprint and its associated sense of entitlement create. One result of all this stress is an increased dependence on external forces to solve our problems. All too often, that enduring stress is focused on our lacking a sense of self-worth, instead of a constructive effort toward leaving a meaningful legacy.

The Listening Circle participants talked about stress a lot, in ways that echoed Sapolsky's observations. Not only were there the logistical stresses of juggling job, family, and changing the cat litter, but there were also the heaviest burdens, the outstanding questions related to self-worth: *Do I have a meaningful place in my community? Am I valued? Does my marriage look acceptable? (And IS it acceptable?) What am I going to do with the rest of my life?* These are all important questions, ones that every human revisits many times throughout their life, yet the pressure to answer them perfectly carries stress in more exaggerated ways today.

We've become highly dependent on other people to measure our worth, and one industry that is particularly benefiting from this cancer of self-hate is Big Pharma.* They've convinced us there is a pill for every problem, and to my maternal grandmother, it was just the message she needed to hear. Nanny, as we called her, was a highly intelligent woman who would have—and arguably should have—chased a career, but she didn't receive much encouragement to do so in the broken home in which she grew up. While raising her four children, and especially afterward, she became bored; the river of self-hating thoughts that boredom generated drove her to constantly seek out an array of doctors that would give her prescriptions for Xanax or Vicodin—anything to numb the disappointment she felt with herself and her life.

Pharmaceutical companies offered my grandmother an escape from her inner turmoil. Rather than use that turmoil as a spur to achieve self-actualization, she chose pills, which offered her a way to detach—an option she embraced. This started a cycle of opioid abuse that ultimately escorted her to her grave.

As our self-disappointment and additional economic pressures snow-ball in an increasingly impersonal society,† living a healthy life becomes even harder. *Deaths of despair* is a phrase first coined by Princeton University researchers to describe the way people in twenty-first-century America so often kill themselves by suicide or more slowly using alcohol or drugs.[86] We sometimes feel lost and spinning in circles because we did what we were told—we checked all of the boxes—yet we still don't feel we're living up to expectations. When we feel helpless in such unbelievably stressed-out times—grounded not only in fear of where the next meal is coming from but also the lack of self-worth—mind-numbing activities of all types, including the ones that we are addicted to, can spare us the pain 🕹. Video games.‡ Blooper videos on Instagram. Or, in my grandmother's case, a pill§ that promised her relief from herself.

---

* "The worldwide market for pharmaceuticals is projected to grow from around $1 trillion in 2015 to $1.3 trillion by 2020."[83] Almost half, $485 billion, comes from the US.[84]

† One out of every five meals in America are eaten alone or in the car.[85]

‡ 42% of Americans play at least three hours of video games a week.[87]

§ We are 4.3% of the world's population, yet we take 75% of the world's oxycodone.[88] I'm pretty sure we don't have 75% of the world's pain.

so, you wanna have a baby

My grandmother is one example of an American woman who was not given enough room by a patriarchal system to blossom into the leader that she could have been. While things have certainly improved for women in America since her time, stories like hers are not rare, even today. In an impassioned speech during the 2016 presidential election, Michelle Obama reminded the world, "The measure of a society is how it treats its women and girls."[89] And, unfortunately, as mentioned earlier, our country is the tenth most dangerous country in the world for women. America's lack of access to healthcare, high rates of women (primarily women of color) dying of pregnancy-related issues, and, the one in four women[90] who are domestically abused by the men in their lives places us just above Yemen, a country whose citizens contend with famine and drone strikes.

Another component of the larger problem is the gender pay gap: White women make $0.77 for every dollar a white man makes, black women just $0.61.* Over the course of a career, that averages out to nearly $840,000 of lost wages for white women; cumulatively that's almost $513 billion[92] a year. Twenty percent of children† in this country are living in poverty. Imagine how much difference an extra $840,000 would make when it comes to paying for school fees and medical bills and mortgages and . . . I don't know, even that $9.00 kale smoothie.

I often heard women in the Listening Circles talk about how they felt trapped because men created and controlled their family's resources. In those households that were also dependent on the woman's income, the women I talked to were sometimes deeply passionate about their careers, and other times felt depleted by their jobs, because of long hours or arduous commutes. I heard from women who admitted to staying in marriages because they weren't sure they could get a job that paid enough to survive if they left. Tears always followed those statements. This was always difficult to hear because of the implicit trade-off: food and healthcare security coming at the expense of staying in an unsafe or unhealthy relationship.

---

* As of the 2017 Census, Asian American women made 85 cents, Native American women made 58 cents, and Latinas made 53 cents.[91]

† For black children, the poverty rate is around 32%; for Asian and Pacific Islander children, the poverty rate is around 11%; and for Hispanic and Latinx children, the poverty rate is around 26%.[93]

As we discussed in chapter two, many of the women in the Listening Circles admitted they'd abandoned what could have been stable, fulfilling careers because they also wanted to stay home with their children in the early years and didn't see a way to juggle both. Indeed, motherhood—the biggest transition laid out on our blueprint—seemed to make or break a lot of the women in the Listening Circles. I, too, struggle; it's *hard*, particularly dealing with the guilt (whichever choice you make), especially when you have the power position in a company or enough money to throw at the logistics of life.

The systemic factors behind this struggle hark back to another era—one where women were expected to remain in the home. The United States is the only country in the "developed world" that does not require employers to provide paid leave for new mothers.[94] In 1993, Bill Clinton signed the Family and Medical Leave Act, which gave eligible workers twelve weeks of unpaid leave to care for a new child. The key words there are "eligible" and "unpaid." According to federal law, "eligible"[95] pregnant women—those who worked approximately 156 days the previous year for companies with fifty or more employees—are allowed to leave work to care for themselves and their newborns without losing their jobs. But their companies are not required to pay them.

By contrast, mothers in Finland get three years of paid leave; the Norwegians get almost two years, Canadians one year, and in the United Kingdom, women get eight months. We push our mothers back to work after twelve weeks, and that's *if* they are "eligible" for leave. Many women are forced to return sooner. I've watched friends hoard vacation days years before maternity leave, even before they're thinking about having children, and ask me bashfully if I think they should try asking their boss for three months' pay.*

For Listening Circle participants, the transition to motherhood was one of the biggest universal forks along their professional roads, as it changed their earning power† and, in the process, the power they had within their homes. One woman, a lawyer who had worked for a prestigious firm, had sacrificed tremendously over the years trying to make partner, and she was on track to get there. When it came time for her to take maternity leave,

---

* Maternity leave is categorized under disability in this country—and determining if that is the right spot for a temporary condition is complicated; see endnotes for more.[96]

† In other words, the ability to make significant financial contributions to household expenses, particularly in comparison to one's spouse.

she was offered the New York State minimum of unpaid leave: up to eight weeks.[97] But because she had many complications after the birth, including trouble breastfeeding and postpartum depression, she took additional disability. When she returned to work, she did not make partner, and unlike past years, her salary increase was smaller. Discouraged, she resigned a year after that salary review and has been out of the workforce since. She and her family rely on her husband's income, which, she admits, though they are in what feels like an "equal relationship, changes the dynamics related to money and power at home."

These circumstances are exacerbated for women of color. Compared to white women, they are more likely to work jobs without any maternity leave allowance. It is one of many tragic racial disparities in US healthcare: black women in the United States are three to four times as likely to die[98] from pregnancy-related causes as their white counterparts*—a maternal death rate higher than in Mexico, where nearly half of the population lives in poverty.[100] Black women are also more likely to suffer complications during pregnancy, birth, and postpartum that keep them out of the workforce. And black babies are twice as likely to die as white babies†—a racial disparity that is wider now than in 1850‡—thirteen years before emancipation— when people wouldn't name their children for the first year because so many didn't make it to that milestone. That's how many American women of color are burying their babies today, compared to white women—more than when their ancestors were enslaved. Even a United States woman of color with an "advanced degree is more likely to lose her baby than a white woman with less than an eighth-grade education."[103]

The US is ranked thirty-second out of the thirty-five wealthiest nations for infant mortality, an inherited problem and a tragic legacy for the next generation. I've concluded that the root cause is not enough women in senior positions of real power, like elected office,§ to advocate for improved maternity conditions across the board.

---

* In New York City, it's twelve times more likely.[99]

† There are 11.3 deaths per 1,000 black babies compared to 4.9 per 1,000 white babies.[101]

‡ Back then, the numbers were 340 deaths per 1,000 black babies compared to 217 per 1,000 white babies.[102]

§ The United States is 77th out of 192 ranked countries for gender parity in elected offices.[104] This is despite the "blue wave" of 2018 that put 112 new female electeds in Congress.[105]

Those women fortunate enough to be raising healthy children shoulder the burden of supporting them at approximately $13,000 per year.* The early years of life require hands-on care, either by daycare or a parent, typically a woman who has stepped out of the workforce. If one parent does leave their job, it means household income drops exactly when baby-related expenses increase[107]—perfect timing. The needs of families, in particular the women doing the crucial work of maintaining the human race, are disregarded in law and by employers, which do the bare minimum to support new parents.

Mothers are idealized in our society, yet employment policies treat them as a weight to be shrugged off—particularly mothers of color. This is yet another example of the structural oppression that white people often choose not to see.

our questions matter

I recognize that I've given you a lot to digest in this chapter. In the Listening Circles, after talking about some of these issues and the complicated cycles of oppression that can be close to impossible to break, participants sit back and say, "I get it." But "getting it" often means feeling equal parts clear about this complex state of our world, and sometimes—for me, at least—demoralized. We were told in school, in movies, on Martin Luther King Jr. Day, that this stuff was already solved—that everyone's rights were protected, that we all had an equal shot. Nope, no we don't.

Again, we are not at fault for the injustices that took place generations ago. But we are responsible for whether or not the injustices happening today continue. And now that we "get it," we have to recognize that we are on the frontlines in ways we may never have assumed. We have to raise our hands to ask more questions. In your OBGYN's office, ask about the horrible statistics I just raised. When you're filling out an application for a home loan at the bank, ask the officer about the denial rates of nonwhite, non-heterosexual couples. Notice the relative ease in which you might navigate the judicial system to expunge your kid's record for the time he got caught buying alcohol underage or when she was carrying her fake ID. Asking those questions and being alert to disparities isn't the sum total

---

* According to the US Department of Agriculture, it costs about $233,000 to raise a typical (keyword) American child from birth to eighteen years—*not* including college.[106]

of this work, but it is a crucial beginning (more on that later). It makes a difference when customers start using their voices to air their concerns; Walmart started to bring in more environmentally friendly options for this very reason. Be a more vigilant critic and move these issues into your orbit, because they are already there.

If this sounds like work, well, it is. Sorry(/not sorry)—you crossed the point of no return when you opened this book. And while you can challenge me on statistics or the precise connections I've made between current struggles dictated by race, gender, and class, what you can't deny is that these struggles are happening—and that you play a role in either perpetuating suffering or actively working to end it. Consider this chapter your reintroduction to society. And then turn the page to see how you can bring your fathers, brothers, husbands, and sons along, too.

CHAPTER SIX

WHAT ABOUT THE BOYS?

When I saw my dad cry for the first time, it was in my brand-new freshman dorm room, after the beds were lofted and the power strips were sorted. He walked out, chin quivering and eyes pooling with tears. The grief and fear I sensed from him didn't match my nervous excitement at the next ginormous chapter of my life. More than that, his sudden weakness suggested a dire malfunction in the system my world was built on. A number of alarms triggered internally: How could my dad—a tough, straight-edged man who had it all together, all the time—be crying?

In retrospect, my dad's behavior was appropriate—it was my assumption that he never needed to emote that was wrong. I had a specific vision of how my father, and how most men in my life, were meant to act all the time, even at heart-wrenching crossroads. That range of fitting reactions didn't include tears. I now understand this vision of mine as an explicit bias—and my rules about how he was allowed to behave represent an inherited blueprint. Like so much else we're unpacking in this book, both originated many generations earlier.

That same blueprint tells boys and men to be tough and doesn't take much issue with fighting. I understood the implicit and explicit guidelines my father was expected to adhere to as well as he did. That's why, that day in my dorm, I was so shocked by his tears, and likely why he walked out so

quickly when they began to fall. Maybe he was embarrassed to be so overcome with sadness, once he'd built the shelving and had nothing left to do
but leave his eldest child behind.

In chapter two, we discussed the perfection myth that tells us how we
should, and shouldn't, act in order to stay in the societally designed lane for
what an acceptable life looks like. It should not be a surprise that our fathers
and brothers and sons have their own rules they are expected to follow, or
that these rules are harming them—and us. They're rules that preserve the
system that keeps us and them trapped in an inauthentic performance.
We've explored several of the never-ending list of racial, gender, and class
(among other) biases we've inherited. Now let's explore another that tends
to hit particularly close to home because it defines how our households,
families, and one-on-one relationships might function: our assumptions
about the men in our lives.*

what about the boys?

Let's take a look at the list of behaviors men perform for their gender blueprint: remain in or gain control, always be brave, be intimidatingly strong,
and be in or at least on their way to a position of power. This blueprint is
known as *toxic masculinity*, because, well, these traits have been *dangerous* for what feels like forever. In a *Psychology Today* op-ed, John Leimer
describes it this way: "Toxic masculinity tells us it's a dog-eat-dog world,
every man for himself and we must have wealth, status, and power by any
means necessary, even if it means hurting or using others."[1] I've seen this
firsthand, as a child, watching boys kick another boy on the playground
while he was already down, or, as an adult, watching one man belittle
another in debate in a conference room.[†]

Another *Psychology Today* writer discusses how these "weaknesses masquerading as strengths" applied to him. Among his admissions were that

---

* Although this chapter is primarily focused on white, American men, I will note occasionally
  how my hypothesis might impact men of color; in this particular context, black and brown
  men are subjected to even more rigid definitions of masculinity than white men due to
  historical emasculation.

† I'm writing from my own heterosexual experience, and this section has an especially
  narrow focus, even within a fairly heterocentric chapter. I fully acknowledge the limited
  scope, and the examples that follow will likely play out a bit differently for other types of
  relationships.

he treated "women as objects for my sexual gratification and confirmation of status/manhood," and that he "began to abuse others weaker than me and bully those smaller than me to get some sense of power back."[2] I know those men. I dated them. I almost married them. And I've recently realized that sometimes I even perform my own versions of toxic masculinity, acting like those men when I'm trying to exert dominance or confidence in a professional setting. Consequently, I'm freaking out about how I'm raising my son, Atlas Oz. He's two years old, can barely form a sentence, yet I've already overheard the men who play key roles in his life telling him to "Stop crying," "Be tough," and worse, "Be a man." I have a front-row seat to a young boy being stripped of his emotional framework, and it's an inhumane show with aftershocks that hurt us all.

As parenting experts now tell us, summarizes the *New York Times*: "Toxic masculinity lies in constant wait . . . Bad porn and frat parties and the sleepwalking of white, male privilege."[3] I look at my baby boy, and as much as I fight for another path for him, I know exactly what's ahead.

arrested development

I was always curious what issues the Listening Circle participants were wrestling with and what concerns they had about our world. They'd list the divisiveness in our country and, often in a more hushed tone, they'd talk about the fears they had for their (white) sons. (Yes, only their sons, even as more and more data shows that one out of three of their daughters will experience sexual assault,* and nearly all are likely to encounter the wage gap.) There is good reason for worry: experts believe our culture's conception of masculinity stunts the emotional growth of men during adolescence. "American society socializes boys and men to conform to a definition of masculinity that emphasizes toughness, stoicism, acquisitiveness, and self-reliance. And that, they say, leads to aggressive, emotionally stunted males who harm not just themselves but their children, partners, and entire communities," says Rebecca Clay.[5] Chest bumps, fist pumps, and the awkward high-five-hug are the only acceptable signs of affection.

---

* According to the Centers for Disease Control and Prevention, one in three women have experienced sexual violence involving physical contact at some point in their lives. Nearly one in five women and one in thirty-eight men have experienced completed or attempted rape in their lifetimes.[4]

This set of social expectations can put white men into what some people call the *Man Box*. Mark Greene, a senior editor for the Good Man Project and author of *The Little #MeToo Book for Men,* describes the Man Box this way: "This 'real man,' as defined by the Man Box, represents what is supposedly normal and acceptable within the performance of American male masculinity. He dominates our movies and television. He defines what we expect from our political leaders. He is the archetypal sports star. He is our symbol for what is admirable and honorable in American men. And if he happens to get aggressive, belligerent, and violent sometimes, well, that's just the price of real masculinity."[6] The only thing he didn't add is *Arrr!* (in a rugged pirate voice).

Patriarchal societies tend to trap *everyone's* social and emotional development in adolescence. When we—of all genders—are between the ages of thirteen and seventeen, we focus on societal conventions as we begin forming deeper relationships beyond our family circle, including peers and friends, romantic partners, groups, and authority figures. Within each of these relationships, we either conform to or rebel against what society expects of us. Everyone who does not belong to "our" group, who is not "one of us," is an "outsider" in this "us vs. them," patriarchal, white supremacist structure we live in—and that includes the parts of our own identities that don't conform to expectations. All of us are raised to suppress emotions and desires that aren't reflective of the blueprint society has given us. For boys, that blueprint is outlined in our textbooks and superhero movies, and in their relationships with the older men and authority figures in their lives.

Men can become all-too-easily disappointed in themselves if they're not meeting unattainable, culturally defined standards. Sound familiar? 💡. Psychologist Avi Klein, who works mostly with affluent white men, says their common issues include "shame at having feelings at all, shame because they believe that there is something fundamentally wrong with them, shame that they are not men, they are just boys."[7] An inability to live up to standards of masculinity can lead to deeply entrenched feelings of shame by the time boys reach adulthood.

Generally, men are trained to believe if they are being steady and unemotional, they are doing it right. And like all humans, they can get defensive when told they might be doing something wrong. Men are not taught to listen and feel, but to stay focused on building, strengthening, and fixing.

Imagine asking a white male in your life to receive gender-sensitive psychological treatment, diversity training, or to read about how white privilege is giving them control and power they have not earned but use. I'm not sure I know many men who would voluntarily sign up for that type of work—the type of work that this book requires—which asks them to question their power and sense of entitlement. It's the same type of work we are doing with ourselves in this book, and it's hard. Who wants to come face-to-face with that type of ignorance? It would mean we'd have to come to terms with using it as a blanket to protect our privilege.

Consequently, as we studied in chapter one, white men—and white women, who have a bunch of white men in our lives—end up doing what humans do best: those cognitive acrobatics, maybe a handstand and an arabesque to excuse their conventionally "male" shortcomings like passive behavior (ignoring the work they don't feel like doing) or complacency. A lot of Listening Circle participants said versions of the following, when discussing their husbands' behaviors: "He really does mean well." As we know, though, good intentions are not a meaningful contribution in themselves unless backed by action. White men's assumption that they know the route, the way to behave, the way to perform, and the way to do—compounded with their sense of righteous indignation—empowers them to step in places where they likely shouldn't be.

the man in the mirror

White men's righteous faith in their own abilities has been handed down from generation to generation through the same patriarchal structures that have protected their power. "White men were always and have remained the rational norm, the intellectual ideal, their dissatisfactions easily understood as being grounded in reason, not in the unstable emotional muck of femininity," writes author Rebecca Traister in *Good and Mad*.[8] I learned at an early age—likely the first time I went to bat for a more efficient recycling system in our family beach home—that regardless of how reasonable (and bipartisan, I might add) my perspectives were, if any of the men in the house wasn't into the idea, it typically didn't come to fruition, and my pleas would be written off as "girlie emotional tree-hugger blah-blah-ness."

My uncles were some of my earliest and toughest sparring partners. As I grew older and committed to pushing back against some of their arguments—as most of their rebuttals were simply lobbed into the center of the discussion for their own entertainment—my tongue became quicker, more articulate, and better sourced. In equal measure, their dismissals became that much louder, more aggressive, and more phlegmy in the sound effects, and more whole body in their fidgets . . . until, typically, they collectively erupted in condescending bully laughter. That laughter, I've grown to understand, is the distress call of toxic masculinity being challenged.

Still, men are quietly beginning to question this hyper-dominant mandate, too, particularly as a result of the #MeToo movement to end sexual violence and support survivors. It is a complicated process, as Traister points out: "We're trying to change the rules with the understanding that those rules have been set up, and our norms have been set up, in ways that are fundamentally unjust to vast swaths of people. So we want to change them. But changing them mid-game means that some people who have been playing by them are going to be called out at having violated rules they were born thinking they could play by."[9]

Many men responded so defensively to the traction of the #MeToo movement. The reason for this, according to Avi Klein, is that "they feel like there's a sense in which whatever they're engaged in, that they're not really in charge of that in some way. It's confusing to them."[10] The way a prominent, widely validated, woman-initiated, woman-led movement makes men feel—a bit insecure, which is human nature—is the exact opposite of how the blueprint tells them they're supposed to feel.

As the long-suppressed realities of modern American life have begun to rattle their Man Boxes, the men who are unwilling or unable to do the type of self-exploration necessary to destroy internal toxic patterns tend to focus on reinforcing the walls that protect both the patriarchy and their own insecurities. Many women play a role in this, too. This was reflected in many of the comments about the #MeToo movement I heard at Listening Circles. I remember one woman lamenting the situation for our "poor husbands now, too! They can't compliment a woman's skirt at work now or take a woman out to a professional lunch!" The men in question seem to be, surprisingly, bewildered by having to learn a new set of standards.

The reason some men have been so adamant about protecting the blueprint, suggests Michael Kimmel, author of *Angry White Men*, "is their sense of entitlement [has been] thwarted by larger economic and political shifts, their ambitions choked, their masculinity lost."[11] Kimmel, a scholar-researcher studying the patterns among men who convert to extremism around the world, spoke with more than 100 male ideological extremists. Writes Kimmel, "Almost all violent extremists share one thing: their gender." He has observed a connection between radical, violent ideology and a desire to feel like a real man. He says of his subjects' determination to be perceived as manly and important: "As they saw it, they'd lost some words that had real meaning to them: honor, integrity, dignity. They'd lost their autonomy, their sense of themselves as 'somebody.' And, as I heard them say it, they'd lost their sense of themselves as men. Real men. Men who built this country and who, in their eyes, are this country."[12] As a result, Kimmel explains that young men who become involved in extremist groups are the ones "who feel small, who resent being made to feel small and who are looking to get big by destroying others."[13] Evidence increasingly suggests that the side effects of this righteous masculinity is resulting in our sons taking their own and others' lives.

Let's take a serious pause here to acknowledge what humiliation and shame can morph into when an individual does not have the language or emotional capacity to articulate and address this pain and confusion. Sometimes the result is shamed silence; sometimes it's rage. Either way, it sometimes comes at the expense of everyone on the planet and should be allowed no excuse. We're often quick to blame bullying, isolation, or even the Man Box for why men are committing senseless crimes, but the fact is, regardless of structural and moral failures, they know what they are doing is wrong.

the stigma of "help"

Author Brené Brown, who researches courage, vulnerability, and empathy, found that shame is the single biggest contributing factor to the toxicity of traditional masculinity.[14] Shame is an admission of vulnerability, and since vulnerability is considered a weakness and not a strength, men can have a hard time taking the essential, even life-saving step of exploring it.

As Klein observes, "In their efforts to manage the feeling of shame, some men numb themselves. Others sink under it and slip into depression or chronic underachievement. And others take the pain that they feel and project it back out into the world with violent words and deeds."[15]

When I see a man get angry and act out that anger on others, I can't help but wonder about the source of that rage—if it's because he feels broken, or irrelevant, or is struggling with self-worth. It's behavior I'm familiar with, because I do the same thing. When I'm disappointed in myself, sometimes I end up taking it out on other people in my life, too. We all know that's not productive for anyone. We know that we shouldn't do it. That's the same for men as it is for women.

But while we're all capable of raging at others when overcompensating for self-disappointment or experiencing poorly channeled pain, men—particularly those of a privileged race and socioeconomic class—have more freedom to act out that rage. They also receive more protection and support when they choose to do so.

This can be a hard truth for white women to confront because we tend to make excuses for their poor behavior—possibly without knowing what exactly we are enabling—all while reinforcing the same blueprint that informs their behavior. In other words, we support the perpetuation of harmful habits. This repression-based performance was a constant concern echoed in the Listening Circle: women were confused about how to "get to" their sons. One woman said she doesn't "believe her husband has had a deep conversation with anyone in years." This might be why one study found that 62%[16] of Americans are really, really lonely in our marriages and 43%[17] of us say our relationships aren't meaningful. There is stigma for men in being vulnerable, particularly in front of other men, and in taking the further step of seeking professional support. We've raised our men over generations to feel weak if they suffer from symptoms like anxiety, depression, or common phobias, or if they are unable to control their anger on their own—as if they can't control their "manliness."

The consequences of this cultural support for violent behavior in men can be severe. Statistically, very few men seek any form of mental support, informal or formal, and many report feeling like they have nobody to talk to.* Men of color, particularly black men, face additional barriers, including racial stereotyping,[19] discrimination,[20] and stigma[21] against the process of seeking mental health support.

Even when men do go to therapy, they can have a hard time expressing their emotions.† Dr. Angela Beard, a clinical psychologist for the Department of Veterans Affairs in Dallas, told *Harper's Bazaar*, "Men have never been taught how to identify what their emotional needs are, their thoughts and feelings, or to express how someone can help fulfill them."[23] Although

---

* According to a 2015 study, 2.5 million men in the United Kingdom admitted to having no close friends and feeling incredibly lonely.[18]

† Also known as normative male alexithymia, which "refers to the fact that traditional masculine role socialization channels many men into ways of being such that their masculine identity conflicts with many emotions they feel and what they feel they are 'allowed' to express."[22]

white boys and men, as a group, hold privilege and power based on gender and race, many of them are also miserable and lonely. This pervasive loneliness and alienation from their own emotional needs has also increased the likelihood of men taking their lives—especially if they're white. Nearly 84% of people who kill themselves are white, and about 77% are men.[24] It makes it even more difficult to confront privilege, and then work to dismantle it, when those who hold it have little self-worth.

One study showed that "of 1,500 young men aged 18–30 . . . nearly 1 in 5 thought about suicide *in the past two weeks.* Which young men were more likely to think about suicide? Those who believed in a version of manhood associated with being tough, not talking about their problems, and bottling up their emotions were *twice* as likely to have considered suicide."[25] These statistics are tough to hear, I know. But keep going.

how we factor in

Because men are trapped in this highly refined definition of manhood that keeps power within that one demographic, women end up paying the price. Some men see women as a source of emotional labor far beyond a loving, egalitarian partnership, which adds another thing to our already jammed to-do lists. Modern romance still encourages women to "save" her man from himself. Boy, do I have stories of men showing up at my feet, looking for me to save them in every underdeveloped lane of their life. We are the unicorns that have to toggle between bestie, lover, stylist, (unqualified) therapist, career coach, constant cheerleader, air traffic control for all of life's logistics, and oh, did I mention we have to remind them how great they are? Been there, done that. In a 2016 tweet, writer Erin Rodgers coined the phrase "emotional gold digger"[26] for men like this, highlighting the burden of unpaid emotional labor that, as a side effect of the patriarchy, many men assume is their due.

Some women in Listening Circles suggested that serving as an emotional crutch for their men gives them purpose; it makes them feel needed. I appreciate that; I like being there for people I love, too. But when I pushed against the women in the group, asking about who was showing up for *them,* the answer wasn't their men. They'd list other women in their lives—friends, daughters, their administrative assistant—adding just another item to those women's to-do lists. As Traister says, "This has been the ask of women, and most especially, of non-white women, since the beginning of time: Take the diminution and injustice and don't get mad about it; if you get mad, you will get punished for it, and then you will be expected to fix it, to make sure everyone is comfortable again."[27] Why don't we expect more for ourselves—and from the men in our lives? How many men do you know who show up for long, engaged conversations about emotions?

Forget being there for *us*—how many are there for each other? I don't mean hanging at the bar watching football, I mean there as in, let's have a deep conversation about the state of my life. In the decade I've been with my husband Jeremy, I have heard about maybe three or four of those types of conversations, and he has loads of male friends. I, on the other hand, and the other close women in my life, have had countless vulnerable conversations in the same amount of time.

And yes, women are raised to build nurturing relationships with each other (thank goodness). It's why it is very easy to fill a room for a Listening Circle. RSVPs fly in when the invitations go out. We're given the freedom to be vulnerable. This isn't because vulnerability is a welcome and universally honored human condition, but because it was a way for the patriarchy to further separate the sexes and convince themselves of—and perpetuate— the myth that women are too emotional (read: unstable) to be in power. Men—and other women—have been saying this throughout history, and you hear it even still today.* Women just let ourselves feel and express our emotions. Although we're trained to think men don't need to do this, too, it's a requirement for mentally stable *Homo sapiens*.

muted

Just as women can become silent and avoidant when we're afraid of not being perceived as perfect, men can fall prey to the same conditions when they can't quickly and easily solve a problem. Their coping method can take the form of *selective hearing*: blocking out anything that induces feelings of inadequacy. Or, lacking a quick fix or the ability to relate to a common life experience—the toddler's temper tantrum or the logistics of juggling

---

* One gentleman told the *New York Times* in the summer of 2019, when Joan Perry, a Republican woman in North Carolina's Third District, ran for Congress: "I want someone who's going to support the president, I think she would do that. But the only thing is, that, as you know . . . women can sometimes be a little emotional, and I'd really have to think about that."[28]

multiple social events in a given weekend—they bow out completely, so they don't have to admit not knowing or risk remaining in uncomfortable territory. This dismissal is a survival defense of the most primitive kind: it's the classic *fight, flight, or freeze* response. It's hard for the brain to process unfamiliar emotions, particularly all the feels they're told not to process to begin with, and a common knee-jerk response is to just *opt out*.

Voluntary opting out can happen both emotionally and physically. Cognitively, men put up a filter—silencing, or "shushing," the speaker. The clearing of a throat, a hand gesture, walking out of the room, telling people to *just get over it!* are all cards men can play to "shush" a voice. "Oh yeah," said one Listening Circle participant, "my husband always tells me 'Not now' to pretty much every subject I want to or need to talk about." For some men, reflecting before acting conflicts with the strong, tough, "everything is under control" attitude; their true feelings, your feelings, and anyone's pain aren't serious variables; they never have been. Feelings are a female thing and are unwelcome when they make their way into men's spaces.

Our partners have to go out of their way to silence us, though, because we often occupy the same places. We are in their cars en route to the Friday night football game, next to them in their cubicles, and beside them as we brush our teeth at two-sink Carrera vanities. But while we technically *can* speak up to the men in our lives, Listening Circles agreed that when we do, we can be actively ignored. Their men, as they described in a half-joking, half-desperate tone, were "really good at tuning in and tuning out when it's convenient." And if sports are on, they said, then forget it.*

My husband, Jeremy, reminds me that I have pretty high expectations for the speed with which light bulbs should be changed or suitcases put away, chores that have been his domain for years. So is that why he "doesn't hear me" when I answer his questions for the fourth time? Because he's been tuning out the other "nags" related to school uniforms or his yearly physical? Does it mean that one day I might scream—to save a life, stop an imminent injury, protect someone from harm—and he will instinctively tune that out, too, because that morning I was bugging him to take out the trash? Some research—most of it conducted by men—says his brain can't multitask the same way mine can.[30] But the freedom men have to opt out

---

* The average 25- to 34-year-old man spends almost seventeen hours a week watching sports.[29] Couldn't they put some of those seventeen hours to work in home maintenance, childcare, listening or, I don't know, having sex?

of listening means real appeals for help might not be heard when they need to be. If he's not listening to me, and I'm on the other side of our shared kitchen table, what other voice begging for help—help that he could actually provide—is he also not hearing? (And, I don't mean to pick on Jeremy directly; he's just one of a lot of white men who do exactly the same thing.)

While this may sound like fodder for another Tuesday night bickering session, selective hearing, and more broadly speaking, this tendency—and cultural permission—to tune out and opt out is very dangerous for more vulnerable populations. Because of the way our maps are drawn, both literally* and metaphorically, women of color are left pleading for help at intersections far, far away from the eardrums of people in power. Their voices aren't making it into the dens of suburban homes. If some of our white men are opting out of listening to the white women with whom they share a garage, how are they going to hear the sound of others in more desperate circumstances, or know how to process that type of pain, when there are no easy solutions?

the injustice

Men's ability to opt out of conversations that involve others' pain or require vulnerability stops the gears of justice from turning. This has been true whether they have been perpetrators of harm, witnesses to it, or decision makers sitting behind Congressional microphones at hearings. Some white men have been raised to have such a shiny, sturdy, superhero-sized shield propped up in front of them that even when they see their wives and their daughters struggling, nothing rocks them; if they don't have a quick fix, they disassociate themselves from their pain. Embarrassed that they don't know how to process others' vulnerability, some men just act oblivious to it. Psychologist Avi Klein says that "shame is the emotional weapon that allows patriarchal behaviors to flourish. The fear of being emasculated [through inability to navigate vulnerable, tense, confusing, guilt-provoking situations] leads men to rationalize awful behavior. This kind of toxic shame is in direct contradiction with the healthy shame that we all need to feel in order to acknowledge mistakes and take responsibility."[31]

As I mentioned, some theories assert that all of us, but men in particular, haven't developed past the adolescent stage of emotional development.

---

* Partly due to redlining, as we learned in chapter five.

This may be because we as a society have never forced them to go beyond the archetypes found on movie screens and in Calvin Klein underwear ads and video games. But the #MeToo movement has changed this for some men. It has put white men in particular into the previously unheard-of position of being challenged, which is forcing them to acknowledge and speak to others' pain—a new concept for some. "This moment has done them a favor," Klein says, "bringing up uncomfortable feelings that they're better equipped to ignore and avoid . . . It's just forced its way in."[32] Just like we white women, white men are in the middle of a reckoning—not just about past wrongs individually and collectively, but also about what gender norms should look like in the future.

quick lil' cartwheel

Let's be clear, though: now that you know all of this, if we pretend to ignore this behavior and thus allow it to continue without encouraging change moving forward, we are also responsible for the consequences. As noted in chapter one, we are excellent gymnasts—those floor routines in which we convince ourselves a husband or father's behavior is "normal" or "not his fault." Sometimes, by rationalizing their choice to opt out, we are also using their complacency as an excuse to avoid dealing with our own guilt, questioning, and other hard feelings we've sedated. We think, "If I don't have to check him, I don't have to check myself." We too become apathetic and indifferent—and that, my friends, is the most dangerous stance in the world to take.

When men blow things off, it gives us permission to do the same—even if inside we're ready to pick up a bat. Our proximity to men with this type of power position—to their ability to opt out without consequence when anything gets too confusing or heavy—gives us the power to do the same. It also protects the patriarchy. If we let men get away with being "too tired," if we say "They just want to watch the game" or "Boys will be boys" or "That joke was just a guy thing, let them bond" or "Of course he's checking her out, she's super cute!" we get a free pass out of the (often hard) work of questioning harmful messages and systems, too.

Our civic behavior shadows this. Research suggests that we—white women—have inherited voting habits from our families that work against our own and other women's interests. Because of the privilege we have, and the way that privilege often depends on the men in our lives, we often fail to see how our rights and freedoms as women are more bound to those of people who are also marginalized or oppressed by society's structures than to white men's. But I bet we'd see it if the rug of our comfortable, power-adjacent position were suddenly pulled out from under us.

The authors of the 2017 article "Gender Linked Fate, Race/Ethnicity, and the Marriage Gap in American Politics" wrote, "Women consistently earn less money and hold less power, which fosters women's economic dependence on men. Thus, it is within married women's interests to support policies and politicians who protect their husbands and improve their status."[33] This dynamic, explored by researchers, can be described as a kind of *linked fate*. As I discussed in chapter one, we want our husbands to maintain their (our) powerful positions, because that secures power for us, too; as a result, we white women defer to our husbands' choice of candidate more than any other demographic in the country. When a man is the household breadwinner, his power is not just financial—it's political, too.

When the subject of political views and perspectives on social issues came up in Listening Circles, there was always charged resistance. Women claimed that they made decisions independently, citing the breadth of territory over which they have control—all of the consumer, religious, and educational decisions, they said, were driven by them. Yet, a few glasses of wine later, the same women admit they feel "out of the loop" and do, in fact, defer to their husbands or other men in their lives when it came to suggested political choices.

One woman in a Listening Circle recalled that on Election Day 2000, she was driving to a polling place, but didn't yet know who she was going to pull the lever for. She tried to pull over to call her dad to confirm: Bush or Gore? The desire for a quick confirmation resulted in a fender bender. The woman, who can now chuckle about it, said, "The whole debacle was like God kicking me in the ass, telling me to make my own damn decision!"

We tend to assume that men are more plugged in to and engaged in objective conversations about the state of the world, particularly if they are in an office or more social with professionals. And, by extension, we believe they are better positioned to make decisions on behalf of our families and others. One research Listening Circle participant said, "[My husband] watches TV and reads news on his phone all the time and listens to political radio and I don't. I'm not educated in politics like he is."

It is true that men likely have more spare time to consume news and engage in political conversations with friends and colleagues (because, as we know, they're not spending that time talking about their feelings or throwing themselves as frequently on the two-year-old's temper tantrums). "This allows men to shape their views, have them reflected back, and reinforced. Women miss these opportunities to develop confidence in their own political decision making," says a GALvanize USA study.

Also, as we know from chapter two, because white women are trained to keep the peace and maintain relationships, we often actively avoid the subject of politics when it does come up in social settings. As the GALvanize report explains, "They equate civic discourse with certain conflict, loss of relationships, and the attendant social and economic penalties . . . Under these conditions, white women experience significant political pressure from their more conservative husbands, fathers, and male authority figures, which they feel ill equipped to withstand."[34]

And it's true—men *are* better, because they have generations of practice at protecting the status quo and knowing what decisions will protect their own power, particularly when they're white and have resources. When their decisions are enacted only with their own interests in mind, it protects both the patriarchy and the white supremacist blueprint.

After listening to women speaking candidly across the country, I now believe that—even in homes where women have loads of academic degrees and are otherwise confident—their husbands still hold an inherited position of appointed authority on politics, finances, and legal matters that determines how these women participate in public debate about subjects in the news. I recognize that deferring to one's husband on politics means there's one less thing to quibble about (sign me up, 😜) as you're clearing the table after dinner. The most honest Listening Circle participant shared that, "My husband told me that, if I wanted those new curtains in the living room I'd been moaning about, I had to vote for lower taxes."

As I said in chapter one, our silence and complicity can give us indirect influence, because we're positioned to benefit from the men we're married to, friends with, and work for, through our proximity to them. And on some level, at least, we know it. A study of more than two thousand women analyzed responses to the following question: "Do you think that what happens generally to women in this country will have something to do with what happens in your life?" Turns out that unmarried women are significantly more likely to answer "yes" than married women.[35] Research shows that marriage alters our perceptions of self-interest because it institutionalizes our partnership with men.[36] And we prioritize the preservation of the marriage, which often requires deferring to men, versus charting a less conventional path.

Sometimes in the Listening Circle we'd break the ice by going around and introducing ourselves. It wasn't rare for participants to weave their husbands' work into their descriptions of themselves. Similarly, in public spaces like hotel check-in desks and event registration tables, I've seen wives demand the power of their husbands' last names ("I'm Mrs. *Blank*") and the access that their status provides, when these resources were inherited or earned by their husbands—not by them.

I get why these married women are particularly proud—they got an A on the part of the checklist outlined in chapter two where we are encouraged to marry rich and powerful men.[*] This is not a game we simply fall for: our parents, grandparents, babysitters, Barbie, the Little Mermaid, and *Real Housewives* all tell us to strive for better circumstances . . . and we might sacrifice a lot to reach that bar.[†] A rising tide lifts all boats, and the benefits of a prosperous partner radiate to those with vested interest.

In Listening Circles, many of the women who choose not to work reported that they can feel "obligated to defer" to their husbands because of it—and that, if they and their husbands do come to an impasse, they are the ones who wind up caving. As one woman said, "We made the unspoken deal that he works and commutes, and I deal with the kids and the house." It's a trade that makes a lot of sense, in terms of making sure everything gets done. But historically, it's meant white women have given their husbands or fathers a second vote.

chief manicurist

I didn't realize how hard my mom worked until I became a mom myself. Typical story, right? I didn't understand how much more we all worked until I started to look into the darkest corners of my own schedule and those of other mothers to see who in the house is doing what.

---

[*] Forget kindness or sexual compatibility, or even their ability to be a decent human being.
[†] And a hand well played results in particularly smooth poolside daiquiris. I get it.

One tiny example: I have cut every single fingernail of both of my children since they were born.* The first thing I did when I walked in the door the day after the 2017 Women's March was grab the nail clippers. I'll never forget the contrast: just the day before, I had been negotiating the movement of satellites in space to better broadcast the event, and troubleshooting with the Washington, DC, Police Department about overflowing train platforms deep in Maryland and as far north as Delaware. But once that was all done, top priority was the meditative practice of wrestling a toddler while nudging sharp blades under her teeny pinky nail.

Keeping score is a favorite game for me and Jeremy—and, apparently, for many of the women in the Listening Circles, as well. Marriage can become a professional game of tit for tat, particularly if children, pets, or a home are in the picture. Who took the dog out in the middle of the night when he was sick, who rescheduled the plumber, whose grandmother's house did we last go to for Sunday dinner, who drove to the most recent away swim meet or took the kid to the last high-pitched birthday party? There are many different potential playing fields for this game, and I'm excellent at finding them.

In these discussions, Jeremy argues that I'm biased, and that our workloads are much more equal than I claim. But unfortunately for poor Jeremy, the research-based evidence is in my (our) favor. Like the fact that women spend two to ten times more hours on unpaid care work than men[37] even when both partners work. That rings true to me, as I've purchased 100% of the toothbrushes and jackets and been in charge of tracking all of both of our children's linguistic, social, and not-pooping-on-the-floor development stages to make sure everyone is hitting those milestones. I once had an epiphany while rocking my son to sleep: if I died, the avalanche of logistics that would fall on Jeremy's head would come close to drowning him. He'd be fine, but the scramble to the surface would be intense. He doesn't know either kid's shoe size, where the bathing suits are, or where I have a hidden duplicate of our son's favorite lovie bunny.

Research finds that globally, women spend an average of 4.5 hours on unpaid labor per day. Men average less than half of that.[38] As a by-product

---

* It's not that I'm better at cutting nails than my husband; it's that there's no choice to opt out of child hygiene. I never even thought about whether or not I wanted the job of household manicurist; I just thought that if I didn't do it, it wouldn't get done (oh, the backflip to give me permission to be a martyr, too).

of our sense of domestic responsibility, we're often forced to choose careers that might not be our dream jobs, but that give us the flexibility to pick up an unexpected sick kid from daycare and contribute to the carpool rotation with other moms who are barely keeping it together themselves. And then, rather than demand a more equitable allocation of duties, we cling to those same gender norms to make ourselves feel better—cue a cognitive acrobatics floor routine with the triple backflip.

As discussed, our biggest obstacle to seeing the patriarchy clearly is our fear of confronting—let alone uprooting—the inequalities in the system we've spent our whole lives playing into, often unknowingly. As Traister points out, "If you're going to look straight at and acknowledge the inequalities on the table, what that means is disturbing some of the most intimate relationships in our lives. It's partners and lovers and spouses, for hetero people. It's fathers and brothers and sons and friends and neighbors and coworkers."[39]

In my research for this book, I started questioning the routines in our home that seemed to "naturally" fall squarely on my shoulders. Chores related to our children's health were at the top of the list—and since we have two very young kids, there is a lot to be done. Since I can't individually change the system, I began assigning Jeremy tasks he could own.*

We started with teaching Jeremy how to braid Ever's hair. It has been a bit of a nightmare—teach your boys this early—but Jeremy was a patient student and Ever was excited to play salon. Our daughter has soft, curly hair, which means when she wakes up in the morning it's a proper "rat's nest," as my mother calls it. Every morning, I used to have to herd her into the bathroom, detangle the knots, then wet, re-brush, and braid her hair. This took up to ten minutes a day, and god forbid the braid is too high or low or I use the wrong color rubber band.

Let's say it was my responsibility to do this every morning until she's ten. That's equivalent to 168 hours of my life just spent braiding one child's hair. I'd be excited to get one of those hours back, but imagine if got a portion of those hours back—that would almost be a month of my professional working life returned. And guess what I could do in a month. I don't know, start to write a book?

---

* Needless to say, being "in charge" of the list of household chores demands substantial emotional labor on its own.

I offer this example because, when these conversations would come up in Listening Circles, women tended to defend their husband's inadequacies by explaining that it's just much quicker and easier for them to do it. And in the short term, that's true. I can get more done, better, in a briefer period of time, and my braids will likely always be better, too. But that's only because the patriarchy has forced us to be better at these things. Even I pushed back on Priya Fielding-Singh, when I spoke with the Stanford sociologist and gender expert, telling her that I'm simply a *much* better cleaner than my husband. Her response? "No, he just never learned how to clean, he didn't watch his father do it—who never saw his father do it, and on and on through much of history." For generations, women have been picking up the slack for what we thought our husbands simply weren't "good at." One of the most common myths, used to explain why women handle meals, is that women are much better cooks than men, yet, as Fielding-Singh pointed out, "Then why are all the most famous chefs in the world men?" Crickets. Men are just as capable of learning to do these things as we are. Gay couples and trans people with partners don't go hungry waiting for a Stepford wife to show up and cook the meals and rotate laundry. And to add insult to injury, when men do learn to do these things, they are, as the cooking example shows, more likely to get lauded for their expertise.

"Stick to what you're good at," one of my uncles always says. But if I did this, it would mean my children would eat cereal for dinner. So, I had to get good—or at least passable enough that my kids won't suffer from malnutrition. Men have the option to opt out of doing the same. As one man once said to me, "I've learned how to load the dishwasher poorly, wrap a messy present, and unsuccessfully put the kids to sleep." Let me translate, in case his message is not crystal clear: Through poor behavior, *he* gets to finagle his way out of all the grunt work.* Well played, sir, well played.

The argument used to support traditional gender roles is often that men and women are *innately* different. But the key difference between men and women is that we are *socialized* differently. There is no genetic difference that makes one person better at school-supply shopping or greeting-card signing than the other. What makes more sense: that men are biologically incapable of cutting kids food at a restaurant or making a kid's doctor's

---

* And in the process, we are already training the next generation of men to pretend the same incompetence, and the next generation of women to just pick up the slack.

appointment, or that no one ever asked them to be competent at these tasks to begin with?

We perform the same kinds of cognitive acrobatics when it comes to the rest of the world, too. Instead of looking at the patriarchally constructed system of inequality for the source of suffering of those not white and male, we blame others for looking for ways to survive—to simply keep their children and themselves alive. We blame the mothers of babies in cages on our borders for having brought them there to begin with. We say social services are just free handouts for the lazy poor, and maybe we should consider rolling those back,* or we suggest that men's advances are uncontrollable urges triggered by women's clothing or behavior. Pointing fingers and using phrases like "you reap what you sow" is way easier than examining deeply socialized and gendered behaviors and then . . . actually doing something about it.

People are incredibly adept at rationalizing complex behaviors that actually compromise our own well-being, when the alternative is contradicting our societal blueprints. It's easier to just tackle the task and get it done the way we like than to convince the men in our life they should be helping, teach them how to do it, and then expect them to remember to do it exactly when the occasion calls for it, especially when we've ended up disappointed in the past. It's *so much easier* to just change how we feel, to "give in" and convince ourselves we're better at something, than to change everyone's behavior.

One Listening Circle participant said that when she went back to work after ten years of being at home with the kids, she told her husband she was not going to do another dish. The first few months, the dishes were left in the sink for days, even "longer than a week one time." She held her ground and didn't touch them. Eventually, he changed his behavior and started loading the dishwasher. What if we all stepped to the side a bit more often, so that the men in our lives had the space (or the requirement) to do more of the labor we shoulder?

---

* If everyone had access to the same-quality healthcare, food, and educational and after-school programs as the wealthy, people could build lives that weren't dependent on getting to the next paycheck, and they could lift themselves out of poverty more easily.

two by two

It's hard to see how we have accommodated the men in our lives in ways we were groomed to believe was appropriate. But, as we look deeper, we might acknowledge that there was always an unsettling, deep in our guts, that told us this isn't really fair. Beginning to notice these rituals of defending, protecting, and justifying our men's behaviors, though, tells us about both what we are denying ourselves and what we are doing to our daughters.

When my son was learning to walk, I caught myself coddling him more than I did with my daughter at the same stage. When he fell, I'd often rush to his side, while with her, I'd be more likely to insist that she stand back up by herself. And every time we treat our children differently, we are sending them a message about what is expected of them, and what isn't. Every time we insist our daughters, but not our sons, clean the dishes after dinner, we take time away from her and give it to him. And I'm not just talking about the twenty minutes it takes that one evening to scrape, soap, rinse, dry, and stack. By telling your children that dishes are something *she* is expected to do and *he* isn't, you're setting your daughter, and any future daughter-in-law, up for thousands and thousands of hours over a lifetime doing dishes while your son or son-in-law spends those thousands and thousands of hours doing something else. When you give your sons the pass on something you expect your daughters to do, it strips future generations of women of an incomprehensible amount of time.

We put our daughters in situations where they are expected to do more household labor than our sons all the time. "Maybe he just needs an activity," an excuse women in my family quickly give when men fly out the front door to tennis after breakfast. We require our daughters to do more physical labor, and we often enable the unequal division of chores ourselves. "It's true!" a Listening Circle participant said. "Whenever my sons walk through the front door, I always offer to make them something to eat. When my daughter comes home, she always ends up doing it herself." When you pick up your son's wet towels or drop off his lunch when he forgets it or micromanage finding his tuxedo for prom, you're pushing those same burdens onto other women and potential partners in his future. Stop.

As the men in our life opt out of doing domestic labor, and we shoulder countless tasks as if nobody else would cut the nails if we didn't, we create a flawed model for our daughters when it comes to emotional labor, as well. Another Listening Circle participant, whose mother was suffering from breast cancer, shared that her adult brother "is allowed to go fishing to 'deal with the challenges of having a mother with cancer,' but I have to manage all of the logistics of getting her to chemo, hold her hand while she's throwing up, wrangle my father who isn't processing what's really going on. The whole time, my brother is trying to hook a fish because that's how he 'deals.'" By silently taking on most of the tough stuff ourselves, rather than demanding that the men in our lives share the physical and mental load, we're overburdening ourselves, and keeping them from having to learn and grow.

Yes, even though it can be much easier to turn our back to all this, we need to stop making excuses for our men's behavior. We also have to recognize the impact this white supremacist, hypermacho, only-be-tough blueprint has on them. We don't just need him to schlep the groceries into the kitchen; we should redefine our expectations to include him completing the task, because yes, he knows exactly where the milk goes. All of the men in my life have room for growth in the laundry room, hair-braiding, and emotional communication departments, but we must add another to-do to our own list. We have to hold ourselves accountable for holding *them* accountable. This doesn't mean they aren't responsible for their own actions—just that a new frontline of ours is holding them accountable too.

Maybe we've kept quiet so far because we weren't making as much money or reading the headlines as often, or because we were tired and it was just one more loaded conversation we could avoid. But if we continue to adjust our behavior so that he is not required to adjust his, the consequence is an affirmation of the same male-driven society that it's always been, which benefits nobody.

the rules have changed

We are not living in simple times—for women or for men. As Rachel Giese, author of *Boys: What It Means to Become a Man*, points out, "We've swung so quickly from permissive (boys will be boys) to panic (what's wrong with our boys?) that it's hard to know what the solution should be."[40] The rules men in particular were raised to live by are changing, and men are confused. I don't blame them. But it's important that the game is being redefined now, because it's in *everyone's* best interest.

One way we can break the cycles that protect the patriarchy, a system that has caused men internal pain and the rest of the world extreme harm, is by ending our tendency to rationalize both his avoidance behavior and our own. Facing the mirror is tough—whether you're looking in it or you're holding it up to someone you love. But remember, we have to find the front lines under our own roofs and in our own relationships and hold ourselves, and men of all ages—including our very young boys—to new, higher standards of emotional intelligence. Let's start with letting them cry and asking them to emote, constantly—please encourage that.

Even *chivalry* can transform into *courtesy*, a more genuinely supportive form of that traditional masculine value. "Holding doors and giving up seats are prime examples of courtesy," says Peter Glick, an expert on sex stereotyping. "Of course those are good things." But the benevolent sexism of how chivalry plays out in modern society—where men are "responsible" for their households and manage the finances, casting women as dependents and stripping them of their power—has been shown in studies to correlate with hostile sexism, with threats to women "who don't fit the idealized mold of women as pure, faithful, and compliant." Glick adds, "It's important to promote a masculinity that's not all about 'protecting women,' but rather about standing up for whoever is vulnerable."[41] And as we know, there are many different ways to define vulnerability.

White men were taught that they had the answers. People who look like them—who, in their heads, they'll be one day—are peering down at them from portraits hanging in museums and the halls of power. Our textbooks, written predominantly by white men, have told the story that white men alone have built and know how to lead this country. Of course there is the occasional Betsy Ross, Rosa Parks, or Eleanor Roosevelt* (thank you, ladies), but for the most part, as we looked at closely in chapter three, white dudes have traditionally saved the spot at the front of the line for themselves.

We all receive the message loud and clear: it's better to be a boy than a girl, and the best way to be a boy is to not act like a "girl."† If you're looking for competence, you want a white man. But, when we do look deeper, listen

---

* Respectively: considered the first seamstress to design and create the first American flag (though the jury is still out on the accuracy of this story); an African American civil rights activist renowned for her central role in the 1955 Montgomery, Alabama, bus boycott; and an American activist responsible for the creation of many international documents grounded in human rights, whose biography in textbooks tends to follow that of her husband, President Franklin D. Roosevelt.

† Which sends a lovely message to our girls about how they're supposed to feel about themselves.

closely, and even sometimes call them out, we know men are constantly questioning what the hell they're doing too (we all live in that purgatory most of the time 😔), even though our patriarchal system keeps handing them the torch of authority.

It's time to recognize how women sometimes enable this dynamic to continue, and how we should expect more from the men in our lives. Starting with small but radical reallocations of emotional labor and domestic work, we can ensure this heteronormative pattern doesn't oppress the next generation.

The good news is that activists and authors are continuing to deepen our awareness, which drags the (appropriate) self-doubts men might have about themselves and their capacity into the public square for questioning. The world seems to be getting a bit fidgety (can we say . . . fragile?) when we talk about this subject. White men, in particular, are understandably sprinting for the golf course.

CHAPTER SEVEN

"US" VS. "THEM"

We all belong to lots of groups that we opt into as members—with certain caveats. I'm a good-ish mom (though I feel slightly less good when I'm having to tell my kids for the fourth time to brush their teeth); a Philadelphia Eagles fan (unless I like the uniform design of the other team better); and a reluctant runner. I'm Team Women; Team New Yorker (but not when the Yankees are in the World Series*); Team Disciplinarian in my household (always, it seems); and Team Human Rights First when it comes to the Arab–Israeli conflict (which makes the conversation with anyone, on either side, long). Being able to casually pick teams without exceptions or disclaimers is a privilege.

Some of the groups we belong to are obvious, longstanding cultural institutions; others, not so obvious. Membership in some comes by blood and others from life experience. Some memberships, whether on a political committee or museum board, or at graduate school, require a fee; the resources to pay the fee and the option to choose where the money goes are both examples of privilege. Other groups we can't opt out of as members. For me, I can't shake my membership in the teams that are daughter,

---

* I just feel like they win a lot, and I'm always Team Underdog.

mother, sister, cousin, niece. I'm white, able-bodied, blue-eyed, of Jewish ancestry. I am also my voting record.

The groups I mentioned above have one thing in common (🫏), but that does not mean I have everything in common with everyone else in any one of them. As the marketing leader at ORGANIZE, I've engaged different demographics to encourage them to register as organ donors. When our team first connected with other organizations doing similar work, I was shocked to see the existing marketing materials on the market for Spanish-speaking audiences were simply English copy translated into Spanish. As we refined our strategy for connecting with Spanish speakers, I kept reminding everyone on our team that addressing the Guatemalan community is very different from speaking to the second-generation Colombian community, which is different from talking with the Puerto Rican community. Cultural context is critical in sending messages; just translating English into Spanish won't always work, and, frankly, it's insulting. It would be like an end-of-life organization sending the same message to Evangelical, Orthodox Jewish, and atheist communities, just because all of the groups' members spoke the same language; they all have different beliefs about what happens after death. When it comes to reaching a specific audience, multiple nuances always must be taken into account.

The same is true of American white women. I have talked with hundreds of women in living rooms across this country and abroad. I've talked with women who, on the surface, "seemed" very much the "same"—they had the same apps organized in the same way on their smartphones (the factory setting, typically), the same Jarlsberg cheese on similar platters, the same charms dangling from wine goblet stems. But to suggest the American white woman—or really, any population—is homogenous is not only inaccurate, but also potentially dangerous.

Take my Jewish identity, as one very personal example. My father was raised Jewish and my mother Christian. As a child, I was naturally very willing to benefit from a dual-religion home, with its deluge of presents, extra days off of school, and springtime Peeps and matzah brei. But I was only eight years old, in the school cafeteria, when I received my first scolding from a Jewish peer: "You're not really Jewish," she lectured, "because your mother wasn't 'technically'"—yes, she finger-quoted—"Jewish when you were born."

Though I was not asking for permission or approval to identify as Jewish, she, and many other people in my life since, even today, seem to enjoy watching me wrestle with their perspective about whether or not I am allowed to be on the Jewish team. I was constantly told I was not Jewish—that I didn't qualify because of an inherited cultural rule about matrilineal descent. I know now that many in the Jewish community believe this rule counters the tenets of Judaism as an inclusive faith. And I understand that this is legacy behavior from times the Jewish community needed to turn inward to protect itself. As I became an adult, and developed my own relationship with my faith, it became clear that this debate was not about helping me find the right "bucket" but about other people's need to "bucket" me. And yet the fact remains that both when I was growing up, and today—even as I am raising my kids in the Jewish faith—there are many who believe that, while I may be among Jewish people, I will never fully belong myself. This is one of the many reasons I was unwilling to take my husband's last name: Goldberg.

In the Jewish community I am the still an "other"—someone outside the group. And while I also had the experience of being othered as a child and a adult with my alopecia-induced baldness—which makes me different from the typical white, cis woman who has her own hair—I can make a choice about viewing myself as Jewish, regardless of my lineage or what other people think. But when you're told you're not allowed and find out you're not included, when you've been left behind and intentionally not factored in, the trust between you and that group is violated. That's what happened to me. So my refusal to take my husband's Jewish last name is a bit of a snub of a community that questions whether or not I belong. That told me that what I believe doesn't matter. That made me feel that no matter what I do, I will never be good enough to join.

Sometimes we voluntarily other ourselves, deciding who we are and aren't; other times, as is true for me with the Jewish community, the world makes those decisions for us. We can feel like we don't connect to moms who go to work or to moms who stay at home. We sense it in yoga classes if our body type makes some poses too hard to hold while they're easy for the chick in front of us. We can feel excluded from family events because financial circumstances mean we can't afford to keep up. If you are alive, it's likely you've felt—whether because of someone else's words or passive-aggressive actions, or just a story about who does belong that we've made up ourselves—"You're not one of us."

Certain ways of being in the world have been built into our DNA over millennia, and our tendency to categorize things is one of them. For primates, categorizing and recognizing poisonous plants ensures they don't eat them. Toddlers know which people are mom and dad. Categorization is useful, and yet, you can see from my own experience, that whenever we group people, we also mask diversity and fabricate hard divisions rather than honoring the multiple and worthy identities people have. You tell me: Are all Episcopalians, New York Jets fans, or, I don't know, Republicans the same? While sorting is a natural function of our brains, it's a function sometimes worth fighting against, because of the way grouping people based on a handful of stereotypes and biases limits us.

A culture of white supremacy and patriarchy prefers that we make sweeping generalizations about each other. It's easier to control people that way: if you're not a man, you're not qualified to lead and protect. If you're not a woman, you can't be nurturing. If you don't have United States documentation, you're not "home" here. If you don't believe in Christ, you're not on the right path to salvation. If you're not rich, you're not smart.

Just as we have to begin exploring and challenging our biases, we also have to question, and ultimately shed, binaries—the belief that something or someone either is or isn't good or bad, right or wrong, true or false, foreign or American, conservative or progressive, a professional or a mother, etc. We know the world is more complicated than that. Sometimes I'm a great daughter, and sometimes I call my mom late on her birthday. Sometimes I'm an amazing listener, and other times I interrupt people before they have a chance to be fully heard. I'm blonde with lots of hair with my wig on, but visibly disabled without it. Reality exists at the intersections. We humans are never wholly one thing or another, *especially* when it comes to morality; we can't really help it. Sometimes whether we are sinner or saint depends on our mood that hour and how well we slept the night before.

So, let's stop bucketing ourselves and each other into fabricated categories. While we might sometimes play for different types of teams at different moments in our lives, one point was clear in every Listening Circle: we all want the same damn thing—happiness for ourselves and each other, and ease along the way. No academic expert, poll,* or religious institution needs to tell me what human beings need: safety, health . . . a bit of humor, and a few dance-filled nights. So if we know we want this for ourselves, and we'd "like" everyone to enjoy these same essentials, why do we chase the satisfaction of watching others lose and fail and construct harsh stories

---

* As if I'll trust a poll again in my whole entire life after the 2016 election. Please.

about other people in our heads, just to make ourselves feel momentarily better about who we are?

grow up

I probably don't need to tell you that Listening Circle participants were heartbroken about the state of our divided country. Everyone seems familiar with this charged atmosphere and the competitive tension many are stoking (particularly some news channels), feeding both the divisions so familiar to our psyches and our implicit biases. This "us vs. them" divide means the majority of Republicans and Democrats strongly believe the other political party is jeopardizing humanity,[1] or is "a threat to the nation's well-being."[2] Stanford University professor Shanto Iyengar's research into how the news media and mass communication play a role in politics today suggests that political identity has become even more pronounced than race as a factor in people's self-reported biases 💀.

My huge, sixty-plus-person extended family used to be a very harmonious, albeit rowdy, bunch, but since 2016, we ourselves have become divided. Those who chose to raise their voices about disconcerting headlines get reprimanded for even raising the topic—they're not following the rules of keeping the peace. There is an increase in the number of people who would be disappointed if their child ended up marrying someone from the other political team, and I'd be lying if I didn't feel this way too, right at this moment—thank God my children are still babies.

In families like mine, as well as in neighborhoods, communities, and comment threads throughout America, we're acting like thirteen-year-olds. In Listening Circles, what inevitably followed participants' expressions of disgust for the insult-slinging to which we all have a front row seat was a common refrain of, "I wish we could all just stop fighting"—as if it were that simple. This, naturally, is a performance women have PhDs in: maintaining civility amid disagreement. But as we now know from chapter one, civility can mean we just repress our own feelings, avoiding important conversations in favor of silence and "playing nice" just to get through a girls' night out or Super Bowl party. Civility is what we pride ourselves on, a well-established social norm, but it's often a performance, and that's not always healthy.

To look more closely at the divisive power systems we've inherited, I've drawn heavily on the interpretations of Dr. James Fowler, a professor of theology and human development at Emory University. In his book *Stages of Faith: The Psychology of Human Development and the Quest for Meaning*, he offers a seven-stage model of how we grow emotionally through the full arc of our lives, in which we learn to divide our world into the "us vs. them" in the early decades and then, as we mature, become more inclusive and less defensive. In the early stages of our development, we thrive on debate and discourse; in the more mature stages, we seek acceptance, inclusion, and empathy. Fowler believes that much of who we are depends on what stage we are in.*

I want to take his model a step further and apply it to the state of our country. I believe we're stuck in his:

Stage 4. Conventionality and Conforming (13–17 years old): Adolescents form relationships with peers, friends, romantic partners, groups, and authority figures. They either conform or they rebel. Everyone who does not belong to "our" group—who is not "one of us"—is out, which is why this stage has a lot of us-them, cliquish perspectives. Most tellingly, the values of other groups are wrong—not just different, but wrong, even evil—and the people in those groups are also viewed as wrong or evil. Adolescents realize that they have ideas and values, but they do not examine the sources. They overreact to the ideas and values of others. Teenagers take everything personally and have exactly *zero* long-term vision. The values of whole groups bring the same response, and members of a group are treated as if they are all identical: all wrong or evil.[4]

I said earlier that we were acting like thirteen-year-olds, and I meant that literally. Our country is, collectively, those annoying teenagers that waltz out of the room with a series of eye rolls.

When I was a teenager, I was convinced adults were ignorant of the emotional intensity of being an adolescent (little did I know they were just opting out of the memory—I totally get it now). The world was full of clear distinctions: You either lived and breathed protecting the whales or you didn't care about anything at all! A side-eye or snarky comment from a peer could bring my world crashing down; there were rarely any gray areas and certainly no space for empathy for other people's insecurities or mistakes.

---

* I've placed Fowler's seven-stage model as interpreted by Chris Largent, Jungian philosophical counselor, and Tracy Halterman in the endnotes—take a look.[3]

In fact, they made me feel stronger. Clearly, my development as a human was far from complete.

The same is true of our eager-to-categorize, eager-to-blame society, which leaves no room for scenarios where marginalized communities are intentionally oppressed. We have to take the next step, into Stage 5 adulthood, which is when we realize we have individual responsibility and a capacity to make a difference in the world around us. This sense of accountability and grounded optimism leads to an even better place: Stage 6, our forties through our late fifties, when we recognize the value of complexity, diversity, and sophistication, and then Stage 7, when we are markedly more inclusive, nonjudgmental, and engaged in our lives and in society. To solve the world's key problems by better understanding how we're standing in the way—how we very literally are the bottleneck—we urgently need to move beyond Stage 4.

gotta pick one (no you don't)

In my world, one particular subject of conversation that seems to universally implode into binary, "us vs. them" thinking, as outlined in Stage 4, is any subject related to the role of American Jews in the Arab–Israeli conflict. For this reason, I organized a number of Listening Circles with white Jewish women in a number of demographic categories: Orthodox, Reform, affluent, urban, rural, young, retired.

There were clearly distinct generational perspectives on the very complicated subject of Arab–Israeli relations. Women born before 1965 had a very specific relationship with the state of Israel. To them, the cries of the younger generations of Jewish people around the freedom and rights of the Palestinians implied their own ordeals were being minimized or forgotten. For one Listening Circle participant, mentioning Palestinians triggered a reference to her parents' tattoos from Auschwitz.* This same woman seemed remorseful that her daughter, who is in her early twenties, cares "more about abortion in the United States than the State of Israel."

The views shared in another Listening Circle, organized around a younger demographic, suggested that younger Jewish people do care more about issues they face here in America. In the words of one participant,

---

* Those held at the Nazi concentration camp Auschwitz and its sub-camps, Birkenau and Monowitz, were tattooed for identification purposes.[5]

"Of course I care more about abortion than Israel—that country has always been safe and secure enough in my lifetime." Another participant said, "I love my faith, but question the Israeli government. I'm told that it is anti-Semitic, but I can't stand seeing endangered children on either side of the line." Another, older participant quickly snapped back, "Jews have been persecuted in every country [where] they've ever existed—there is literally no place where they are safe; if you don't defend Israel, you're anti-Semitic."

This is when the conversation spins in circles; Listening Circle participants feel, at times, even more divided on this particular issue when they leave than when they entered the room, 😔. At the same time, participants sometimes mentioned desperately wanting to find a unified pathway forward. They recognized that an emotionally charged stalemate can stall any possibility of progress, as we've seen over decades in the region.

Lately, we've seen neo-Nazism on the rise in the US, from the Pier One tiki torch rally in Charlottesville, Virginia, where participants chanted "Jews will not replace us,"* to, as one woman put it, the "swastikas spray-painted on my daughter's school bus in a suburb of NYC." Yet the Jewish community is still so focused on who is and isn't "technically" (I'm using the air quotes—just like the girl who ridiculed me in the cafeteria when I was eight) on the Jewish bench, and allowed to speak on behalf of the community. And that futile exercise is distracting from the urgent work we have to do. It's also excluding interest, willingness, and efforts like mine to seek involvement in the midst of this frightening crisis.

Unfortunately, Americans are becoming comparably divided over topics that do not have nearly as fraught a history or as important a set of consequences, like sewage systems and Starbucks versus Dunkin' Donuts coffee—you know, stuff not even mentioned in the Old Testament. Some of these questions do not need a fight. It's like being asked to choose between "Does the United States need more faith?" and "Does the United States need more science?" Um, yes. The problem is when we're reducing each other to memberships, it causes conflict that could lead to possible bloodshed. Our knee-jerk antagonism and division are the problem.

---

* The "Unite the Right Rally," commonly referred to as the Charlottesville Riot, was a demonstration in that Virginia city, during the summer of 2017. The rally included white nationalists, Klansmen, and members of the alt-right protesting the removal of a Confederate statue and aiming to promote the white supremacist agenda. Ultimately a counter-protester, Heather Heyer, was killed.

Kwame Anthony Appiah, British-born Ghanaian American philosopher and cultural theorist, believes that in all these identity wars, we keep making the same mistake: exaggerating our differences from other groups and then doubling down on our similarities with people we think are like us. As outlined in his book *The Lies That Bind: Rethinking Identity*, his observations suggest we see ourselves in monolithic groups, at war with each other, rather than being skeptical of social divides. According to Appiah, if we don't find a way to transform narrow identities—whether political affiliations, sports team preferences, SoCal or NoCal, vegan or carnivore—our nation will continue to fracture.[6]

Here's an example of the arbitrary oppositions we've allowed to creep into our worldviews. In his recent essay, "Against Identity Politics," American political scientist, economist, and author Francis Fukuyama writes about how "us vs. them" plays out across political divides. He says the left has defined itself recently around "promoting the interests of a wide variety of groups perceived as being marginalized," whereas the right "is redefining itself as patriots who seek to protect traditional national identity."[7] I'm both. I deeply care about marginalized communities and have spent my professional career focused on them. I also care about who we are as a "we," as these United States, and what we want to be for ourselves and the rest of the world moving forward. Fukuyama fears today's *identity politics* "has become a cheap substitute for serious thinking." The reason why we're often left wondering how we have any cohesive sense of national identity is because we have become so focused on our differences. When we hold these theories of separation at our center, it justifies our separation from each other, which is the lazy way out. Countries cannot survive like that; in fact, that is how countries crumble into civil war.

It's the same in foreign policy. When we create walls around our country, we create a "forced choice between globalism and patriotism," says Appiah. We conveniently forget that a modern, pluralist democracy like America is "not a fate but a project"—a project that takes work from all of us. The structures that govern our lives today can seem like they are set in stone, but actually, they require refashioning to fit the society we want today.

us-and-them in politics

It's worth noting that this deeply venomous "us vs. them" mentality has run through the veins of our nation since the very beginning. George

Washington took notice of this tendency and warned against it in his presidential farewell speech, more than two hundred years ago.* Still, today, our nation's limited, two-party, blue-versus-red conversation makes it hard to live in the many shades of purple where most of us reside. An either/or choice is deeply entrenched in our political system that is supposedly designed to be representative, even though each of us is a complex human who, apparently, needs hundreds of yogurt options.

In the Listening Circles, I found that American white women perform cognitive acrobatics not just for our men, but also our political parties. After the release of the recording of then-candidate Donald Trump telling Billy Bush that he grabbed women "by the pussy," I saw interviews of white women at rallies who brushed it off, saying, "Eh, boys will be boys." I don't care where you fall on the political line or who you voted for in 2016—no one wants our daughters to be grabbed anywhere on their bodies without their consent, let alone their genital area. We are at least in agreement on that, yes?

Many women in the Listening Circles said the 2016 presidential campaign was so acrimonious, they just voted the same ticket they always had just to be done with it. That's where we are: thanks to our either/or politics (paired with our reluctance to engage with complexity), we are picking sides and toeing a party line, even when we might not agree with it, just to avoid the hailstorm of contentious debate in our heads or with the people around us.

I'm not saying another political party or candidate could be perfect if we made space for them—I hope I made it clear that this is an impossibility in chapter two—but it's clear our current two-sided system is not working. You only have to look at the way that people are now going at it in social media and op-ed comment feeds, calling each other out on language, facts, and perspectives as if they're falling on some public sword for their followers to see. Oh, the heroism.

"*Call-out culture*"—publicly shaming someone for offenses committed—has become another tool to split communities into factions. As David

---

* "The alternate domination of one faction over another, sharpened by the spirit of revenge, natural to party dissension, which in different ages and countries has perpetrated the most horrid enormities, is itself a frightful despotism . . . the common and continual mischiefs of the spirit of party are sufficient to make it the interest and duty of a wise people to discourage and restrain it." Basically, he's saying that two parties won't work, because the "us vs. them" brings out the worst in us.[8]

Brooks, *New York Times* columnist, suggests about the harm caused by call-out-culture, "you've reduced complex human beings to simple good versus evil. You've eliminated any sense of proportion."[9]

Call-out-culture is sometimes the only form of justice many marginalized communities have because they've been denied it institutionally, and social media is "making it easier for the powerless to collaborate, coordinate, and give voice to their concerns," in the words of Malcolm Gladwell.[10] Yet we need to find other methods of restorative justice that don't rely on rage and vengeance that can ruin lives while still holding people accountable. While it can be helpful to share your perspective online, because it can broaden other people's awareness (and I want to emphasize "people," since so many comments today are made by bots*), social psychology tells us that when people feel threatened, they are much less likely to listen or change.[12] It's like what we saw last chapter: when some of our men aren't sure how to navigate conflict, they opt out (and then make excuses for why opting out was the right way to handle the conflict). And when they *do* engage, the subject that triggers the most contentious dogfights is . . . well, anything that the political ringmasters want us to be divided over, which pushes us deeper into our own camps.

We have to debunk the two-sides myth, especially when it comes to political parties. This seems like an idea we could dismantle: we know there aren't only two kinds of people in America. This idea that there are only two ways to run a country, two teams you can be on, and two sides to every issue is a contradiction of human existence and suggests intellectual laziness.

I recognize that there is a long way to go before a third party becomes a serious contender, but can we break the mindset of either/or politics? Can we look for policies you agree with on both sides, and stop just assuming people on the "other" side will always disagree? Either/or politics have built up another obstacle that keeps us silent and unwilling to engage with anyone we perceive to be "other."

---

* Some estimates suggest that Instagram has 95 million fake accounts posing as real people. These accounts, known as bots, respond like humans, and post comments based on an analysis of the photo's characteristics, other people who have responded to it, and keywords in the post or comment threads. According to TwitterAudit, only 40 to 60% of Twitter accounts are real people. This makes it difficult to tell who is a homemaker in Salt Lake City and who is a bot, or someone sitting in a troll farm outside of St. Petersburg, Russia.[11]

the wedge (not the salad)

Sometimes issues on the voting ballot are used as bait to divide us in ways that aren't always immediately obvious in the midst of the headline fire hose. Divisiveness helps those in power stay in power. And historically, white women have been the queen on this chessboard—and not just because we tend to like the idea of wearing tiaras. We see this in the way political parties emphasize issues they can spin to resonate with women: reproductive rights, for example, or the human rights crisis of minors crossing the border. But the skewed messaging around those issues can have the dangerous effect of driving us much further apart than we actually are.

Wedge issues are those that are emphasized, deliberately and expertly, to further separate us into political factions. Most modern-day wedge issues are easy to identify. Just think about the most divisive political issues of our time—gun control, immigration, or one of the most famous and effective wedge issues ever manufactured, abortion. Political parties have drawn well-defined lines in the sand on these topics. According to them, you are either on one side or the other.

Focusing on abortion, little (if any) nuance finds its way into this discussion. "Abortion kills babies" versus "Women should retain control of their bodies" is the binary we usually hear. And there's no stronger "us vs. them," right/wrong, "the other side is completely immoral" issue in political life today. Consequently, many of us just avoid the conversation altogether. But let's look at the history of this wedge issue briefly, to explore how it's been manipulated by cynical political operators to influence voters over time.

As you may know, *Roe v. Wade* was decided in 1973, with seven Supreme Court justices voting in favor of a woman's right to choose. Keep in mind, a conservative-majority court handed down this decision. Republicans at the time, who overwhelmingly viewed reproductive issues as a private matter between a woman and her physician, were actively involved with efforts to legalize abortion. Democrats, which included a huge percentage of the country's Catholic voters, were largely opposed.

Starting in the late '70s, the parties began to slowly flip sides on this issue. Republicans were looking for more women voters, and images of dead babies were a quick and easy way to bring in women who were undecided.* The Republicans—who, let me reiterate, were up to this point

---

* Danger to babies tends to trigger hormones related to the desire to protect in women more so than men. A 2013 study stated, "Women interrupt mind wandering when exposed to the sounds of infant hunger cries, whereas men carry on without interruption."[13]

pro-choice—quickly won a number of seats in key districts, and ultimately the 1980 presidential campaign, by using abortion to flip white, female, religious voters. And they did it by picking a subject—babies—they thought would res-onate with their target demographic, and building a message that, ironically, contradicted their previous position just to win the seats and stay in power.

Abortion was one subject everyone actively avoided in Listening Cir-cles, though one brave woman said she is always so torn on presidential candidates that she "just votes for whichever ticket is most anti-abortion." The wedge issue worked; it's kept her "wedged" on one side of the political line for decades.

On this issue and many others, we're under the belief we're so divided, but I'm not sure we truly are. In one Listening Circle, made up of predom-inantly eighty-plus-year-old conservatives, we tackled the question: what would you be willing to fight for besides your kids and family? One woman shared how she has marched in pro-life marches in Washington, DC, for the past ten years. A few hours later, I posed another question: what if a mother of two, juggling two jobs to make ends meet, found out she was pregnant and wished to terminate but she didn't have the approximately $500 to complete the procedure; would you help her? The vocally pro-life woman yelped from the back of the room, "Absolutely!"

I asked her to clarify: "Just confirming I understand what you're saying: you are pro-life, but you would help another woman terminate an unwanted pregnancy?"

She said: "Yes. I know how hard it is to be a mom. Abortion isn't for me—but I understand why that woman would." She further explained that, as a rule, she distrusts governments and large institutions, which is why she doesn't funnel money to women through existing organizations like the one I made up. This is a position many of us can sympathize with. There is a common sense of distrust of systems across the board—government agen-cies, large nonprofits, electeds—and we've become committed to the idea that we are all being played, that someone is pulling a fast one on us . . . because they are.

And since I just dragged abortion into this book—let's talk about immi-gration, a subject that has everyone scurrying to their sides and mounting their defenses. The varied demographic makeup of this country used to be a point of pride; we were a collection of human beings whose ancestors came here in search of freedom and hope.* My great-great-grandfather

---

* Unless their ancestors always lived here, or they were brought here against their will.

Johan arrived from Sweden, built a potato farm near Princeton, New Jersey, and had eleven children. Eleven! That's a lot of desks his children took up over the years. When he found out immigration authorities were rounding up undocumented individuals, he hung himself. My other great-great-grandfather, Sam, came from Russia fleeing Jewish persecution; he was trying to go to Germany, but the US is where he landed. His son, also Sam, drew people's portraits on the sidewalk in Times Square to make a living. And because we let them in and they raised families here, their children, their children's children 🫂, and so on down the line have been able to take advantage of opportunities that helped not just them, but *us*, as a country prosper.

In early 2019, I spent a brief moment with a group of young moms in Mexico City who were carrying their babies to the United States border. They were adamant they would be killed if they stayed in their home communities. One woman told me, "They raped my sister and we can't find her, they skinned my brother, and my parents are both dead, all because my great uncle, who I never met, had a position in local politics that influenced the police."

Imagine packing a backpack, with your baby in your arms, and leaving all you know in the world to venture north for a tiny chance at a safer life. These women knew the risk: transportation on the tops of trains, drunk strangers at midnight, a lack of diapers and clean water—but still they carry, walk, and pray north. I can say with certainty: they're not casually showing up at our borders looking for a general "upgrade" in life. They're showing up at our borders because if they don't, they will die. Period.

Turning these people away violates the law* of our country—as well as our religions and hearts—which mandates we take in people who are persecuted. It's our country's most successful advertisement, embodied by Lady Liberty.† But the reason many people are fleeing the only homes they've ever known is the result of United States foreign policy decisions

---

* Seeking asylum in the United States is a statutory right established in the Refugee Act of 1980.

† "'Give me your tired, your poor, / Your huddled masses yearning to breathe free, / The wretched refuse of your teeming shore'" writes Emma Lazarus in "The New Colossus," a poem transcribed onto the pedestal of the Statue of Liberty.[14] Lazarus wrote the poem in 1883, amid a time of anti-Chinese United States immigration policy, European colonialism, and an influx of Jewish refugees fleeing anti-Semitism in Russia.[15]

over the decades.* Today, more than sixty-eight million† people are displaced worldwide.‡

Immigration will remain a wedge issue, causing constant division, as long as political parties can keep constituents focused on the big picture, "us vs. them," rather than the human costs. Too often, the debate doesn't focus on the complicated effort to create a humane practice at the borders. A balance, one that is constantly being explored and iterated, is required, but to suggest that it's a line drawn in the sand is oversimplifying a herculean task. The wails of the children separated from their mothers at the border did rattle the conscience of the country—and particularly that of American parents—so much so that an executive order was issued to reverse the "zero tolerance" border separation policy. Also known as the Family Separation Policy, it officially lasted from April 2018 to June 2018.§ There's another layer to the recent immigration issue: it can be seen as an attempt to dehumanize an entire group of people based on nationality and race (they're all "criminals, drug dealers, rapists,"[19] according to the forty-fifth president) to justify a violent response. Arbitrary characteristics are used to determine whether an individual in search of a better life is a "good" or "bad immigrant. This performance of cognitive acrobatics allows Americans to make exceptions for the immigrants in their lives and communities they know and love, and carve out exceptions for why those immigrants can "stay," while assuming everyone else is not worthy. Our human instinct encourages us to protect those we know and care about; our political teachings tell us to ostracize those we don't.

In chapter three, we talked about Bacon's Rebellion, in which the elite found ways to divide people so that they could not unite to fight back—and

---

* The United States has triggered so much of the conflict in Central and South America from which the refugees at our border are escaping. According to the Council on Foreign Relations, the "U.S. interventions during the Cold War—including support for a coup in Guatemala, brutal government forces in El Salvador, and right-wing rebels based in Honduras known as the Contras—helped destabilize the region."[16]

† 44 internally displaced (staying within their home countries but lacking anywhere to go), 25 million refugees (people leaving or fleeing their country), and 3 million asylum seekers. United Nations High Commissioner for Refugees.[17]

‡ Syria is considered a climate crisis.[18]

§ There are still babies and children being separated from their parents as I type this and some have lost their lives in the process—including one eleven year old girl who tried to take her own life while detained.

so all the power remained in their own hands. Back then, the divisions were about race—a manufactured construct. Today, that is still the case, though we've also allowed ourselves to become divided based on things like who we love and how we pray. Whenever we are presented with a new issue to divide us, it's essential to question the messenger, be it a leader, influencer, celebrity, snappy teenager, and, of course, any company that is looking to make money off of our being divided. How do they benefit from our division? In many cases these days, the answer is through profit and power.

someone is making $$$

I would often leave a Listening Circle feeling as if the participants were marching to the beat of whatever drum had been pounded on the news channel they watched the night before. It was crystal clear who watched which channel, based on the way they spoke—as if the television pundits had provided a cultural script for viewers to recite in relevant conversations.*

The problem is, news is the first draft of history. Talking heads are asked to draw quick conclusions and save the rationalizing for afterward. Also, news outlets are under financial pressure to attract and keep our attention. Because their employers, the news media outlets, keep the lights on by selling our time and attention—our most precious commodity—to advertisers, they must keep us riveted. *This* is why television networks and newspapers and online news websites play up the controversy and a sense of constant urgency—to keep us hooked. They have to make sure that the "Breaking News" graphic is always positioned on the bottom of the screen. They have to make sure you cannot look away, so they can bill advertisers accordingly.

We're all subject to this manipulation, and as a result, we end up living in an atmosphere of media-manufactured crisis. (There *is* urgent news, but it often isn't covered.) In our current news climate, findings are exaggerated, and data selectively emphasized in order to make content stickier and to keep you coming back for more. Not to mention the growing evidence that outside forces, which may or may not be controlled by governments, are working to manipulate what information you're exposed to.

You've probably heard about Cambridge Analytica, the United Kingdom-based data analysis firm hired during the 2016 United States presidential

---

* I can be guilty of the same thing, as I'm also not an expert on Social Security or trade or climate science, for example, and rely on outlets I trust.

election to specifically target Facebook accounts they considered mallea-ble. Based on your Facebook behavior (say, for instance, "liking" an animal shelter page or a Confederate flag page), Cambridge Analytica would direct micro-targeted ads your way that were designed to appeal to your specific personality profile based on those "likes." And once you clicked on those ads, you were potentially exposed to misinformation.

I'm not subscribing to off-the-wall conspiracy theories here. I used to buy ads all the time at ORGANIZE, trying to get people to register to be organ donors, so I know first-hand that there are software plugins available on the open market with algorithms that use your behavioral data to learn who you are, how to find you, and what to say to get you to click on that ad. It's why, for example, ads for that shoe you were looking at a couple of days ago are now on every website you click on.

I also learned, while at ORGANIZE, how two seemingly aligned groups could end up telling two very different—even contradictory—stories using the same set of data. Both my team and the established Organ Procurement Organization's wanted to collect more organs, but the latter was saying "We are really good at our jobs, we couldn't possibly do better, though please continue to donate" and the former, ORGANIZE, was saying, "There is room to do better." We both interpreted and positioned the data on death rates and organ donor conversions very differently to meet our objectives.* Marketers do this all the time, but lately mainstream media has been doing the same thing, pushing drama—including the drama of political division—in order to capture the most attention.

Let's silence all of this noise for a minute to consider how we are actually more similar to each other than we are usually led to believe. Like the pro-life woman willing to help a woman in crisis who needed to terminate a pregnancy, most of us can find common ground even with a seeming oppo-nent. According to the Hidden Tribes Report, 67% of Americans are part of the "Exhausted Majority," "flexible in their views and willing to endorse dif-ferent policies according to the precise situation rather than sticking ideo-logically to a single set of beliefs."[20] I always imagine what the overlap might

---

* The number of people who die while waiting for a transplant and the number of lives we save with organ transplants are very concrete. But I have seen two different factions within the organ donation community (which is supposed to be focusing on saving lives, I might add) take an identical piece of data (the increase in organ recovery rates) and reinterpret it to take credit for them being better at their jobs, when in fact it's due entirely to another crisis (the opioid epidemic).

be in a Venn diagram on headline issues—my hunch tells me it's much larger than media conglomerates and political parties want us to believe. We know 77% of Americans say the Supreme Court should uphold *Roe v. Wade*,[21] 83% agree with background checks for sales of firearms between private parties and at gun shows,[22] and 68% think we should provide afford-able healthcare for all.[23] But the way we vote often doesn't demonstrate that unity, because we are wedged to one side or the other, thanks in often large part to the news that finds us and the products their advertisers want us to buy.

the goat

Another way that people in power maintain that power is by creating *scapegoats** —by telling a story that blames the suffering of one group on the actions of another group. It gives those in control the air cover to justify oppressive decisions, like stop-and-frisk policies† or even billing inmates for calls home to their children.

History is littered with examples of people in power dehumanizing oth-ers in order to seize greater control, or just to maintain the control they have. In American history, European settlers used the term "savage"[25] to describe indigenous peoples as justification for killing them and taking their lands, and they had to see Africans as property to enslave them. Nazis saw Jews as not worthy of life, and some children's books compared them to poi-sonous mushrooms,‡ to justify gas chambers. The Khmer Rouge saw ordi-nary Cambodians as completely expendable in their quest for an entirely classless society where only the rulers had power; anyone who posed a real or perceived threat had to be slaughtered to ensure unquestioned loyalty to

---

* The word comes from Judaism, from when a rabbi, during Yom Kippur, used to bring a goat to the altar and everyone would metaphorically shower the goat with their sins. The goat then is sent into the wilderness, along with all of the sins it absorbs from the people (Leviticus 16:21–22).

† These policies overwhelmingly target communities of color, specifically people who are black and Latinx. In New York City, according to the ACLU, "nearly nine out of ten stop-and-frisked New Yorkers have been completely innocent."[24]

‡ In a children's book intended to distribute Nazi propaganda titled *The Poisonous Mushroom*, written by Ernst Hiemer and published by virulently anti-Semitic Nazi propagandist Julius Streicher, one story said, "Just as it is difficult to distinguish between a poisonous mushroom and an edible mushroom it is difficult to distinguish between a good Jew and a lying, thieving Jew."[26]

the state and the state alone. The Hutus in Rwanda called the Tutsis cock-roaches to justify that genocide.

The creation of superficial boundaries that divide members of a society into "good/worthy" and "bad/unworthy" is deadly, and not just for the people serving as the scapegoat. I believe America is on the brink of implosion like we've seen in some of these places before. Experts have suggested that our country's polarized, hyper-identity-based behavior is similar to that seen in countries worldwide, including during our own Civil War. For example, Shamil Idris, executive director of Search for Common Ground, the largest conflict-resolution organization in the world, identifies the risk: "The modern manifestation of political and racial polarization in the U.S., combined with the widespread delegitimization of institutions that have historically played a unifying role for the nation, presents an altogether new and profound challenge to the country's unity and governability. Without serious and sustained intervention, any nation whose citizens turn on one another to this extent while rejecting all sources of unifying authority will eventually give way to disintegration." Disintegration. Lovely.

Hey, reader, we can stop this.

We are walking a fine line between forward progress and civil war right now, if we haven't already crossed it. Violence caused by white supremacists is now being considered terrorism, just like attacks from ISIS or al-Qaeda.[27] One terrorist* who stabbed a black man on a New York City sidewalk was attempting to start a "race war."[29] From the 2015 Charleston church massacre that took the lives of nine African Americans, to the Tree of Life Synagogue shooting in Pittsburgh in 2018 that resulted in the deaths of eleven Jewish worshippers, our fellow Americans are being slaughtered again and again specifically because of our growing division.

The resolution of "us vs. them" (my team is better than yours) conflicts, in contrast to "interest-based" conflicts (for example, who has control over a body of water), can take generations to reverse. And even then, something has been lost that can never be regained. After the assault by Nazis on American soil in Charlottesville, author Nathan Englander wrote in a 2017 *New York Times* op-ed, "I am reminded of a notion that our rabbis taught us:

---

* Murders committed by white supremacists have more than doubled in 2017, with far-right extremist groups and white supremacists "responsible for 59% of all extremist-related fatalities in the US in 2017," according to the Anti-Defamation League. These groups were responsible for 20% of these fatalities in 2016.[28]

The theft of time is a crime like any other. Back then it was about interrupting class—one minute wasted was a minute of learning lost. But multiply that minute by everyone in the room, and it became 15, 20 minutes, half an hour's worth of knowledge that none of us could ever get back. Saturday in Charlottesville was just one day, but think of that one day multiplied by all of us, across this great country. Think of the size of that setback, this assault on empathy, the divisiveness and tiki-torched terror multiplied by every single citizen of this nation. It may as well be millions of years of dignity, accessibility, of progress lost. Just from that one day."[30]

"you are not stuck in traffic, you ARE traffic"[31]

We've established that white women have a significant controlling influence on much of America's dominant culture. We tend to be grouped as an "us" by advertisers, pollsters, and hey, even the author of this book. And it's true that just by being white, we are likely to have a common set of expectations and biases.

We all engage with the world looking for our own biases to be confirmed. We look for and most easily recall information that confirms our already-formed beliefs. I know I do it in my personal relationships; if I've written off someone as being rude, I might fail to give them credit for giving a coworker a ride to the ER. Similarly, if we believe our political party is the most righteous, we are more likely to process only news that proves our perspective, and to ignore or overlook policies we don't agree with. We are experts at proving our arguments right; we are constantly on alert for evidence to make our case. This is known as *confirmation bias*—and, thanks to today's plethora of news sources and talking heads, it's easier than ever to comfortably cherry-pick information to confirm the verdict already in our head. In the *echo chambers* of social media and politically motivated news outlets, we hear only what we want to believe, and so end up believing it more deeply.

A sense of supremacy of any kind, based on race or gender, requires first a clear and obvious affiliation with one team over another, and second, the belief that your team is not just different from the other one, but *better*. With that belief in your own supremacy in place, the "them" becomes a threat. The idea that "they" might actually be worth listening to complicates our binary mindset and our previous sense of comfort that we are on the "winning" team. This is as true for entire nations as it is for individuals. And it's why exploring and questioning our group memberships, and our divisiveness in general, can feel so threatening to the people and groups currently in power. Ridding ourselves of this binary system is the only way to be able to hear and respect all people. Because the idea that there is only one right way, group, perspective, pathway, outcome? It's simply not true.

Neither is the assumption that many Americans have today, that if we start extending housing, education, and medical care to other people, there won't be enough left for them. This sensation will be familiar thanks to any commercial running around Halloween through Christmas that screams "only while supplies last!!!" This *scarcity mentality* is built into our supremacy culture—if we don't get "it," and keep "it," then someone else does, and we lose "it," along with our power.

"People with a *scarcity mentality* have a very difficult time sharing recognition and credit, power or profit—even with those who help in the production. They also have a very hard time being genuinely happy for the successes of other people—even, and sometimes especially, members of their own family or close friends and associates," says Stephen Covey, author of *The 7 Habits of Highly Effective People.* Their sense of worth comes through comparison with others'; they see another person's success as their failure.[32] Only so many people can be "A" students; only one person can be "number one." To "win" simply means to "beat"—and if you're not winning, you aren't following the blueprint.

The attitude that there isn't enough to go around is a big part of the anti-immigration narrative: the idea that those seeking refuge will take your jobs, and your kids' school desks and doctors' appointments. This is in contradiction to the widespread worker shortage in the US for the first time in two decades, according to the Department of Labor.[33]

When I told certain people, particularly people of color, I was writing this book, the reaction always included a bit of exasperation—primarily among people who have been marginalized by our society. Then sometimes a sarcastic "Good luck" would fall out of their mouths. I continued to seek clarity on their impression of white women (and what they thought their assumptions were, as you'll learn more about in chapter ten). But one idea that came up a lot was the belief that, in the words of one friend, "white people believe they are entitled to everything just because they are white— the best schools, getting immediate attention at the doctor's office, or from the hostess at the restaurant. I always wonder who they think they are, acting like everything is theirs—as if they have a right to something the rest of us don't."

We all know she's right. I have witnessed this not only in my family and in professional spaces, but also within Listening Circles. There *is* a sense of entitlement that seems to come with being white. It's similar to what we discussed in chapter three with regard to the Doctrine of Discovery—how white Christian men (and by proximity, the white Christian women close to them) accepted it as their God-given right to just take what they wanted regardless of the impact on others. We resist the idea that we have a responsibility toward others whose names we don't know, whose gods we don't pray to, whose children we don't love. We don't want to pay for other people's food (outside the school canned-food drive), gender transitions, special education needs, or rehabilitation services for those suffering from addiction, because that's "our money." Or we may say, "Why are we spending money protecting another country? Let's keep it all here!"

I see it when I drive through suburbs, some studded with palatial homes—most of which hold a family of five, max. There seems to be this ingrained ambition to hoard space, separateness, and status, and a lack of commitment to preserving and sharing. We seem to forget, time and time again: there is enough opportunity to go around. And if that wasn't always true before, then certainly advances in technology, education, and healthcare make it much more certain today.* Plus, when other people are protected and have their basic needs met, as discussed in chapter five, everyone is safer and better off.

If we're concerned about where we are going to get the money, maybe we could reclaim some from our billionaires. The wealthiest Americans have the lawyers and resources to move fortunes between shell companies and offshore accounts, meaning they can evade having their fortunes accurately assessed for the IRS. Or maybe we could trim the federal government's spending a tad. We recently placed an order for one hundred B-21[†] bombers at a "discount rate" of $550 million each—a tiny total of $55 billion.[34] The United States also spent $175 million on maintaining vacant

---

* "Humanity is now entering a period of radical transformation in which technology has the potential to significantly raise the basic standards of living for every man, woman and child on the planet," write scientists Peter H. Diamandis and Steven Kotler in their book *Abundance*.

† Each of these stealth bombers has the capacity to carry both conventional and thermonuclear weapons, which of course begs the follow-up question: What parts of the planet are we planning on gutting, and, while we are at it, what are the chances, then, that we'll die, too?

government buildings[35] and $28 million a year printing 4,500 Congressional records a day[36]—they're also available online.

What if we reallocated some of that money, maybe just one or two planes' worth, to better equip classrooms, fund more drug rehabilitation centers, or build more low-income housing?

The *scarcity mentality* is the belief that taking care of other people and having enough for yourself is mutually exclusive. It's not. It's a myth. We don't need fear-mongers to bully us into buying into their interests. The same applies to media outlets, social media algorithms, and big-box stores that are bent on feeding the scarcity mentality. Our rights, our stuff, and our freedom will not be ensured by watching a particular channel, buying a specific brand, or depriving others of basic human rights. If we think in such self-centered ways, we'll continue to destroy our communities, the planet, and our relationships abroad—not to mention our bank accounts.

As I explained in the Introduction, many astronauts have remarked on the Overview Effect: that slightly out-of-body experience of viewing our planet and species without borders, divisions, or separations. Individualism is an illusion on this tiny planet of ours. Our world belongs to all of us, and to none of us. Nothing is for you that is not also for someone else—no classroom, no lane on the highway, no grant or job opportunity. In other words: Not one of us is born exceptional.

i'll get my own damn dignity

Human beings have become very adept at hurting one another—both physically and psychologically, individually and on an international scale. What tongue-lashing arguments between sisters who know exactly where the pain points are, and international disputes that result in large-scale violence, have in common is that both are aimed at the most vulnerable parts of our humanity—our dignity and sense of worth.

Dignity comes from basic human rights being protected, and ideally secured, in some way by the government or state. It's like we looked at the scarcity mentality at a super-top level, looking down thirty thousand feet, and now we're looking at what an individual needs in their heart—in their chest, in their certainty about who they are and what they hope for themselves.

Synonyms for "undignified" include "humiliating," "shameful," and "unworthy," like the way I felt the time a bully tried to pull off my wig in eighth grade to embarrass me in front of my peers, or what my brother must have felt like when I was so mad at him that I told him my parents loved me more. We humans are great at being mean, and if you let us close enough to see where it hurts, we'll not only stab you, but then twist the knife after. "Whether we are aware of it or not," says Donna Hicks, conflict resolution expert and author of *Dignity: Its Essential Role in Resolving Conflict*, "when we inflict wounds on one another, they are meant to make us doubt the very core of who we are. They leave us with the question, 'Am I good or bad?' The truth about wounds to our dignity is that they don't go away."

Stripping people of their dignity, through isolating them or blocking their access to a stable, fulfilling life, is a common, long-used tool in warfare. And recent conflicts show that nothing much has changed over the centuries. As I write this, hospitals in Aleppo,[37] Syria, are being targeted; Rohingya Muslims in Myanmar are being systematically killed, and buried in mass graves, or being forced to watch their homes burn to the ground;[38] and in Yemen, one of the worst humanitarian crises of our time, 85,000 children may have starved to death.[39] Not one child—*85,000*.

And taking away the dignity of others isn't just a part of how conflicts play out; it's also very often their source. As Hicks explains, "In over 20 years in conflict resolution and international field work, every conflict I've seen, big and small, involved underlying, unaddressed dignity wounds."

Humans are really good at being vicious to one another.

My studies in graduate school revolved around the rehabilitation and reconciliation of children involved in armed conflict. I was especially fascinated by the transition that nine- and ten-year-olds were asked to make from being violent militia back to "normal," everyday lives. Communities would often design cleansing ceremonies as part of the reintegration process. Sometimes these practices included breaking an egg over the child's head or pouring chicken blood on their feet to cleanse their sins. These baptism-like ceremonies were important for both child and community so that the child, who was sometimes both a victim and perpetrator, would no longer be seen as "contaminated."[40] Both child and community worked together to reestablish social norms and restore the child's dignity, the child forgiving themselves and the community recognizing the child's violence was due to the failed responsibilities of adults.

We have to be careful, however, when we suggest restoring dignity to a person who has experienced trauma is a simple process; there is no simple fix. In the United States there are homeless shelters, empowerment programs, and campaigns that use the term *dignity* in their titles or mission statements. While those initiatives—be it to provide a meal or a warm place to sleep—can be necessary to sustain life, we have to be careful not to suggest that we are "restoring" someone's dignity by giving them tangible goods. Helpful? Yes! "Re-dignifying" someone? Probably not. People want jobs that pay so they can afford their own shelter and peace of mind. At the risk of stating the obvious, soup is not enough.

Poverty is the intended by-product of systems designed to exclude some to the gross benefit of others. That system yields imbalance; the system itself is not broken but rather is producing the exact results it was designed to (similar to the Constitution we discussed in chapter three). And while we sometimes talk about poverty as stripping people of their dignity, when those in power are prioritizing themselves over those who are less fortunate, whose dignity should really be under a microscope? When we allow ourselves to keep believing that it's all okay, when we tune out the suffering of others, and behave as if we're the only ones who deserve a fair shot—it is our dignity that is in jeopardy. The only way to repair our nation's dignity is to equalize access to opportunities—not by performing one-time, well-intended acts of charity, but by calling into question, and working to change, the systems that have benefitted us but that have kept the poor poor. We must push our systems to support all of us, and not just some of us.

the greater "we"

Our innate urge to be part of an "us," to feel a part of something bigger than ourselves, can be a key tool in protecting and, in some cases, restoring dignity. As john powell said, "The human condition is one about belonging. We simply cannot thrive unless we are in relationship. When you look at what groups are doing, whether they are disability groups or whether they are groups organized around race, they are really trying to make a claim of, 'I belong. I'm a member.'"[41] It's what I'm hearing in Listening Circles, too—desperation to have more of these hard conversations. To become a more authentic, welcoming "we"—a "we" that might actually be able to heal the divided "us"es.

It's becoming increasingly clear that if this country is going to shift from "us vs. them" to a "we," we have to put aside our pride—our inflated egos, desperate to protect us from our insecurity of not being perfect long enough to let other people in. Dismantling the perfection performance, necessary for us to get closer to each other, can be painful. It requires we be more vulnerable . . . and less committed to pretending everything is exactly the way it's supposed to be. It's an unfamiliar slap on the hand to be reminded that we aren't uniquely deserving of that closer parking spot, or that our kid shouldn't have more playing time on the soccer field than his peers. And that can feel scary. If our belief in our own entitlement gets challenged or torn down, it means we as white people might need to redefine parts of our identity. We might have to reclaim a part of our roots, our humanity, that our ancestors exchanged when they turned their backs on the enslaved children working their fields two hundred years ago, or that we silenced ourselves last week at the mall when we swiped our credit card for another shirt that we don't need, but that let us continue hiding in our cloud of ignorance.

We'll have to learn how to get out of our own way—get back to human, which requires holding up the mirror and changing our behavior. Rejecting the pressure to follow proper protocol and breaking the cycle of entitlement is hard yet oh-so-necessary for us all to move forward together.

It's also worth pointing out that as we look more deeply at our own perspectives and habits, and thus get into more authentic relationships, the rules that previously protected the wealthy and powerful will inevitably get adjusted. Consequently, the fears of some white supremacists'—that more voices of color will get heard and shape the world—will come true. And that prospect is more real every day, for the most positive of reasons. As powell says, when "you bring people together, they will actually learn to love each other. Some of them will marry and have children. And so it will, actually, change the fabric of society."[42]

Future Census projections state the population of people who are of mixed race will be the fastest-growing racial or ethnic group in America over the next several decades.[43] As powell points out, the legalization of gay marriage, the increased presence of Latinx people, and the continued inclusion of immigrants from around the globe, will all change the US. "The other is going to change us, but we're going to change the other. And if we do it right, we're going to create a bigger 'we,' a different 'we.'"[44] I know I'm excited about it—and trust me, so are your kids.

This is what we want the world to look like. This is part of the American story and identity that I'm proud of: many creeds and religions and races and genders and disabilities (and, and, and) have created art and science and medicine and systems (and, and, and) that have benefitted all of humanity. The collections of individuals who have come before, who are here today, and will come in the future require this diversity to thrive and push the human race—please, dear god—forward.

if we don't force it, something else will

The good news is that we already know how to drop the "us vs. them" to form a "we." When our survival depends on it, we almost instantly revert to our best, most human selves. As Rebecca Solnit points out, "When all the ordinary divides and patterns are shattered, people step up to become their brothers' keepers. And that purposefulness and connectedness bring joy even amidst death, chaos, fear, and loss."[45]

When humans are forced into the present moment by the immediacy of needing to pull drowning people out of floods or dig children out from under rubble, connection is a matter of life and death—and there is very little room left for notions of difference. As Solnit puts it, this can be a "violent gift." When we're forced into the experience of common humanity, there's a "shared experience with everyone around you, and you often find very direct but also metaphysical senses of connection to the people you suddenly have something in common with."[46] It's that Overview Effect astronauts get—without ever having to leave the ground!

Some thinkers believe human nature and society are tending toward progress, as Harvard psychology professor Steven Pinker argued in his book *The Better Angels of Our Nature.* There are also compelling arguments that such theories are naive, since violence has been a constant through human history, and by focusing on who was able to survive in the past, we often ignore those who weren't. But what we *can* determine is whether we do the work to make our own lives tend toward justice. The question is not whether we are capable of connecting with a broader community and developing a positive global identity that embraces diversity, rather than dwelling on superficial differences, but rather how we get honest enough with ourselves to do so.

We also don't have to put the pressure entirely on ourselves to find the answers. Humanity has already learned so much about how to take care of each other—we start receiving these messages early, in children's story books, and see them later on as adults, as in philosopher's deathbed pronouncements. What we need to ask ourselves is my outstanding question from chapter three: Are we ready to take what has been learned from the past and apply it to the future?

And even though I just outlined the danger of oversimplifying any group of people based solely on race, gender, or class, I do want to remind you what we learned earlier in this book: the American white woman is the most powerful political, consumer, and cultural force in the whole entire world. If you see places where our collective fabric is starting to fray, can you look in the mirror and set aside your insecurities—because you know you're not alone in this work—and conjure the bravery to raise your hand and do something about our polarized country?

We know how to break up meaningless spats: we do it all the time with our children and coworkers. We know how to speak up when we hear people talking negatively about someone we love. We know how to be fierce—like, scary fierce—when we have to protect our babies. Let me take this moment to remind you that you are on the frontlines of the fight to end this divisiveness, whether you like it or not—it's happening at your holiday dinner tables and water coolers at work and your friend's fiftieth birthday party, and on, and on, and on.

Which side of the fight will you be on? Are you smack in the middle of a fruitless effort to keep the peace, or in the trenches with us? I know you'd prefer to cheerlead someone else in this work, but unfortunately, that's my role here, cheering you on as you help bring people back to their senses.

CHAPTER EIGHT

YOU, THEM, WE

A s we have discussed, and you know intimately, we white women swallow a tremendous amount of discomfort in our relationships for the sake of keeping the peace. In one Listening Circle, a woman said, "I don't like to talk about politics with people I care about"—and in today's world, 🫤.

Research is now starting to show that white women feel isolated, lack confidence, and are desperate to avoid conflict at all costs, particularly with the conservative men in their life, who may lash out when questioned— which, though inexcusable, may partly also arise from feelings of shame, as we saw in chapter six. As one woman said in the GALvanize USA Report, "If I tried to communicate with my husband about some of my beliefs, he says, 'You've been listening to too much fake news.' I mean, he's right and everyone else is wrong."[1]

Remember the turmoil in my tight-knit family around the election? Leading into November 8, 2016, we slung memes back and forth in a private Facebook group. After the election, there was a short silence, followed by screeching phone calls to the family matriarch, asking "How could they possibly?!" and, many evenings, leaving the poor woman in tears. It can be very frightening and risky to have hard conversations with the people we care for, particularly when you feel like the harmony of the family unit is at stake.

When we choose not to engage, however, we turn our backs on a leadership role for which we are uniquely qualified. White women are in positions of extreme influence in the families they are trying to protect. The same influence is at work in the voting booth and the workplace, as well as in groups of high school girlfriends or classroom moms. But a significant part of this same demographic, as long as we've had the option, has chosen silence, for the sake of keeping things moving and getting through life's next logistics puzzle. How many more generations have to suffer because we're too intimidated to say the wrong thing—or can't be bothered?

In these moments, I always think back to the white women on antebellum plantations. How did they just stand there and watch the plight of the enslaved? Some very likely found a way to justify the abuse, but many others must have chosen silence because it was simply too much to take on. I know there were also women who fought back, helping to free the enslaved* and even sacrificing their own lives to help them escape. I see the spirit of those women still at work today, in the actions of those standing between children and Immigration and Customs Enforcement (ICE) agents; I see it in the hundreds if not thousands of women virtually leaping out of their seats to run for office; I saw it on so many determined faces the day of the Women's March; I see it at the conclusion of so many Listening Circles when the women seem to plead, "Now what?"

However, I also see women today who I imagine are similar to those who stood idly by when indigenous peoples were slaughtered and ten-year-old African girls were ripped from their mothers' arms to work in the fields many states away. These women send me private text messages raging about the state of the world, but won't post a similar statement publicly on social media or volunteer for the causes they claim to care about. I see it in the women who sit quietly in the heated discussions I have with their husbands: one part of them is dying for the conversation to be over, the other part—hanging on every single word being uttered—knows that someone has to take him on.

I could list all of the atrocities that happened on the watches of strong, well-intentioned women. I know many have tried to fight back, for instance,

---

* For instance, Sarah and Angelina Grimké, sisters who grew up on a plantation and ultimately became fervent feminists and abolitionists.[2]

by harboring refugees, taking in orphans and raising them with their love and on their dollar. Those people have existed during every humanitarian crisis in history. But I still can't wrap my head around HOW there weren't more of them and how MORE women didn't scream MORE loudly to the people that had power in their hands. I know some were too scared to speak truth to power, because they were under threat themselves;* I also realize many liked to be close to that power.

I get it: we have our own lives to look out for, and some of us have families to feed, which might require accommodating a man and his job and his boss, who are all employed by a company driven by profits, not justice. That is the social instinct, but we can't let it be the only instinct we respond to. The other one, the primal instinct—the same one that pushed millions of people to the streets in the days after the 2017 inauguration—suggests that if we as a species don't act promptly in response to the collective instinct inside that is telling us something is wrong, we might be on the brink of something catastrophic.

While people are no longer legally enslaved on plantations or in households, we know they are confined in a system that refuses them home loans and their children a quality education. And while there aren't people being carted off on trains to incinerators, as I'm writing this book there are people, many of them children, falling ill or dying in *concentration camps*† along the southern border in Texas because there isn't enough room to lie[4] down and they lack access to water.[5]

If you ever look back at the horrific moments of history and wonder, *how the hell could people let that happen?*, then let me be clear: whatever you are doing now is exactly how you would have behaved then.

Can we all link arms, metaphorically speaking, turn around to our great-great-grandmothers and all the other women who have gotten us to this exact moment, thank them, and then say, "I'm going to do better. I won't do what so many other privileged women throughout history have

---

* For some privileged white women in today's society, the potential consequences of speaking up might, frankly, be minimal: hurt relationships or angry feelings, at most. Some of us are physically safe, and able to control our own money and property. Going against one's spouse a hundred or even fifty years ago carried different weight. Women without that safety and economic security risk a much worse outcome, even today.

† "A place where large numbers of people (such as prisoners of war, political prisoners, refugees, or the members of an ethnic or religious minority) are detained or confined under armed guard."[3]

done: protect my comfort at the expense of someone else's basic human rights. That cycle stops with me."

This is a scary thing to do, because we don't know the best way forward. But we have to remember that we're reinventing our behavior patterns for ourselves as well as for the little girls and boys in our future who will already have similar tendencies encoded from an early age. And, in those moments of possible self-doubt, know you're not the only one searching for these frontlines and yanking them closer to you. So many of our sisters are stepping up to power in ways we've never been allowed to before. Come, join us.

So, the next time you dodge difficult subjects or avoid moments of confrontation—the same way other privileged women from the past have avoided conflict and let other people die because of it—know that there may be little girls and women in our future who might wish that you had been braver, right here, right now.

In the rest of this chapter, we're going to walk through a series of concrete steps and scripts for having difficult conversations, not just with others, but with ourselves, too. Doing this type of work is about healing through intensified communication with ourselves, loved ones, and those with whom we may not expect to share much common ground. Indeed, extending the kindness of an open, questioning, noncombative dialogue to other people—especially those we don't agree with—is the most revolutionary and constructive work of all.

My aim is to provide practical tools to use as we start listening with open hearts to others and inviting them to listen to us in the same manner—as, instead of calling people out, we start calling them in. We must put aside the urge to win—or maybe just redefine what winning means. We're not stirring the pot with the goal of a neat resolution or a concrete answer; rather, we want to start uncomfortable conversations for the sake of urgently needed exploration. This can be hard to fully internalize. Yet this hard work is the most essential antidote to the polarization widening the rifts in society and within ourselves.

"The intimate and civilizational questions that perplex and divide us will not be resolved quickly. Civility, in our world of change, is about creating new possibilities for living forward while being different and even continuing to hold profound disagreement." This quote is from a guide, "Daring Discussions,"[6] that I cowrote with a handful of my Women's March family to help navigate potentially explosive conversations. But while the work itself isn't easy, the rules for getting started with it are.

rules to life (as if it were this easy)

So you can start engaging with the people in your life about touchy subjects—even while you muster the confidence (life. long. work.) to instigate difficult conversations—here are five rules I've learned from working with social change activists over the years:

> **Rule 1: Ask questions.** This is the number one rule in this chapter (and, arguably, for your life moving forward). People are more interested in the questions you ask than the statements you make. Statements are all about you, but questions focus conversations on them. They'll not only deepen your understanding: they'll connect you to others, too. As Jimi Hendrix once said, "Knowledge speaks but wisdom listens."

> **Rule 2: Always stay in the curious crouch.** According to some theologians, the cornerstone of keeping a thriving Judaism alive is the practice of constant debate. A tremendous number of rabbis over the centuries spent their days debating tiny words and punctuation marks in the Torah. To debate is to continue to knead life in all its glory. Don't let the desire for understanding die down; remember, a retreat to silence often means we're drifting back into our ignorance cloud. When a debate seems intractable or even pointless, stick with it. Asking questions for the sake of understanding isn't the end of this work; it's the beginning.*

> **Rule 3: There's no easy answer.** A lot of subjects in the headlines don't have easy answers—or we'd have arrived at them sooner. There are sometimes several right answers,† or there might not be an answer at all. We can share a goal and still approach a situation from drastically different places. The goal is to hold your values while making room for those of others.

---

* It's like my three-year-old in the forever spiral of whether unicorns prefer pink or purple—we've talked in circles about that subject, with in-depth analysis and properly prepared arguments on both perspectives. When Ever allowed red into her repertoire, our heads were about to explode, but we are still committed to the discussion.

† A unicorn might prefer pink one day, and purple the next.

Rule 4: Relearn. Try to start at square one, as if you don't have any context for the subject at hand. Extend the possibility that your framework on a topic might need an adjustment. For example, learning that an anti-abortion Listening Circle participant trusts individual women, but dislikes institutions governing reproductive rights, gave me a new grasp of why she holds her positions. Be open to starting over. This isn't about throwing away your knowledge; it's about being willing to reorganize the information that you already have to understand someone else's perspective.*

Rule 5: Choose vulnerability. Ask for help. This isn't about playing the damsel in distress to bolster the ego of the person you're talking with. Instead, it's about encouraging all parties to admit to being flawed humans in a process of constant growth, to recognize the limits of their understanding, and to take ego out of the equation. This is not a weakness; instead, it is a willingness to be surprised by the consideration of another and to allow them to feel meaningfully engaged. Humans want to be there for others; we just aren't often invited in, because everyone's busy protecting their own egos.

Now that you've had a chance to absorb these guidelines, let's dive deeper into what it looks like when you put them into effect.

YOU

learn to be wrong (i'm growling in defense already)

Being wrong, hurting someone's feelings, or saying something inappropriate can all be excruciating, especially for perfectionists 🫠. Our self-disappointment and guilt can be a dangerous mix. When I screw up enough, I get particularly fragile; I long to commit to a life of silence to avoid messing up again. (First I contemplate monasteries, which I quickly discard, and then I consider committing to my current life . . . just in silence. This is when I'm being particularly mature.) Being scolded for wrongdoing, by

---

* Be willing to relearn, constantly, as Ever will have to once it occurs to her how glitter could factor into the unicorn debate.

others or—worse—ourselves, can deter us from stepping up to the plate again. The key is not to let our guilt or shame prevent us from learning from what we did wrong or trying to do better the next time. Yes, this book is written by a white, privileged, constantly recovering perfectionist. And given that I'm still licking my wounds from instances when I didn't know the right answer or was bullied for presenting a truth that wasn't welcome, being honest with myself about falling short is really hard for me.

After a public mistake, I spend hours (🌑) or years (🌑, 🌑) replaying scenes, wishing I'd had a quicker comeback or chosen different words or gestured a tad differently to suggest that none of what was happening was actually eating me alive inside. I have spent so much time wishing I had behaved differently—performed better.

Too many of us are busy luring other people's validating comments (about a recipe or a wallpaper, or the much longed-for "Look at Super-woman, juggling it all!"). We want to hear that we aced the test. So, when someone tells us that we hurt their feelings; asked an inappropriate question; used the wrong word; said something offensive or shallow based on difficult-to-navigate subjects like race, gender, or class; crossed a line; or otherwise behaved in a way that doesn't feel aligned with our understanding of our own morals, we can get rattled. We're suddenly getting graded on a test we didn't even know we were taking and likely aren't prepared for, because we didn't study this in school—heck, this book might be your first experience with some of these topics. And then, forget it—time to retreat, lick our wounds, and off to the monastery we go.

But that "A" we were looking for would've been an evaluation of the performance, not an assessment of whether we had the courage to take action to begin with. The misstep lies in our ego's tendency to center our own feelings instead of staying focused on the larger meaning of the work. I'm asking us to participate more. And while we strive to be appropriate in our timing, language, and thoughts—we can always be better—I'm suggesting the act of engaging warrants the pat on the back, no matter the grade. It's like a priest saying, "You don't have to pray perfectly at church; that is a lifetime's worth of practicing. I'm simply asking you to just show up every Sunday—let's just start there."

When you do have those inevitable foot-in-mouth moments—when you share a hurtful observation aloud, make a misplaced assumption about someone, or blurt out a blanket statement about an entire group—take a breath, apologize, *silently* talk yourself out of the corner your insecurities (and ignorance) backed you into, and keep going. Do better the next time. This work necessitates stripping back our egos and focusing on the harm caused.

People way smarter than us have no doubt told you, when you fall down, don't tap out for good; get back up. Failure isn't a life sentence. One mediocre performance—or a dozen, or a hundred—doesn't dictate how you will perform in perpetuity. And it surely doesn't dictate who you are in character—that is something we're always refining.

As my friend Reshma Saujani, author of *Brave, Not Perfect,* says, "We have to keep stepping up to the plate. We have to keep flexing our bravery muscles. The more we do, the less our failures will impact us. The more we practice bravery, the more joyful and free we'll be." If you are not uncomfortable, then you're not moving in a productive direction.

be uncharacteristically flexible

Part of the binary, blueprint-driven, perfectionist mindset has us believing that there is always a right and wrong. Yet some questions and conundrums have no clear resolution. We must get comfortable in the confusion. Sometimes I'm feeling particularly savvy about a subject, only to find out that my understanding of that subject is all wrong—like with the particularly popular, and as we know now, very inaccurate, "I don't see color" claim we discussed in chapter four. Stand corrected. Keep going. Plenty of ideologies and strategies and words evolve over time, and we have to evolve with them.* Even if something *was* "correct" one day, it might not be the next. Just deal.

"Well, what is it?" asked one Listening Circle participant. "Black or African American?!" It can be both, I explained. African is an ethnicity, black is a race. Some black Americans have ancestors from places other than Africa, or cannot reliably trace their heritage to anywhere in particular. Some just prefer to be known as black rather than African American; others prefer to be known by their African heritage.

---

* We don't tell children to sit in "Indian style" anymore because (1) "Indian" is not how the indigenous community wants to be known, and (2) seven billion people sit cross-legged, but the term suggests that only "Indians," whether from the Native Nations or the country of India, sit cross-legged (because they don't have furniture to sit on—the root of the description); it's thus a myth. We've been corrected. Boom, done, and moving on.

I have the privilege to know the countries in Europe from which my ancestors came. At any point I could request that people, when they describe who I am, not just say, "American," but instead say Russian, Romanian, Swedish, Scottish, Irish (I'm a mutt, I could go on) American, because that is part of my identity, too.* Some people who are Christian are perfectly happy being known as that; others prefer to clarify their specific denomination—Catholic, Protestant, Coptic, Methodist, Episcopalian, Congregational, and so forth. Similarly, there is a spectrum of ways to identify gender and sexuality that may or may not evolve throughout a person's life. Human beings get to decide what they want to be called and when. When I'm not sure, I often just ask people how they want to be identified.

If different people identify in different ways, how do you always have the "right" language? You don't. You do the best you can with what you already know, and allow your understanding to change and be flexible, depending on context. You ask for clarification (but see the next section for a big caveat). There's no one right answer you can learn or know; you can only get better at understanding and responding to more people's experiences. This is one area where we are going to be corrected our whole lives; let's welcome that as the opportunity it is.

Part of the process of being an engaged citizen is building stamina for grappling with constantly evolving rules. I'll say it again: there is no end to this learning. While that may seem exhausting, it can also be incredibly rewarding. You can strive for excellence and also welcome the world's helpful editing, too—like yoga or sex, we're always in development. Maybe, like me, you'll find new freedom in the lack of exactness within this ongoing conversation; we're all students together, constantly learning from each other. You can never ace this test, but you *can* perfect your willingness to learn.

This is the work we were cut out to do. Our understanding of anything at all is incomplete, at best, but we should always strive to make our understanding more complete.

---

* Some black Americans have ancestors from places other than Africa. Others can't trace their heritage to a specific part of the continent. As is true for all of us, they each get to decide whether they want to be known by their African heritage or to choose some of the words that signal racial identity in the US, such as "black" or "brown," or something else. It is up to them.

guilt to Google

For years I wondered how I was supposed to understand the challenges that people of color face if nobody was willing to teach me. I was blessed to have women of color and from different demographic groups who were willing to offer me guidance, but they also reminded me that it wasn't their job to educate me.

I remember one conversation in particular, the evening after the 2016 presidential election. I was among activists of color who were as shocked by the outcome as it seemed the entire world was. One black woman, with tears streaming down her face, said, "It is not my job to educate white people any more! They're not listening!" I kept thinking, *If she doesn't help us, how the hell are we going to know what to do?*

It wasn't until I was trying to educate a male friend about the effects on women of well-intentioned men's nonetheless misogynistic* behavior that I understood what that tearful activist was talking about. I spent hours talking and emailing with my friend, trying to explain to him the gauntlet women constantly navigate in relationship with the men in their lives, particularly in social and professional spaces. He asked me over and over to prove with new facts the pain women shoulder, and I opened up old scars of verbal and sexual abuse (which I prefer to only revisit in safer spaces, on my own terms) to use as evidence in a desperate attempt to help him "see." Whether I succeeded or failed is still unclear: the point is, it demanded a *lot* of my energy.

How tired and unvalidated I felt from helping just one man understand how and why the #MeToo movement applied to all women—by calling him in, rather than calling him out—left me with a new appreciation for the burden I was putting on people of different faiths, races, classes, genders, or disability status every time I need to be corrected or casually request a conversation. Also—and I'll be a broken record about this—women and others from all backgrounds have been raising their voices for generations, and the privileged among us often choose to ignore them, convincing ourselves why their claims aren't universally applicable. It's unfair to expect marginalized people to revisit on command the harm that's been done to

---

* Kate Manne, a Cornell University philosophy professor, defines "misogyny" as the punishment of women who defy the patriarchal status quo (and the reward of women who reinforce said status quo). In other words, misogyny is a consequence of a patriarchal system that also enforces that system.[7] When a man rolls his eyes when a discussion of maternity leave is raised at work, that's misogyny.

them, just because we're finally ready to listen. We need to tackle our own urge to refute their positions or put their perspectives on trial.

What I've learned is that I should not ask anybody who might be suffering under systems of oppression to answer questions that can be answered by first putting my Google search bar to work.

If my male friend had spent fifteen minutes internet-searching for one of the, I don't know, twenty-five thousand articles about gender-based discrimination or domestic abuse, he could have spared me the exhaustion of walking him through the lived experiences of so many women on the planet.

In other words: Don't ask me to guide you through Alopecia 101; don't tell me, wide-eyed, that you "can't imagine" what it's like; instead, do a little googling on your own or when I'm not looking, and let's spend our time together having heartfelt conversations about what it's like to live in a vain society when you're bald.

The right answer might not be the top hit when you first plug in questions like: *Why shouldn't I use the word "articulate" in describing a person of color?* or *What's the difference between* queer *and* trans? or *Do people of short stature prefer* dwarf *or* little person? But dig in there, nevertheless*: scroll, read, reflect, and you'll find many perspectives by people who have volunteered educational materials on their own terms. And, remember, despite educating yourself, understand that individuals are the experts of their own lives; different groups of marginalized people have different opinions on how they would like to be described or what justice looks like for them and their communities. You should never contest an individual on the terms and experience of their own identity, regardless of what you've been told or found in your research.

Our conceptions about race, gender, class, and other facets of identity are learned and shaped over time, just like they are with something like religion. If you are of the Christian faith, and you choose to teach your children about Jesus, you don't do it just once—you do it over many years, even a lifetime. When your child is three, you might not focus on the crucifixion, but instead on the major moral messages that define your relationship with Him.

The evolution of society and our understanding about not just ourselves but every community of individuals is ever changing. This book, for example,

---

* 📖. To help guide this ever-evolving conversation, I will be regularly updating all of my social media channels with resources, and linking to leaders whose voices we should listen to and follow.

is time-stamped, the ideas suspended in air from the day it's published; but because there is so much debate, discovery, and evolution about every one of these subjects, it will likely require a revised edition further down the line. But we are here with what we know now—let's build off of it.

THEM

now or never

There will be moments when we see harm happening in real time, and we'll need to resist our peacemaking tendencies and instead do something about it. It's risky to challenge someone who is saying something insensitive about race, gender, religion, class, or disability. As I've made a point to confront my own biases, I've increased my ability to be brave and gently but firmly point out the biases of others, particularly when I don't want to be the one to confront them and even if the audience is larger than I want it to be.

I'll go to my favorite tactic—asking questions to grab ahold of the conversation or an unclear moment. (Have I mentioned this is the secret weapon?) I'll say, "I'm confused" (be vulnerable, let the other person "save"* you), "Where did you get that idea from?" Often the other person will try to pivot and back out of the conversation with some version of, "C'mon, it was just a joke!" or the incredibly demeaning bluff, "Really? Are you serious? Chill."† (Yes, I'm always serious about this work.)

Depending on the circumstance, the audience, and everyone's safety, I continue to engage, asking more questions, even though my natural impulse is to walk away. If I'm in a really generous mood, I might offer a shared experience of a time when I used to have the same opinion: "I've been there before. I totally get what you're saying. I've spent a lot of time recently learning about different perspectives and life experiences, and my outlook has shifted—here is what I think . . ."

As the situation and stakes allow, sometimes you can table the conversation until you're feeling on firmer ground—say, later that evening or the next day—so that you can approach the other person more calmly or when

---

* But be authentically curious. While you might know a statement is inappropriate, asking why they think it *is* appropriate may help them see why it's not.

† By which they essentially mean, "Oh no, she might be right and now I have to make her feel stupid to get out of this corner I'm backed into."

you think they may be more receptive: "I've been wrestling with something you said/did the other day and I couldn't quite figure out why, but now I know. Do you have a few minutes for a quick chat?" I then typically stumble through my feelings, using some of the tactics from this chapter.

I'd be surprised if you were proud of how you performed in your first few attempts to push back against an idea that you know to be wrong. My own first at-bat was in a FedEx parking lot, after I saw a car with a number of inappropriate bumper stickers. I stumbled through explaining my concerns to the driver and passenger as they were getting in the car—why the "Women belong in the kitchen" sticker didn't seem to reflect the values we all share. I ended up getting emotional, snot included (as I was rummaging in my jacket pocket for a tissue that definitely wasn't there). The conversation ended with them speeding out of the parking lot while giving me the finger. My heart was racing for an hour afterward, and I replayed the conversation over and over with more refined and piercing arguments. Though I had been less coherent than I'd wanted, I knew just having done it was a turning point for my confidence regarding my place on the new frontlines. I knew firsthand what it felt like to challenge dangerous ideas in everyday scenarios—and as it turned out, I could get through it. I knew I wouldn't be so intimidated next time.

There is a big difference, in terms of stakes (they're higher) and safety (it depends), between confronting a stranger in a parking lot and correcting a loved one's language across the dinner table. Even so, when these moments do arrive, I can guarantee it will be when you're least prepared and most exhausted, and really don't feel like engaging. It's like how kids always find the most inappropriate times to ask life's most difficult questions. Ever did this recently, while I was unloading the groceries from the car. "When people die, why can't you just plug them in like a phone?" she asked. Perfect timing.

We have to engage, even when it's inconvenient, because a lot of people in this country, as we discussed, don't have the access, or the safety, to have these types of urgent conversations.* Speak your truth even if your voice shakes 🫱, you cry 🫱, and you're scared 🫱.

After one Listening Circle, a participant and I ran into her husband, who was out walking the dog. He asked how the conversation went, and she was bursting with ideas, trying to stumble through an explanation of

---

* Be safe. Don't confront potentially violent strangers.

all that we had just uncovered. And then, in the midst of her efforts, she stopped herself, turned to me, and said, "Well, Jenna, you just explain it to him. You're better at it."

While she was right that I had a bit more experience explaining concepts like white supremacy and patriarchy to an audience, it isn't as helpful for me to share our experience with her husband. Just as you can—and should—lean on friends and teachers, she could have enlisted me for help. But if she uses her own words, the ideas are more likely to resonate with him. He already knows and loves her, which makes her a much more powerful messenger than just another woman he doesn't know who has her own agenda.

Wrestle that self-doubt; don't shy away from where you are in this type of self-development work. Be honest with yourself and your audience. If you have a moment to share a new fact or insight, put it in your own words. I'm a pro at saying, "I might stumble through this . . ." before I try to dive into a subject that I'm still learning; I also ask the listener "to forgive me as I try to articulate this [fill in the blank]."

However, it is worth remembering that there *are* times when we may not be the best and most effective messenger. For example, I was recently with a number of friends, and one of them was questioning a recent #MeToo allegation. One of the men in the party, when building an argument, was using an analogy that absolutely did not work. Some of the women at the table pushed back on his response. Several looked at me, knowing I'd be chomping at the bit, but instead I started kicking Jeremy, my husband, under the table.

He gave me a slightly annoyed look, which I could understand; I'm tired of having these conversations, too. But he knew that my kick meant I thought our friend would listen to him, another male, more than he would listen to the women at the table. It's not that the man with the poor analogy didn't have respect or admiration for his female friends, or that he isn't horrified by the state of the world. But it seemed impossible for us, women, to bring him to a place where he could understand our grief. With this particular man, I knew that having another man put into words a woman's experience was the best way to ensure the point resonated.* The women at

---

* People like this—who have worked to identify their blind spots—can be useful in educating others who are unwilling to engage. It's like me and writing this book: I was once a white lady who "didn't see color"; today, I might be a helpful messenger for those who think the way I once did.

the table could reason with or scream at him all day; however unfortunate, the voice of a fellow man carried weight that ours didn't.

It's important that we hold other people accountable for speaking up, too—they might just need a gentle nudge (or kick under the table) to be reminded that we are all in this together. Sadly, I find that men often resist less strongly if another man protests an offensive joke or statement, so I don't hesitate to give Jeremy a strong stare when he needs to step in, too.

center vulnerability like a fruit basket

Tempers can easily flare during uncomfortable conversations. If a resolution is not in sight—often the case at times like these—there is inevitably an element of friction or frustration. But as long as we resist being manipulated into a binary or partisan battle, these conversations can also be some of the most productive and insightful of our daily lives.

Rebecca Traister describes her own strategies for getting through a difficult conversation: "I say, 'I really care about our relationship, so tell me, can I push back on something right now? Or is that too much for you?' I let them decide: Can they hear it or not? And then, once they hear it, I tell them, 'When I hear you say something like that, I think you're obscuring what really happened, so can we look at that together?' And then afterward I say, 'I'm appreciating that we have a relationship that's based in honesty,' just to start to shift what's happening. In the end, my actions are driven by my own need for integrity, not a need to correct or change someone else."[8]

For most of my professional life, I've trained with a communication coach, Charlie Hauck, who has gotten me out of a number of . . . binds, shall we call them?* Along the way, he has shared some strategies for defusing one constant in our lives: really tense, fact-slinging conversations, of the type we'd never need to have if we were all actually perfect. The key is to navigate these conversations from a place of curiosity, not just so others feel heard but so you can genuinely understand where they are coming from and move forward together. We're constantly making assumptions about why people believe the things they do; instead, let's get clarity so we can have smarter, more compassionate and productive exchanges.

According to Charlie, there are three main steps to starting these conversations:

---

* Breaking up with boyfriends, quitting jobs, etc.

1. *Ask for permission to have the conversation.* Something like, "Hey, I want to have a conversation with you. Can you spend an hour with me sometime? It's okay if you tell me it's too uncomfortable or you don't want to talk about it." Chances are they'll agree to talk, because most humans want to help other humans. In the event that they are unwilling, gently keep trying. Even though this can be hard to do, we have to help hold each other accountable for the work that our ancestors didn't do.

2. *Tell them (again) that they might be uncomfortable with the discussion.* Human beings have a greater capacity for discomfort or pain when they know what's coming. Historically, people have always hated going to the dentist. Then the American Dental Association realized that, if dentists gave patients a heads-up, explaining the procedure step by step, they didn't have to strap patients to their chair anymore when the drill revved. Humans can withstand a lot when they are given advance warning and know what to expect—that's as true for emotional discomfort as it is for physical discomfort.

3. Finally (here's your black-belt move), *plop your vulnerability smack in the middle of the table like it's a fruit basket—by starting with an apology* (stick. with. me. here): Apologize* in advance for not knowing how to perfectly navigate a complicated conversation. Remind them that you are eager to *listen* and *learn* even though you might stumble over your perspectives and language. Ask them, "Is that okay?"—let them "rescue" you.

Drawing from these tactics, here is a script of sorts, should you want concrete language for navigating sensitive conversations. When I'm on a call having these types of discussions, I always have the following guiding sentences laid out in front of me:

1. For the millionth time, *lead with questions*. They are more powerful than statements—always. The most powerful questions are the ones that invite the participants to the other side of the table (or through the phone) to come and rescue you from confusion and curiosity. Ask them to help you see their point of view:

---

* Which feels *beyond* infuriating for Type-A American-born perfectionists, particularly when we've convinced ourselves, whether it's true or not, that we know how to navigate the world.

- "I'm sure I'm missing something about this. Can you take some time to explain your view so I can see what you are seeing?"
- "I have a problem." "I need your help." "It's my fault for not getting this." (You're lifting responsibility for any lack of clarity off their shoulders, a place they don't want it to sit. This shouldn't be done as a disingenuous "trick": it's a way to set aside any defensiveness and focus on the task at hand.)
- "I don't quite understand. Can you give me more details?"
- "I'm afraid that my answer will upset you. What should I do?" I use this one a lot. It gives people the heads-up that they won't be pleased with my response, which never ends up being as bad as they then think it is going to be. Remember: A heads-up about discomfort or awkwardness keeps tension contained.

2. *Put your confusion on the table first.* "I'm struggling with something." Boom, vulnerability. It's your ace card.

3. *Don't engage in a fact war.* You can cherry-pick academic research* to support any agenda. Not using examples might feel counterproductive when there is so much evidence about the suffering of others that could make powerful arguments. The problem is, you can't start any constructive conversation with any human on the planet with, "Here is a long list of all the reasons you are terribly wrong." It would be like asking an Orthodox Jew and a Baptist to engage in a conversation about faith and then kick off the conversation by asking whether Jesus was the Messiah. Everyone has their soundbites that keep them, arguably, more firmly positioned on their side. When you start slinging facts, you give the person one option: agree or disagree. Unless you are the only leading expert in the whole entire world on a subject, someone can always find evidence to refute your claims. Start with broad questions and if the conversation is calm and moving forward, sure, add a few key statistics that might help clarify your point.

4. *Remember: You're not there to change someone else's opinion.* This is counterintuitive, and may sound like I'm giving a pass to bigotry or hate

---

* The reward system in academic research incentivizes groundbreaking results over rigor. Consequently, outcome switching in clinical trials seems to be a newly admitted, serious problem. The top five medical journals from 2015–2016 were reviewed to see if they misreported findings, and it was shown that only nine of sixty-seven trials were accurately reported. It seems that researchers weren't reporting data that might not support their argument.[9]

speech, but please stay with me. The philosophy behind this "inviting through questions" approach lies in the belief that the most productive way forward is engagement itself, not who can out-debate the other. Altering another person's stance will not come from strong-arming them to your side, but by encouraging them to question themselves and practice openness by reflecting those behaviors yourself. This is not a manipulative process, as tempting as it is sometimes to try and "convert" someone to your way of thinking. You're there to give the other person—and yourself—a chance to *relearn* a particular subject or experience differently. This is not about perfectly entering the conversation, perfectly convincing them you are right, and then perfectly exiting stage left. It's about relearning a position, even if it's one you are diametrically opposed to—a new opportunity to explore something that you may have thought you understood, and through that exploration, help someone else see what they might not have as well. The objective is the engagement, keeping the conversation going as long as possible: that's where the power for change can happen.

You do not have just one at-bat when you are in conversation with people, when you're refining your understanding or participating in the education of another. We, white women, don't spend a lot of time in these courageous conversations, so the moments to sneak in our perspectives and to ask the hard questions have been limited. But since the new frontline is creating space for these conversations and learnings way more often, you don't have to worry about getting it right the first time. Focus on learning. Focus on growing.

"I'm sorry"

Don't assume people, particular those in marginalized communities, who have suffered at the hands of white ignorance are going to automatically trust you because you're doing this work now. Think of it this way: just because the man you just met seems trustworthy doesn't necessarily mean you feel comfortable riding in a car with him late at night.

For this exercise, let's pretend you caused harm while talking with someone whose demographics differ from yours, and you need to apologize. Though we all theoretically learned how to say we're sorry as a child, this is a tricky task. People who are deeply affected every single day by

systemic discrimination have to deal with difficult situations and conversations more frequently than you do; as I've noted, they might be exhausted
at the prospect of one more. They put more emotional labor into our society
than you do, and an apology from a more privileged person may just open
old wounds. It can immeasurably impact their life, and we'll never really
understand their frustration over it.

Keeping all that in mind, first do some deep thinking about what you
can contribute and research current conversations about the topic, including asking close friends (who might have deeper knowledge about the
subject) how they might help you interpret your perspective and actions
differently. Then, you can reach out to the person you offended by saying,
as Robin DiAngelo suggests in *White Fragility*, "Would you be willing to
grant me the opportunity to repair the [racism, misogyny, anti-Semitism,
etc., etc. . . .] I perpetuated toward you in that conversation [or wherever/
however you did what you did]?"

You must be prepared for the person to deny your request. (If you can't
accept "no" for an answer, it's unlikely you were truly ready to hear the other
person's point of view to begin with.)

If you do get the chance to talk to someone you feel you've wronged,
tell them that you are sorry for what you did, without—and this is really
important—justifying your action in any way. You are not allowed to say
that you "just thought it was a joke" or that you were "trying to share your
opinion." Avoid long monologues about what got you to that moment or
assigning blame to others or to circumstances. You now know a lot about
your bias, but don't try to explain it away—they get it, whether it came from
textbooks, *Sex and the City*, white supremacy, blah, blah, blah. You know,
they know—let's keep going. They likely do get the many layers of your bias
and how it affects them far better than you do.

What often works best is to keep your apology simple and focused. Tell
the person that you "are working to do better" and tell them you are open to
more feedback, should they want to share.

Recently I posted something on Instagram about entertaining my kids
for the weekend while Jeremy was on a work trip. In the post I casually
called myself a "single mom" for those days I was rolling solo.

I received a comment from a woman about the flippant use of the term,
when being short a co-parent for a brief period of time does not qualify me
as single mom: essentially, "It's not the same as being totally responsible,
physically, emotionally, and financially, for a child." As much as I wanted to

say, "Yeah, but [fill in the blank with whatever excuse I might have had]," I was wrong. My response? "Thank you for the note, I really appreciate the edit. Let me know if there is anything else. The feedback must not have been easy, and I'm sorry."

I was embarrassed—ashamed of my mistake and frustrated of a light-hearted post gone wrong, particularly when I harbor such deep respect for single moms. Those feelings come with being human, and research suggests they serve as a healthy boundary check. Carry these reminders with you as you respond with maturity and grace. Remind yourself that some mistakes are inherited behaviors your ancestors sculpted, some are a life-time of unchecked biases at work,* and others are our own lazy ignorance.

That "Let me know if there is anything else" is important. Asking, as DiAngelo says, "Is there anything else I missed that is problematic?"—closing the conversation by asking if there is anything more that needs to be shared to move the relationship and learning forward—shows you care about sustaining a meaningful connection with them.

Even when I talk to friends about something ignorant I did years ago, or last week, that really hurt them, I still have a physical response when they provide feedback—and I likely always will. Recently, I was receiving feed-back, and after I hung up the phone, I gagged (lovely, I know), as though my body were rejecting something deep and vile. After a hard conversation, go to the bathroom, close a door, and let your body respond if it needs to, with silent screams or clenched fists. Think of it as your body cleansing itself of generations of white supremacy (more on that later).

Then keep going, by reminding yourself that no one gets it right all the time. In *White Fragility*, DiAngelo describes how people of color are look-ing to engage with white people around the subject of race. "What they are looking for is not perfection, but the ability to talk about what happened, the ability to repair. Unfortunately, it is rare for white people to own and repair our inevitable patterns of racism. Thus, relationships with white peo-ple tend to be less authentic for people of color."

That restorative process starts with us, with our sincere and true apol-ogy for hurts inflicted and our willingness to acknowledge how the systems that protect our privilege have benefitted us. The best apology is changed behavior. Only then can the conversation move forward.

---

* Textbooks, news outlets, tabloid magazines . . . our preachers or rabbis or swamis, or, or, or . . .

WE

if you build it, she will come

When you tell another human, "You have a seat at my table," you remind them they belong. What a gift; there are so many ways to show a person they belong.

As we learned in chapter seven, human beings yearn for community 🌐. We are longing to belong to something bigger than ourselves. Inviting people into the conversation—calling each other "in" versus calling each other "out"—is key to our survival. But that doesn't only need to happen in the wake of an awkward statement, bumper sticker, or post-election conversation. We need to share ideas and seek out the perspectives of others in our communities, throughout our lives. We're no longer allowed to go back to sleep no matter who is in the White House or how fair the world suddenly becomes. Being a citizen is active, hard, constant work.

There are many, many different ways to build community. A friend of mine, author and activist Kris Carr, did something brilliant for her fortieth birthday. She invited a number of friends to dinner and announced at the meal that, as her birthday present to herself, she was giving herself all of us. She was putting us all on one email thread, and when she had a question about mascara or an accountant or needed to vent, she was emailing us all. In other words, she manufactured a digital environment where she wanted to belong.

That group morphed naturally into something from which we all benefited. Each of us posed questions, which became more intimate as time went on. Someone would write, "My boss is being an ass and I just needed to tell someone. So now you all know. Love you ladies!" Other times people would share their most intimate pain, asking for recommendations for divorce lawyers . . . which led to drinks together that night. Others shared the grief of being unable to conceive . . . which led to suggestions of when to have sex and what special tea to drink and which color candle to light after doing both (red, apparently).

Another group of my friends are political fanatics; they read every article and listen to every podcast they can get their hands on. I'm so grateful for them. They share links to important information on a group text, some that I've seen and some I've missed altogether. Yes, we banter about weekend plans, but I can also count on these friends to send me an insightful podcast with the exact minute of the relevant point we all need to hear.

You might be wondering whether or not there are people in your life who qualify for these types of conversations. Obviously, I can't answer that for you. But I have found that we overthink the roles people in our orbit are meant to play. For example, we assume someone doesn't want to be bothered with a subject, or worry they will judge us, or that we'll look stupid to someone we respect. But often we're partly or completely fooling ourselves. That other classroom mom or new colleague a few cubicles down whom you started to befriend might be as interested in a news article about a local social issue as you are. All too often, instead of taking the trouble to find out, we opt to do nothing.

Friends and relatives with whom I've spent years talking about fluff become suddenly generous with information and perspectives just because I texted them an article link. It may feel simple and insignificant, but a gesture like this invites them to participate in conversation. You're making room for them at the table and you're telling them they belong, even if it's just the two of you figuring out what the hell is happening down the street. Doors for deeper types of relationships with different types of people will open, if you just take the first step.

We're all trying to figure out how to make the world a better place. But that doesn't mean we have to reinvent the wheel with every conversation we have. Can we focus first on coming back to each other, to make our burdens less heavy and our evolution (and joy) a collective experience?

We've been fed a particular vision of what strength looks like, but the real bravery is in being vulnerable. This allows others to do the same—to lean on each other for help outside of superficial requests. I'm concerned about the country, the world, the future, and, as it's probably clear at this point, the way we interpret the past. My "headline groups," as I call them, are their own mini-democracies: they help me see what I miss when I'm busy juggling two sniffly kids with fevers or have back-to-back meetings or school lunches to pack. I need these group emails and text chains to help me keep my head above the information overload.

My favorite part about these types of groups is their simplicity. Thank you, Steve Jobs* and the multitude of apps and devices we now use every day—we don't all have to be physically together to be in community. A quick text with a thought, complaint, or link to an article brings me quickly

---

* An organ recipient, I might add—a quick little plug for how the entire world has deeply benefitted from a liver transplant. Just saying.

into community with my sisters, who are doing their own juggling in the middle of their own circus acts.

However, the danger of relying on tech platforms for sharing info and calling others in makes it easy to look away when something is shared that makes us uncomfortable, or that otherwise isn't completely aligned with our perspective. It's easy to not jump into a heated text exchange, and instead sit the tension out for a few days. It's in these moments, though, that it is most important for us to resist the urge to be silent and the desire to avoid conflict and instead start the gentle questioning.

The other danger of having these conversations over text or email is that tone can get quickly misinterpreted on these platforms. If you think something you or someone else has said feels a bit passive-aggressive (we all have very finely tuned radars for that), pick up the phone.

One of the headline news text groups I'm on got heated about anti-Semitic tweets swirling in the news. Being the only Jewish woman in this group, I shared my messy thoughts. I was in the minority with my perspectives, and there were some difficult back-and-forths. I admit I turned away from the group for a few days, not because I was giving up but because this conversation is profoundly difficult. A few days later I responded with, "Hey, let's get dinner and continue this conversation. Too much to say on text." We picked a date, and the online conversation pivoted for the time being to my botched eyebrow wax job. What I'm saying is that we *can* juggle all the different facets of our complex lives; we can have crucial, life-changing discussions in parallel with sharing advice for finding a new eyebrow aesthetician. We are built to handle the constant juxtapositions of life, and community helps us do that.

The most rewarding communities to build and call-in are the in-person types. These are also the most intimidating, though, and can require a bit of a dance, particularly if you are looking to center complex subjects. Even with my family, who sees me in my bathing suit and all my cellulite glory all summer long, find difficult my suggestions of a "nontraditional, structured conversation about [fill in the blank of some controversial headline]."

Years ago, I was telling a close friend of mine about the Listening Circles I wanted to start having with a very specific demographic: white, middle- and upper-class women. We were standing in the kitchen during a party, and she slapped me on the arm with her cell phone and said, "What the hell are you waiting for? Go!" That evening I texted all of the women in my family who I was going to see that weekend and said, "Nine AM, women's-only coffee talk on Saturday morning . . . just to chat about . . . stuff" (what "stuff," exactly, I had no idea at the time).

The conversations I'd had with family members since the 2016 election had been unproductive, but I knew we could do better. I wanted to talk about the state of the American white woman, and since I had no full concept of where I'd land, I just led with questions. (As the Listening Circles evolved, so did the questions: *How have you disappointed yourself? What are your greatest regrets? What stereotype about you is true/false? What part of the idea of America has failed you? How do you self-sabotage?*) As we talked, I began to see my family members from a different angle. Unsurprisingly, my assumptions about their world views were shattered a bit.

That was my first Listening Circle. Could you host your own? Could you bring people together and pose similar types of questions for the sole purpose of bringing people back into authentic community? One message I heard over and over in the Listening Circles was how earnestly all of the participants wanted to share heartfelt conversations more frequently. If you're interested in hosting a Listening Circle in your own community, please see the Listening Circle Guide at the end of this book, and the resources online at www.raisingourhands.com.

The communication frequency in every digital or in-person group I belong to ebbs and flows. Sometimes it's a fire hose of information, tears, and LOL emojis in a single day, and sometimes it's radio silence for weeks or even months. Some groups have a short lifespan—a school year, maybe, or the time leading up to a specific event. Some groups last lifetimes. Don't put too much pressure on any one of these groups to be the new circle of friends you've been craving for a decade. Don't expect everyone to want or need the conversation and resources the same way you do. Just let these groups evolve organically; they might grow to include more people, or die because the energy wasn't right. Don't enforce your need for perfection on these communities, either.

We are in dire need of more small-d democratic* conversations in this country. Even if we don't reach a clear place of resolution, these dialogues will keep us learning and show us how to live out the values we hold dear. We barely know how to have these conversations with ourselves, let alone one another, but they are necessary to get closer to that "idea" of America.

---

* That is, committed to the free exchange of ideas, rather than the party with a donkey as the mascot.

'tis true

I may have just given you a lot of instructions, but they're just tips. You have exactly what is needed right now: keep it simple, lead with your confusion and vulnerability, and give others permission to help you see something new. Thank you again for being here.

"What if we were exactly what's needed?" Rachel Naomi Remen, author and family medicine doctor, asks. "What then? How would I live if I was exactly what's needed to heal the world?"[10]

I'm here to slap you in the arm with my cell phone and say, "What the hell are you waiting for? Go!" The next stage of your life will demand a new version of you as you seek and step up to the new frontlines. Please rise to her level—we are all waiting.

Let's draw each other closer into community. "This is the way we need to move forward in a world that is so interested in being comforted by the damp blanket of bad stories," says Irish peacemaker Pádraig Ó Tuama. "We need stories of belonging that move us towards each other, not from each other; ways of being human that open up the possibilities of being alive together; ways of navigating our differences that deepen our curiosity, that deepen our friendship, that deepen our capacity to disagree, that deepen the argument of being alive. This is what we need. This is what will save us. This is the work of peace. This is the work of imagination."[11]

Acknowledging that difficult conversations need to be had—and that *we* are the ones who must have them, holding space for the complexity of issues we face and granting other people the space to share how they feel, too—is an essential step forward. As we try, and fail, and get up and try again, we need to walk the line between standing strong in our convictions and retreating into self-righteousness. What helps is remembering how vulnerable and in need of authentic human connection each of us is—even, yes, that guy in the FedEx parking lot.

CHAPTER NINE

THE FRONTLINE—HOLD

old the line. It's the easiest yet most intimidating stance.

At ORGANIZE, my team members and I sometimes used to get scathing or bullying reactions from the organ donation establishment. And when we were cut down, or being intimidated, it was tempting to just run away to do something safe, like making witty memes about the power of organ donation (we did that anyway). But instead, in those moments, someone would scream, "Hold the line!" (We were poking fun at that scene from the movie *Braveheart,* when the main character gallops on horseback in front of his army before an ensuing battle, with his face painted blue and his hair all wild, screaming the very same thing.) And instead of doing the safe thing, we'd craft a substantial, evidence-based response—we'd hold the line.

The battle against complacency does not look like we see in movies, with soft, rolling hills on a misty morning, with all of us lined up in rows. It's already happening, in the hearts and minds of so many of us. Our weapons aren't swords and rifles. They're words—ones we use to fight back against jokes about "running like a girl," or how we make excuses for our sons' rambunctious behavior, political candidates, or the messaging in traditional children's storybooks like the *Berenstain Bears,* in which I'm sadly finding Mama Bear permanently busy in the kitchen. In her blue polka-dot dress.

These moments—the joke, the threatening emails from the angry donation establishment, story time—are some of the tiny frontlines we walk up to every day. And we must always, exhausted and confused or not, hold the line. Because if we stay silent, we guarantee that we are perpetuating norms we've inherited that still cause harm.

There are some suggestions for immediate use in everyday life in this chapter, like catching the jokes that are hovering close to an inappropriate line and leading with your vulnerability: "I don't understand why that's funny." We can spontaneously rewrite the stereotypes out of traditional stories—Jeremy and I always talk to our kids about the meeting Mama Bear Berenstain had that day in Washington, DC, and how Papa Bear just finished baking banana bread for brother and sister bear. We can start shifting this mountain of bias and division in tiny, quiet, but immediately impactful ways.

Then, of course, there are the heavier tasks, the ones that require all of us to think, question, donate, and vote differently. The new level of mindfulness we must all arrive at—the one where we're not just thinking about incremental changes but work that is perspective shifting and narrative adjusting. The main tenet here is to adopt an inquisitive and intentional approach; take the time to question why things function the way they do, and make choices that align with how you believe the world should look. Don't automatically trust people and institutions just because it's the easiest route and you know of no other path—one does exist.

Humanity has been in this predicament before, with the emergence of a new way of thinking that challenges the very basis of everything we believe. Humans used to believe that the ocean tides were contingent on Poseidon's mood, that infertility meant the god Juno was pissed at you, and that volcanoes, home of the god Vulcan, erupted on days when he was cranking out lots of blacksmithing assignments. We invented countless systems (gods, in the Greeks' case) to explain the unexplainable and to create a sense of order and function in societies. As scientists realized that the tides arose from the gravitational pull of the moon, identified key times of the month to conceive, and understood the pressure of the molten-core layer of the earth, our reliance on that portfolio of gods for explanations decreased. All of these discoveries put people like Poseidon out of a job. Still, when long-held beliefs suddenly no longer make sense, things can get tense; power shifts are messy. And that, my friends, is exactly what is happening today. The tectonic plates of our society are moving, and we know what happens when earthquakes hit: buildings crumble, sometimes with innocent lives sleeping soundly inside.

This is the frontline, the one we are all standing on, and I'm on horseback, pacing up and down, though Ever would probably prefer a unicorn (though, as discussed, purple or pink hair is still unclear), asking you to hold the line, because to topple white supremacy and the patriarchy, a few key battles lie ahead.

my search for the "answer"

I started work on this book because I was looking for an answer to a question I kept asking myself, once I realized the conflict of values raging around us: What am I supposed to do right this instant? My perfectionist, master-the-checklist personality was searching for coaches, people who didn't have the same life experiences as I did, politicians, tarot card readers*—anyone who was going to hand over some instruction manual for how to live authentically. I was looking for someone to help me fix what I felt responsible for as a white woman growing up in these United States. I was looking to pay down the moral debt of being a person who continues to experience privilege because of my race.

The answer to how we can best fight this battle, I learned, is more than simply a set of moves or a field strategy. It is a mindset shift, an adjustment of our long-held assumptions and reactions. And while there are some short-term changes we can make, we, as white women residing in the United States, have to reset our understanding of our identities. It's time to turn the prism through which we see ourselves in the world so we can more deeply understand our position in society and what responsibility comes with that type of influence. We must shift our perspective, and I hope this book does that for you, indefinitely.

As you know, and as I can't say enough, the work I—and you—have to do is right in front of us—right there in the room you're sitting in. It's not just in the halls of Congress or on the streets in protest. The frontline is also in the small moments, in conversation with a semi-estranged neighbor or in the discussion with your brother about his confusion over the trans community wanting to use the bathroom of their choice or crossing the street

---

* Let me be honest—I have a full Rolodex of psychics, astrologers, and seers (yeah, that's a thing—like full-blown people who say they can see and predict eeeeevvverything).

when you see a black man approaching, locking your car doors or grasping your purse a bit tighter.

I know that you're on the frontlines in a way you might not want. I get it: raising my hand to do this work is a lot harder than sipping that margarita that's waiting for me on my best friend's kitchen counter while we check in on ex-boyfriends on social media. I also acknowledge that what I'm proposing is not straightforward, and that there will be times that all of the trying you're doing will not feel like enough. It's like when you decide to get fit and start planning your workout schedule 🏋 and someone says, health is not just about the treadmill, it's about that shot of Starbucks vanilla simple syrup you keep pouring in your coffee.

We need to challenge our need for a blueprint, and also remind ourselves that it's not always about *doing* what we believe to be traditional activism or our civic duty—like having discussions about end-of-life wishes.* Sure, vote, march, donate money, call your elected officials—that's important, just like, yes, running on that treadmill is important, too. But in order to fully address inequality, we must pay equal attention to the other frontlines, the ones we might not have been looking for until now: our thoughts, who we hire, where we donate that money, how we respond to a passing comment, the roles and discussions we model for the next generation, what kinds of conversations we're having (or not having) and with whom, and so on.

I'm not asking you to stop organizing fundraisers for your kid's pre-school.† Instead, I'm asking you to be aware of the work you can do in spaces you are already intimately familiar with: your head and your home.

---

* 80% of our medical costs in this country are incurred during end of life. Please stop avoiding the inevitable and have end-of-life conversations with your next of kin. Let's talk with each other about what we want our deaths to look like. 96% of the citizens of La Crosse, Wisconsin, have an "advance directive," a document outlining their end-of-life wishes, compared to just 30% nationally.[1] La Crosse residents spend 32% less than the average Medicare patient in the last six months of their lives.[2] Additionally, there is a significant decrease of caregiver stress, anxiety, and depression after the sudden death of a loved one when they know the deceased's end of life wishes.[3]

† As a former teacher who spent almost a quarter of her salary on supplies, I'm so grateful to the parents who offered to show up with cannolis and do a fifteen-minute segment on their Italian family legacy, or the times I needed to give certain students special attention and parents and grandparents occupied the rest of the class with a story for ten minutes. Those tiny gestures mattered and helped. I am also posing the question, though: is there another school that could use your attention? Yes, your kids' teachers are exhausted, but

There's more than one way to do this work. Some people are excellent conveners. Great! Do (even) more. Invite groups of people to your home to have conversations about issues (maybe even seek out an expert to join) and "what to do next." Be a catalyst for change by creating spaces for people to communicate with each other. Other people are givers—and have the means to give. If that's you, donate money to organizations run by people who don't look like you in places that aren't within arm's reach and where nobody expects you to go.

In short, I am asking you to remember that our power comes from our ability to participate in ways we haven't been compelled to do so, to stop being oblivious to the frontlines and pull them into our lives, to the very tips of our toes. I'm asking you to admit our shortcomings and work to understand our blind spots and biases; to raise your hand for courageous conversations with people, both those you are close with and those whose names you might not know; to build community with one or two people, or cast the net wide and invite more people in. Most importantly, confront the new frontline that challenges the idea that we are "all knowing," make that effort to work for deeper clarity, and be corrected along the way. Learn how to say, "Sorry, I got that wrong. What can I do to make it better?"

This requires that we question it all. Whose voice hasn't been considered in the establishment of certain laws* or your maternity policy at work? Who is not sitting in that board room? Where was the voice of that exhausted single mom that you know would have loved to be at the PTA meeting—can you send her notes? That youth soccer registration fee of $37—could you pay that for a few other kids who aren't able to afford it, even if they are better athletes and will get more playing time than your children? Mustering the stamina to question spaces and systems we haven't yet takes courage, and "courage is courageous," as Ana Maria Archila said in regard to her bravery in confronting Senator Jeff Flake in the elevator during the confirmation hearing of Supreme Court Justice Brett Kavanaugh. She credited the strength she drew from all of the other protestors

---

speaking from firsthand experience, the more resource-scarce the community, the more difficult the teaching task is, because you're juggling the side effects of people who've been neglected in ways that are different from those in the suburbs. I promise, it's harder for those teachers and they need your help.

* Every reproductive law has primarily been proposed, designed, and passed by men.

filling the streets and halls of Congress for giving her the courage to speak her truth, despite feeling petrified.

Take turns being brave so we can drag each other through. If the ways our systems are working aren't up to your standards for everyone (which they're not), it's not enough to complain and point fingers. It's time to do something about it.

we can do this

Yes, that is a rallying cry. We have been complicit, and so have our ancestors, but we also come from strong stock: capable, willing, and phenomenal people. You are the descendent of a long line of women who carried us all to this moment—even if you've been raised in a country that hasn't given some of your female ancestors the recognition they deserve.

We have talked a lot in this book about what is holding us back—about the expectations placed on us by others and by ourselves. We've internalized that unless we can perfectly enter a conversation, offer a winning argument, and gracefully exit, then it's best if we don't participate. That's why almost half of white women—48%—"find it hard to express or defend [their] political views,"[4] according to GALvanize USA.

But now you know better. You know that you're not alone in the way that you feel. You know that you're part of one of the most educated demographics in the world. And if you still don't feel like you know enough about what you want to talk about, remember that you have more resources in that smartphone in the palm of your hand than were in the Apollo 11 module that landed on the moon. You can learn.

For generations now, women have been seizing more and more opportunities to prove that we belong—in the conversation, on the podium, on the screen, in the Capitol, behind the Roosevelt Desk in the Oval Office—regardless of the fact that the Constitution makes approximately zero mentions of a "her" or "she." It's still worth remembering that part of the reason why white women are plagued by the belief that we aren't capable and that we don't belong is because the women who looked like us and who accomplished monumental achievements are often footnotes in our history, if present at all. White women are proportionally well represented in textbooks, compared with women of color, but Listening Circle participants still struggled to cite any. "Who are your female heroes?" I often ask them. Their first response was typically a clarifying question because . . . you know, they're buying time to chase the perfect answer. When I push them, they'll start listing predominantly women of color—Oprah, Sojourner Truth, Harriet Tubman—all obviously women worthy of the "hero" accolade. When I ask if they have any white female heroes, some will say Hillary Clinton or their moms, but most just stare blankly and wait for me to move on to the next subject.

Historically, white women have had more freedom and thus, more power, than women of color; they have been able to climb into different professional and political spaces with greater ease. Nevertheless, white women still weren't often allowed to take credit for their accomplishments and therefore aren't often memorialized in visible places.* Men have won prizes, became idolized for breakthrough discoveries, earned incredible wealth, and cemented themselves in the boys' club that is our history books. All the while, women of genius, dexterity, artistry, and resourcefulness were footnoted, at best—and this is why, when I ask white women about their *white* female heroes, I often get blank stares. You can't be what you can't see.

For example, British chemist and X-ray crystallographer Rosalind Franklin captured a breakthrough image of the structure of DNA that was stolen from her and shared with two other scientists, James Watson and Francis Crick, who later went on to win the Nobel Prize for their work on the double helix. Rosalind's name was barely attributed to the study.[6]

Hedy Lamarr, in addition to being a well-known actress in the '30s and '40s, also developed a radio guidance system that the United States military stole, patented, and incorporated into a host of new weapons systems. Oh, and it was her work that is the foundation for Wi-Fi and Bluetooth wireless technologies.[7] Do you know her name? My guess is no.

Or, Anna Jarvis who created Mother's Day—a day she hoped would mobilize mothers in community parks to discuss peacemaking efforts. She was inspired by her own mother, who organized mothers from the Confederate and Union sides to work together toward ending the Civil War;

---

* Quick anecdote: Central Park has twenty-three statues of historical figures, and not one of them is a real woman—Alice, from Lewis Carroll's *Alice in Wonderland*, is the only female figure memorialized in the park. Elizabeth Cady Stanon, Susan B. Anthony, and Sojourner Truth are scheduled to be added by the end of 2020.[5]

however, President Wilson was the one who made it a national holiday, so he gets the high-five.*

Another theory is that white women continuously chose traditionally safe forums to raise their activist voices or break new ground professionally, which is why the accomplishments of their counterparts, women of color—who were often forced to operate outside of societally approved lanes—are more radical and noteworthy. Though overused, the quote "well behaved women seldom make history" could not be more true. Rather than joining the protests and divesting from the systems that historically oppress people, white women attempted to work from within these systems, appealing to the dormant ethical consciousnesses of their male superiors—all attempts that ultimately ended in vain even when they were successful. White women are coming to understand what women of color have known for centuries: you cannot expect the same people and systems that keep you down to also free you. Instead, to be a trailblazer, you have to deviate from the path already set before you and step outside of the usual, well-ordered power system.

Ultimately, recognizing achievements is about so much more than points on the scoreboard. As Eric Chase reminds us, in reference to the labor strikes of the 1800s when protesters lost their lives resisting unfair working conditions, we benefit from the legacies of brave revolutionaries every day. "Truly, history has a lot to teach us about the roots of our radicalism. When we remember that people were shot so we could have the 8-hour day; if we acknowledge that homes with families in them were burned to the ground so we could have Saturday as part of the weekend; when we recall 8-year old victims of industrial accidents who marched in the streets protesting working conditions and child labor only to be beat down by the police and company thugs, we understand that our current condition cannot be taken for granted—people fought for the rights and dignities we *enjoy* [my emphasis] today, and there is still a lot more to fight for. The sacrifices of so many people can not be forgotten or we'll end up fighting for those same gains all over again."[9]

---

* Meanwhile, greeting card and floral companies paid to keep Jarvis in a mental institution at the end of her life because she was, you guessed it, kicking and screaming that the day was being hijacked for corporate profit, when she meant it to focus on gratitude for and peacemaking by women.[8]

Though few of us today know who those demonstrators were, we stand on their shoulders when we freely take our children to the playground, drive to the store to return an item, or casually walk into the booth to vote for president.

Every step *we* take will also support a thousand descendants. If we take this for granted and overlook the responsibility to future generations, we and our granddaughters will end up fighting for those same gains all over again, and they, too, might shake their heads at our delusions, the same way we do when we think of the Greeks with regard to Poseidon controlling the tides.

The right to live in a democracy requires civic participation that is often inconvenient or uncomfortable—particularly when it requires a perspective shift that can't be solved just by pulling a voting lever. Our survival as a nation, now more than ever, demands we face hard truths about both the problems and the benefits of our society. The frontlines have moved into our homes and workplaces and schools, into our very psyches, and we have no choice but to step up and throw down, in ways that are uniquely ours, by having the difficult conversations with ourselves and with the people we love.

My conversations in Listening Circles across this country prove that white American women are changing in a way that could shift the course of human history. We are seeing what we haven't before. We are hearing the pleas of our fellow sisters in closer proximity and more comprehensively than previous generations did.

Though these pleas aren't any different from the ones made in previous centuries, we are just willing to listen differently—in part due to our political climate, but also because we have greater proximity to these voices, thanks to the internet. The perspectives we casually hear are no longer restricted to our often-homogeneous neighborhoods.

And we are seeing more change makers that do look like us—women like gun-safety champions Shannon Watts and Nicole Hockley, as just two examples of white women who are living, sledgehammer-swinging examples of our activist foremothers, showing through their brave actions and words the conviction and strength that we have in our bones, too.

Now that we're familiar with the blueprints around us, it's time we commit to breaking new ground, so that we can build on all the work of those women behind us. Amy Richards, a third-wave-feminist writer, puts it very clearly: "Feminism's crusade remains unfinished because examining the 'personal' is far more threatening than condemning the political." By reading this book, you have admitted that there is a problem. You've raised your hand in all of your complicity and, now, bravely, you've committed to set us all on a new course. Let's turn now to the things we actually *can* do—an array of actions we can take together to shake our dependency on ignorance for good.

the white supremacy diet

As I mentioned, the transition into this part of the book is hard for me, because I'm still so eager to find and follow a blueprint. The Type-A perfectionist in me wants someone else to design a clear set of rules for me to follow. I want to know that the answer is out there, within arm's reach, if I just worked a bit harder, performed a bit better . . . if I were just a tad more perfect.

We know now that part of the system that we have to break is our search for a perfect answer all of the time; that's literally been the objective of every major religion, university, and hallucinogenic drug that has ever existed. Unfortunately, those easy answers don't exist. This is the frontline—fighting against our reliance on the blueprint and working so hard to keep our heads out of the cloud of ignorance we've been living in—and we must hold ourselves there in perpetuity. That's why, instead of delivering some perfect solution (which I really wish I had for you), I'm going to suggest we go on a diet—a white supremacy diet.

This may strike you as a frivolous way to describe the work ahead of us (I recognize I am pushing a metaphor here, stay with me), since the task is no less grand than changing the way we think, speak, and live. But, personally, I have found it helpful to have a way to think about the concrete, everyday changes we can make. It's a place to start—not the be-all and end-all. Anyone who has tried a diet to solve all their problems, 🫤, knows it's not a cure-all. But whether a diet involves no longer eating gluten or sugar or drinking more water, it's less about the specific rules and more about deciding to take better care of your body. This diet asks you to stop doing things that you had been doing that you might have thought were insignificant or not that big of a deal—you know, the moral equivalents of eating highly processed white bread.

The surface-level rules of this diet are sometimes very specific: language that you are and aren't supposed to use, and a bare-minimum set of things that, as an American citizen, you're responsible for doing (like *actually* showing up for jury duty* and paying taxes[†]). What the diet won't do is provide detailed instructions for how to move through the heaviest, most complicated obstacles we collectively face. Because, like any diet, it doesn't make over-carbohydrated brunch buffets or gooey cheese pizza disappear from Earth forever; it only offers guidance for how to make the simple, easily identified behavior changes we can all raise our hand to make. The real tectonic shift will be the way we understand our complicity in the systems we operate and how we can work to counteract it—that's the varsity-level work.

We know no diet can provide a systemic fix for our relationship to food, but it can provide some quick ground rules for moving toward a healthier life. Just as there are immediate dos and don'ts to a successful diet, there are similar steps we can take to adjust our behaviors for a more equitable world.

Speaking of temptation, the first ingredient we have to purge from our diet is our dependency on ignorance; we must pop our heads out of that foggy cloud for good. Sometimes we seek refuge there because society is sending us messages that we're not good enough or not needed. But it's also on us to be honest about choosing behaviors that are easier and less work—marathoning reality TV versus reading a book—and I don't mean the escapist kind. I, too, get excited when I board a plane and find a tabloid magazine in the seat pocket that the cleaning crew missed. Sometimes I want nothing more than to watch the Kardashians, and yes, there are many nights I announce I'm going to bed and an hour later my husband finds me lying in the darkness, wide awake with my phone screen five inches from my face, scrolling through nothing useful. You live in a free society, and you have the privilege and right to do all of those things. But now you know that

---

* If you want the right to a fair trial, show up to jury duty. I've watched many, many white ladies with very expensive hand bags make emotional arguments to a judge about how they can't serve on a jury, they have a kid that needs to be picked up from karate practice. I have been in that position before, when eleven out of eleven babysitters aren't available. Please work really (really) hard to find a way to figure out how to show up for another citizen in their most vulnerable state. One day you might need a fair trial and you'll want everyone showing up with deliberate intentions to review the evidence as justly as possible.

† Taxes can be a loaded subject depending on the city and state where you live. My point in flagging it here is that many women in Listening Circles would reference selecting a political party based on tax policy. At risk of stating the obvious, the only reason we get ambulances when we call them or paved roads to drive to work or a military is because of our contribution to the tax pool.

by hiding in that ignorance cloud, you're turning your back on the front-line—that "checking out" of the difficult conversations, ignoring the news, and opting out of working on ourselves means other people suffer.

Our ignorance comes partially from our textbooks, news channels, and society's generations-old broken-record message that if you are financially stable and influential enough, then you earned the freedom to check out. We know full well that "making it" is largely dependent on the zip code in which we were born and the color of our skin—no meritocracy involved there. I believe that well-off people are so quick to check into the cloud of ignorance because there is a belief of invincibility (nothing can really harm me; if I'm in a rut, I can swipe my credit card or call my influential friend). We also believe that we have earned, through our own grit, a well-deserved laissez-faire life.

This is not to say that you shouldn't take moments to "smell the roses," or take deep breaths to center gratitude for the blessings you do have—that game of cards, roller coaster rides, and, what I get a lot these days, the always-on three-year-old ballet performance that requires my full attention whenever the appropriate background music starts playing. And, yes, enjoy that margarita on a breezy porch, those long walks in nature, massages, or latest TV series everyone is talking about. As you do this work, it is essential to care for yourself and figure out how to sustain your efforts. It's easy to become overwhelmed, find yourself burnt out, and sink into apathy on the other side. In doing this work, you must create and make space for joy, too—whatever it takes to remain engaged. Just don't check out too long: come back. You are needed on the frontlines next to us.

None of us has earned the right to just sit back and relax. There is simply too much to do to coast through life as if we've already won a Nobel Prize or an Olympic medal—as if our assignment is complete. Even people with extraordinary accomplishments are still on the field playing, working, moving forward. I heard it over and over from our elders in the Listening Circles: do everything you can to give back now, or you'll be kicking yourself in your twilight years. One in particular mentioned what we already know but never hurts to hear again: "Your legacy, how you leave the world a bit better, is what will outlive you and give you the greatest peace with yourself toward the end." Amen, grandma.

The longer-term white supremacy diet asks us to start using what you've learned in previous chapters of your daily life. To begin the life-long exercise of questioning the things we take for granted; of catching ourselves mid-cartwheel as we perform cognitive acrobatics on behalf of our inse-curities, our history, our institutions, and our sons or husbands; of digging deeper into the soundbite versions of politics and history. And when you find yourself slipping, put yourself right back on the frontline—we're here waiting for you.

put the donut down

Part of the White Supremacy diet is holding ourselves accountable. Always. Even during those inevitable moments when I'm 100% vegan and refuse to buy single-use water bottles,* except when I'm at a BBQ festival with my husband and I'm thirsty after my ribs.

You have to be real with yourself when you mess up, and always strive to do better the next time. Once a nutritionist says, "Hey, Jenna, did you know Krispy Kreme donuts are really bad for you?" I can't promise I won't ever eat another one. But I won't be able to pretend I don't know what I'm eating when I bite into one of those glorious fried dough confections.

In this book, I might be your very first anti-white-supremacist nutri-tionist telling you the very basics, but I shouldn't be your last.† Now there is no turning back—you know what the stakes are every time you make an assumption about someone because of their race, religion, disability, or gender, turn on your favorite cooking show and not the news, or "have no words" when there is another mass shooting in a first-grade classroom to avoid butting heads with your gun-owning relatives. All of those reac-tions are proof that we are dodging the work that our times so desperately require. We live in a new world now. Welcome.

The most important thing you can do to make sure you stay on this diet is put systems in place to catch counterproductive thoughts and behaviors.

Jerry Kang, the vice chancellor for equity, diversity, and inclusion at UCLA, explains that it's impossible to "scrub" implicit and explicit bias; we

---

* A million plastic bottles are purchased every minute, about 20,000 per second. Globally, more than 480 billion plastic water bottles were bought in 2016.[10] Less than half of these are recycled, leaving the rest in landfills and our oceans to outlive us all. By 2050 the world's oceans will contain more plastic bottles per weight than fish.[11]

† I'm not even qualified; I'm just your average white woman telling you to eat the apple instead of the bagel. Now that you're doing this life-long work, it's time to start seeking out the other issue-area experts—they're brilliant and beyond inspiring.

can't Clorox it from our psyches. Instead, he suggests we have to change our behavior to accommodate all that we've subconsciously been taught.

This work on explicit and implicit biases is like cleaning a kitchen. We know that every day, possibly multiple times a day, the kitchen gets messy, as we use it to prepare meals for ourselves and our family. And so every day, possibly multiple times a day, we have to clean it and put it back together again. Over time, you might build systems to help you expedite the clean-up process, be it the position of the trash can or the proximity of the dish cabinet to the dishwasher. But regardless of how organized our kitchen is, everyday life continues to mess it up.

You need a similar approach for catching and addressing your biases. You can't avoid them; they're too ingrained in the structure of our country and the ways in which we've been raised to look at the world. But over time, you will become more efficient at sorting through the mess in your head and then cleaning it up. You'll see the bias more quickly and label it as such. Maybe you'll get so comfortable with the experience that you'll start to investigate the source of bias, study it, and put it in the trash. Keep doing it even when it somehow gets dragged back out of the trash—so many biases are difficult to discard, and get shoved back into the depths of the cabinets despite our efforts to purge them. Eventually, that bias might stop showing up, and if not, at least you'll know how to trash it when it does surface. With implicit and explicit biases, you'll have to do it over and over.

Recent research into long-term psychological change suggests that at the rate society is evolving, implicit racial bias might be neutralized 57 or 107 years from now.* We either wait for the generations to age it out—which I'm not convinced is realistic, since new generations are constantly absorbing micro-messages that perpetuate those biases via every TV show and new Instagram influencer—or we start participating in society more actively and stop them in their tracks. Each piece of media we mindfully improve, each new bit of representation, changes the messages girls and younger women get.

The toughest moment is when you realize you have biases you weren't previously aware of. At this moment, while reading this book, you might

---

* This research also predicts that implicit sexuality biases might be neutralized in 9 or 29 years, implicit disability bias will take 150 years, and implicit body-weight biases will never disappear.[12]

think you know what your lapses are. I have bad news for you: there are more you don't know you have 🫧. The good news is, we might be at a time in history, as I've alluded to repeatedly throughout the book, where we can catapult our thoughts and behaviors that—fingers so tightly crossed—the changes we need won't take 107 or even 57 years.

The goal moving forward: Be anti-hypocrisy. For example, if you really care about starving children, then only buy the amount of food that you need.* Not because that large cardboard tray of croissants from Costco could otherwise suddenly be transported to Yemen—I'm confident you would take the food off your plate and give it to those babies if you could— but because buying more food or things than we need has environmental (and financial) impact that matters.

Overbuying food,† like many of our consumer habits, can sometimes be about us feeling productive or keeping busy when we might not actually need all of the items in our shopping carts. Retailers have certainly convinced us that more is better. But we don't need all the baby contraptions we're encouraged to buy; most children survive on a swaddle and their mother without the vibrating symphonic bouncer. Or, unless you run a professional kitchen, there is no need for the vegetable chopper that one infomercial convinced you to add to your wedding registry. Just use your knife—all those machines will just end up in landfills eventually, while life without them passes by with perfect function. Stop being played by retailers. And stop numbing yourself to avoid the real work of accepting your imperfections and wrestling with your self-doubts.

how to show up

You may have heard words like "ally," "advocate," "activist," and "accomplice" used in conversations about reaching out across race, gender, religious, and class lines. All four roles are important, but they are not synonymous.

This, too, is part of the white supremacy diet: being clear about which camp you likely fall into, at any given point.

---

* Stop wasting. We're going to struggle to produce enough food for everyone as it is. We'll need to feed 3 billion more people over the next thirty years, and croplands and pastures already account for 60% of the world's vegetated lands.[13]

† According to the United Nations Food and Agricultural Organization, 1.3 billion tons of food, or roughly 30% of global production, is lost or wasted annually.[14]

An *ally* might be actively working to understand her biases and privileges, and is committed to finding ways to become more educated and responsible for dismantling broken systems. Reading this book and getting to this page qualifies you as a rising ally. You are peeling back the onion to understand how both you and society operate, and raising your hand 🤚 to move forward with that knowledge for the rest of your life.

An *advocate*, on the other hand, is somebody who is willing to take what they've learned from books, like this one and others from experts they've sought out, and make significant and tangible changes in her life to break the cycles of oppression in their life and society more broadly. You are an advocate when you adopt a movement or group's political and social agenda as your personal agenda. You might donate money or vote for legislation to support social justice causes in your constituency.

An ally is someone who aligns themselves with a group politically or ideologically. An advocate speaks up to advance, protect, or uplift the welfare of a group. Allyship can be solely internal; advocacy is very visible.

An *activist* takes it a step further: she seeks out specific spots in the system that need improvement and actively works to identify solutions. Activists lend actual labor by organizing, launching campaigns, and building coalitions for constituencies of advocates and allies, but also by showing up to help the work of other activists.

An *accomplice* goes further still. At the direction of oppressed individuals and groups, an accomplice works to dismantle structures that cause harm. She is a partner in crime in strategies designed and set forth by those most impacted by those structures.

Here's a simple way of thinking about it. Being an "ally" means you speak highly of an actress. Being an "advocate" means you pay to go see her films on opening weekend. Being an "activist" means you petition a movie studio to cast her in more films. Being an "accomplice" means taking specific direction from the actress on how she would like you to support her work. It's different degrees of "talking the talk" and "walking the walk."

In any case, it's less important to declare ourselves as being in one of these categories than it is to put our heads down and do the work—and not expect to have any of these titles bestowed on us. We can talk about striving to be an ally, advocate, or activist—that's the end goal, if we're really going to break these systems—but we aren't the ones to dub ourselves with these terms, no more than we get to decide whether we are good Christians or gymnasts, because that judgment is up to God and the judges (or both).

One way to do the work is to show up in person—not to co-opt attention from the issue at hand, but to use your body to take up physical space and make a statement, even if it's not particularly convenient. Showing up may not be the most impactful course of action, compared to donating money, shelter, or other tangible resources, but doing it sends a message— to lawmakers, to naysayers, to your friends and family, to the press—that you are paying attention.

But sometimes doing the work also means refraining from taking up space in other ways. Just because we show up doesn't mean that we should speak on behalf of someone else and their needs, if they are there to speak for themselves. It's like a guy "mansplaining" gender inequality: just by doing so, often he is silencing a more qualified voice—a woman's. Also, you can and should speak on behalf of your life experiences and the many intersectional challenges that determine how you operate in the world. But you also need to be mindful of whose voice yours might be drowning out. It's a frustrating habit of some white women who want to be a part of the solution to push for the prioritization of subjects related to their welfare in the public forum over and at the expense of the welfare of others.

For example, after the 2016 presidential election, white women furious with the results suddenly became more vocal about their concerns with their country, some for the first time, while others hadn't marched in the streets since the '60s (even though there have been plenty of worthy reasons to march since then). The sudden enthusiasm with which white women were willing to organize—and the media attention many of them immediately received—was frustrating for communities of color that had been organizing and challenging administrations for decades.

One activist and writer, ShiShi Rose, told the *New York Times*, "I needed [white women] to understand that they don't just get to join the march and not check their privilege constantly."[15] This is the constant work of the white supremacy diet and the long-term mindset shift. As white women, we should constantly put our whiteness and the power and privilege it comes with under scrutiny, asking how we benefit in any given moment, particularly complex ones.

Four days before the 2017 Women's March, Jamilah Lemieux wrote in her article, "Why I'm Skipping the Women's March," "Will the Women's March on Washington be a space filled primarily with participants who believe that Black lives matter? I'm not sure, especially considering the attitudes of some who have publicly stated that they don't want to hear calls for attendees to check their White privilege at the proverbial door." Lemieux continued, "It's time for White women to come together and tell the world how their crimes against Black women, Black men and Black children have been no less devastating than the ones committed by their male counterparts."[16]

This is what some activists describe as the difference between *white feminism* and *intersectional feminism*. White feminism has historically revolved around white, middle-class women's issues, like reproduction and equal pay, while intersectional feminism includes those but is also much broader, encompassing many other issues that affect white women less than women of color: to name just a few examples, access to healthcare, education, and transportation, and safety from law enforcement.

Some women don't identify as "feminists" because they do not recognize themselves in the white feminist definition. "It wasn't that I didn't believe in liberation for all genders," writes Dr. Melissa C. Brown, a post-doctoral fellow for gender research at Stanford University who writes about black feminist thought and intersectionality. "Rather, I didn't see myself as part of a movement where no one looked like me."[17] To have an impact that lives up to its ideals, our feminism must be universal. It must include all races, genders, classes, and disabilities. And our job is to make sure we are constantly centering the voices and needs of the most marginalized first.

As you move forward from this book, below is a diagram inspired by The 519, a Toronto-based nonprofit working within LGBTQ2S* communities, to help you think about the different kinds of positioning, both literally and figuratively, you can take in different scenarios.

---

* The "2S" at the end of the acronym refers to "Two Spirit," which is a term that is used within some indigenous communities to describe gender-nonconforming individuals who identify as having both a masculine and feminine spirit. This is different than trans or non-binary identities because those terms are typically tied to culturally specific conceptions of gender.[18]

DIFFERENT WAYS TO SUPPORT

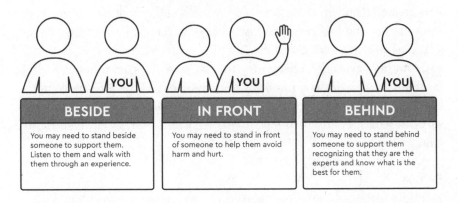

BESIDE	IN FRONT	BEHIND
You may need to stand beside someone to support them. Listen to them and walk with them through an experience.	You may need to stand in front of someone to help them avoid harm and hurt.	You may need to stand behind someone to support them recognizing that they are the experts and know what is the best for them.

Beside

Standing beside an oppressed person means lending your voice, time, energy, and physical presence to advance their cause. It can also mean not accepting certain privileges that oppressed groups aren't afforded, or ones that you receive at the expense of an oppressed group's well-being. One example is actress Jessica Chastain, who insisted on an equal salary as her costar Octavia Spencer when she found out how much less women of color make in Hollywood; her protest resulted in Spencer's pay being quintupled.

If you see members of an oppressed group speaking up for themselves and privileged groups attacking them, intentionally mistaking their words or accusing them of exaggeration (very common on social media platforms), you can jump into the conversation, validate the oppressed person's concerns, and speak to their opposition directly. Though it is unfortunate, your privilege gives you credibility in the eyes of other privileged people, and they are more likely to listen, try to understand, and ultimately believe you.

In Front

Standing in front of an oppressed person means utilizing your position of power and privilege to protect them, or putting yourself in a position that would be unsafe for (or unavailable to) other groups of people. One powerful example is from Hermitage, Tennessee: when ICE officials showed up to collect a man and his son in July 2019, their neighbors quickly mobilized. The targeted people stayed in their car, which ICE officials aren't legally allowed to enter, while neighbors kept refueling it with gas and brought food and water that they slipped through the car windows. Later that day the neighbors created a human chain between the car and the front door of the home so the father and his son could safely get from the car into the house. ICE left. This story gives me the chills. Americans can do this for one another.

Another example relates to the #OwnVoices movement, where "authors share a diverse, minority, or marginalized trait with their protagonist."[19] If you're in a position to amplify the voices of such people as a teacher, writer, editor, producer, publisher, event host, or faith leader, use your power for good.

Behind

Standing behind an oppressed person means supporting them and looking to them for leadership. Members of oppressed groups are perfectly capable of speaking for themselves, but people in power aren't always willing to listen to or acknowledge them. Rather than speaking over or on behalf of oppressed groups, you can uplift their voices simply by showing up, standing behind them, and helping command the attention they might otherwise be denied. One example of this is when a passerby stops to video police who are interacting with someone from a vulnerable group. Without saying anything or antagonizing anyone, this holds people in power accountable and helps reduce the likelihood of harassment, because someone is bearing witness.

A true ally, advocate, or activist is not motivated by ego. Before you promote your own ideas and agendas, look to people within the oppressed group you want to support who have already been doing the work. They are the most informed teachers, as they understand their conditions best and can explain how, why, and when they need support. Be honest about the limitations of your knowledge on certain topics; look to activists who have lived experience to guide your own activism, then promote their work.

When it comes to dismantling white supremacy, white people *can* be allies, advocates, and activists, but part of being great co-conspirators means remembering that we are afforded privileges—even if we don't want them—that come at the expense of other people's basic rights. I know how discouraging that sounds. But instead of feeling like the mountain of white supremacy is too big and deciding to not even try, we should start chipping away at pebbles and boulders, and let our shared goals of a just society (not a perfect one) motivate our actions.

the gig is up

White people have finally begun to realize that something is not right. This demographic now owns the highest rates of suicide and the emerging, deadly disease of loneliness. Now that 1% of our society is holding almost all of the wealth in the world* and increasing that wealth at double the speed of anyone else (it takes money to make money), we are starting to realize there is no such thing as a pure meritocracy. We aren't exceptional because we are white; we made up rules to the game as we went along and were winning, but now the gig is up.

American citizens are now questioning our theory of higher education—like universities that have billions of dollars in endowments† but still charge $250,000 for a diploma that might not actually be needed. We're questioning the quick-fix, "pain-free" lives Big Pharma promises us through their drugs, while 130 families bury their loved ones per day because of our abuse of opioid medications.[22] We are questioning why men have freedoms to speak and take and control that women can't, when we know we are just as capable. It's now clear that success doesn't depend on hard work but about access to opportunity—and the outstanding question for those in our privileged demographic always to ask themselves is: Do we believe everyone should have these opportunities? And, if so, what are we doing to make that a reality?

The "white-lash," as Anthony Kapel "Van" Jones, an American news commentator and author, described the results of the 2016 presidential election,[23] was the white American player trying to find that ace card and play it again. The catch is the other players in the game already know the card is no longer available. We all know we're biased. Most employers are no longer hiring based solely on GPA and a school logo at the top of some piece of paper. And women aren't waiting anymore for men to tell us what to do.

---

* The share of national income flowing to the wealthiest 1% has tripled since 1980. Since the 2008 recession, 90% of the recovery's financial gains have landed in the pockets of the 1%. Average income has stayed relatively the same (adjusted for inflation) while CEO salary has increased tenfold. Of course, most of the federal tax breaks apply only to the wealthiest 5%.[20]

† Despite their multibillion-dollar endowments, in 2015 Harvard ($38 billion) and Yale ($26 billion) spent more money on private equity managers than they did on providing students financial aid.[21]

a word about voting—the most obvious exercise

By now you're crystal clear that being a responsible citizen cannot merely mean living within the speed limits, tax rules, or watching fireworks on the Fourth of July. It's about questioning everything, including the truths that you personally hold as self-evident. Still, I must spend a few minutes on our mandatory homework: voting. As we discussed in chapter two, some white women opted out of voting because they didn't see a "perfect candidate" on the ballot. In chapter six, we explored how some of us developed voting habits from our father's and husband's strong suggestions, even when it meant pulling the lever against our own best interests.

I get it. It's not always easy to see the repercussions of your vote, and sometimes it's cold in early November. But the awesome power of voting is undeniable—and not "awesome" in the cool-dude definition, but "awesome" in the extraordinary, awe-inspiring power. A century ago, women suffered in jail cells, with maggots in their food, so that they and you, your daughters, and granddaughters could have a voice. Does it help to know that so many people in different parts of the world have a huge stake in who becomes our president? Maybe the hundred thousand people who apply for citizenship in the United States every year, or the peacekeeping operations that help secure innocent lives, or the life-saving medicine we distribute to the most remote corners of the earth. I meet people constantly in my travels abroad who know more about our politics than some Americans I know. What we, white women, do in the voting booth reverberates well beyond the borders of this country, especially since white women make up 42% of all American voters—the most powerful voting demographic in the country.* Despite all this, some of us just don't show up to vote.

I have repeated this point—and this statistic—because I believe it's one that demonstrates your extreme influence on every life today and all those to come. This cannot be taken for granted; whether you want that power or not or still aren't sold isn't relevant. You have it.

You've had teachers and PSAs and influencers and countless proud sticker-wearing family members and coworkers bug you to vote. My chiming

---

* The next largest demographic is white men at 37%, 7% African American women, 5% Hispanic women, 4% African American men, 3% Hispanic men, 1.4% Asian or Pacific Islander women, and 1.2% Asian or Pacific Islander men.[24]

in may not be what gets you off your couch on a wintry Tuesday. But now you know more, and I need to remind you of the power you hold.

It's *good* to see voting as an exercise. Yes, it's one that we've been able to do—and hopefully have been doing—for a few generations, and yes, we still need to continue doing it.* To keep all these health analogies going: think of voting like holding a plank pose instead of doing a few quick push-ups. Same idea, but more evolved and focused on the big picture. Because it's not the fact of the vote that matters, it's the quality of the vote—and understanding that the results of each election are, for some, the difference between life and death.

We must constantly question how and on behalf of whom we are voting—even if, because of our race and our resources, it is likely that who wins the American presidency may not significantly impact our lives in any way. That's right: The white women's voting bloc represents 77% of women's votes nationwide;[28] yet we aren't nearly as impacted by policy as more marginalized demographics, both in the United States and elsewhere. The moms who are pregnant behind bars, the moms who are fleeing gang violence in the streets, the moms who beat themselves up every night because they can't fill their children's stomachs—can we vote for them?

My younger cousin, in a debate with her father, told him that she "will never be voting on behalf of myself; I don't really need the government to do anything for me. I'll always vote for the women and their babies who I'll never know—here and abroad—they need the social support that I don't have the means to give them. I don't need my vote, she does." She understands her power. Even in forty years, when white people will be a minority in the United States, white women will still be the majority of the electorate in twenty-eight states, controlling fifty-six of 100 Senate seats. We will still maintain the most

---

* While I'm leaning here on the importance of white women voting, it is also critically important that we support getting more disenfranchised voters into voting booths. In the 2016 presidential election, 120,000 people were not eligible to vote because of voter suppression—discriminatory and partisan-rigged district mapping that kept marginalized people's voices from being heard.[25] Most recently, voter suppression was prevalent in North Dakota, Florida, Texas, and Georgia—all key states in the electorate.[26] Voter purging is also an issue. Various studies show that people in communities of color and low-income areas are more likely to be removed from the voter rolls than those living in majority white, wealthy zip codes. There's also malfunctions in the voting equipment, and cultivating voter confusion by sending out misinformation through texts and mailers. And yes, voter intimidation and harassment, closures, and long lines still occur in the good ol' USA.[27]

influence in 2060.[29] So let's stop pretending like our participation doesn't really matter and start using the powerful magic wand we're holding.

My hunch, however, is that if you made it to this paragraph in the book, you're not really interested in what your country can do for you anymore (oh dear God, please be true), but are eager to see how you can change on behalf of everyone.

So I am not only asking you to commit to voting, always. I am asking that, because the white woman's voting bloc is not only the most powerful in the country—now and for a very long time—but also the most powerful in the world, you think more deeply about what goes into that decision.

five hundred years from now

One of my favorite stories is about a dining hall at Oxford University that needed to replace the large oak beams that supported the ceiling. The architects of the renovation, unsure of where they could source new beams of that size, asked the groundskeeper, who responded with (say this with your best British accent), "Well sirs, we was wonderin' when you'd be askin'." The groundskeeper shared a message that had been passed down for five hundred years: a series of oaks were planted when the original dining hall was constructed, in preparation for their *replacement*, hundreds of years into the future.

Every time I retell this story, I'm impressed with the selfless foresight of the architects and groundskeepers, as they began preparing to sustain their building five hundred years and more into the future. Can we likewise invest in this country and ourselves now to ensure more stability then?

There are the easy requests: when you see the opportunity to make a conversation more inclusive, diverse, or simply aware of the structural bias supporting it, use your voice. When you feel the need to make your household's division of emotional and domestic labor more egalitarian, do so. Enough with the red keg cups, zip-shut plastic bags, and paper plates because they're easier to clean up—and when you do use your reusable flatware, require him to help clean up, too. No more swallowing your objections and accepting "tradition" as law; those cognitive acrobatics have harmed many people in the past and still do today, including our daughters.

There are the less convenient asks, the ones you might struggle with for a while. Hold yourself and others accountable when you see lazy, complacent behavior in your homes and tennis clubs—those are the frontlines of where change needs to happen. Vote, channel money into new ideas carried by people who don't look like you, grab your biases by the tail and put them under a magnifying glass. Don't let yourself or anybody else off the hook regardless of intention or age or position of power. Ask smarter questions, and don't be so desperate 🙊 to give the smartest answer, speak up and shut up, and show up just to bear witness.

Enough with the excuses for why you are or aren't worthy, can or can't do something, or don't have enough time. We do things we don't want to all of the time because our patriarchy tells us if we don't do it, nobody else will: fold the laundry, organize the church fundraiser, shoulder the burden of an unwanted pregnancy. And the patriarchy is right: if we, women, don't raise our hand, generation after generation, to deal with those chores, nobody else will. Can we demand more boundary-setting for ourselves, the kind that says to men: you take the birth control shot, you find money for the church—or that single sock? You go find its match; check behind the dryer. Can we take back our time and increase our output for the members of our society whose names we'll never know?

There are people across the country and world who are filling the gaps, committing their lives to meager nonprofit salaries, marching in the streets when they, too, would prefer to be at a beach or with their loved ones. They are challenging the status quo on behalf of you and your children. Can we participate in the bare minimum tasks of keeping a democracy alive, and then create new ideas, movements, institutions, and companies that propel us to a morally right future at the maximum? Yes. Yes we can.

Here's a first step, as we feel that familiar hesitation coming from a place of wanting to keep the peace and ensuring others are comfortable. Instead of asking ourselves, "How can I be good?" let's start asking:

> What would change if I owned the fact I have power,
> and acted accordingly?

These questions, or even all of these behavior changes I've laid out above, can't single-handedly reverse all of the oppressive systems that have been built to compartmentalize the most vulnerable people and render them invisible. But, if we all pull our attention to the frontlines where we stand together and individually, we can begin to plant trees for which our children's children's children will thank us. Together we can end the cycle of privileged women who, for generations, just opted out. Not anymore.

CHAPTER TEN

THE RECKONING

M y family and I are avid card players. When we spend time together, typically in the summer at my great-grandmother's beach house in southern New Jersey, we constantly play a fast-paced game called Nertz. Nertz is a combination of Solitaire and Spit and requires copious amounts of focus and aggression. The objective is to get rid of your cards while accumulating points as fast as you can. If you deal yourself one or more aces, the likelihood that you'll win the hand is high.

In a fair game, the card order is random, and winning comes down to chance and the skill with which individuals play the cards they've been dealt. But there's the possibility someone could cheat by stacking the deck, arranging for themselves to get those aces quickly.

As the past nine chapters have hopefully made clear, the deck of cards from which some people's hands are dealt, particularly ours as white people, has had a number of aces pre-positioned—giving us a leg up despite our being no more skilled than anyone else. You now know that we—not because of any natural aptitude, but simply due to the circumstances of our births—are better positioned to win the game of life. And we are now faced with the moral question of how to play that game, knowing the people who came before us were able to cheat, thanks to white supremacy, so that we could have those aces in our hand.

As filmmaker and activist Abby Disney says, "The rich and the poor are living on different planets. One on their private planes and with no wait at a doctor's office. The reality for the other," as she discovered, to her horror, was the case for Disney employees, "forages for food in other people's garbage." She continues, "The rich have short-circuited the system [and] they can't fathom that a $400 bill could get in the way of medical care—that's couch cushion money for the rich."[1]

Just by virtue of being white, our hand of cards has been pre-stacked. If you are also cisgender, nondisabled, free to practice any religion you choose or none at all; if you were born into a family with a roof you could all sleep under safely, have a source of life-sustaining income or inherited money, have access to clean water and a place to buy affordable, healthy foods; if you have a high school and/or college diploma, and parents with similar degrees; if you're part of a dual-parent household; if you're a United States citizen—just to name a few privileges—your hand has been rigged even further. We need to subvert our stacked decks by starting to play the game differently—so that we can more broadly serve each other, find greater meaning in our lives, and leave this world a bit better.

This is not about taking food out of your children's mouths or handing over the keys to your dream house so that a less fortunate family can move in. Instead, it's about asking, is there a way we can stop prioritizing *just* our own comfort? Can we clear our lives of performance chores, take just what we need, and stop obsessing over how we appear to the outside world in order to prove to ourselves that we are enough? Can we show up for others as a pathway to securing not just our own salvation, but an entire country's?

un-stacking our Constitution

The Constitution is working. And that's not always good.

As we discussed in chapter three, "We the people" has never meant ALL the people, even though we've gotten very good at pretending like it *might*.

Over generations, we have tried to edit the Constitution to broaden its scope and make it more inclusive. But it's not working; people are still suffering at the hands of our white supremacist system. And we aren't being honest with ourselves that the "all" in "liberty and justice for all" really only means "all of the people who look like me." We know not ALL people have access to water without lead. We know not ALL kids have music and art and gym class in their schools. We know not ALL families have access to the top oncologist at the top cancer hospital when they need it. We know all of that, right?

So do we just make excuses, those good old cognitive acrobatics, and say, "Everything happens for a reason" or "God has a plan," or hide behind Martin Luther King's quote: "The Arc of the moral universe is long, but it bends towards Justice"?* Do we say, "Oh, my life isn't all fairytales, either" or "I work my ass off, too" (🙄), as one Listening Circle participant said?

I'm not sure those sentiments are welcomed by people who have to bury their loved ones because of gun violence or malaria or overflowing levees. I'm not an atheist, but I can't hide behind the notion that all the chips will eventually fall where they may morally and ethically because of some divine intervention or cosmic influence—that's too easy of an excuse, enabling us to pop into our ignorance cloud and let ourselves off the hook. I refuse to pretend this performance of "it will all be okay." I invite you to do the same. Instead, let's yank that arc toward justice, and for the religious among us, act on that free will God gave us.

I am privileged beyond measure, primarily because of the color of my skin and the socioeconomic class in which my parents were raised—and, I admit, I want the same comforts for my children. I dream about living in a home with a foyer, maybe one large enough for one of those circular tables that always has fresh flowers—I'm thinking peonies. But I'm not willing to accept that others can't share in the same ease, and that my access to it depends on their deprivation. I know there are children moaning for a meal in so many nutrient-poor communities not just abroad, but here at home. I'm finding it harder to balance on this tightrope, and the older I get, the heavier it all becomes and the harder it is to balance.

Our Constitution is among the oldest still-operating governing documents on the planet,[3] which tells you something: it's probably time to revisit. There have been twenty-seven amendments to the Constitution, but there is a very lively debate at the moment among constitutional experts and political scientists about whether we should keep tweaking it or scrap it

---

* King was actually reinterpreting part of an 1853 sermon delivered by abolitionist minister Theodore Parker, an influential Unitarian preacher. In that sermon, Parker said, "I do not pretend to understand the moral universe. The arc is a long one. My eye reaches but little ways. I cannot calculate the curve and complete the figure by experience of sight. I can divine it by conscience. And from what I see I am sure it bends toward justice."[2]

completely. Going back to the house analogy in chapter two, are you going to renovate the home (our country) room by room, or should we just knock it down and start over? If the latter gives you a tinge of anxiety (🫣), it's probably worth considering whether fears about how your life might change are the reason why. And while this book isn't about what to do with our Constitution—I certainly have no idea—it *is* about making sure we know there are some serious leaks and mold in our national identity that require our immediate attention.

The American democracy is more fragile than it's been in generations, yet that same American democracy is more primed than ever for a regeneration. The good news is that this is something that our much-revered Founders did see coming. Apparently, when Ben Franklin was leaving Independence Hall in Philadelphia after the Constitutional Convention in 1787, a pedestrian passed him on the street and asked what he had just helped create. Franklin replied, "A republic, if you can keep it." A working republic requires constant iterating, protecting, morphing, dismantling, and rebuilding, all while holding ourselves accountable to our core values. In 2017, the United States was demoted as a democracy* because voter suppression is so rampant and because two recent presidential candidates have won the popular vote but didn't become president thanks to the structure of the Electoral College. Historian Bernard Bailyn wrote, "Free states are fragile and degenerate easily into tyrannies unless vigilantly protected by a free, knowledgeable, and uncorrupted electorate working through institutions that balance and distribute rather than concentrate power."[5] We have to tend to this republic, our democracy, as if it is a living, breathing thing. This work is 100% on us. Always has been, always will be.

Our country looks the way it does because of the way the privileged and powerful think and act. And that means when we change the way we think and act, we change the country. In his recent book, *You Are More Powerful Than You Think: A Citizen's Guide to Making Change Happen*, author and activist Eric Liu says, "We in the United States have an opportunity now to create the planet's first mass multicultural, democratic, republic. Ancient Athens was a democracy but not mass, multicultural, or a republic. Rome's republic was multicultural and democratic but not mass. The Soviet Union was mass, multicultural, and a republic but not democratic.

---

* *The Economist's* Intelligence Unit Democracy Index ranked the United States below Uruguay, Mauritius, and Spain.[4]

No nation has ever hit all four marks, including the United States. And it is unclear whether the United States will."[6] The outstanding question for us is whether or not we are open to forming a new America with flexible systems capable of accommodating our further evolution as we work toward equity.

The organizers of the Women's March saw this opportunity. My friend Paola Mendoza, artist and activist, describes the role of the organizers of the 2017 Women's March as midwives to a moment, and the role of the people who spilled onto the streets in 667 marches worldwide as birthing a movement. Can we deliver a set of ideals that fairly govern this land's 300-million-plus souls, all of whom seek equal access to safety and an opportunity to prosper?

As my friend Valerie Kaur, author of *Revolutionary Love,* says in reference to our tumultuous times, "What if this is not the darkness of the tomb but the darkness of the womb?" She encourages us all to keep pushing toward clarity.

inherited trauma

"History is not the past," said James Baldwin, one of the writers who shaped my thinking most during this book's journey. "We carry our history with us. We are our history." To root myself a bit more in the painful truth of my country's past, the tales and facts I wish weren't true, I needed to ground myself in the tangible. So while I was researching this book, in addition to spending a lot of time in living rooms, I also—and this is way more creepy— found myself walking through graveyards. I was searching for unmarked and mass graves,* places where white Europeans would have buried dead indigenous people, or where slave owners would have discarded the bodies of the enslaved.

I spent some time with a groundskeeper at one graveyard I visited in Pennsylvania, which was connected to a Quaker meeting house. Apparently it's not often that a New Yorker with oversized sunglasses knocks on this groundskeeper's door, asking for the secrets of his cemetery. We spent a few hours together, and in the course of our conversations I told him a bit about the book; he was particularly curious about chapter six, and my thoughts on the state of the American white man.

---

* Three or more human corpses in a single grave, which may or may not have been defined as such pre-burial.

We walked the rows of tombstones, back and forth, as he summarized stories of the deceased. We spent a lot of time hypothesizing over the parts of the cemetery, where he had come to believe, after working there for forty-plus years, a number of graves might contain more than one body.

The Quakers played a role[7] in the construction and maintenance of the Underground Railroad,* secretly helping escaping enslaved people travel north from southern states. Not all of them survived the journey. The Quakers avoided filing death certificates or registering the gravesites with the state in an effort to protect their participation in others' flight to freedom.

As I was reversing out of the driveway, waving goodbye to the groundskeeper with my window rolled down, he started urgently running after the car. I slammed on the brakes, giving him a chance to catch up. When he did, he said, panting, "The reason all of our men are killing themselves is five thousand years of emotional oppression."

"Pardon me?" I responded.

"The reason our [white] men are taking their lives and are fighting so hard to justify not caring, is because they have caused thousands of years of trauma and have been actively suppressing that as well as self-hatred associated with those actions generation after generation, and now it's catching up to them. To us."

I was skeptical. Isn't it just as easy to explain these behaviors as "nurture" rather than "nature"? As performing what is modeled for us, and not some preprogrammed set of responses?

And then I witnessed Ever—at the time she had just turned three—who was one moment casually standing in the kitchen of my parent's home and the next, shrieking and leaping into my father's arms with such voraciousness her life seemed to depend on it. She'd spotted a small centipede but thought it was a snake. She had never encountered a snake in the wild and most certainly had never been harmed by one, which would've validated such a shocking reaction. When did she develop her fear of snakes, and how did she know to respond that way when her mother and grandmother—who are equally afraid of snakes—have gone above and beyond to declare our love for them the few times the subject came up?

---

* A term used to describe an intricate network of secret places, people, and routes during the early to mid-1800s that aided enslaved African Americans as they escaped slavery in the South and fled to northern states and Canada. The Underground Railroad was supported by slavery abolitionists and allies.[8]

With the groundskeeper's hypothesis haunting me, I dove into that rabbit hole and found brilliant minds on the case. I learned about a new field of study known as *epigenetics*: how the way our genes express themselves can be altered by our environment, and how these alterations—known as *epigenetic changes*—can then be passed on to our children. Epigenetics suggests that the experiences our ancestors endured might still be encoded in us at a molecular level, thus impacting how we respond in similar instances today. In this school of thought, is Ever's (mine and my mother's) fear of snakes a result of traumatic engagement our ancestors had with these reptiles?

Scientists are also studying the epigenetics of inherited trauma,[9] looking at the possibility that both being the victim of trauma and being the one perpetrating trauma changes bodies at a molecular level.* Some psychologists suggest that Ashkenazi Jews are particularly anxious because of intergenerational trauma from World War II.[11] Another study suggests that sons of Union Army soldiers imprisoned during the Civil War under particularly grueling conditions were more likely to die young than the sons of soldiers who weren't held captive.[12] "The stresses of war were getting passed down between generations," despite the sons being born well after the war was over.[13]

This research has huge implications on our reckoning—on our coming to terms with exactly what work we have ahead of us. It means that part of rectifying our history must include addressing how that history might have become inscribed on our DNA. And while our collective priority must be the currently marginalized communities suffering from this kind of generational trauma, we might also consider what has been written in the DNA of those of us who are privileged at the expense of others and how that

---

* Resmaa Menakem, in her book, *My Grandmother's Hands: Racialized Trauma and the Pathway to Mending Our Hearts and Bodies* explains, "Trauma always happens *in the body*. It is a spontaneous protective mechanism used by the body to stop or thwart further (or future) potential damage . . . In the aftermath of highly stressful or traumatic situations, [our brain] may embed a reflexive trauma response in our bodies . . . Such overreactions are the body's attempt to complete a protective action that got thwarted or overridden during a traumatic situation. The body wanted to fight or flee, but wasn't able to do either, so it got stuck in freeze mode. In many cases, it then develops strategies around this "stuckness," including extreme reactions, compulsions, strange likes and dislikes, seemingly irrational fears, and unusual avoidance strategies. Over time, these can become embedded in the body as standard ways of surviving and protecting itself. When these strategies are repeated and passed on over generations, they can become the standard responses in families, communities, and cultures."[10]

might be impacting our current behaviors. Could apathy and complacency be inscribed in our DNA as a coping mechanism for when the suffering of others, and its benefits for us, are too great to justify? And are we allowing that coping mechanism to silence the voice inside us that would otherwise challenge our ignorance? Is the resulting self-hatred from causing others so much harm now boiling to the surface after generations of being suppressed? Is the anger we take out on others, and ourselves, our last-ditch effort at keeping the better angels of our nature muzzled just a bit longer?

Rachel M. MacNair, an activist and psychologist, describes in her book on perpetration-induced traumatic stress (PITS)[14] what she believes is the underdescribed side of the trauma coin: the long-term psychological consequences on those responsible for the suffering or death of another. McNair points out that PITS is not uncommon in religious texts and poetry. Heck, even Shakespeare claims that being haunted by the pain we've caused is the worst of all fates. Socrates says, "He or any other who like him has done wrong and has not been punished, is, and ought to be, the most miserable of all men; and that the door of injustice is more miserable than the sufferer." This does not suggest we should feel bad for those who perpetrate harm. But it does imply that the knowledge of unearned privilege may carry its own kind of trauma, one that could have changed us, too, on a molecular level. What effect, if any, did the violence of previous generations have on its perpetrators? Has the abuse they inflicted changed them in some way?

My intention in visiting with the graveyard keeper was to talk about a few of the mass graves scattered across our country, which have been effaced by in-ground pools and football stadiums. The question I walked away with, delivered by a quiet man who spends his days weed-whacking tombstones and cleaning up beer bottles from teenage after-dark shenanigans: Are we all living with the consequences of our history, even those who benefited most from inequality?

To be clear, this doesn't excuse our apathy or cognitive acrobatics. But it may give weight to what Baldwin says—that when white people stop hating themselves, there won't be a "Negro problem."* And it makes this work even more important for *all* of us to do as we search for undiscovered frontlines.

---

* "White people . . . have quite enough to do in learning how to accept and love themselves and each other, and when they have achieved this—which will not be tomorrow and may very well be never—the Negro problem will no longer exist, for it will no longer be needed."[15]

i don't know either, and that's okay

Part of the reason why I wanted to write this book was, as I mentioned in chapter nine, to find an "answer" to the problems I was seeing all around me. But it was also because I wanted to find good deeds I could do to drown out the guilt I felt over my privilege.

I don't think I'm unique, either, in feeling this shame and the desire to do better at doing better. I'm just a human being with normal (whatever that means) levels of compassion and empathy. I give up my seat on the subway when someone else needs it more. I lend people a hand when they've dropped something out of their bag. I know I can be tough, snappy, and impatient at times, but I don't want my personal failings to harm others. In this, I'm sure we're a lot alike.

I was taught that success meant having answers good enough to pass life's big tests, and having a sufficiently decorated life, with the photos to prove it. I was also taught that I had to keep summiting—which mountain didn't really matter; I always had to have my eye on the next peak.

So it feels strange and inadequate to admit that in my search for an answer, the best I could come up with was to question that blueprint: to have tough conversations and keep asking challenging questions of myself and the world around me. I am learning to embrace that I'm not always sure how to think, speak, act, sing (you don't want me doing that), or cry. I am learning to see insecurity as the excuse we use for chasing our ego-driven personal agendas. It creeps into every stage of our lives, from grades to sports to social media followers to job titles to the distance our guns can shoot and the speed our cars can drive. It's seeing the voice inside me that says *I am not enough* as the devil it is. That voice shuts up when we serve others, when we act on behalf of the greater good, when we sit in silence so that we can understand ourselves better, and when we scream at the top of our lungs to make the lives of others easier. It quiets when we change our behavior to do these things not just in our personal lives, with our words or our credit cards, but wherever we wield influence: in our business decisions or corporate policies, in our law firms or classrooms or medical offices or religious institutions. In whatever our sandboxes are, we can be radical in ways that quickly restructure paradigms. The white supremacy diet requires us to look at those moments when our biases translate into action, call them what they are, and chip away at our habits to make a change. The same process applies to reshaping this country.

We're not in this to find constant happiness—and our desire for the same is another result of our warped blueprint. Trying to be "happy" all the time is futile. It's like saying you want to be having an orgasm every moment of your entire life. Not only is it impossible; it would eventually become agonizing.* Rather than wishing the world constant happiness, I pray for humans to be safe enough—from each other's pain, from natural disasters—to live their self-chosen paths, for them to be confident enough to ask hard questions of powerful people and institutions, and for them to have enough ease. I want us to be able to fully embrace moments of joy: the glee in watching a child belly-laugh, the beauty in a magenta sunset, the grace in holding the door for a stranger, the warmth of holding someone's hand. Being of service is fundamental to our humanity, and we can do that through many different paths—and on the new frontlines where we must hold ourselves every day.

I laid out some ground rules in this book, which I hope got you to this point. You have what it takes to continue the work, but here are a few last guidelines, drawn from the chapters you've just read, to keep in mind:

- Embrace silence for answers and to make space for others, but get loud when you must.
- Break the habit of doing performance chores, and elevate others' wellbeing over following the rules.
- Ask the hard questions about past stories and today's headlines.
- Confront your biases.
- Stop protecting our men and sons at the expense of others, including our daughters.
- Stop living by the binary.
- Consistently call yourself and others in, and build community.
- And last, I beg you: believe you are worthy. I don't even know your name, yet I want you, I *need* you here. Can you extend yourself the same consideration?

---

* There are actually people who suffer from constant orgasms. It's not as awesome when you're filling the car up with gas or giving a speech.

opening the gate of the white picket fence

My hypothesis in writing this book is that I, a white woman, could speak to the experiences—good and bad—of other white women. That because I am like you, at least in some ways, I might be able to contextualize these issues in a way that feels familiar and easier to understand. And my hope is that this book has given you clarity and confidence, and has served as a spark of motivation for you to continue doing this work, by seeking out and learning from the true experts.

Still, it's hard for me to reconcile taking up space in this inequity conversation when we should be listening to marginalized voices, who are closest to the problem, and therefore closest to the solution. So this is where I step aside and let a few of the voices that we all need to hear come through—where I open the front gate to that white picket fence we've built around ourselves for generations, and ask you to step out.

Hopefully, after putting down this book, you'll seek out voices like this on your own. They won't fall in your lap; your current circles might not include people who aren't, largely, like you. And as I mentioned in chapter four, we don't have time to wait for socioeconomic systems to evolve enough to put us in the kind of proximity to each other that would help break down our current biases. (Not to mention, as we saw in chapter nine, researchers believe it could take more than a century for these biases to disappear—that's just too long.)

I'm privileged to have had relationships with many teachers who represent several marginalized communities, and I want to share some of their guidance here. I asked these contributors, "If you could make a statement to and a request of white women, what would it be?"

———⟍ ———

Get used to being uncomfortable. If you're really ready and willing to do this work—welcome the discomfort that so many have faced for so long. The first thing I learned when getting into community organizing is that you should spend extensive time just listening and learning from those that came before us. This learning must be done proactively and intentionally. Push the boundaries of your comfort zones and examine why you are uncomfortable. Because often your discomfort comes from the insidious nature of privilege. It remains silent, waiting for you to push down against the truths that are oppression and inequality.

Come with open minds and hearts. We have been waiting for you to join us in this fight. But make sure you're willing to use your whole self in the cause. Folks cannot remain timid in fighting for equality and justice. There can be no fence straddling, no both sides. If you join us, keep your head in the game and do the work that is needed.

—Mia Ives-Rublee, disabled Korean American activist

You white women don't seem to have context for how much power you have and what you could do with it. It's time for you to wake up and own your influence in all the ways your ancestors protected for you, except now it's time for you to work on behalf of all of us. We are here, waiting for you.

—Ron Finley, known as the Gangsta Gardner,
agricultural and restorative justice activist

The nannies, house cleaners, and home care workers who work in our homes do the caregiving and cleaning work for our families that makes everything else possible in our society. And yet, in the United States, they have, historically, been undervalued and explicitly excluded from basic rights that most of us take for granted when we go to work. This workforce, predominantly women of color hailing from places in the Caribbean, Latin America, Asia, and Africa, are at risk of unpredictable hours, stagnant wages, lack of benefits, lack of job security, and limited rights. In households around the world, domestic workers are often considered family, and their contributions staples in the successes of our lives, yet they can hardly care for themselves or their own families doing this work. My request is that we honor the lives and contributions of women who do this work, by ensuring they earn living wages and have clear work agreements, with time off and access to benefits.

—Ai-jen Poo, director, National Domestic Workers Alliance;
labor activist; author of *The Age of Dignity:
Preparing for the Elder Boom in a Changing America*;
and MacArthur Genius Award recipient

As a marine biologist and conservation strategist, my career has granted me a front row seat to watching ecosystems and our climate system fall apart. The climate emergency and sixth mass extinction mean we need all hands on deck, all solutions and all solvers. And despite their impressive track records of moving mountains with very few resources, women leading environmental work are woefully underfunded. Yes, most especially women of color.

At the same time, the last decade has seen the shift that now, over half of the private wealth in the United States is controlled by women. So I'm calling on you to connect these dots. To ensure a habitable planet, you simply must fund women climate leaders. And you must divest your assets from funding fossil fuels.

I'm also calling on you to live lighter on the planet. Not just to recycle and buy more sustainable products. But to think about the "5 R's" that should come before recycling: refuse, reduce, reuse, repurpose, and repair. Ditch the bottled water. Don't just consume differently, consume less. Buy food grown nearby and without pesticides. Reduce your carbon footprint. Your individual decisions are not nearly enough, but your influence in your homes and in your communities and with your elected officials really can shift the status quo.

The good news is that we already have the environmental solutions we need. We just need you to step up and support the women and people of color leading the way—with your dollars and your influence.

—Dr. Ayana Elizabeth Johnson, marine biologist and founder of Ocean Collectiv and Urban Ocean Lab

I spent sixteen years in prison, some in solitary confinement, serving life for murdering a man. After a few years I stopped getting visitors; every time they would call visiting hours I would walk to my cell and read a book, too heartbroken to face the feeling of abandonment. I laid there, wondering how the world just chose to forget about me. Yes, I committed a crime, yes I deserve punishment, but no, I'm not the worst thing I've ever done—I still have something to give the world. Don't forget about the people who are locked up; they're ashamed and remorseful and often didn't have many options of surviving outside of the crimes they committed. Don't forget about us; we long for our mother's touch and the forgiveness of strangers. Don't forget about us.

—Chris Wilson, anti-incarceration activist and author of
The Master Plan: My Journey from Life in Prison to a Life of Purpose

I have been living with multiple chronic illnesses for over twenty-eight years, and the National Health Council states that there will be over

157 million people in the US who will have a chronic condition by 2020. Health is one of those things that you don't realize how lucky you are to have it, until it's gone. If you know someone who is battling their health or struggling in mental and physical ways, I urge you to show up for them. Don't know how? *Ask* them what they need. Especially for our women of color who often don't have the financial resources to get the care they need, and even when they do they show up to appointments they are ignored or not taken seriously just because of their race. Women are dying all over the world because of this and it needs to stop—we must pay closer attention and look out for all of them. Talk about this with your medical professionals, offer to accompany women of color to a doctor's appointment, flow money to organizations focused on the healthcare of marginalized populations. We all have to take care of each other.

—Nitika Chopra, chronic illness activist
and founder of Chronicon

I wish white women would pay attention to stories about what is happening to our children—our sons and daughters. Yeah, they seem to know that more black men are dying at the hands of law enforcement than white men—but do they know their names, are they watching their mother's weep and families unravel? It's hard to look at any pain, I get it, but my request is for people to bear witness, see and carry the burden of the pain as means for action in ways they haven't been willing to in this country's history. It's easier than ever to pay attention—please, look.

—Shaun King, activist, journalist, and CEO of The NorthStar,
a media company that grew out of a nineteenth-century
antislavery newspaper founded by Frederick Douglass

I immigrated to the United States at the age of two. I came with my mother and older brother. We were following in the footsteps of what millions of immigrants had done before us, striving for our American Dream.

In the first months of our American Dream we were homeless, on welfare, and went to bed hungry more times than I can count. Somehow in the most impossible circumstances my mother was able to find us a place to live, get a job, and make sure we never went to bed hungry again.

My mother made miracles happen every day. I love her dearly for all that she gave us and everything she sacrificed, but she is by no means unique in her journey. My mother, like the hundreds of millions of immigrants before her, is the living embodiment of what it means to be American.

We must celebrate the resiliency, grit, love, and bravery of immigrants because without them and their legacy, there really isn't an America.

—Paola Mendoza, filmmaker, artist,
author of *Sanctuary*, activist, and mother

The Constitution protects white, Christian, land-owning men, and how many of those boxes you can check determines how well you can access the system. I'm male, but not white. Reader, maybe you're white but not male—we both have different types of access points to the system because of it. Women on Native Reservations are not white, not male and, because they live on a reservation, which is held in Federal Trust, they cannot own land. They are at the bottom of the list and a lot of them are being killed or disappearing every year in a crisis known as "missing and murdered indigenous women and girls" #MMIWG. Native women have absolutely no entry point to buy and sell into the system whatsoever, so they're scraping together whatever they can to survive. Yes, you white women, and some white men, may be treated unjustly, but do not operate as if you're living your injustices in a silo. The racial dynamics in a country should not just be black and white and antislavery. My request is for you to take notice of how the marginalized populations of this country—yourself as a woman included—are tied closely together because of white supremacy and patriarchy because the Doctrine of Discovery came out of the Vatican and trickled through the Christian church. My request of white women: raise your hand to learn the truth about why our systems look the way they do, and raise your hand for my native sisters.

—Mark Charles, Native activist, former pastor, and coauthor of
*Unsettling Truths: The Ongoing, Dehumanizing Legacy
of the Doctrine of Discovery*

Dear reader, I'm so grateful you're here. Born in northern Uganda, I spent twenty-one years of my childhood as a refugee in camps where we barely survived off of one meal a day. The violence we were fleeing displaced three million people, and 60,000 of my fellow brothers and sisters were forcefully abducted, including my own brother. We'd go to sleep at night wondering where the rest of the world was, why they didn't seem to care. I know my country might feel far away, but we're not; we want the same thing for our children that you do. Just like you are navigating your way out of post-colonialism, we are doing the same here—so much of our conflicts are outcomes of a time when colonial powers were trying to claim our lands as their own. There are generational wounds we can heal together. Thank you for showing up—we are here waiting for you.

—Victor Ochen, Ugandan activist. The organization he founded, African Youth Initiative Network, has so far provided reconstructive medical repair to over 21,000 war victims of rape, mutilation, and gunshots. Ochen bravely led the campaign against child-soldier recruitment amid the war in northern Uganda. He is the first Ugandan and the youngest-ever African nominated for the Nobel Peace Prize,* in 2015.

from where we've come

While I was writing this book, I was on a parallel journey of trying to understand a part of my ancestry that I hadn't been privy to because my father was adopted at birth. I purchased a number of DNA kits as holiday gifts for family members, and when we received the results, we were able to reconstruct my father's biological paternal family tree, thanks to an internet that makes almost everyone very findable. I enjoyed learning about my paternal grandfather, Bill Cahan, a thoracic surgeon who was one of the leading medical professionals to connect smoking to lung cancer and who spent decades taking on big tobacco;[16] he died in 2001. I'm proud of the work of my step-grandmother, Grace Mirabella, who, when she became the editor of *Vogue* in 1971, demanded the magazine not just cover hemlines,

---

* Victor was nominated by a Quaker organization, which makes me particularly giddy: the American Friends Service Committee, an organization that promotes peace and justice as a practical expression of faith in action.

introducing long-form articles about the broadening role of women and other social issues;[17] and of my great-grandmother, Flora Gomperts, who was one of the first activists to protest companies selling German goods at the start of World War II. But for some months we were stuck on finding my father's biological mother—until a relative on the same site reached out to my dad with an email that said, "I thought I knew all of my first cousins, but apparently not!"

A number of weeks of friendly back-and-forth followed, with slightly awkward attempts to summarize our lives via email. We were most curious about whether my grandmother, Anne, was still alive. She was—ninety-two and living in Providence, Rhode Island. According to GPS, she was three hours and twenty-four minutes from my front door. And the more I learned about her, the more excited I was at the idea of becoming acquainted with this family member, who might also help explain some of my characteristics. For instance, we found out Anne started homeless shelters and animal rescue clinics, and had been studying to be a Catholic nun—well, until she and my very suave grandfather crossed paths.

I'd spent the past thirty years of my life daydreaming about her: *Did I look like her? Does she cry easily, too? Did she also have alopecia, and if so, how did she deal? Did she ever think of us?* Now I had an opportunity to find out, and I was excited.

For about two weeks, we and a number of our "new" relatives did the impossible dance of figuring out how and when to make ourselves known to her. We spent a lot of time debating how best to be mindful of our sudden appearance—after all, she was frail, nearing the edge of life—and we equally wanted to be respectful of the five children she raised years after turning my father over to his adoptive parents.

So together we fabricated a set of rules that would help govern how we should proceed, even knowing her age meant she could take her last breath at any moment. And while we negotiated what we thought would be proper performance protocol for a family we had never met, and for a woman who had made an impossible decision sixty-seven years earlier, we found out that she had suddenly passed away.

My grief—wails and slapping the floor, behavior that I had only ever seen in photos of women from far-off places who had lost loved ones in conflict—shocked me. After all, I had lived a comfortable life never knowing her. But my grief lay not only in not being able to meet and touch the warm hand of this ancestor who was responsible for passing on to me so much of my strength and determination, but also in how the reason we'd lost that chance was all the time we'd spent on fabricated performance chores about the best way to proceed. We'd known her name and home address for three weeks while over and over, we played the game of how, when, and who.

We've since made contact with her children—the rest of my father's siblings. They said that toward the end of her life, she was constantly praying out loud, asking for forgiveness; not knowing about my father, they'd struggled to understand what she was beating herself up over for so long. Given her Catholic values, they thought maybe it had been because she had sex before she met their father. And, well, yes, that, but also 🫤.

I'm still angry with myself. I'd wanted to tell her that the hardest decision she had ever made resulted in my father having a safe and joyful life filled with soccer games and art classes. That she passed her grit on to two additional grandchildren, and that she has four great-grandchildren now running after soccer balls and drawing on their mother's walls—just like her first son did. That we survived, and that we wanted her to know we forgive her.

But we missed that opportunity. We left her to have to forgive herself.

We missed the opportunity for a crucial relationship, however short-lived it would have been, because we made up rules about what we could and couldn't do. We wanted to wait until my book was submitted. Until my dad and cousin were back on the East Coast. Until . . . until . . . Our tasks got in the way of our real work—the work of being human, of connecting, of asking questions and extending compassion for what must have felt impossible.

I'll spend the rest of my days wondering "what if." And I don't want you—I don't want us—to suffer from missed opportunities anymore.

We don't have time to defer the work of restorative justice for another decade. We have to be honest about our history, study the current-day consequences, and reconsider our social structures not as a thought exercise but as a way of identifying opportunities for change. Moms whose kids are drowning don't wait to learn how to swim—they jump in. Grab my metaphorical hand and let's go.

Don't imagine you'll eventually reach a blissful end to your to-do lists where you can finally, peacefully, figure out how to contribute. We need you *now*.

We, the American white woman, are key to the world's survival, and we can't pretend the world isn't a frail ninety-two-year-old that might take its last breath at any moment. We are literally at the end of the line; we need to get in the car and drive to Providence right away, because she might die any second.

go, now

Humanity is a paradox. Sometimes we choose the destruction of ourselves and others. Other times we choose to express incredible kindness and generosity. The potential for both always exists within us, and part of our continued work is to recognize which impulse is guiding us. Yet we cannot let this duality that dwells within us—and that drives the wider world—become an excuse for inaction.

We're in the midst of a historic, tectonic reckoning. The past is tapping us on the shoulder and whispering, *Take another look*. Because we can't really move forward until we understand exactly where we've been. The journey to fully deconstruct white supremacy and the patriarchy will be long, and while I hope this book has helped you start, reading these pages is not enough. We must stop walking in the tracks we have been contentedly strolling in for many generations, pivot, and take bold new strides in a drastically different direction.

Our sins aren't the entirety of what defines us; our willingness to escape from our ignorance and find grace—that is our measuring stick. We must begin to rewrite our stories, even if we're not yet completely clear on what that new, better story will look like.

Let's step off our self-righteous pedestals and make room for the new us. Roar when you need to drown out those stifling whispers of insecurity, but cloak yourself with the insight of silence when women who aren't like you use their voices to speak. Unstick yourself from the performance of perfection. Look deeply at our past and connect the dots to the suffering we see today. Toggle past the social media fluff and into the headlines of the day. Monitor your biases, humbly accept your mistakes, and do better. Redraw the lanes the men we love so deeply have been allowed to walk. Call each other *in*, while holding vulnerability sacred and central; it's the fastest way to the productive, courageous conversations of your future.

What I believe is here to stay, now that you've finished this book: the questioning of who we've been, and focus on a more considered, more equitable destination.

I write these last paragraphs convinced that you are powerful and worthy. Now that you know how much needs to be done, and how needed and wanted you are, I trust you to get out of your own way and act. That every time you come face to face with harm on the new frontlines—in your heart, in your home, at your club, in your school, boardroom, gas station, stationery store, spin class, voting booth, lawyer's office, or toll booth on the highway—you step up with the fierceness of all of those women who have handed down their ingenuity and strength and commitment from generation to generation. Everything they've done, everything you have in your bones, has prepared you to raise your hand in this moment.

This is my rallying cry to my privileged family, to my community whom I love, yet who often seem preoccupied with performing for whatever fake audience they've assembled in their mental bleachers: we have to show up for this battle. Now. The way we live our lives and the way our country functions isn't good enough; people are still suffering and dying because of it. Calling it the battle of a lifetime falls short—this is the battle of a species—our species.

We have to give space to the new world that wants to be born, by getting out of our own way as well as blocking and tackling dangerous ideas and outdated institutions. We have to wrestle ourselves and society to let the saint, not the sinner, blossom. Most everyone in the Listening Circles, despite political party or religion, is waiting for that new world to arrive—they all wanted more of the "better world" they thought was within arms' reach. Let's all be the midwives that help her arrive quickly.

It's time for us to be a little bit scared and a lot brave together, because nobody else is coming. Who we are now is not who we will become—go be the women who are waking up inside you. The women throughout history who died for our rights, or who were too endangered by others or too afraid of their own power to raise their hands—let's make them proud. And let's spare future generations from looking back and wondering where we were when they needed us. Go, now.

HOW TO FACILITATE A LISTENING CIRCLE

> Be brave enough to start a conversation that matters.
> —Margaret Wheatley

've spent the past couple of years crisscrossing the country, having closed-door conversations with American white women. The conversations I facilitated and participated in, which I call Listening Circles, were lightly structured, based on inquiry, with no objective but to increase personal understanding of a subject or another's perspective. In some cases, these conversations marked the participants' first attempts to articulate their feelings about something happening inside them or out in the world.

The conversations had challenging moments, but all who participated were eager to engage more in just this type of dialogue—one that calls people in to this kind of collective work. I received messages for months, even years, after initial Listening Circles from people who were continuing to have these conversations, saying how much meaning the discussions continued to bring them.

Following is a suggested blueprint for igniting similar conversations with the people in your own life. If you're considering facilitating a Listening Circle as part of a reading group, you may choose to hold that circle after the group has read the book, using chapter topics as conversation prompts, in addition to the questions suggested below.

While I'm not qualified to facilitate conversations on race, gender, class, disability, sexuality, or other complex subjects (as I've said, I'm still very much a student), and so did not include these as explicit discussion topics in the Listening Circles I held, the topics often surfaced anyway. When they did, I'd lean into participants' curiosity with further questioning, encouraging them to spend some time researching the subject and then share their findings and sources with the group over email. Before holding your own Listening Circle, you may find it useful to re-read chapters eight and nine for further support navigating tense conversations, in case these topics surface in your discussions, too.

At the beginning of a Listening Circle, I set the stage with a few specific ground rules:

1. Everything is off the record.*
2. Strip yourself of the need to perfectly articulate a perspective or point—just speak, even if its messy. Everyone has the right to edit their words or refine their points over the course of the conversation, and after. We are here to learn; our vocabulary and ideas will evolve. Your stance will shift.
3. Don't enter this conversation as if it's going to be a complete activity. These are the first few hours of a lifelong conversation.
4. This conversation is meant to make space for everyone to participate; please keep your thoughts brief so we can make sure everyone has a chance to be heard. I always tell the participants that if they do start to ramble, I'll do my best to break in gracefully, although the interruption is typically clunky. I apologize in advance for what might feel like me cutting them off (since technically I am).

---

* In the ones I held, if someone said something I wanted to share after the conversation or quote publicly, I would circle back with them, make sure I understood their point, and confirm whether the language they used then was still what they meant to say.

5. Avoid "facts." When a wedge issue or other complicated subject sur-
   faces, participants often retreat to a specific script distributed by a
   news outlet, political party, or non-profit. Rarely have I found debating
   the facts helpful in Listening Circles; the conversation usually turns
   into a fact war, with people competing over who can recite more statistics. And let's be real—nobody has a break in the conversation to verify
   the data or vet how it was collected to begin with. Try to stay away from
   talking points that aren't your own.

I like to start Listening Circle conversations with an ice-breaker question; there are great ones available with a simple Google search. I always
enjoy asking people about their "dream jobs," with the pre-requisite that
they can't say their current profession (mine would be the interior designer
of restaurants).

Since these conversations are meant to bring people together and help
us see our common struggle as humans, I keep the questions very top level.
Here are some of the questions I used during the research for this book:

- Why are you here? What motivated you to participate in this
  conversation?
- What is happiness for you?
- What are your regrets? How have you disappointed yourself?
- What stereotype about you is true? What stereotype about you is
  false?
- What part of the American narrative do you feel most tied to?
- How do we participate in and contribute to the world, outside of
  the jobs we have?
- Do you think any part of the "idea of American" has failed? If so,
  which parts?
- Where is it that you belong? How do you think of your place in
  society, beyond being an individual or being part of a family?
- What is it that you are most afraid to face in your own life?
- Who is your hero?
- What would you be willing to fight for (besides your children/loved
  ones)?
- What is your legacy (besides family/job) if you feel like you have
  one? What would you want it to be?

- What would you want to be different about humanity? About yourself?
- What internal suffering do you work the hardest to avoid dealing with?
- Do you think you are understood by others?
- Is there something you hope people will understand about you that you feel they currently do not?
- What do you hope comes out of this discussion?
- What are you most hopeful about when you think of the future?

The most important thing is to come to this work in the spirit of civic responsibility, looking to engage in constant conversation with each other as we work forward. Thank you for doing this—it is the urgent work of our time.

ACKNOWLEDGMENTS

Attempting to summarize words of gratitude feels like a futile attempt, but let me try, as so many fingerprints made this book a reality.

To my children, who are too young to know how much of our precious time I traded to write these words—I did this for you. To my future children whose names I do not know, thank you for waiting just a bit longer.

To my family: I thought I was just overwhelmingly lucky for the first thirty-eight years of my life—I didn't realize how lucky until the last two. I'll be searching my whole life for teachers, but you *all*, in your pajamas and drinking coffee at 214 will always be my most sacred classroom. You've given me just the insight and encouragement I need to venture out and question everything. Thank you, in particular, to my aunts (for raising me!) and female cousins, for your vulnerability during this process, and I apologize for not being as graceful in the past with my opinions as I hope I was in these pages.

To all my ancestors, whom I thank with tears streaming down my face, you arrived and departed at just the right time. I didn't appreciate the weight of the torch I was carrying until I also became a Cahan/Pierik in the spring of 2019. Your commitment to doing better blew wind in my sails at exactly the moments I didn't think I could or *should* go any further. Thank you for giving me what I got to get this done.

There are too many cherished relationships and groups of people to possibly list in this section who have been formative in sculpting my thoughts and encouraging me to be brave. My teachers as far back in elementary school, particularly Ms. Sommerfeld, who helped me finally figure out how to read at the age of eleven.* Abington Friends School for the Quaker ideals woven so carefully into their curriculum, which launched me on the social justice path I continue to try to walk.

My Dot2Dot family, who, over the past decade, ushered me to my own frontline, the blank sheet of the first page of this book. In no particular order: Cole B, dream hampton, Adeporo Oduye, Erica Williams, Jamira Burley, Angela Rye, Carmen Perez, Michelle Minguez, Paola Mendoza, Tamika Mallory, Linda Sarsour, Valerie Kaur, Ayana Johnson, Anjali Kumar, Nia Batts, Reshma Saujani, Nitika Chopra, Albert Sykes, Alexis Jones, Clemantine Wamariya, Sean Carasso, Jamison Monroe, Geena Rocero, Janaye Ingram, Sarah Stillman, Alida Garcia, Ramy Youseff, Emily Tisch Sussman, Jie-Song Zhang, Sean Carasso, Melissa Kushner, Mike de la Rocha, and Michael Skolnik and Rachel Goldstein for bringing us together to begin with.

To my advisors and guardian angels always willing to take a call to help me sift through facts and figures or to explain a concept to me one more time: David Goldberg, Simon Sinek, Amanda Disalvatore, Sarah Sophie Flicker, Chris Wilson, Chris Largent, Tracy Halterman, Kerri Kelly, Erica Ford, Jess Morales, my Women's March Family, Charlie and Sarah Hauck, Ron Finley, and Amichai Lau-Lavie.

To those who mulled over concepts and comma placement with me: Sarah J. Robbins, Jane Wulf, Liz Parker, Jennifer Holder, the team at Kevin Anderson Agency, Sam Horn, and Stephanie Gorton.

To the sensitivity editors who shouldered the burden to help me not cause more harm, with a particular acknowledgment to Treasure Brooks, whose insight and guidance pushed me, and the reader, into spaces of deep reflection. To Mia Ives-Rublee, thank you for the constant education and reminder of all that we need to do for the disabled community, and for holding on to my membership card until I'm ready to come get it. To Mark Charles (and his generous parents, Ted and Evie Charles), whose bravery and insight has helped me see, both figuratively and literally, Turtle Island a bit more clearly. To Holly Baird for helping us navigate the gauntlet that is the world today.

To the wonderful agents at Park & Fine—Celeste Fine, Sarah Passik, and John Mass—whose commitment to seeing this book come to fruition was noble.

---

* The average age is six, by the way. I suffered from severe dyslexia as a child.

To the wise voice of reason coming from BenBella who raised their hand to take a risk with this book, specifically Leah Wilson, Jennifer Canzoneri, Jessika Rieck, Glenn Yeffeth, Adrienne Lang, Sarah Avinger, and Alicia Kania. To Krista Tippett for additional wisdom and being an initial source for a lot of research. To Jenai Wadia—for your input on the cover design.

Additional unquantifiable support and those whom I love, who raise the bar so we can all follow: Blowback Productions, Leelee Groome, Rachel Sklar, Susan McPherson, Glynnis MacNicol, Nicole Patrice Johnson, Sophia Bush, Kriss Carr, Marie Forleo, and Victor Ochen. My girlfriends who kept reminding me some mountains can be moved, particularly Abby Brody, who is climbing the most heartbreaking of all slopes. To my supportive in-laws Ken, Sharon, Josh Goldberg, and Veronica Landry; my little brother, Thomas; and my cherub nephew and niece.

To my parents, for sacrificing so much to build a life that afforded me the clarity and chance to raise my hand to do this work that I feel so drawn to. The sacrifice is not lost on me; I hope I make you proud.

My husband, Jeremy, who takes a bit of heat in the pages of this book on behalf of so many men. Thank you for raising your hand so we could find the space and resources needed to push this book into the world. Your tight hand-squeeze when I was feeling incapable, your offering the tissue box when I was really a mess, your constant vote of confidence in this message— thank you for pushing me out the door to my desk many mornings.

To Karma, who has shouldered so much in this life on behalf of injustices in her home country of Tibet and her family, yet still finds space in her heart for my Ever and Oz. Thank you for raising my children to have your strength. May the outcome of our collective work swiftly circle back to the people of your homeland.

ENDNOTES

INTRODUCTION

1. Erica Chenoweth and Jeremy Pressman, "This Is What We Learned by Counting the Women's Marches," *Monkey Cage* (blog), *Washington Post*, February 7, 2017, https://www.washingtonpost.com/news/monkey-cage/wp/2017/02/07/this-is-what-we-learned-by-counting-the-womens-marches.
2. Dana R. Fisher, Lorien Jasny, and Dawn M. Dow, "Why Are We Here? Patterns of Intersectional Motivations across the Resistance," *Mobilization: An International Quarterly* 23, no. 4 (2018): 451–468.
3. Megan Angelo, "16 Unforgettable Things Maya Angelou Wrote and Said," *Glamour*, May 28, 2014, https://www.glamour.com/story/maya-angelou-quotes.
4. Jeffrey M. Humphreys, *The Multicultural Economy 2018* (Athens, GA: Selig Center for Economic Growth, Terry College of Business, University of Georgia, 2018), pp. 5, 9.
5. Inclusionary Leadership Group, "Women Influence 83% of All Consumer Spending in the US," February 10, 2017, http://genderleadershipgroup.com/the-inclusionary-leadership-blog/210.
6. Krystle M. Davis, "20 Facts and Figures to Know When Marketing to Women," *Forbes*, May 13, 2019, https://www.forbes.com/sites/forbescontentmarketing/2019/05/13/20-facts-and-figures-to-know-when-marketing-to-women/#469971231297.
7. Sam Ellison, "Win over Women, and the Men Will Follow," *Branding: Guardian Small Business Network* (blog), *The Guardian*, July 21, 2015, https://www.theguardian.com/small-business-network/2015/jul/21/win-over-women-men-follow-marketing.
8. Center for American Women and Politics, *Gender Differences in Voter Turnout*, September 16, 2019, https://cawp.rutgers.edu/sites/default/files/resources/genderdiff.pdf.
9. World Bank, "Air Pollution Deaths Cost Global Economy US$225 Billion," press release, September 8, 2016, https://www.worldbank.org/en/news/press-release/2016/09/08/air-pollution-deaths-cost-global-economy-225-billion.
10. Corey Flintoff, "The 'Coalition Of The Willing' Winds Down In Iraq," *NPR*, December 16, 2008, https://www.npr.org/templates/story/story.php?storyId=98025667.

11. James Baldwin, "On Being White . . . and Other Lies," *Essence*, April 1984, 1–3.
12. Becky Ferreria, "Seeing Earth from Space Is the Key to Saving Our Species from Itself," October 12, 2016, https://www.vice.com/en_us/article/bmvpxq/to-save-humanity-look-at -earth-from-space-overview-effect.
13. Ibid.

CHAPTER 1: SILENCE(D)

1. GALvanize USA, "How Do We Reach White Women?" 2019.
2. Ibid.
3. Wendy Wang, "Parents' Time with Kids More Rewarding Than Paid Work—and More Exhausting," Pew Research Center, October 8, 2013, https://www.pewsocialtrends.org/2013 /10/08/parents-time-with-kids-more-rewarding-than-paid-work-and-more-exhausting/.
4. OECD Stat, "Time Use," Organization for Economic Co-Operation and Development, accessed May 16, 2019, https://stats.oecd.org/Index.aspx?datasetcode=TIME_USE.
5. Thomson Reuters Foundation, "The World's 10 Most Dangerous Countries for Women 2018: USA," poll2018.trust.org, accessed November 18, 2019, http://poll2018.trust.org /stories/.
6. Thomson Reuters Foundation, "The World's 10 Most Dangerous Countries for Women 2018: USA."
7. "How Do We Reach White Women?"
8. US Census Bureau, "2018 Population Estimates by Age, Sex, Race and Hispanic Origin," table 2a, accessed March 22, 2020, https://www.census.gov/newsroom/press-kits/2019/ detailed-estimates.html.
9. Andrew Therriault, Joshua Aaron Tucker, and Ted Brader, "Cross-Pressures and Political Participation," Southern Illinois University Carbondale OpenSIUC, 2011 Conference Proceedings, https://core.ac.uk/download/pdf/60534850.pdf.
10. Ibid.
11. Cassandra Nemzoff and Kalipso Chalkidou, "Are Other Countries to Blame for High US Drug Prices?" Center for Global Development, November 13, 2018, https://www.cgdev.org /blog/are-other-countries-blame-high-us-drug-prices.
12. Sheena Malhotra and Aimee Carrillo Rowe, eds., *Silence, Feminism, Power* (London: Palgrave, 2013); Kathy Caprino, "Renowned Therapist Explains the Crushing Effects of Patriarchy on Men and Women Today," *Forbes*, January 25, 2018, https://www.forbes.com/sites /kathycaprino/2018/01/25/renowned-therapist-explains-the-crushing-effects-of-patriarchy -on-men-and-women-today/#3398ead82161.
13. Private conversation with Dr. Priya Fielding-Singh.
14. S. Ballakrishen, P. Fielding-Singh, D. Magliozz, "Intentional Invisibility: Professional Women and the Navigation of Workplace Constraints. Sociological Perspectives," *Sociological Perspectives* (2018), https://gender.stanford.edu/publications/intentional-invisibility -professional-women-and-navigation-workplace-constraints.
15. Darcy Lockman, *All the Rage: Mothers, Fathers, and the Myth of Equal Partnership* (New York: Harper, 2019), 16.
16. Max Lawson et al., "Public Good or Private Wealth?" Oxfam International, January 21, 2019, http://www.oxfam.org/en/research/public-good-or-private-wealth.
17. OECD, "Gender Equality: Balancing Paid Work, Unpaid Work, and Leisure," May 3, 2018, https://www.oecd.org/gender/balancing-paid-work-unpaid-work-and-leisure.htm.
18. Pew Research Center Social & Demographic Trends Project, "How Working Parents Share Parenting and Household Responsibilities," November 4, 2015, https://www.pew

socialtrends.org/2015/11/04/raising-kids-and-running-a-household-how-working-parents-share-the-load/.

19. *The Economist,* "Are Women Paid Less Than Men for the Same Work?" August 1, 2017, https://www.economist.com/graphic-detail/2017/08/01/are-women-paid-less-than-men-for-the-same-work.

20. Jill E. Yavorsky, Claire M. Kamp Dush, and Sarah J. Schoppe-Sullivan, "The Production of Inequality: The Gender Division of Labor Across the Transition to Parenthood," *Journal of Marriage and Family* 77, no. 3 (2015): 662–79, https://doi.org/10.1111/jomf.12189.

21. Rebecca Solnit, "Feminism Silence and Powerlessness Go Hand in Hand—Women's Voices Must Be Heard," *The Guardian,* March 8, 2017, https://www.theguardian.com/commentisfree/2017/mar/08/silence-powerlessness-womens-voices-rebecca-solnit.

22. US Bureau of Labor Statistics, "Labor Force Statistics from the Current Population Survey, Household Data, Annual Averages, 18. Employed Persons by Detailed Industry, Sex, Race, and Hispanic or Latino Ethnicity," accessed October 28, 2019, https://www.bls.gov/cps/cpsaat18.htm.

23. Ohio Humanities, "Betty Freidan: The Three Waves of Feminism," *Ohio Humanities,* April 27, 2018, http://www.ohiohumanities.org/betty-friedan-the-three-waves-of-feminism.

24. Gilborn, "Rethinking White Supremacy: Who Counts in 'WhiteWorld,'" *Ethnicities* 6, no. 3 (2006): 318–40.

25. Vann R. Newkirk II, "The Language of White Supremacy," *The Atlantic,* October 6, 2017, https://www.theatlantic.com/politics/archive/2017/10/the-language-of-white-supremacy/542148/.

26. Race Forward: The Center for Racial Justice Innovation, *2015 Race Reporting Guide,* version 1.1, June 2015, https://www.raceforward.org/sites/default/files/Race%20Reporting%20Guide%20by%20Race%20Forward_V1.1.pdf.

27. The Civil Rights Project, "New York Schools Most Segregated in the Nation," press release, March 26, 2014, https://www.civilrightsproject.ucla.edu/news/press-releases/2014-press-releases/new-york-schools-most-segregated-in-the-nation.

28. Charlotte Higging, "The Age of Patriarchy: How an Unfashionable Idea Became a Rallying Cry for Feminism Today," *The Guardian,* June 22, 2018, https://www.theguardian.com/news/2018/jun/22/the-age-of-patriarchy-how-an-unfashionable-idea-became-a-rallying-cry-for-feminism-today.

29. UNCHR, "UN Conventions of Statelessness," accessed December 18, 2019, https://www.unhcr.org/en-us/un-conventions-on-statelessness.html.

30. Stuart Jefferies, "Jacqueline Rose: A Life in Writing," *The Guardian,* February 3, 2010, https://www.theguardian.com/culture/2012/feb/03/jacqueline-rose-life-writing.

31. US Bureau of Labor Statistics, "Labor Force Characteristics by Race and Ethnicity, 2017," *BLS Reports,* August 2018, https://www.bls.gov/opub/reports/race-and-ethnicity/2017/home.htm.

32. Brittany Rico, Rose M. Kreider, and Lydia Anderson, "Growth in Interracial and Interethnic Married-Couple Households," United States Census, July 9, 2018, https://www.census.gov/library/stories/2018/07/interracial-marriages.html.

33. Caprino, "Renowned Therapist Explains."

34. Layla F. Saad, *Me and White Supremacy: Combat Racism, Change the World, and Become a Good Ancestor* (Naperville, IL: Source Books, 2020).

35. Judith N. Shklar, *American Citizenship* (Boston: Harvard University Press, 1998).

36. Calipher, "The Qualities that Distinguish Women Leaders," accessed December 14, 2019, https://www.calipercanada.com/portfolio/the-qualities-that-distinguish-women-leaders.

37. Catherine Hakim, *Erotic Capital: The Power of Attraction in the Boardroom and the Bedroom* (New York: Basic Books, 2011).

38. Bob Sherwin, "Why Women Are More Effective Leaders Than Men," *Business Insider*, January 24, 2014, https://www.businessinsider.com/study-women-are-better-leaders-2014-1.

39. Marianne Williamson, *A Return to Love* (New York: HarperOne, 1996).

40. Rebecca Traister, *Good and Mad* (New York: Simon & Schuster, 2018).

41. Soraya Chemaly, "Why Women Don't Get to Be Angry," *Medium*, September 18, 2018, https://medium.com/s/story/rage-becomes-her-why-women-dont-get-to-be-angry-b2496e9d679d.

42. Lenny Bernstein and Kimberly Kindy. "Trump Administration Seeks to Make Thousands More Transplant Organs Available," *Washington Post*, December 17, 2019, https://www.washingtonpost.com/national/trump-administration-seeks-to-boost-organs-available-for-transplant/2019/12/17/0b76a264-20d4-11ea-bed5-880264cc91a9_story.html.

CHAPTER 2: PERFORMANCE CHORES, PERFECTION & PRIVILEGE

1. Jaison R. Abel and Richard Deitz, "College May Not Pay Off for Everyone," *Liberty Street Economics* (blog), Federal Reserve Bank of New York, September 4, 2014, https://libertystreeteconomics.newyorkfed.org/2014/09/college-may-not-pay-off-for-everyone.html.

2. Zack Friedman, "Student Loan Debt Statistics In 2019: A $1.5 Trillion Crisis," *Forbes*, February 25, 2019, https://www.forbes.com/sites/zackfriedman/2019/02/25/student-loan-debt-statistics-2019/.

3. Ronald Brownstein, "Admissions Scandal Reveals 'Aristocracy Masquerading as a Meritocracy,'" *CNN*, March 20, 2019, https://www.cnn.com/2019/03/19/politics/college-education-scandal-inequality-higher-education/index.html.

4. US Equal Employment Opportunity Commission, "New Gallup Poll on Employment Discrimination Shows Progress, Problems 40 Years After Founding of EEOC," December 8, 2005, https://www.eeoc.gov/eeoc/newsroom/release/12-8-05.cfm.

5. Jennifer L. Berdahl, "Prescriptive Stereotypes and Workplace Consequences for East Asians in North America," *Cultural Diversity and Ethnic Minority Psychology* 18 (2012): 141–52, https://doi.org/10.1037/a0027692.

6. Brando Simeo Starkey, "Why We Must Talk About the Asian American Story Too," *The Undefeated*, November 3, 2016, https://theundefeated.com/features/why-we-must-talk-about-the-asian-american-story-too/.

7. Paul Sullivan, "The Rising Costs of Youth Sports, in Money and Emotion," *New York Times*, January 17, 2015, https://www.nytimes.com/2015/01/17/your-money/rising-costs-of-youth-sports.html.

8. Bob Cook, "Reminder to Parents: All That Money You Spend Probably Won't Get Your Kid A Scholarship," *Forbes*, April 23, 2019, https://www.forbes.com/sites/bobcook/2019/04/23/reminder-to-parents-all-that-money-you-spend-probably-wont-get-your-kid-a-scholarship/#6e03c0042836.

9. Gretchen Livingston, "Stay-at-Home Moms and Dads Account for About One-in-Five U.S. Parents," *FactTank* (blog), Pew Research Center, September 24, 2018, https://www.pewresearch.org/fact-tank/2018/09/24/stay-at-home-moms-and-dads-account-for-about-one-in-five-u-s-parents/.

10. W. Bradford Wilcox and Lyman Stone, "The Happiness Recession," *The Atlantic*, April 4, 2019, https://www.theatlantic.com/ideas/archive/2019/04/happiness-recession-causing-sex-depression/586405/.

11. Sady Doyle, "Gwyneth, Ivanka, and the End of the Effortless White Woman," *Medium.com*, July 31, 2018, https://medium.com/s/story/gwyneth-ivanka-and-the-end-of-the-effortless-white-woman-9d8c4e01a026.

12. Claire Clain Miller, "The Gender Pay Gap Is Largely Because of Motherhood," *New York Times*, May 13, 2017, https://www.nytimes.com/2017/05/13/upshot/the-gender-pay-gap-is-largely-because-of-motherhood.html.
13. "Female Clergy in U.S. Increased Significantly Over Last 40 Years," EthicsDaily.com, https://ethicsdaily.com/female-clergy-in-u-s-increased-significantly-over-last-40-years/.
14. Reynolds and Amanda Shendruk, "Demographics of the U.S. Military," Council on Foreign Relations, April 24, 2018, https://www.cfr.org/article/demographics-us-military.
15. Claire Zillman, "The Fortune 500 Has More Female CEOs Than Ever Before," *Fortune*, May 16, 2019, https://fortune.com/2019/05/16/fortune-500-female-ceos/.
16. Susan Faludi, *Backlash: The Undeclared War Against American Women, the 15th Anniversary Edition* (New York: Broadway Books, 2006).
17. Dr. Dilts, "Gödel's Incompleteness Theorems," *Infinity Plus One Math is Awesome*, August 4, 2017, https://infinityplusonemath.wordpress.com/2017/08/04/godels-incompleteness-theorems/.
18. Doyle, "Gwyneth, Ivanka, and the End of the Effortless White Woman."
19. Maria Konnikova, "How Facebook Makes Us Unhappy," *The New Yorker*, September 10, 2013, https://www.newyorker.com/tech/annals-of-technology/how-facebook-makes-us-unhappy.
20. Ibid.
21. Thomas Frank stamped this onto the back cover of Jonathan Metzl's book *Dying of Whiteness* as a blurb. Jonathan Metzl, *Dying of Whiteness: How the Politics of Racial Resentment Is Killing America's Heartland* (New York: Basic Books, 2019).
22. Julie Scelfo, *The Women Who Made New York* (New York: Seal Press, 2016).
23. Ibid.
24. Ibid.
25. Nell Irvin Painter, *The History of White People* (New York: W.W. Norton & Company, 2010), 48.
26. Ibid., 362.
27. Ibid.
28. Yolanda Moses, "Why Do We Keep Using the Word 'Caucasian'?" *Sapiens*, February 1, 2017, https://www.sapiens.org/column/race/caucasian-terminology-origin/.
29. Staceyann M. Chin, on Facebook, May 30, 2019, https://www.facebook.com/staceyann.m.chin/posts/10156220418900404.
30. World Health Organization, "Mercury in Skin-Lightening Products," 2011, https://apps.who.int/iris/handle/10665/330015.
31. Ibid.
32. Marian Liu, "Skin Whiteners Are Still in Demand Despite Health Concerns," *CNN*, September 2, 2018, https://www.cnn.com/2018/09/02/health/skin-whitening-lightening-asia-intl/index.html.
33. Mary-Rose Abraham, "Skin Lightening: The Dangerous Obsession That's Worth Billions," MosaicScience, August 29, 2017, https://mosaicscience.com/story/skin-lightening-whitening-India/.
34. Ronald Hall, "Black America's 'Bleaching Syndrome,'" *The Conversation*, February 2018, https://theconversation.com/black-americas-bleaching-syndrome-82200.
35. Lexy Lebsack, "Skin Bleaching Is Poisoning Women—but Business Is Booming," *Refinery29*, May 28, 2019, https://www.refinery29.com/en-ca/2019/05/233892/skin-bleaching-lightening-products-safety-controversy.
36. Rose Abraham, "Dark Is Beautiful: The Battle to End the World's Obsession with Lighter Skin," *The Guardian*, September 4, 2017, https://www.theguardian.com/inequality/2017/sep/04/dark-is-beautiful-battle-to-end-worlds-obsession-with-lighter-skin.
37. Abhay Deol, "Let's Talk About Racism: Our Ads Preach We Will Get Jobs, Find Love if We Are Fairer," *Hindustan Times*, May 23, 2017, https://www.hindustantimes.com/india-news

/lets-talk-about-racism-our-ads-preach-we-d-have-better-jobs-marriages-if-we-are-fairer -says-abhay-deol/story-LKAB5eGLi5vOQVkZ4jUTOO.html.

38. Hall, "Black America's 'Bleaching Syndrome.'"

39. Katheryn B. Davis, Maurice Daniels, and Letha A. Lee See, "The Psychological Effects of Skin Color on African Americans' Self-Esteem," *Journal of Human Behavior in the Social Environment* 1, no. 2–3 (1998): 63–90, doi:10.1300/J137v01n02_05.

40. Ibid.

41. Peggy McIntosh, "White Privilege and Male Privilege: A Personal Account of Coming to See Correspondences Through Work in Women's Studies," 1988, accessed October 28, 2019, https://www.collegeart.org/pdf/diversity/white-privilege-and-male-privilege.pdf.

42. Gus Lubin, "Queens Has More Languages Than Anywhere Else in the World—Here's Where They're Found," *Business Insider*, February 15, 2017, https://www.businessinsider .com/queens-languages-map-2017-2.

43. Kaiser Family Foundation, "Key Facts About the Uninsured Population," December 7, 2018, https://www.kff.org/uninsured/fact-sheet/key-facts-about-the-uninsured-population/.

44. Krista Tippett, "john a. powell: Opening to the Question of Belonging," *On Being*, June 25, 2015, last updated May 10, 2018, https://onbeing.org/programs/john-a-powell-opening-to -the-question-of-belonging-may2018/.

45. United States Census Bureau, "Voting and Registration in the Election of November 2012," May 2013, Report Number P20-568, https://www.census.gov/data/tables/2012/demo/voting -and-registration/p20-568.html.

46. Krista Tippett, "Rebecca Solnit: Falling Together," *On Being*, May 26, 2016, updated December 14, 2017, https://onbeing.org/programs/rebecca-solnit-falling-together-dec2017/; Rebecca Solnit, "Silence and Powerlessness Go Hand in Hand—Women's Voices Must Be Heard," *The Guardian*, May 8, 2017, https://www.theguardian.com/commentisfree/2017 /mar/08/silence-powerlessness-womens-voices-rebecca-solnit.

CHAPTER 3: WHITE LIES

1. University of Turku, "Social Laughter Releases Endorphins in the Brain," June 1, 2017, https://www.sciencedaily.com/releases/2017/06/170601124121.htm.

2. James Baldwin, "On Being White . . . and Other Lies," *Essence*, April 1984, 1–3.

3. Turner, "Why Schools Fail to Teach Slavery's 'Hard History,'" *National Public Radio*, February 4, 2018, https://www.npr.org/sections/ed/2018/02/04/582468315/why-schools-fail-to -teach-slaverys-hard-history.

4. Interview with Mia Ives-Rublee, Disabled Korean American activist.

5. NYU Furman Center, "Focus on Poverty in New York City," *The Stoop* (blog), June 7, 2017, https://furmancenter.org/thestoop/entry/focus-on-poverty.

6. Robin Hood Foundation homepage, accessed November 20, 2019, https://www.robinhood .org/.

7. Lorraine Boissoneault, "Humans May Have Arrived in North America 10,000 Years Earlier Than We Thought," *Smithsonian.com*, January 31, 2017, https://www.smithsonianmag.com /science-nature/humans-may-have-arrived-north-america-10000-years-earlier-we-thought -180961957/.

8. Hansi Lo Wang, "The Map of Native American Tribes You've Never Seen Before," *National Public Radio*, June 24, 2014, https://www.npr.org/sections/codeswitch/2014/06/24/323665644 /the-map-of-native-american-tribes-youve-never-seen-before.

9. Klein, "10 Things You May Not Know About Christopher Columbus," *History.com*, October 5, 2012, updated August 31, 2018, https://www.history.com/news/10-things-you-may-not -know-about-christopher-columbus.

10. Colleen Connolly, "The True Native New Yorkers Can Never Truly Reclaim Their Homeland," *Smithsonian.com*, October 5, 2018, https://www.smithsonianmag.com/history/true-native-new-yorkers-can-never-truly-reclaim-their-homeland-180970472/.

11. Vincent Amoroso, "Peter Minuit and The Purchase of Manhattan Island," *The Culture Trip*, October 20, 2016, https://theculturetrip.com/north-america/usa/new-york/articles/peter-minuit-and-the-purchase-of-manhattan-island/.

12. Matt Soniak, "Was Manhattan Really Bought for $24?" *Mental Floss*, October 2, 2012, http://mentalfloss.com/article/12657/was-manhattan-really-bought-24.

13. Tanay Warerkar, "Manhattan's Average Price per Square Foot Surpasses That of Other Major U.S. Cities," *Curbed New York*, October 2, 2012, https://ny.curbed.com/2017/8/21/16179926/manhattan-average-square-foot-price.

14. Intersections International, "Healing Turtle Island," *Intersections.org*, n.d., accessed November 20, 2019, http://www.intersections.org/healing-turtle-island-0.

15. National Museum of the American Indian, "Harvest Ceremony: Beyond the Thanksgiving Myth. A Study Guide," accessed November 20, 2019, https://americanindian.si.edu/sites/1/files/pdf/education/NMAI_Harvest_Study_Guide.pdf.

16. Michelle Tirado, "The Wampanoag Side of the First Thanksgiving Story," *Indian Country Today*, November 23, 2011, https://newsmaven.io/indiancountrytoday/archive/the-wampanoag-side-of-the-first-thanksgiving-story-TmMLTgQs40aJT_n9T3RMIQ/.

17. Julian Brave Noisecat, "Tommy Orange and The New Native Renaissance," *The Paris Review*, June 29, 2018, accessed May 12, 2019, https://www.theparisreview.org/blog/2018/06/29/tommy-orange-and-the-new-native-renaissance/.

18. Maya Salam, "Everything You Learned About Thanksgiving Is Wrong," *New York Times*, November 21, 2017, http://www.nytimes.com/2017/11/21/us/thanksgiving-myths-fact-check.html.

19. Barbara Maranzani, "How the 'Mother of Thanksgiving' Lobbied Abraham Lincoln to Proclaim the National Holiday," *History*, November 19, 2019, https://www.history.com/news/abraham-lincoln-and-the-mother-of-thanksgiving.

20. Mark Charles and Soong-Chan Rah, *Unsettling Truths: The Ongoing, Dehumanizing Legacy of the Doctrine of Discovery* (Downers Grove, IL: Intervarsity Press Books, 2019).

21. Steve Newcomb, "Five Hundred Years of Injustice," *Shaman's Drum* (Fall 1992): p. 18–20.

22. Mark Charles and Soong-Chan Rah, *Unsettling Truths.*

23. Steve Newcomb, "We the People of the Dominated Native Nations," Indianz.com, February 11, 2019, https://www.indianz.com/News/2019/02/11/steven-newcomb-we-the-people-of-the-domi.asp.

24. Mark Charles and Soong-Chan Rah, *Unsettling Truths.*

25. R. Miller, *Native America, Discovered and Conquered: Thomas Jefferson, Lewis and Clark, and Manifest Destiny* (University of Nebraska Press, 2008).

26. Lisa Wade, "U.S. Schools Are Teaching Our Children That Native Americans Are History," *Pacific Standard*, June 14, 2017, https://psmag.com/social-justice/u-s-schools-teaching-children-native-americans-history-95324.

27. Maureen Costello, Southern Poverty Law Center's Teaching Tolerance Project (Turner 2018), https://www.npr.org/sections/ed/2018/02/04/582468315/why-schools-fail-to-teach-slaverys-hard-history.

28. Alexa Lardieri, "Despite Diverse Demographics, Most Politicians Are Still White Men," *US News*, October 24, 2017, https://www.usnews.com/news/politics/articles/2017-10-24/despite-diverse-demographics-most-politicians-are-still-white-men.

29. Jamelle Bouie, "The Senate Is as Much of a Problem as Trump," *New York Times*, May 10, 2019, https://www.nytimes.com/2019/05/10/opinion/sunday/senate-democrats-trump.html.

30. Stacy Jones, "White Men Account for 72% of Corporate Leadership at 16 of the Fortune 500 Companies," *Fortune*, June 9, 2017, https://fortune.com/2017/06/09/white-men-senior-executives-fortune-500-companies-diversity-data/.

31. Nathan Robinson, "Rich White Men Rule America. How Much Longer Will We Tolerate That?" *The Guardian*, May 20, 2019, https://www.theguardian.com/commentisfree/2019/may/20/rich-white-men-rule-america-minority-rule.

32. "Women CEOs: Ask Catalyst Express," Catalyst, January 1, 2020, https://www.catalyst.org/research/women-ceos-resources/.

33. Michael Harriot, "From Most Hated to American Hero: The Whitewashing of Martin Luther King Jr," *The Root*, April 4, 2018, accessed October 26, 2019, https://www.theroot.com/from-most-hated-to-american-hero-the-whitewashing-of-m-1824258876.

34. Martin Luther King, Jr., "Letter from a Birmingham Jail," https://www.africa.upenn.edu/Articles_Gen/Letter_Birmingham.html.

35. Peter D'Errico, "Native American Genocide or Holocaust?" *Indian Country Today*, January 10, 2017, https://newsmaven.io/indiancountrytoday/archive/native-american-genocide-or-holocaust-f9BbVANPQEOn_BzVGhOJ5g/.

36. Dennis Gaffney, "'American Indian' or 'Native American'?" *Antiques Roadshow*, April 24, 2006, https://web.archive.org/web/20190717171237/http://www.pbs.org/wgbh/roadshow/fts/bismarck_200504A16.html.

37. Max Brantley, "Bill Introduced to Ban Howard Zinn Books from Arkansas Public Schools," *Arkansas Times*, March 2, 2017, https://arktimes.com/arkansas-blog/2017/03/02/bill-introduced-to-ban-howard-zinn-books-from-arkansas-public-schools.

38. Helmut Richard Niebuhr, "The Story of Our Life" from *The Meaning of Revelation* (Louisville, KY: Westminster John Knox Press, 2006).

39. "Navajos Weigh Return to Old Name: Dine," *New York Times,* December 17, 1993, https://www.nytimes.com/1993/12/17/us/navajos-weigh-return-to-old-name-dine.html.

40. Mark Charles and Soong-Chan Rah, *Unsettling Truths.*

41. National Congress of American Indians, *Tribal Nation and the United States: An Introduction* (Washington, DC: National Congress of American Indians, January 15, 2015), http://www.ncai.org/resources/ncai_publications/tribal-nations-and-the-united-states-an-introduction.

42. Mark Charles and Soong-Chan Rah, *Unsettling Truths.*

43. Individuals like Mark Charles and Mahtowin Munro, one of the leaders of the organization United American Indians of New England, call what happened to indigenous people in America a genocide. Many people who study the treatment of indigenous people in California, in particular—like scholar Benjamin Madley—consider their especially brutal treatment there from 1846 to 1873 an attempt at genocide. And historians David Stannard and Ward Churchill have also written books characterizing what happened to indigenous people in America as a genocide. Scholar Jeffrey Ostler predicts that researchers in genocide studies may become increasingly interested in looking at what happened to populations in North America, which hasn't really been a focus in genocide studies up to this point. (Which I think supports our argument, in this book, that there's all sorts of history we as a culture haven't really explored.) (Andrew Buncombe, "Thanksgiving 2017: Natives Americans Reveal What They Think About the Day," *The Independent*, November 22, 2017, https://www.independent.co.uk/news/world/americas/thanksgiving-2017-native-americans-videos-what-do-they-think-racism-columbus-redskins-a8070611.html; Richard White, "Naming America's Own Genocide," *The Nation*, August 17, 2016, https://www.thenation.com/article/naming-americas-own-genocide/; Jeffrey Ostler, *Surviving Genocide: Native Nations and the United States from the American Revolution to Bleeding Kansas* (New Haven, CT: Yale University Press, 2019).)

44. "Genocide: Background," https://www.un.org/en/genocideprevention/genocide.shtml.

45. As Mark Charles and Soong-Chan Rah put it in *Unsettling Truths*, "In 1492, at the start of the War of Discovery and Manifest Destiny the estimated Native population of Turtle Island (North America) ranged between 1.2 million and 20 million. For the sake of argument, we

will use the median of the two numbers which is 9.4 million. Then excluding the approximately 3–4 million who lived in what is now Canada and Alaska, we will estimate the Native population of the lower continental United States in the year 1500 to be 6 million people. Between 1492 and 1900 the estimated population of indigenous peoples in the continental United States dropped to 237,000. That gives the War of Discovery a 96% rate of genocide (i.e. 96% of the Native population was wiped out during the ongoing war). From 1800 to 1900, often referred to as the century of expansion, the indigenous population of Turtle Island was depleted from 600,000 to 237,000. Giving the War of Manifest Destiny a genocide rate of 60%." [Mark Charles and Soong-Chan Rah, *Unsettling Truths* (Madison, WI: IVP Books, 2019)].

46. Alysa Landry, "Abraham Lincoln: Enigmatic President, and Full of Contradictions," *Indian Country Today*, April 19, 2016, https://newsmaven.io/indiancountrytoday/archive/abraham-lincoln-enigmatic-president-and-full-of-contradictions-YujERMz8AkOl_Etug3JfIw/.

47. Khan Academy, "Indian Removal," accessed December 14, 2019, https://www.khanacademy.org/humanities/us-history/the-early-republic/age-of-jackson/a/indian-removal.

48. Joseph Bruchac, *Navajo Long Walk: Tragic Story of a Proud People's Forced March from Their Homeland* (Washington, DC: National Geographic Children's Books, 2002).

49. Sherry Salway Black, "Lincoln: No Hero to Native Americans," *Washington Monthly*, January/February 2013, https://washingtonmonthly.com/magazine/janfeb-2013/lincoln-no-hero-to-native-americans/.

50. Jennifer Major, private conversation with the author, May 2019.

51. KF Baugh, "The Long Walk," *Westnowthen* (blog), October 10, 2017, http://westnowthen.com/blog/2017/10/10/the-long-walk.

52. Jon Wiener, "Largest Mass Execution in US History: 150 Years Ago Today," *The Nation*, December 26, 2012, https://www.thenation.com/article/largest-mass-execution-us-history-150-years-ago-today/.

53. Lisa Wade, "US Schools Are Teaching Our Children That Native Americans Are History," *Pacific Standard*, December 3, 2014, updated June 14, 2017, https://psmag.com/social-justice/u-s-schools-teaching-children-native-americans-history-95324.

54. Fred de Sam Lazaro, "How Off-the-Grid Navajo Residents Are Getting Running Water," *PBS.com*, June 20, 2018, https://www.pbs.org/newshour/show/how-off-the-grid-navajo-residents-are-getting-running-water.

55. Rachel A. Leavitt, Allison Ertl, Kameron Sheats, et al., "Suicides Among American Indian/Alaska Natives—National Violent Death Reporting System, 18 States, 2003–2014," *Centers for Disease Control and Prevention Morbidity and Mortality Weekly Report* 67, no. 8, March, 2, 2018, https://www.cdc.gov/mmwr/volumes/67/wr/pdfs/mm6708a1-H.pdf.

56. Naomi Schaefer Riley, "One Way to Help Native Americans: Property Rights," *The Atlantic*, July 30, 2016, https://www.theatlantic.com/politics/archive/2016/07/native-americans-property-rights/492941/.

57. St. Paul Interfaith Network, "Denominational Statements," 2016, accessed November 20, 2019, https://spinterfaith.org/healing-minnesota-stories/doctrine-discovery/denominational-statements/.

58. William A. Link and James L. Broomall, *Rethinking American Emancipation* (Cambridge, UK; Cambridge University Press, 2015).

59. "Go Deeper: Race Timeline," *RACE—The Power of Illusion*, Public Broadcasting Service, accessed November 20, 2019, https://www.pbs.org/race/000_About/002_03-godeeper.htm.

60. National Park Service, "African Americans at Jamestown," *Historic Jamestowne*, updated August 9, 2019, https://www.nps.gov/jame/learn/historyculture/african-americans-at-jamestown.htm.

61. Debra Meyers and Melanie Perreault, *Colonial Chesapeake: New Perspectives* (Lanham, MD: Lexington Books, 2006).

62. Francis C. Assisi, "Indian Slaves in Colonial America," *India Currents*, May 16, 2007, https://indiacurrents.com/indian-slaves-in-colonial-america/.

63. David W. Galeson, "The Rise and Fall of Indentured Servitude in the Americas: An Economic Analysis," *The Journal of Economic History* 44, no. 1 (1984):1–26, doi:10.1017/S002205070003134X.

64. WGBH, "From Indentured Servitude to Racial Slavery," *Africans in America* (website), Public Broadcasting System, https://www.pbs.org/wgbh/aia/part1/1narr3.html.

65. Ibid.

66. Facing History and Ourselves, "Chapter 2: Inventing Black and White," *Holocaust and Human Behavior*, accessed November 20, 2019, https://www.facinghistory.org/holocaust-and-human-behavior/chapter-2/inventing-black-and-white.

67. Ibid.

68. Galeson, "Rise and Fall of Indentured Servitude."

69. Michelle Alexander, *The New Jim Crow: Mass Incarceration in the Age of Colorblindness* (New York: The New Press, 2010).

70. WGBH, "From Indentured Servitude to Racial Slavery," *Africans in America* (website), Public Broadcasting System, https://www.pbs.org/wgbh/aia/part1/1narr3.html.

71. Sowande' M. Mustakeem, *Slavery at Sea: Terror, Sex, and Sickness in the Middle Passage* (Urbana: University of Illinois Press, 2016).

72. Nicholas Boston, "The Slave Experience: Living Conditions," *Slavery and the Making of America*, accessed November 20, 2019, https://www.thirteen.org/wnet/slavery/experience/living/history.html.

73. Curtis Harris, "The Loathsome Den: Sexual Assault on the Plantation, #MeToo of the 19th Century," *President Lincoln's Cottage*, accessed November 20, 2019, https://www.lincolncottage.org/the-loathsome-den-sexual-assault-on-the-plantation-metoo/.

74. G. Parsons, *Inside View of Slavery* (Boston: John P. Jewett & Company, 1855).

75. 1661: Virginia passes law stating that any free person, regardless of race, could enslave others. This was clarified in a 1670 law to except Indigenous or black people.

    1662: Virginia passes law stating: if you owned a slave, they were yours for life.

    1669: Virginia passes law stating: if an enslaved person dies resisting his master, the death will not be considered the master's fault.

    1672: Virginia passes law making it legal to kill enslaved people who resist arrest. People owning enslaved Africans or others, whose slaves are killed, will receive compensation for their loss—reinforcing the sense that enslaved humans are property.

    (Ariana Kyl, "The First Slave," *Today I Found Out*, August 23, 2013, http://www.todayifoundout.com/index.php/2013/08/the-first-legal-slave-owner-in-what-would-become-the-united-states-was-a-black-man/; Colonial Williamsburg, "Slavery and the Law in Virginia," 2019, accessed November 20, 2019, https://www.history.org/history/teaching/slavelaw.cfm.)

76. William G. Thomas, "Been Workin' on the Railroad," *Opinionator* (blog), *New York Times*, February 10, 2012, https://opinionator.blogs.nytimes.com/2012/02/10/been-workin-on-the-railroad/.

77. Alexander Lane, "The Legend of Slaves Building Capitol Is Correct," *PolitiFact*, January 19, 2009, https://www.politifact.com/truth-o-meter/statements/2009/jan/19/nancy-pelosi/legend-slaves-building-capitol-correct/.

78. Rachel Elizabeth Cargle, "How Racism and Patriarchy Is Taught at School," *Harper's Bazaar*, October 16, 2018, https://www.harpersbazaar.com/culture/politics/a23732907/school-history-teaching-children-racism-patriarchy/.

CHAPTER 4: GO WHITE-SAVIOR YOURSELF

1. Mark Dolliver, "US Time Spent with Media 2019," EMarketer, May 30, 2019, https://www.emarketer.com/content/us-time-spent-with-media-2019.
2. JoAnn Miller and Marilyn Chamberlin, "Women Are Teachers, Men Are Professors: A Study of Student Perceptions," *Teaching Sociology* 28 (2000): 283, https://doi.org/10.2307/1318580.
3. Krista Tippett, "john a. powell: Opening to the Question of Belonging," *On Being*, June 25, 2015, last updated May 10, 2018, https://onbeing.org/programs/john-a-powell-opening-to-the-question-of-belonging-may2018/.
4. Tom Vanderbilt, "Opinion: The Psychology of Genre," *New York Times*, May 29, 2016, https://www.nytimes.com/2016/05/29/opinion/sunday/the-psychology-of-genre.html.
5. Tippett, "Opening to the Question of Belonging."
6. Jessica Nordell, "Is This How Discrimination Ends? A New Approach to Implicit Bias," *The Atlantic*, May 7, 2017, https://www.theatlantic.com/science/archive/2017/05/unconscious-bias-training/525405/.
7. Phyllis A. Katz and Jennifer A. Kofkin, "Race, Gender, and Young Children," in *Development Psychopathy Perspectives on Adjustment, Risk and Disorder*, ed. Suniya S. Luthar, Jacob A. Burack, Dante Cicchetti, and John R. Weisz (New York: Cambridge University Press, 1997): 51–74.
8. Patricia Ramsey and Leslie R. Williams, *Multicultural Education: A Source Book*, 2nd ed. (New York: RoutledgeFalmer, 2003), 83.
9. Patricia G. Ramsey, "Children's Responses to Differences," *NHSA Dialog* 11, no. 4 (2008): 225–37, doi:10.1080/15240750802432607.
10. Lousie Derman-Sparks and Patricia G. Ramsey, *What If All the Kids Are White? Anti-Bias Multicultural Education with Young Children and Families*, 2nd ed. (New York: Teachers College Press, 2011), 106.
11. Ramsey, "Children's Responses to Differences."
12. C. J. Averhart and R. S. Bigler, "Shades of Meaning: Skin Tone, Racial Attitudes, and Constructive Memory of African American Children," *Journal of Experimental Child Psychology* 67, no. 3 (1997): 363–88.
13. Cheryl Staats, Kelly Capatosto, Robin A Wright, and Danya Contractor, *State of the Science: Implicit Bias Review 2015*, Kirwan Institute, 2015, http://kirwaninstitute.osu.edu/wp-content/uploads/2015/05/2015-kirwan-implicit-bias.pdf.
14. *Variety*, "Beyoncé Surprises Colin Kaepernick to Present SI Muhammad Ali Legacy Award," *NBC News*, December 6, 2017, https://www.nbcnews.com/news/us-news/beyonc-surprises-colin-kaepernick-present-si-muhammad-ali-legacy-award-n826986.
15. Robin DiAngelo and Michael Eric Dyson, *White Fragility: Why It's So Hard for White People to Talk About Racism* (Boston: Beacon Press, 2018).
16. Ibid.
17. Ibid.
18. Tema Okun, *From White Racist to White Anti-Racist: The Life-Long Journey*, n.d., accessed November 20, 2019, https://www.fammed.wisc.edu/files/webfm-uploads/documents/diversity/LifeLongJourney.pdf.
19. *Open Education Sociology Dictionary*, s.v. "Meritocracy," accessed November 20, 2019, https://sociologydictionary.org/meritocracy/.
20. Michael B. Sauter, "16 Most Segregated Cities in America," *24/7 Wall St*, July 21, 2017, https://247wallst.com/special-report/2017/07/21/16-most-segregated-cities-in-america/.
21. Ibid.
22. DiAngelo and Dyson, *White Fragility*.

23. Eula Biss, "White Debt," *New York Times*, June 12, 2015, https://www.nytimes.com/2015/12/06/magazine/white-debt.html.

24. Ibid.

25. Donald E. Pease, "American Exceptionalism," *Oxford Bibliographies*, June 27, 2018, https://www.oxfordbibliographies.com/view/document/obo-9780199827251/obo-9780199827251-0176.xml.

26. Christine E. Sleeter, *Keepers of the American Dream: A Study of Staff Development and Multicultural Education* (London: Farmer, 1992).

27. Kenneth M. Zeichner, "Educating Teachers for Cultural Diversity," paper presented at the annual meeting of the American Educational Research Association, Atlanta, 1993.

28. DiAngelo and Dyson, *White Fragility*.

CHAPTER 5: KKK & KALE SMOOTHIES

1. Minderoo Foundation, "Walk Free," accessed November 20, 2019, https://www.minderoo.com.au/walk-free/.

2. History.com, "Ku Klux Klan," October 29, 2009, updated May 22, 2019, https://www.history.com/topics/reconstruction/ku-klux-klan.

3. History.com, "Jim Crow Laws," February 28, 2019, updated March 13, 2019, https://www.history.com/topics/early-20th-century-us/jim-crow-laws.

4. Ibid.

5. "Prison Labour Is a Billion-Dollar Industry, with Uncertain Returns for Inmates," *The Economist*, March 16, 2017, https://www.economist.com/united-states/2017/03/16/prison-labour-is-a-billion-dollar-industry-with-uncertain-returns-for-inmates.

6. Caroline Winter, "What Do Prisoners Make for Victoria's Secret?" *Mother Jones*, July/August 2008, https://www.motherjones.com/politics/2008/07/what-do-prisoners-make-victorias-secret/1165/.

7. Isabelle Chapman, "Prison Inmates Are Fighting California's Fires, but Are Often Denied Firefighting Jobs After Their Release," *CNN*, October 31, 2019, https://www.cnn.com/2019/10/31/us/prison-inmates-fight-california-fires-trnd/index.html.

8. Nathan James, *CRS Report for Congress: Federal Prison Industries*, Congressional Research Service, RL32380, updated July 13, 2007, https://fas.org/sgp/crs/misc/RL32380.pdf.

9. "Prison Labour Is a Billion-Dollar Industry," *The Economist*.

10. Chris Wilson, *The Master Plan: My Journey from Life in Prison to a Life of Purpose* (New York: G.P. Putnam, 2019).

11. PrisonPro, "How to Save Money on Prison and Jail Phone Calls," accessed November 22, 2019, http://www.prisonpro.com/content/how-save-money-prison-jail-phone-calls.

12. Ava DuVernay and Spencer Averick, *13th*, directed by Ava DuVernay (Netflix, October 7, 2016), https://www.netflix.com/title/80091741.

13. Vinay Basti, and Kara Gotsch, "Capitalizing on Mass Incarceration: US Growth in Private Prisons," August 2, 2018, http://sentencingproject.org/publications/capitalizing-on-mass-incarceration-u-s-growth-in-private-prisons/.

14. World Prison Brief, "Highest to Lowest—Prison Population Rate," accessed December 14, 2019, https://www.prisonstudies.org/highest-to-lowest/prison_population_rate?field_region_taxonomy_tid=All.

15. Ibid., accessed November 22, 2019.

16. Chris Mai and Ram Subramanian, "The Price of Prisons: Examining State Spending Trends, 2010–2015," Vera Institute of Justice, May 2017, https://www.vera.org/publications/price-of-prisons-2015-state-spending-trends.

17. Kelly M. Hoffman, Sophie Trawalter, Jordan R. Axt, and M. Norman Oliver, "Racial Bias in Pain Assessment and Treatment Recommendations, and False Beliefs About Biological Differences Between Blacks and Whites," *Proceedings of the National Academy of Sciences of the United States of America* 113, no. 16 (2016): 4296–301, https://www.pnas.org/content /113/16/4296.long.

18. Kate Torgonovick May, "The Hidden Victims of the Bail Crisis? Women," Ideas.TED.com, April 12, 2019, https://ideas.ted.com/the-hidden-victims-of-the-bail-crisis/.

19. Margaret Goff, "Three Ways Mass Incarceration Affects Women of Color," Urban Institute, March 30, 2018, https://www.urban.org/urban-wire/three-ways-mass-incarceration-affects -women-color.

20. Michael Harriot, "Why We Never Talk About Black-on-Black Crime: An Answer to White America's Most Pressing Question," *The Root*, October 3, 2017, https://www.theroot.com /why-we-never-talk-about-black-on-black-crime-an-answer-1819092337.

21. Daniel Angster, "Video: What Happens When Local News Over-represents African-Americans as Criminals," *Media Matters for America*, March 24, 2015, https://www.mediamatters.org/ legacy/video-what-happens-when-local-news-over-represents-african-americans-criminals.

22. Nikole Hannah-Jones, "Taking Freedom: Yes, Black America Fears the Police. Here's Why," *Pacific Standard*, April 10, 2018, updated May 8, 2018, https://psmag.com/social-justice /why-black-america-fears-the-police.

23. German Lopez, "How Systemic Racism Entangles All Police Officers—Even Black Cops," *Vox*, August 15, 2016, https://www.vox.com/2015/5/7/8562077/police-racism-implicit-bias.

24. Federal Bureau of Prisons, "Inmate Race," accessed November 22, 2019, https://www.bop .gov/about/statistics/statistics_inmate_race.jsp.

25. United States Census Bureau, "Quick Facts: United States," accessed November 22, 2019, https://www.census.gov/quickfacts/fact/table/US/PST045218#PST045218.

26. German Lopez, "Research Says There Are Ways to Reduce Racial Bias. Calling People Racist Isn't One of Them," *Vox*, updated July 30, 2019, https://www.vox.com/identities /2016/11/15/13595508/racism-research-study-trump.

27. United States Sentencing Commission, "Demographic Differences in Sentencing: An Update to the 2012 Booker Report," November 2017, https://www.ussc.gov/sites/default /files/pdf/research-and-publications/research-publications/2017/20171114_Demographics .pdf.

28. "Honoring Officers Killed 2019," Officer Down Memorial Page, accessed January 2, 2020, https://www.odmp.org/search/year?year=2019.

29. FEMA, "Firefighter Fatalities in the United States in 2018," September 2019, https://www .usfa.fema.gov/downloads/pdf/publications/firefighter_fatalities_2018.pdf.

30. "School Shootings This Year: How Many and Where," accessed January 2, 2020, https://www .edweek.org/ew/section/multimedia/school-shootings-this-year-how-many-and-where.html.

31. Eli Hager, "A Mass Incarceration Mystery," *The Marshall Project*, December 15, 2017, https://www.themarshallproject.org/2017/12/15/a-mass-incarceration-mystery.

32. K. K. Rebecca Lai and Jasmine C. Lee, "Why 10% of Florida Adults Can't Vote: How Felony Convictions Affect Access to the Ballot," *New York Times*, October 6, 2016, https:// www.nytimes.com/interactive/2016/10/06/us/unequal-effect-of-laws-that-block-felons-from -voting.html.

33. Lucius Couloute and Daniel Kopf, "Out of Prison & Out of Work: Unemployment Among Formerly Incarcerated People," *Prison Policy*, July 2018, https://www.prisonpolicy.org/reports /outofwork.html.

34. German Lopez, "Research Says There Are Ways to Reduce Racial Bias."

35. Susan Leicher and Thompson & Columbus, Inc., "Blueprint for Investing in Women Ages 25–59," New York Women's Foundation, November 2018, https://www.nywf.org/wp -content/uploads/2018/11/VFTF_25-59_Full-Report_v6-FINAL.pdf.
36. GLAAD, "Transgender FAQ," accessed November 22, 2019, https://www.glaad.org/ transgender/transfaq.
37. Kenneth Haynes, "Are Women Better Shooters Than Men?" *NRAFamily.org*, January 15, 2019, https://www.nrafamily.org/articles/2019/1/15/are-women-better-shooters-than-men/.
38. "A Map of Gender-Diverse Cultures," *Independent Lens*, August 11, 2015, http://www.pbs .org/independentlens/content/two-spirits_map-html/.
39. Chella Man, "What It's Like to Be Trans and Live with Gender Dysphoria," *Teen Vogue*, September 21, 2018, https://www.teenvogue.com/story/what-its-like-to-be-trans-and-live -with-gender-dysphoria.
40. "In Pictures: 13 Silliest Uses of Taxpayer Money. 2. $930 Million: On Unnecessary Printing Costs," *Forbes*, accessed November 22, 2019, https://www.forbes.com/pictures/ejde45i/930 -million-on-unnecessary-printing-costs/.
41. William V. Padula, Shiona Heru, and Jonathan D. Campbell, "Societal Implications of Health Insurance Coverage for Medically Necessary Services in the US Transgender Population: A Cost-Effectiveness Analysis," *Journal of General Internal Medicine* 31, no. 4 (2016): 394–401.
42. Henry Louis Gates Jr., "The Truth Behind '40 Acres and a Mule,'" *The African Americans: Many Rivers to Cross*, January 6, 2013, https://www.pbs.org/wnet/african-americans-many -rivers-to-cross/history/the-truth-behind-40-acres-and-a-m.
43. Evan Comen, "Detroit, Chicago, Memphis: The 25 Most Segregated Cities in America," *USA Today*, July 20, 2019, https://www.usatoday.com/story/money/2019/07/20/detroit -chicago-memphis-most-segregated-cities-america-housing-policy/39703787/.
44. Michael B. Sauter, Evan Comen, and Samuel Stebbins, "16 Most Segregated Cities in America." *24/7 Wall Street*, July 21, 2017, https://247wallst.com/special-report/2017/07/21/16 -most-segregated-cities-in-america/.
45. Ibid.
46. Emily Badger, "How Redlining's Racist Effects Lasted for Decades," The Upshot (blog), *New York Times*, August 24, 2017, https://www.nytimes.com/2017/08/24/upshot/how-redlinings -racist-effects-lasted-for-decades.html.
47. Dahlia Lithwick, "The Convention from the Cheap Seats," *Slate*, July 27, 2004, https://slate .com/news-and-politics/2004/07/the-convention-s-cheap-seats.html.
48. Erin Blakemore, "How the GI Bill's Promise Was Denied to a Million Black WWII Veterans," *History.com*, June 21, 2019, updated September 30, 2019, https://www.history.com /news/gi-bill-black-wwii-veterans-benefits.
49. US Air Force, "Born of Controversy: The GI Bill of Rights," June 24, 2008, https://www. af.mil/News/Article-Display/Article/123186/born-of-controversy-the-gi-bill-of-rights/.
50. Ita Katznelson, *When Affirmative Action was White* (New York: W. W. Norton), 122.
51. US Census Bureau, "Real Median Household Income by Race and Hispanic Origin: 1967 to 2017," accessed November 22, 2019, https://www.census.gov/content/dam/Census/library /visualizations/2018/demo/p60-263/figure1.pdf.
52. Erin Blakemore, "How the GI Bill's Promise Was Denied to a Million Black WWII Veterans."
53. Ira Katznelson, *When Affirmative Action Was White*.
54. Selena Hill, "Cities with the Highest Percentage of Black Homeowners," *Black Enterprise*, June 5, 2019, https://www.blackenterprise.com/cities-highest-percentage-black-homeowners/.
55. Karen K. Ho, "Why It Costs More to Borrow if You're Black," *WealthSimple*, February 28, 2019, https://www.wealthsimple.com/en-us/magazine/data-racial-borrowing-gap-us.

56. Aaron Glantz and Emmanuel Martinez, "Kept Out: How Banks Block People of Color from Homeownership," *AP News*, February 15, 2018, https://apnews.com/ae4b40a720b74 ad8a9b0bfe65f7a9c29/Kept-out:-How-banks-block-people-of-color-from-homeownership.

57. Aly J. Yale, "Black Home Buyers Denied Mortgages More Than Twice as Often as Whites, Report Finds," *Forbes*, May 7, 2018, https://www.forbes.com/sites/alyyale/2018/05/07/ mortgage-loan-denials-more-common-with-minorities-new-report-shows/.

58. Hua Sun and Lei Gao, "Lending Practices to Same-Sex Borrowers," *Proceedings of the National Academy of Sciences of the United States of America* 116, no. 9 (2019): 9293–302, https://www.pnas.org/content/116/19/9293.

59. Joint Center for Housing Studies of Harvard University, "The State of the Nation's Housing 2018," accessed December 14, 2019, http://www.jchs.harvard.edu/sites/default/files /Harvard_JCHS_State_of_the_Nations_Housing_2018.pdf.

60. Matt Bruenig, "The Top 10% of White Families Own Almost Everything," *The American Prospect*, September 8, 2014, https://prospect.org/api/content/3137ed77-ab82-5a87 -b28f-52b6f40b4afc/.

61. US Census Bureau, "Historical Households Tables," accessed October 26, 2019, https:// www.census.gov/data/tables/time-series/demo/families/households.html.

62. National Wellness Institute, "About Wellness," accessed November 22, 2019, https://www .nationalwellness.org/page/AboutWellness.

63. Rina Raphael, "These 10 Market Trends Turned Wellness into a $4.2 Trillion Global Industry," *Fast Company*, October 8, 2018, https://www.fastcompany.com/90247896/these -10-market-trends-turned-wellness-into-a-4-2-trillion-global-industry.

64. WELLread, "WE GOT GOOP'D," n.d., CTZNWELL, accessed November 22, 2019, https://mailchi.mp/ctznwell/wegotgoopd?e=67b5d6a3eb.

65. Raj Chetty, Michael Stepner, Sarah Abraham, et al., "The Association Between Income and Life Expectancy in the United States, 2001–2014," *JAMA* 315, no. 16 (2016): 1750–66, https://doi.org/10.1001/jama.2016.4226.

66. Vann R. Newkirk II, "America's Health Segregation Problem," *The Atlantic*, May 18, 2016, https://www.theatlantic.com/politics/archive/2016/05/americas-health-segregation-problem /483219/.

67. Ibid.

68. Jill Cornfield, "Just 4 in 10 Americans Have Savings They'd Rely on in an Emergency," *Bankrate*, January 12, 2017, https://www.bankrate.com/finance/consumer-index/money -pulse-0117.aspx.

69. Dan Mangan, "Medical Bills Are the Biggest Cause of US Bankruptcies," *CNBC*, June 25, 2013, https://www.cnbc.com/id/100840148.

70. UNOS, "Transplant Trends," accessed December 14, 2019, https://unos.org/data/transplant -trends/.

71. National Kidney Foundation, "What Is Dialysis?" December 24, 2015, https://www.kidney .org/atoz/content/dialysisinfo.

72. Nancy Kutner, Tess Bowles, Rebecca Zhang, et al., "Dialysis Facility Characteristics and Variation in Employment Rates: A National Study," *Clinical Journal of the American Society of Nephrology* 3, no. 1 (2008): 111–16, https://doi.org/10.2215/CJN.02990707.

73. The Planetary Society, "What Is NASA's Budget?" accessed November 22, 2019, https:// www.planetary.org/get-involved/be-a-space-advocate/nasa-budget.html.

74. National Institutes of Health, "Budget," January 24, 2019, https://www.nih.gov/about-nih /what-we-do/budget.

75. Department of Homeland Security, "President's Fiscal Year 2020 Budget Fortifies DHS Operations, Supports Frontline Personnel, Secures Our Borders and Confronts

EmergingThreats,"March 18, 2019, https://www.dhs.gov/news/2019/03/18/president-s-fiscal -year-2020-budget.

76. "US Department of Agriculture, Economic Research Service, "Key Statistics & Graphics," last updated September 4, 2019, https://www.ers.usda.gov/topics/food-nutrition-assistance /food-security-in-the-us/key-statistics-graphics.aspx.

77. Do Something, "11 Facts About Food Deserts," accessed November 22, 2019, https://www .dosomething.org/us/facts/11-facts-about-food-deserts.

78. Sarah Treuhaft and Allison Karpyn, *The Grocery Gap: Who Has Access to Healthy Food and Why It Matters* (Philadelphia: The Food Trust, 2010), http://thefoodtrust.org/uploads /media_items/grocerygap.original.pdf.

79. Gary D. Sandefur, "American Indian Reservations: The First Underclass Areas?" *Focus* 12, no. 1 (1989): 37–41, https://www.irp.wisc.edu/publications/focus/pdfs/foc121f.pdf.

80. Partnership with Native Americans, "Combating Food Insecurity on Native American Reservations," April 2017, http://www.nativepartnership.org/site/DocServer/2017-PWNA -NPRA-Food-Insecurity-Project-Grow.pdf?docID=7106.

81. Do Something, "11 Facts About Food Deserts."

82. Sanjay Gupta, "One Nation Under Stress," *HBO*, 2019, https://www.hbo.com/documentaries /one-nation-under-stress.

83. International Trade Administration, "2016 Top Markets Report: Pharmaceuticals," Top Markets Series, US Department of Commerce, n.d., accessed November 22, 2019, https://legacy .trade.gov/topmarkets/pdf/Pharmaceuticals_Executive_Summary.pdf.

84. "Global Pharma Spending Will Hit $1.5 Trillion in 2023, Says IQVIA," *Pharmaceutical Commerce*, January 29, 2019, https://pharmaceuticalcommerce.com/business-and-finance /global-pharma-spending-will-hit-1-5-trillion-in-2023-says-iqvia/.

85. Cody C. Delistraty, "The Importance of Eating Together," *The Atlantic*, July 18, 2014, https:// www.theatlantic.com/health/archive/2014/07/the-importance-of-eating-together/374256/.

86. Sanjay Gupta, "One Nation Under Stress."

87. "More Than 150 million Americans Play Video Games," L' Agence Française pour le Jeu Vidéo, April 15, 2015, https://www.afjv.com/news/5038_more-than-150-million-americans -play-video-games.htm.

88. Sanjay Gupta, "One Nation Under Stress."

89. Michelle Obama, "US Election: Read Michelle Obama Speech in Full," *BBC News*, October 14, 2016, https://www.bbc.com/news/election-us-2016-37651657.

90. National Coalition Against Domestic Violence, "National Statistics," accessed November 22, 2019, https://ncadv.org/statistics.

91. "Equal Pay Day for ALL Women Should Be on December 31, but It's Not," Equal Pay Day, accessed November 22, 2019, http://www.equalpaytoday.org/equalpaydays.

92. Charisse Jones, "Women Lose $513 Billion a Year in Wages Due to Gender Pay Gap and Math Is Worse for Some," *USA Today*, October 23, 2018, https://www.usatoday.com/ story/money/2018/10/23/women-lose-500-billion-year-because-stubborn-gender-pay -gap/1728870002/.

93. Kids Count Data Center, "Children in Poverty by Race and Ethnicity in the United States," accessed December 14, 2019, https://datacenter.kidscount.org/data/tables/44 -children-in-poverty-by-race-and-ethnicity#detailed/1/any/false/37/10,11,9,12,1/324,323.

94. US Mission to the Organization for Economic Cooperation & Development, "What Is the OECD?" accessed November 22, 2019, https://usoecd.usmission.gov/our-relationship/ about-the-oecd/what-is-the-oecd/.

95. Findlaw, "FMLA Eligibility," accessed November 22, 2019, https://employment.findlaw .com/family-medical-leave/fmla-eligibility.html.

96. Although people who aren't pregnant might see nine months of childbearing as a disability, suggesting an expectant mother might face similar barriers to disabled people may seem inappropriate, and any suggestion that she can't "handle" pregnancy's mental and emotional burdens is outright sexist. However, as Korean American disability activist and writer, Mia Ives-Rublee, suggests, "Would I say that pregnant people are disabled in terms of identity? No. Disability as an identity means an individual has a lived experience with a disability that has affected every aspect of their life and they decide to actively identify with the disability community. But do they share some of the same or similar barriers to society due to *ableism*? Yes. Ableism, a systematic prejudice against disabled people or people perceived to have a disability or medical condition, manifests itself in a spectrum of noxious ways, believing that if you can't do something in the perceived 'normal' way you are less than a person without a disability or medical condition. Pregnant people can be victims of ableist systems. However, pregnant people often do not face lasting barriers due to their medical condition (unless they have complications). Thus they often do not identify as disabled and classifying pregnancy as a disability may result in much confusion for individuals seeking legal protections." (Despite the Americans with Disabilities Act being adopted in 1990, many public businesses still lack wheelchair-accessible entrances. Students with disabilities still struggle to receive accommodations in school, and the pay gap between nondisabled and disabled persons is still alarmingly high; Bhattacharya and Heather Long, "America Still Leaves the Disabled Behind," *CNN Money*, July 26, 2015, https://money.cnn.com/2015/07/26/news/economy /americans-with-disabilities-act-problems-remain/.)

97. "New York State Maternity Leave: Everything Expectant Parents Need to Know About the New Paid Leave Law," *Working Mother*, accessed May 15, 2019, https://www.working mother.com/New-york-maternity-leave.

98. US Centers for Disease Control and Prevention, "Pregnancy Mortality Surveillance System," October 10, 2019, https://www.cdc.gov/reproductivehealth/maternalinfanthealth /pregnancy-mortality-surveillance-system.htm.

99. The Editorial Board, "Easing the Dangers of Childbirth for Black Women," *The New York Times*, April 20, 2018, https://www.nytimes.com/2018/04/20/opinion/childbirth-black -women-mortality.html.

100. Nina Martin, "Black Mothers Keep Dying After Giving Birth. Shalon Irving's Story Explains Why," *NPR*, December 7, 2017, https://www.npr.org/2017/12/07/568948782/black-mothers -keep-dying-after-giving-birth-shalon-irvings-story-explains-why.

101. Linda Villarossa, "Why America's Black Mothers and Babies Are in a Life-or-Death Crisis," *New York Times*, April 11, 2018, https://www.nytimes.com/2018/04/11/magazine/black -mothers-babies-death-maternal-mortality.html.

102. Ibid.

103. Ibid.

104. "Percentage of Women in National Parliaments," Inter-Parliamentary Union, October 2019, accessed November 22, 2019, http://archive.ipu.org/wmn-e/classif.htm.

105. Li Zhou, "It's Official: A Record-Breaking Number of Women Have Won Seats in Congress," *Vox*, November 7, 2018, https://www.vox.com/policy-and-politics/2018/11/7/18024742/mid term-results-record-women-win.

106. Mark Lino, "The Cost of Raising a Child," US Department of Agriculture, March 8, 2017, https://www.usda.gov/media/blog/2017/01/13/cost-raising-child.

107. Alexandra Stanczyk, "What Changes in Household Income Around a Baby's Arrival Tell Us About the Importance of Paid Family and Medical Leave," *Urban Wire: Families* (blog), February 5, 2018, https://www.urban.org/urban-wire/what-changes-household-income-around -babys-arrival-tell-us-about-importance-paid-family-and-medical-leave.

CHAPTER 6: WHAT ABOUT THE BOYS?

1. Samantha Smithstein, "Toxic Masculinity: What Is It and How We Can Change It," *Psychology Today*, October 2, 2018, https://www.psychologytoday.com/us/blog/what-the-wild-things-are/201810/toxic-masculinity-what-is-it-and-how-do-we-change-it.

2. Ibid.

3. David McGlynn, "In the #MeToo Era, Raising Boys to be Good Guys," *New York Times*, June 1, 2018, https://www.nytimes.com/2018/06/01/well/family/metoo-sons-sexual-harassment-parenting-boys.html.

4. US Centers for Disease Control and Prevention, "Preventing Sexual Violence," last reviewed March 12, 2019, accessed November 28, 2019, https://www.cdc.gov/violenceprevention/sexualviolence/fastfact.html.

5. Rebecca A. Clay, "Redefining Masculinity," *American Psychological Association* 43 no. 6 (2012): 52.

6. Mark Greene, "The Man Box: The Link Between Emotional Suppression and Male Violence," *The Good Men Project*, October 2, 2018, https://goodmenproject.com/featured-content/megasahd-man-box-the-link-between-emotional-suppression-and-male-violence/.

7. Krista Tippett, "Rebecca Traister and Avi Klein: #MeToo Through a Social Lens," *On Being*, December 6, 2018, https://onbeing.org/programs/rebecca-traister-and-avi-klein-metoo-through-a-solutions-lens-dec2018/#transcript.

8. Rebecca Traister, *Good and Mad* (New York: Simon & Schuster, 2018).

9. Tippett, "Rebecca Traister and Avi Klein."

10. Ibid.

11. Michael Kimmel, "Almost All Violent Extremists Share One Thing: Their Gender," *The Guardian*, April 8, 2018, https://www.theguardian.com/world/2018/apr/08/violent-extremists-share-one-thing-gender-michael-kimmel?CMP=Share_iOSApp_Other.

12. Michael Kimmel, *Angry White Men: American Masculinity at the End of an Era* (New York: Nation Books, 2017).

13. Kimmel, "Almost All Extremists."

14. Andy Hinds, "'Messages of Shame Are Organized Around Gender,'" *The Atlantic*, April 26, 2013, https://www.theatlantic.com/sexes/archive/2013/04/messages-of-shame-are-organized-around-gender/275322/.

15. Avi Klein, "What Men Say About #MeToo in Therapy," *New York Times*, June 30, 2018, accessed May 13, 2019, https://www.nytimes.com/2018/06/30/opinion/sunday/men-metoo-therapy-masculinity.html.

16. Guy Winch, "Together but Still Lonely," *The Squeaky Wheel* (blog), *Psychology Today*, June 28, 2013, https://www.psychologytoday.com/us/blog/the-squeaky-wheel/201306/together-still-lonely.

17. Mia de Graaf, "Loneliness Epidemic Sweeps the US," *Daily Mail*, May 1, 2018, https://www.dailymail.co.uk/health/article-5679315/Loneliness-epidemic-sweeps-Huge-study-reveals-HALF-Americans-feel-time.html.

18. John Bingham, "2.5 Million Men 'Have No Close Friends,'" *The Telegraph*, November 14, 2015, https://www.telegraph.co.uk/men/active/mens-health/11996473/2.5-million-men1-have-no-close-friends.html.

19. Chandra White-Cummings, "Handle with Care: A Conversation with Black Men on Mental and Emotional Health," *Ourselves Black*, June 5, 2016, https://ourselvesblack.com/journal/2016/6/5/handle-with-care-a-conversation-with-black-men-on-mental-and-emotional-health.

20. Rob Whitley, "The Mental Health Impact of 'Blame a Black Man Syndrome,'" *Psychology Today*, November 16, 2017, https://www.psychologytoday.com/us/blog/talking-about-men/201711/the-mental-health-impact-blame-black-man-syndrome.

21. Erlanger A. Turner, "#YouGoodMan: Black Men and Mental Health," *Huffington Post*, June 27, 2017, https://www.huffpost.com/entry/yougoodman-black-men-and-mental-health_b_5951de6ae4b0c85b96c65c3d.

22. Gregg Henriques, "Why Is It So Hard for Some Men to Share Their Feelings?," *Psychology Today*, November 13, 2014, https://www.psychologytoday.com/us/blog/theory-knowledge/201411/why-is-it-so-hard-some-men-share-their-feelings.

23. Melanie Hamlett, "Men Have No Friends and Women Bear the Burden," *Harper's Bazaar*, May 2, 2019, https://www.harpersbazaar.com/culture/features/a27259689/toxic-masculinity-male-friendships-emotional-labor-men-rely-on-women/.

24. American Psychological Association, *APA Guidelines for Psychological Practice with Boys and Men* (Washington, DC: American Psychological Association, 2018), https://www.apa.org/about/policy/boys-men-practice-guidelines.pdf.

25. Gary Barker, "Why Do So Many Men Die by Suicide?" *Slate*, June 28, 2018, https://slate.com/human-interest/2018/06/are-we-socializing-men-to-die-by-suicide.html.

26. Hamlett, "Men Have No Friends."

27. Rebecca Traister, "Serena Williams and the Game That Can't Be Won (Yet)," *The Cut*, September 9, 2018, https://www.thecut.com/2018/09/serena-williams-us-open-referee-sexism.html.

28. Michael Barbaro, "The Plan to Elect Republican Women," *The Daily* (podcast), produced by Alexandra Leigh Young and Eric Krupke, https://www.nytimes.com/2019/07/10/podcasts/the-daily/republican-women-north-carolina-election.html?.

29. Duncan Stewart, "Does TV Sports Have a Future? Bet on It," Deloitte, December 11, 2018, https://www2.deloitte.com/us/en/insights/industry/technology/technology-media-and-telecom-predictions/tv-sports-betting.html.

30. Ana Sandolu, "Why Men Might Find Multitasking More Challenging," *Medical News Today*, November 20, 2016, https://www.medicalnewstoday.com/articles/314219.php.

31. Klein, "What Men Say About #MeToo in Therapy."

32. Ibid.

33. Stout, Kretschmer, and Ruppannear, "Gender Linked Fate."

34. Ibid.

35. Ibid.

36. Ibid.

37. Veerle Miranda, "Cooking, Caring and Volunteering: Unpaid Work Around the World," OECD Social, Employment and Migration Working Papers No. 116, Organization for Economic Cooperation and Development, September 20, 2011, http://www.oecd.org/officialdocuments/publicdisplaydocumentpdf/?cote=DELSA/ELSA/WD/SEM(2011)1&doclanguage=en.

38. Olga Khazan, "The Scourge of the Female Chore Burden," *The Atlantic*, February 28, 2016, https://www.theatlantic.com/business/archive/2016/02/the-scourge-of-the-female-time-crunch/470379/.

39. Tippett, "Rebecca Traister and Avi Klein."

40. Rachel Giese, "Why We Need a New Model for Raising Boys," September 1, 2018, https://www.todaysparent.com/family/parenting/why-we-need-a-new-model-for-raising-boys/.

41. McGlynn, "In the #MeToo Era."

CHAPTER 7: "US" VS. "THEM"

1. Jessica Taylor, "Republicans and Democrats Don't Agree, or Like Each Other—and It's Worse Than ever," *NPR*, October 5, 2017, https://www.npr.org/2017/10/05/555685136/republicans-and-democrats-dont-agree-dont-like-each-other-and-its-worst-than-eve.

2. Carroll Doherty and Jocelyn Kiley, "Key Facts About Partisanship and Political Animosity in America," *Fact Tank* (blog), Pew Research Center, June 22, 2016, https://www.pewresearch .org/fact-tank/2016/06/22/key-facts-partisanship/.

3. I have abridged the Seven Stages below based on Chris Largent, Denise Breton, and Tracy Halterman's work as they've sculpted this content over many decades. The foundation of much of this copy draws from James Fowler's 1981 book *Stages of Faith: The Psychology of Human Development and the Quest for Meaning*, though the idea of equating our psychological development to human life stages goes as far back as oral Native teachings.

Stage 1. Security (Birth–3 years old): The world is experienced as safe or unsafe, depending on how parents treat a child. To be secure, a child needs to feel loved. If a child does not feel loved, insecurities and fears about survival begin.

Stage 2. Transformation (4–7 years old): Children hear family, cultural, and world stories. The "monsters" of the stories are either transformed and redeemed or they still lurk outside the immediate family and social circles, threatening the child and the world. If negative things (monsters, crises, challenges) can be transformed into positive things, the child feels confident that change is possible. If threats remain unresolved, an either-or, us-them perspective is created, which is a primitive form of moral dualism. (*Moral dualism* is a basic mindset in which we divide the world and people into two categories: the benevolent and the malevolent. There are two moral opposites at work and they often conflict with each other.) The child version of us-them is based on fear, which may feed the us-them perspective in Stages 3 and 4.

Stage 3. Defining Good and Bad (8–12 years old): Children begin to define their world by taking stories literally and sorting the real from the unreal, the good from the bad, and the just from the unjust (with justice as punishment—society punishes bad people, who are extensions of the "monsters" in Stage 2). Facts, people, groups, ideas, values, and even deities are literal things and more concrete objects than, for example, processes or systems. Values are absolutely right or absolutely wrong. There is no alternative, and all attempts to find alternatives signal weakness or confusion.

Stage 4. Conventionality and Conforming (13–17 years old): Adolescents form relationships with peers, friends, romantic partners, groups, and authority figures. They either conform or they rebel. Everyone who does not belong to "our" group—who is not "one of us"—is out, which is why this stage has a lot of us-them, cliquish perspectives. Most tellingly, the values of other groups are wrong—not just different, but wrong, even evil—and the people in those groups are also viewed as wrong or evil. Adolescents realize that they have ideas and values, but they do not examine the sources. They overreact to the ideas and values of others. Teenagers take everything personally and have exactly zero long-term vision. The values of whole groups bring the same response, and members of a group are treated as if they are all identical: all wrong or evil.

Stage 5. Individual Responsibility (18–40 years old): Young and mid-aged adults free themselves from external authority and form their own ideas and values, creating their own individualities and inner authority, including responsibility. But decisions, values, and people are still like things, so these adults respond by determining whether or not they conform to values and ideas. Adults in this stage convince themselves that their ideas and values are right, which they must do to develop a worldview that feels valid. At the same time, they encounter their own controlling, dogmatic tendencies, which they project onto others—the most noticeable of which is passing judgment on people and events (🤬).

Stage 6. Complexity, Diversity, and Sophistication (40–50 years old): Adults acknowledge that perspectives other than their own are valid. They encounter, discuss, and accept the validity of new ideas and values. If, however, they don't see how to apply their new insights and values, they can become passive or cynical. They can also be overwhelmed by the complexity of stepping outside their comfort zones. If this happens, it's tempting to return to the easier, "us vs. them" decision-making of earlier developmental stages.

Stage 7. Nonjudgmental, Engaged (50 years old and beyond): Elders develop universal thinking and apply life-strategies to be all-inclusive and active in their lives and the world. The complexity of the world appears to be beautifully sophisticated and informed by organizing principles at all levels. This perspective allows elders to have penetrating insights and keen perceptions (which earlier-stage thinkers confuse with judgments).

Problem solving and learning from mistakes are natural extensions of creative expression (not a struggle with "failures," a notion from earlier stages). Elders apply their values automatically through living integrated lives, so they do not struggle with apparent moral dilemmas and paradoxes, though they appreciate that other people, wedded to socially conventional thinking, see the world this way, which they do not judge (since they judge nothing). As a result, they make outstanding mentors, an important function during our current era, which is deeply transformational.

4. Summarized from James W. Fowler, *Stages of Faith: The Psychology of Human Development and the Quest for Meaning* (New York: HarperCollins, 1981).

5. Ritu Prasad, "The Tattooist of Auschwitz—and His Secret Love," *BBC*, January 8, 2018, https://www.bbc.com/news/stories-42568390.

6. Kwame Anthony Appiah, *The Lies That Bind: Rethinking Identity* (New York: Liveright, 2018).

7. Francis Fukuyama, "Against Identity Politics—The New Tribalism and the Crisis of Democracy," *Foreign Affairs*, September/October 2018, https://www.foreignaffairs.com/articles/americas/2018-08-14/against-identity-politics-tribalism-francis-fukuyama.

8. OurDocuments.gov, "Transcript of President George Washington's Farewell Address," accessed November 29, 2019, https://www.ourdocuments.gov/doc.php?flash=false&doc=15&page=transcript.

9. David Brooks, "The Cruelty of Call-Out Culture," *New York Times*, January 14, 2019, https://www.nytimes.com/2019/01/14/opinion/call-out-social-justice.html.

10. Malcolm Gladwell, "Small Change: Why the Revolution Will Not Be Tweeted," *The New Yorker*, September 27, 2010, https://www.newyorker.com/magazine/2010/10/04/small-change-malcolm-gladwell.

11. Janet Burns, "How Many Social Media Users Are Real People?" Gizmodo, June 4, 2018, https://gizmodo.com/how-many-social-media-users-are-real-people-1826447042.

12. German Lopez, "Research Says There Are Ways to Reduce Racial Bias. Calling People Racist Isn't One of Them," *Vox*, November 15, 2016, https://www.vox.com/identities/2016/11/15/13595508/racism-research-study-trump.

13. Nicola De Pisapia, Marc H. Bornstein, Paola Rigo, et al., "Sex Differences in Directional Brain Responses to Infant Hunger Cries," *Neuroreport* 24, no. 3 (2013): 142–46, https://doi.org/10.1097/WNR.0b013e32835df4fa.

14. Lit2Go, accessed October 26, 2019, https://etc.usf.edu/lit2go/133/historic-american-documents/4959/the-new-colossus/.

15. Walt Hunter, "The Story Behind the Poem on the Statue of Liberty," *The Atlantic*, January 16, 2018, https://www.theatlantic.com/entertainment/archive/2018/01/the-story-behind-the-poem-on-the-statue-of-liberty/550553/; Katie Mettler, "'Give Me Your Tired, Your Poor': The Story of Poet and Refugee Advocate Emma Lazarus," *Washington Post*, February 1, 2017, https://www.washingtonpost.com/news/morning-mix/wp/2017/02/01/give-us-your-tired-your-poor-the-story-of-poet-and-refugee-advocate-emma-lazarus/.

16. Amelia Cheatham, "Central America's Turbulent Northern Triangle," Council on Foreign Relations, last updated October 1, 2019, https://www.cfr.org/backgrounder/central-americas-turbulent-northern-triangle.

17. "Figures at a Glance," accessed October 26, 2019, https://www.unhcr.org/figures-at-a-glance.html.

18. Guy J. Abel, Michael Brottrager, Jesus Crespo Cuaresma, and Raya Muttarak, "Climate, Conflict and Forced Migration," *Global Environmental Change* 54 (2019): 239–49, https://www.sciencedirect.com/science/article/pii/S0959378018301596.

19. *BBC News*, "'Drug Dealers, Criminals, Rapists': What Trump Thinks About Mexicans," August 31, 2016, https://www.bbc.com/news/av/world-us-canada-37230916/drug-dealers-criminals-rapists-what-trump-thinks-of-mexicans.

20. Stephen Hawkins, Daniel Yudkin, Míriam Juan-Torres, and Tim Dixon, *Hidden Tribes: A Study of America's Polarized Landscape*, More in Common (New York: More in Common, 2018), https://hiddentribes.us/pdf/hidden_tribes_report.pdf.

21. Domenico Montanaro, "Poll: Majority Want to Keep Abortion Legal, but They Also Want Restrictions," *NPR*, June 7, 2019, https://www.npr.org/2019/06/07/730183531/poll-majority-want-to-keep-abortion-legal-but-they-also-want-restrictions.

22. Laura Santhanam, "Most Americans Support These 4 Types of Gun Legislation, Poll Says," PBS, September 10, 2019, https://www.pbs.org/newshour/politics/most-americans-support-stricter-gun-laws-new-poll-says.

23. Ana Campoy, "Democrats and Republicans Agree on Some Surprising Issues, but Not on How to Solve Them," *Quartz*, March 21, 2019, https://qz.com/1577711/the-surprising-issues-republicans-and-democrats-agree-on/.

24. NYCLU, "Stop-and-Frisk Data," accessed November 30, 2019, https://www.nyclu.org/en/stop-and-frisk-data.

25. Duane Champagne, "Noble Savages and Noble Nations," IndianCountryToday.com, January 15, 2014, https://newsmaven.io/indiancountrytoday/archive/noble-savages-and-noble-nations-7_IANhujjEeZ-9A1RkuYBw/.

26. *Wikipedia*, s.v. "Der Giftpilz," last modified October 11, 2019, https://en.wikipedia.org/wiki/Der_Giftpilz.

27. Mallory Simon and Sara Sidner, "Tackle White Supremacism As Terrorism, Experts Say," CNN, May 15, 2019, https://www.cnn.com/2019/05/14/us/white-supremacy-terrorism-soh/index.html.

28. Anti-Defamation League, "ADL Report: White Supremacist Murders More Than Doubled in 2017," January 17, 2018, https://www.adl.org/news/press-releases/adl-report-white-supremacist-murders-more-than-doubled-in-2017.

29. Deloris Rubin, chair of Manhattan Community Board Four, to NYC District Attorney Cyrus R. Vance Jr. and New York City Police Commissioner James O'Neill, "Re: White Supremacist Assassination of Timothy Caughman, March 20, 2017—36th Street and Ninth Avenue, Manhattan," April 13, 2017, http://www.nyc.gov/html/mancb4/downloads/pdf/april_2017/28-EXEC-Letter-to-DA-NYPD-re-hate-crimes-terrorism-occurring-in-Community-Board-4.pdf.

30. Nathan Englander, "What Jewish Children Learned from Charlottesville," *New York Times*, August 15, 2017, https://www.nytimes.com/2017/08/15/opinion/jewish-charlottesville-anti-semitism.html.

31. Carlton Reid, "You Are Not Stuck in Traffic, You Are Traffic," *Forbes*, December 3, 2018, https://www.forbes.com/sites/carltonreid/2018/12/03/you-are-not-stuck-in-traffic-you-are-traffic/.

32. Stephen Covey, *The 7 Habits of Highly Effective People: Powerful Lessons in Personal Change* (New York: Simon & Schuster, 2004).

33. US Bureau of Labor Statistics, "Job Openings and Labor Turnover Summary," accessed October 26, 2019, https://www.bls.gov/news.release/jolts.nr0.htm.

34. Oriana Pawylk, "New Air Force's Stealth B-21 Bomber Getting Ready for Its First Flight," *Business Insider*, April 10, 2019, https://www.businessinsider.com/new-air-forces-stealth-b-21-bomber-getting-ready-for-its-first-flight-2019-4.

35. US Government Accountability Office, *Federal Real Property: Progress Made in Reducing Unneeded Property, but VA Needs Better Information to Make Further Reductions* (Report GAO-08-939, September 2008), Washington, DC: Government Accountability Office, https://www.gao.gov/assets/290/280516.pdf.

36. "In Pictures: 13 Silliest Uses of Taxpayer Money. 2. $930 Million: On Unnecessary Printing Costs," *Forbes*, accessed November 22, 2019, https://www.forbes.com/pictures/ejde45i/930-million-on-unnecessary-printing-costs/.

37. Scott Pelley, "When Hospitals Become Targets in Syria's Civil War," *CBS 60 Minutes*, August 5, 2018, https://www.cbsnews.com/news/when-hospitals-become-targets-in-syria-civil-war-60-minutes/.

38. "Rohingya Muslims Fleeing Myanmar Watch Homes Burn," *CBS News*, September 14, 2017, https://www.cbsnews.com/news/rohingya-muslims-fleeing-myanmar-watch-homes-burn/.

39. Palko Karasz, "85,000 Children in Yemen May Have Died of Starvation," *New York Times*, November 21, 2008, https://www.nytimes.com/2018/11/21/world/middleeast/yemen-famine-children.html.

40. Beth Verhey, *Child Soldiers: Preventing, Demobilizing and Reintegrating*, Africa Region Working Paper Series Number 23 (Washington, DC: World Bank, November 2001), http://documents.worldbank.org/curated/en/284531468770734839/pdf/multi0page.pdf.

41. Krista Tippett, "john a. powell: Opening to the Question of Belonging," *On Being*, June 25, 2015, last updated May 10, 2018, https://onbeing.org/programs/john-a-powell-opening-to-the-question-of-belonging-may2018/.

42. Ibid.

43. Bill Chappell, "Census Finds a More Diverse America, As Whites Lag Growth," *The Two-Way* (blog), NPR, June 22, 2017, https://www.npr.org/sections/thetwo-way/2017/06/22/533926978/census-finds-a-more-diverse-america-as-whites-lag-growth.

44. Tippett, "john a. powell: Opening to the Question of Belonging."

45. Krista Tippett, "Rebecca Solnit: Falling Together," *On Being*, May 26, 2016, updated December 14, 2017, https://onbeing.org/programs/rebecca-solnit-falling-together-dec2017/.

46. Ibid.

CHAPTER 8: YOU, THEM, WE

1. Jackie Payne, "Unlocking the Power of Women to Advance Progress for All," Galvanize USA, n.d.

2. National Women's History Museum, "Woman's Rights Emerges Within the Abolitionist Movement," Fall 2015, accessed December 8, 2019, http://www.crusadeforthevote.org/abolition.

3. *Merriam-Webster OnLine*, s.v. "concentration camp," accessed December 8, 2019, https://www.merriam-webster.com/dictionary/concentration%20camp.

4. Josh Dawsey and Colby Itkowitz, "'This Is Tough Stuff': At Texas Detention Facility, Pence Sees Hundreds of Migrants Crammed with No Beds," *Washington Post*, July 12, 2019, https://www.washingtonpost.com/politics/pence-tours-detention-facilities-at-the-border-defends-administrations-treatment-of-migrants/2019/07/12/993f54e0-a4bc-11e9-b8c8-75dae2607e60_story.html.

5. Adam Serwer, "A Crime by Any Name," *The Atlantic*, July 3, 2019, https://www.theatlantic .com/ideas/archive/2019/07/border-facilities/593239/.

6. Carmen Perez, Cassady Fendlay, Reshma Saujani, et al., "Daring Discussions" (Google Docs file), January 2017, https://drive.google.com/file/d/1U-zG0fOSoqkIZA2omvfa3oJxN JtYM9SB/view (site discontinued).

7. Sean Illing, "What We Get Wrong About Misogyny," *Vox*, December 5, 2017, https://www .vox.com/identities/2017/12/5/16705284/metoo-weinstein-misogyny-trump-sexism.

8. Krista Tippett, "Rebecca Traister and Avi Klein: #MeToo Through a Social Lens," *On Being*, December 6, 2018, https://onbeing.org/programs/rebecca-traister-and-avi-klein-metoo -through-a-solutions-lens-dec2018/#transcript.

9. B. Goldacre, H. Drysdale, A. Powell-Smith, et al., "Tracking Switched Outcomes in Clinical Trials," accessed December 10, 2019, *The COMPare Trials Project*, http://compare-trials .org/.

10. Krista Tippett, "Rachel Naomi Remen: The Difference Between Fixing and Healing," *On Being*, November 22, 2018, https://onbeing.org/programs/rachel-naomi-remen-the -difference-between-fixing-and-healing-nov2018/#transcript.

11. Krista Tippett, "Pádraig Ó Tuama and Marilyn Nelson: Choosing Words That Deepen the Argument of Being Alive," *On Being*, September 6, 2018, https://onbeing.org/programs /padraig-o-tuama-marilyn-nelson-choosing-words-that-deepen-the-argument-of-being-alive -sep2018/#transcript.

CHAPTER 9: THE FRONTLINE—HOLD

1. Craig Hatkoff, Irwin Kula, and Zach Levine, "How To Die in America: Welcome to La Crosse, Wisconsin," *Forbes*, September 23, 2014, https://www.forbes.com/sites/off whitepapers/2014/09/23/how-to-die-in-america-welcome-to-la-crosse/#63d57c88e8c6.

2. Dartmouth Atlas of Health Care, "Total Medicare Reimbursements per Decedent, by Interval, Before Death," accessed December 10, 2019, https://www.dartmouthatlas.org /interactive-apps/?ind=23&loct=3&tf=20&fmt=45&ch=1.

3. Rajesh R. Tampi, Deena J. Tampi, and Lisa L. Boyle, eds, *Psychiatric Disorders Late in Life: A Comprehensive Review* (New York: Springer, 2018).

4. GALvanize USA, "How Do We Reach White Women?" (Google Docs PDF), https://drive .google.com/drive/folders/1yWd5doV7ps5UdnEGOtU5mJSm17UnNT60 (site discontinued).

5. Michele Debczak, "Female Suffragettes Memorial Will Mark Central Park's First Statues of Women in History," *Mental Floss*, October 25, 2019, https://www.mentalfloss.com /article/604870/female-suffragettes-statue-central-park.

6. Jane Lee, "6 Women Scientists Who Were Snubbed Due to Sexism," *National Geographic*, May 19, 2013, https://www.nationalgeographic.com/news/2013/5/130519-women-scientists -overlooked-dna-history-science/.

7. David A. Tomar, "9 Women Who Changed History . . . and the Men Who Took Credit," *The Quad*, accessed December 11, 2019, https://thebestschools.org/magazine/brilliant -woman-greedy-men/.

8. Jonathan Mulinix, "Why Mother's Day Founder Anna Jarvis Later Fought to Have the Holiday Abolished," *Mental Floss*, May 7, 2019, https://www.mentalfloss.com/article/30659 /founder-mothers-day-later-fought-have-it-abolished.

9. Eric Chase, "The Brief Origins of May Day," Industrial Workers of the World, 1993, accessed December 11, 2019, https://www.iww.org/history/library/misc/origins_of_mayday.

10. Sandra Laville and Matthew Taylor, "A Million Bottles a Minute: World's Plastic Binge 'As Dangerous as Climate Change,'" *The Guardian*, June 28, 2017, https://www.the

guardian.com/environment/2017/jun/28/a-million-a-minute-worlds-plastic-bottle-binge-as
-dangerous-as-climate-change.

11. Ellen MacArthur Foundation, *The New Plastics Economy: Rethinking the Future of Plastics*, 2016, https://www.ellenmacarthurfoundation.org/assets/downloads/EllenMacArthur
Foundation_TheNewPlasticsEconomy_Pages.pdf.

12. Tessa E. S. Charlesworth and Mahzarin R. Banaji, "Patterns of Implicit and Explicit Attitudes: I. Long-Term Change and Stability from 2007 to 2016," *Psychological Science* 30, no.
2 (2019): 174–92.

13. "World Population Projected to Reach 9.8 Billion in 2050, and 11.2 Billion in 2100," United Nations, June 21, 2017, https://www.un.org/development/desa/en/news/population/world
-population-prospects-2017.html.

14. Chris Arsenault, "30% of the World's Food Wasted," *Al Jazeera*, October 31, 2014, https://www.aljazeera.com/indepth/features/2014/10/thirty-percent-world-food-wasted
-2014103192739208584.html.

15. Farah Stockman, "Women's March on Washington Opens Contentious Dialogues About Race," *New York Times*, January 9, 2017, https://www.nytimes.com/2017/01/09/us/womens
-march-on-washington-opens-contentious-dialogues-about-race.html.

16. Jamilah Lemieux, "Why I'm Skipping the Women's March on Washington," *Colorlines*, January 17, 2017, https://www.colorlines.com/articles/why-im-skipping-womens-march-washington
-opinion.

17. Melissa Brown, "Ready to Ditch White Feminism? 6 Black Feminist Concepts You Need to Know," *Everyday Feminism*, January 18, 2017, https://everydayfeminism.com/2017/01/ready
-ditch-white-feminism/.

18. "Two Spirit Community," Re:searching for LGBTQ Health, https://lgbtqhealth.ca/community
/two-spirit.php.

19. Bran Ayres, "What Does #OwnVoices Mean for Authors and Readers?" *Jami Gold* (blog), April 24, 2018, https://jamigold.com/2018/04/what-does-own-voices-mean-for-authors-and
-readers-guest-bran-l-ayres/.

20. Eric Liu, *You're More Powerful Than You Think: A Citizen's Guide to Making Change Happen* (New York: Public Affairs, 2017), 5.

21. Victor Fleischer, "Stop Universities from Hoarding Money," *New York Times*, August 19, 2015, https://www.nytimes.com/2015/08/19/opinion/stop-universities-from-hoarding-money.html.

22. US Centers for Disease Control and Prevention, "Opioid Overdose: Understanding the Epidemic," last modified December 19, 2018, https://www.cdc.gov/drugoverdose/epidemic
/index.html.

23. Josiah Ryan, "'This Was a Whitelash': Van Jones Take on the Election Results," *CNN*, November 9, 2016, https://www.cnn.com/2016/11/09/politics/van-jones-results-disappointment-cnntv
/index.html.

24. "How Do We Reach White Women?" GALvanize USA, n.d.

25. Ari Berman, "Welcome to the First Presidential Election Since Voting Rights Act Gutted," *Rolling Stone*, June 2016, https://www.rollingstone.com/politics/politics-news/welcome-to
-the-first-presidential-election-since-voting-rights-act-gutted-179737/.

26. Terry Gross, "Republican Voter Suppression Efforts Are Targeting Minorities, Journalist Says," *NPR*, October 23, 2018, https://www.npr.org/2018/10/23/659784277/republican
-voter-suppression-efforts-are-targeting-minorities-journalist-says.

27. Matt Vasilogambros, "The Messy Politics of Voter Purges," Pew, October 25, 2019, https://
www.pewtrusts.org/en/research-and-analysis/blogs/stateline/2019/10/25/the-messy-politics
-of-voter-purges.

28. Jackie Payne, "Unlocking the Power of Women to Advance Progress for All."

29. Ibid.

CHAPTER 10: THE RECKONING

1. Abigail Disney, correspondence with the author, November 27, 2019.
2. NPR, "Theodore Parker and the 'Moral Universe,'" *All Things Considered*, September 2, 2010, https://www.npr.org/templates/story/story.php?storyId=129609461.
3. George Anastaplo, "The United States Constitution of 1787: A Commentary," *Loyola University Chicago Law Journal* 18, no. 1 (1986): 15, http://lawecommons.luc.edu/luclj/vol18/iss1/3.
4. *The Economist*, "The Economist Intelligence Unit's Democracy Index, 2017, https:// infographics.economist.com/2018/DemocracyIndex.
5. Geoffrey Galt Harpham, *What Do You Think, Mr. Ramirez?: The American Revolution in Education* (Chicago: University of Chicago Press, 2017).
6. Eric Liu, *You're More Powerful than You Think: A Citizen's Guide to Making Change Happen* (New York: PublicAffairs, 2018).
7. "Quakers and the Underground Railroad," World History, August 8, 2017, https://world history.us/american-history/quakers-and-the-underground-railroad.php.
8. National Underground Railroad Freedom Center, "History," accessed October 26, 2019, https://freedomcenter.org/enabling-freedom/history.
9. Olga Khazan, "Can Trauma Be Inherited Between Generations?" *The Atlantic*, October 16, 2018, https://www.theatlantic.com/health/archive/2018/10/trauma-inherited-generations /573055/.
10. Resmaa Menakem, *My Grandmother's Hands: Racialized Trauma and the Pathway to Mending Our Hearts and Bodies* (Las Vegas: Central Recovery Press, 2017).
11. Olga Khazan, "Can Trauma Be Inherited Between Generations?"
12. Dora L. Costa, Noelle Yetter, and Heather DeSomer, "Intergenerational Transmission of Paternal Trauma Among US Civil War Ex-POWs," *Proceedings of the National Academy of Sciences of the United States of America* 115, no. 44 (2018): 11215–220.
13. Ibid.
14. Rachel MacNair, *Perpetration-Induced Traumatic Stress: The Psychological Consequences of Killing* (New York: iUniverse, 2005).
15. James Baldwin, "Letter from a Region of My Mind," *The New Yorker*, November 17, 1962, https://www.newyorker.com/magazine/1962/11/17/letter-from-a-region-in-my-mind.
16. W. Cahan, *No Stranger to Tears: A Surgeon's Story* (New York: Random House, 1992).
17. Grace Mirabella, *In and Out of Vogue* (New York: Doubleday, 1995).

INDEX

ABOUT THE AUTHOR

Jenna Arnold is an educator, entrepreneur, activist, and mother who lives in New York City with her husband and two children, who are anti-sleep. Oprah named Jenna one of her "100 Awakened Leaders who are using their voice and talent to elevate humanity" for her professional portfolio of work across education, entertainment, and activism.

Jenna is currently the Chief Impact Officer for impact investing platform Rethink, which funds companies working to solve some of the world's most complex problems: equitable education, food distribution, climate sustainability, community growth, and women's and minority-population empowerment. She is the cofounder of ORGANIZE, a nonprofit focused on ending the waitlist for organ transplants in the US. ORGANIZE launched the country's first central organ donor registry, was awarded an Innovator in Residence position in the Office of the Secretary of Health and Human Services beginning in 2015, and cohosted the White House Organ Donation Summit, which, in addition to other initiatives, launched $300 million worth of commitments across multiple sectors. Since then, an executive order has been signed and legislation proposed to increase the number of life-saving, transplantable organs. For her work at ORGANIZE, Jenna was named one of *Inc.*'s "20 Most Disruptive Innovators." The *New York Times* called ORGANIZE one of the "Biggest Ideas in Social Change," and the organization has been covered by CNN, *Washington Post, NPR, US News, FastCompany, Forbes,* ESPN, *Slate, SELF,* UpWorthy, HBO's *Last Week Tonight,* and *Full Frontal with Samantha Bee.*

Previously, Jenna was the executive producer and creator of one of MTV's hit TV shows, *Exiled!,* which took spoiled American teenagers to live with indigenous cultures around the world. She was the youngest American to work at the United Nations, where she created multi-platform programming for MTV and Showtime with A-list celebrities like Jay-Z and Angelina Jolie.

Jenna received a graduate degree from Columbia University's Teachers College in International Education Development and a BS.Edu and minor in astrophysics from the University of Miami. She has taught in thirteen countries with a laser focus on citizenship education, and has authored fifteen different curricula.

Jenna sits on a number of boards, including the Sesame Workshop Leadership Council, and is a member of the Council on Foreign Relations. She is also an emeritus World Economic Forum Global Shaper and a Women's March Global Board Member.

Her husband, Jeremy, is the president of LeagueApps, a technology platform to equitize youth sports, and her two children, Ever Alula and Atlas Oz, keep pointing to the encyclopedias on the shelf, asking, "Is that the book you're writing?" (which, at times, has felt accurate). Jenna can't wait to be an elementary school teacher again, but has a few things to do before she formally returns to the classroom.